The HISTORICAL RENAISSANCE

The

HISTORICAL

RENAISSANCE

New Essays on Tudor and Stuart Literature and Culture

Edited by Heather Dubrow and Richard Strier

The University of Chicago Press
Chicago and London

HEATHER DUBROW, professor of English at Carleton College, is the author of *Genre* and *Captive Victors: Shakespeare's Narrative Poems and Sonnets*.
RICHARD STRIER, professor of English at the University of Chicago, is the author of *Love Known: Theology and Experience in George Herbert's Poetry*.

The University of Chicago Press, Chicago 60637
The University of Chicago Press, Ltd., London

© 1988 by The University of Chicago
All rights reserved. Published 1988
Printed in the United States of America

97 96 95 94 93 92 91 90 89 88   5 4 3 2 1

Library of Congress Cataloging-in-Publication Data

The Historical renaissance : new essays on Tudor and Stuart literature
and culture / edited by Heather Dubrow and Richard Strier.
    p.   cm.
  Bibliography: p.
  Includes index.
  ISBN 0-226-16765-8. ISBN 0-226-16766-6 (pbk.)
    1. English literature—Early modern, 1500–1700—History and
criticism.   2. Literature and society—Great Britain—History—16th
century.   3. Literature and society—Great Britain—History—17th
century.   4. Literature and history.   5. History in literature.
6. Renaissance—Great Britain.   I. Dubrow, Heather, 1945–   .
II. Strier, Richard.
PR418.S64H57 1988
820'.9'003—dc19   88-10686
                                                                CIP

To Herschel Baker

Contents

Acknowledgments

We are grateful for a generous grant from the Hyder E. Rollins Fund of the English Department of Harvard University to aid in the publication of this volume. We also wish to thank Carleton College and the University of Chicago for defraying some of our expenses.

Our dedication of the volume to Herschel Baker acknowledges another type of debt. Herschel Baker's commitment to the uses of history is manifest in all his work. *The Dignity of Man, The Wars of Truth,* and *The Race of Time* are wide-ranging analyses of intellectual and religious history; his anthologies give literary and nonliterary texts equal place. Yet it was not only as a scholar that Herschel Baker contributed to historically oriented English Renaissance studies but also as a teacher. His students found him witty as well as thoughtful, humane as well as rigorous. This volume is intended as a tribute to him by two of these students.

H.D.
R.S.

Introduction
The Historical Renaissance

> There are some other rather peccant humours than formed diseases [of Learning] . . . The first of these is the extreme affecting of two extremities; the one Antiquity, the other Novelty: wherein it seemeth the children of time do take after the nature and malice of the father. For as he devoureth his children, so one of them seeketh to devour and suppress the other; while antiquity envieth there should be new additions, and novelty cannot be content to add but it must deface.
>
> Francis Bacon, *The Advancement of Learning*

The title of this collection is intentionally ambiguous. By "the historical renaissance" we mean both the actual historical era termed the Renaissance and the remarkable recent efflorescence of historical studies of English Renaissance culture. Our aim is, in a very general sense, polemical, but it is not, in any sense, partisan. We want at once to demonstrate and to advocate the fruitfulness of a historical approach to English Renaissance (and all) literature and culture, but we do not wish to argue for any particular kind of historical approach. We aim, instead, to present something of the variety of approaches and concerns that can legitimately be termed historical and that can be seen to produce historical insight. We hope to represent the extraordinary range of ways that contemporary scholars are fruitfully conducting the historical study of Tudor and Stuart literature, culture, and politics.[1]

It is no accident that such a book should appear now rather than, say, a decade earlier. A heightened interest in history and politics is the most salient characteristic of literary studies of the English Renaissance and of other fields in the 1980s. In some ways this interest is a reaction against earlier approaches: many critics would maintain that their predecessors variously neglected or misinterpreted the relationships between literature and history in the English Renaissance. To a large extent such accusations are justified. The New Critical platform that dominated literary studies in the fifties and sixties and remained influential through much of the seventies rigidly separated what were sometimes termed "intrinsic" textual issues from "extrinsic" social ones and opposed combining the two on several grounds.[2] Rooted in I. A. Richards's views on the differences between poetic and nonpoetic discourse, New Criticism distinguished and privileged "literary" language; the characteristic richness and ambiguity with which literature was associated was seen to render it a far fitter object of study than other types of texts, such as descriptions of cities or political tracts. The New Critics united T. S. Eliot's observations on the impersonality of literature with an emphasis on its universality. Literary works were viewed as exploring general human emotions and doing so in a way that was accessible to all properly attentive readers. Hence, although New Criticism itself developed in part as a response to a particular Southern milieu, its exponents often neglected or downplayed the ways in which authors, texts, and readers were shaped by the local and particular stresses of their cultures. And though structuralism affected Renaissance studies in this country far less than New Criticism had, the structuralist emphasis on the synchronic rather than the diachronic also fostered neglect of the local and particular.

Yet generalizations like these, though essentially sound, are partial in more than one sense. Concerned to distinguish their stance from that of their predecessors, contemporary critics often oversimplify the work they are rejecting, much as contemporary architects are prone to oversimplify the achievements and the limitations of the International Style. It is much easier to supplant or suppress the fathers if they can be parodied as bogeymen or reduced to straw men. Despite the theoretical dogmas of New Criticism, some of its proponents did in fact comment acutely on social, historical, and political issues; and many "new critics" resolutely refused to distinguish between "internal" and "external" approaches. Consider, for example, the corpus and curious career of that dean of New Criticism, William Empson. Empson's work is at least as close to Kenneth Burke's as it is to Cleanth Brooks's, though Empson's kinship with Burke is rarely acknowledged.

Similarly, when we scrutinize the ways history and literature did interpenetrate in the work of earlier critics, we are sometimes prone to misread that work, offering our own exaggerations and distortions in place of others. It is true that a (loosely) Burckhardtian notion of the Renaissance—an interpretation that populated the period with energetic, optimistic overreachers, unfettered by religious concerns—was influential.[3] It is also true that E. M. W. Tillyard's *The Elizabethan World Picture,* now notorious for its homogenization of a much messier scene and its "law and order" perspective, enjoyed an inordinate status in many quarters. Yet it is not true, as contemporary critics sometimes assert, that these views swept the field. The criticism of Shakespeare's history plays, for example, involved a whole range of approaches to Elizabethan culture, including some that drew attention to the kinds of tensions and inconsistencies that interest many of us today.[4] Hence, as the essays in this volume would suggest, the line between the "old" and the "new historicism" is notoriously difficult and often not very profitable to draw. Indeed, the term "cultural poetics," coined by Stephen Greenblatt, describes contemporary work more precisely than does his other coinage, "new historicism," while avoiding the misleading and invidious implication of a radical discontinuity between contemporary scholarship and everything that preceded it.[5]

Nevertheless, however one defines the critical climate prior to the current one, it is clear that today scholars of the English Renaissance are intensely concerned with the connections between literary texts and social and historical phenomena—and, indeed, with collapsing the boundaries suggested by those very distinctions. Several currents have contributed to this shared contemporary project. The most obvious influence is the movement alluded to above as the "new historicism." Describing that school is as tricky as attaching a name to it, but it is fair at least to begin by observing that, influenced in particular by the anthropology of Clifford Geertz and the historiography of Michel Foucault, new historicists examine both "literary" and "nonliterary" texts as both implicated in and generative of a cultural milieu.[6] The conceptual shift from speaking of "works" to speaking of "texts" has helped break down disciplinary and generic boundaries, as has the conception of literary production as one among many complex cultural practices.[7] Certain branches of feminism, in their scrutiny of how power operates within a patriarchal culture and how authors support or undermine the assumptions of that culture, have also contributed to the historical emphasis that characterizes contemporary Renaissance studies.[8] And if deconstruction is, as many of its critics have observed, apolitical in some of its implications and applications, it can be intensely political in others. The deconstructionist emphasis on how language can undermine its ostensible meanings lies behind many contemporary studies of the tensions that political pressures create in Renaissance texts.

Influenced by schools and movements like these, many of the essays in this book reflect certain shared assumptions. As we have already seen, one assumption common to much contemporary study of the English Renaissance is that the division between the historical or social on the one hand and the literary on the other is problematic. Rather than distinguishing between text and context, the literary foreground and the social or political background, many critics collapse those distinctions, stressing instead the qualities common to all forms of discourse and the ways in which cultural institutions and practices of various sorts shape each other. Jean Howard states the goal of new historicism thus: "instead of a hierarchical relationship in which literature figures as the parasitic reflector of historical fact, one imagines a complex textualized universe in which literature participates in historical processes as in the political management of reality."[9] If contemporary Renaissance scholars often insist that the text is not autonomous, not independent of its cultural milieu, they approach the inhabitants of that milieu from a similar perspective: the persons of Renaissance England are seen as constituted by their culture.

But these generalizations, like those we made about the work of earlier scholars, also demand refinements and qualifications. First of all, just as the lines between historical and literary texts blur, so too do those between the "old" and the "new" historicism. As we have already observed, many contemporary scholars who would consider themselves new historicists are doing work that is closely related to that of their predecessors. Moreover, the "old" historicism—that of the nineteenth- and early twentieth-century scholars and antiquarians who put together the variorum editions, edited the old books as historical curiosities, and found the sources for Shakespeare and others—is very much present in the new. The new historicism is in a sense dependent upon the old. It is not primarily an archival movement; its triumphs are not discoveries of new documents but stunning and suggestive reinterpretations and reconfigurings of existing materials, of materials that the "old" historicism discovered (Samuel Harsnett's presence in *Lear*, Simon Forman's remarkable journals, James's hatred of crowds, etc.). This is part of the reason why invidious contrasts are uncalled for. It would be a very positive effect of the new historicism to encourage archival work, the oldest historicism of all. Meanwhile, much significant and original historical work is going on substantially unaffected by the newer critical and historical movements. Some of the "new" assumptions, moreover, are present in work that might not normally be so labeled, which again calls the value of the label into question.

It might be said, too, that there are a number of new historicisms. The contemporary British movement known as "cultural materialism" is one. This movement is rather different from American new historicism. Cultural materialism is more involved in twentieth-century culture than is the new historicism, and while the influence of Althusser, particularly his notion of literature as an ideological state apparatus, is evident in the new historicism, cultural materialism is generally more overtly Marxist in its assumptions and orientations than its American counterpart.[10] And even within American new historicism, as Louis Montrose among others has pointed out, generalizations about the movement or school are themselves dubious because the practitioners of that movement differ among themselves on important issues.[11] One of the central differences concerns the nature and extent of subversion within a dominant ideology. Some students of the field see all rebellions as contained, even authorized, by those in power, while others emphasize instead the power and the achievements of the subversive. These positions are not, of course, the only ones the issue permits; for instance, as Jonathan Dollimore recently observed, "although subversion may indeed be appropriated by authority for its own purposes, once installed it can be used against authority as well as used by it."[12] This debate relates to another one: to what extent does one see the Elizabethan court and culture as monolithic, and to what extent, on the other hand, does one emphasize conflicting voices and ideologies? New historicists also disagree on the crucial questions of causation and agency, on what or who shapes the contours of a culture—an issue on which Foucault's work is similarly reticent and ambiguous. To what extent does one emphasize the influence of an individual, whether a figure with political power or a poet? To what extent, on the other hand, does one see persons merely as vessels for cultural codes and cultural tensions?

However one resolves these and related controversies, they find their analogues in some of the preoccupations of contemporary history and anthropology, hence facilitating connections between these fields and literary studies. Rather than celebrating their own objectivity as Ranke and other nineteenth-century historians were prone to do, many contemporary social scientists are concerned to explore the reasons why objectivity is impossible. Similarly, a number of historians have commented on the rhetoricity of their own language. Hayden White has done pioneering work on these and related issues, but a traditional historian like J. H. Hexter shares this concern. As Hexter puts it, "rhetoric is ordinarily deemed the icing on the cake of history, but . . . it is mixed right into the batter."[13] Similarly, the anthropologists who have downplayed the functional and material bases of culture in favor of its symbolic and ideological dimensions are evidently opening avenues for connections with contemporary movements in literary studies (which are partly going in the other direction). The essays in this volume exemplify both the ways these and other debates about history and politics are currently affecting Renaissance studies, and the ways in which traditional scholarship continues to prosper and develop.

In our opening section, "The Mid-Tudor Scene," Janel Mueller and Donald Kelley investigate from the perspective of the mid-Tudor period a number of issues currently central to Renaissance studies: the (potentially related) issues of political subversion and of female political and literary authority. Mueller explores the content, context, and inner structures of Queen Katherine Parr's neglected devotional masterpiece, *Lam-*

entation of a Sinner. She conclusively demonstrates that Erasmus was a less central influence on this text than scholars have assumed and that Parr was building on the affective, psychological, and social discourse of the strong English Protestantism of Tyndale, Cranmer, and, especially, Latimer. Recognizing the discursive and political contexts of Parr's work serves to illuminate Parr's political and religious project and her concept of her own female, Protestant authorship. Donald Kelley's essay, "Ideas of Resistance before Elizabeth," charts the development among the Marian exiles of distinctive and radical theories about resisting political authority. Emphasizing the social as well as the intellectual contexts of writers like Ponet, Goodman, and Foxe, Kelley argues that radical "resistance theory" developed through a process that cannot be adequately explained in terms of conventional political models. Instead, we must acknowledge that the process included several stages: religious and doctrinal protests, the socialization of protest, and the amassing of authorities to give a broad-based intellectual legitimacy to the new position.

Our second section focuses on Shakespeare's conceptions of and relations to history and politics. In "Descanting on Deformity: Richard III and the Shape of History," Marjorie Garber maintains that Shakespeare saw in Richard III's deformity the deformities inherent in history and history writing. In analyzing these deformations, she adduces Nietzsche's observations on the use and abuse of history and thus exemplifies the powerful influence Nietzsche has had on contemporary critical theory and practice. Richard Strier's essay, "Faithful Servants: Shakespeare's Praise of Disobedience," shows the ways in which some of the ideas situated by Donald Kelley, together with some complementary ideas in the humanist tradition, can be seen at work in Shakespeare's plays, especially *King Lear.* Using the tools of intellectual history and literary analysis together with an awareness of social history and of recent work on the texts of Shakespeare's plays, Strier offers a strongly revisionist view of Shakespeare's commitment to the hegemonic official ideology of order and obedience. Leah Marcus's essay takes up the vexed question of specific topical references in Shakespeare. Focusing on a key case, in *"Cymbeline* and the Unease of Topicality" Marcus analyzes the contradictions and apparent faults in *Cymbeline,* with regard especially to the successes and the problems in reading the play as referring to James I and the controversial Project for the union of England and Scotland. The "riddling" mode of the play, Marcus suggests, demonstrates the way in which Shakespeare both invites and resists topical readings of his plays. Taken together, these essays present Shakespeare in powerful dialogue with his culture on issues of historiography, ideology, and authority.

The third section, "Poets, Courtiers, and the Monarchy," continues the investigations of power and authority by focusing on the symbolically and in many ways literally central institution of the Tudor and Stuart social world, the monarchy. In "Sidney and His Queen," Maureen Quilligan adduces the theories of the anthropologist Pierre Bourdieu to investigate Sidney's reactions to various forms of power, whether it be that of the earl of Oxford in a tennis court incident, that of Penelope Rich (Sidney's "Stella"), or that of the Virgin Queen herself. This essay, like Mueller's, exemplifies the interplay between feminist and historicist concerns—both "new" and "old"—that is currently emerging in Renaissance studies. Heather Dubrow explores the perplexing epithalamium that Donne composed for the wedding of Frances Howard and the earl of Somerset, finding in its complex language responses to patronage that range from uncritical sycophancy to covert but intense rebuke. A close examination of this lyric, she suggests, offers guidelines for studying the attitudes toward patronage in other texts as well. Brian Levack's contribution to the volume aptly demonstrates the ways in which the work of historians can supplement and inform that of literary critics. His essay traces one of the roots of the absolutist ideology that the literary texts explored in this section of the book variously support and critique (or both). Levack's research indicates that the political theories of a number of late Elizabethan and early Stuart writers and thinkers, including Francis Bacon, were shaped to a surprising extent by their study of the traditions of civil law. In his essay on Herbert and authority, Michael Schoenfeldt argues that an awareness of courtly strategies characterizes the life and work not only of "secular" types like Sidney and Bacon, but also of Bacon's friend and translator, "holy Mr. Herbert." Seeing the religious discourse of George Herbert's lyrics as both "contaminated and enriched" by Herbert's interactions with secular authority (which Schoenfeldt analyzes), Schoenfeldt charts a number of parallels between Herbert's responses in the religious and the secular arenas, focusing especially on a repeated slippage between submissiveness and rivalry, a slippage that is widespread in the period.

The final section, "Humanism and Its Discontents," approaches the relationships between history and texts by exploring the controversies in—and the controversies engendered by—Renaissance humanism. Richard Helgerson argues that the movement in favor of quantitative meter is more culturally significant than scholars have hitherto seen. Helgerson finds in the Spenser-Harvey correspondence on meter alternative models for *national* self-fashioning. Arthur Kinney's essay opens by suggesting the number of influences that converged to produce Sidney's responses to history, including his reading of ancient historians, especially Thucydides, and his own political experience. The essay proceeds to juxtapose the Old and the New *Arcadia* to demonstrate Sidney's increasing commitment to elucidating particular political concepts, especially the crucial notions of equity and conscience. Clark Hulse's "Spenser, Bacon, and the Myth of Power" opens by investigating a methodological problem central to new historicism: the workings of power in relation to the discourses of a culture. Hulse develops this discussion by contrasting Spenser's mythological renderings of power with Bacon's demythologized, analytical approach to it. As this summary would suggest, his explorations are closely related to those raised in the previous sections of the volume. In "From Matron to Monster: Tudor-Stuart London and the Languages of Urban Description," Lawrence Manley examines the ways in which Renaissance conceptualizations of a social reality, drawn primarily from classical sources, struggled to come to terms with the unprecedented conditions of early modern London. Manley's study culminates in a contrast between Defoe's representation of London and the Renaissance conceptualizations that preceded it. Manley demonstrates the limits of this realm of Renaissance discourse, and his essay therefore serves as a fitting close to the volume.

If many of the essays in this volume explicitly demonstrate the ways contemporary scholars are splicing the concerns of literature, history, and politics, they also implicitly demonstrate potentialities for future work. What strengths of current scholarship should be maintained, what problems addressed and redressed?

An emphasis on the workings of power is one of the principal contributions of contemporary Renaissance scholarship. Yet, as the new historicists have themselves acknowledged, this is also one of the principal areas that demands more scrutiny. We would suggest that in our current preoccupation with the symbolic manifestations of power we may sometimes lose sight of the more practical and material manifestations, even though they are closely related to the symbolic. Perhaps Mao Tse-tung was oversimplifying matters when he said that power comes out of the barrel of a gun, but (as one would expect) he had a point, and one which much contemporary discourse about power, more mindful of Foucault than of Mao, oddly elides. The *Annales* school is more mentioned than followed in contemporary literary and cultural studies; we need to focus on inheritance practices as well as coronation ceremonies, on the courts as well as on the court. (Similarly, some contemporary anthropologists have been suggesting that the pendulum in their field has swung too far in one direction: they maintain that we need to complement the current preoccupation with symbolic anthropology with a renewed interest in the functional questions that concerned an earlier generation of anthropologists. Recognizing that marriage may serve to transfer property or establish kinship ties should stimulate, not stifle, investigations into its symbolic languages.)

A review of contemporary investigations of power suggests another and related area for future work: we tend to concentrate too exclusively on centralized power. How much power accrued to a Catholic landowner on his Northumberland estate despite—or because of—his problematical relationships to the central power? How much to a wealthy widow in a Suffolk village? Given their positions in other milieux, how would (and did) such people react to the symbolic and tangible operations of power at court? How did the presence of such alternative power bases complicate those at court and, indeed, complicate the very notion of power?

We would also benefit from reconsidering and expanding the ways in which we borrow from other fields. For all their distrust of authority and authorship, contemporary literary critics are sometimes prone to rely uncritically on a single representative of another discipline, neglecting the ways his or her work has variously been reinterpreted, revised, or criticized by other members of that discipline. Lawrence Stone's work on the aristocracy and the family, for instance, will and should continue to inform our own, but we should also recognize that some of his fellow historians consider Stone's work on these subjects as problematic as it is provocative. Many scholars have found evidence in earlier eras of the qualities Stone ascribes to companionate marriage; others have questioned whether Protestantism did indeed affect marriage in the ways Stone asserts. Perhaps we have skirted problems like these in part because Stone so conveniently supports our own assumptions about patriarchy. In any event, however we evaluate the critiques of Stone's work, which admittedly are themselves controversial, we need at least to acknowledge and address the questions raised by such historians as Ralph Houlbrooke, Alan Macfarlane, and Keith Wrightson.[14]

We must be careful, moreover, not merely to substitute Foucault for Tillyard, a new Elizabethan world picture (read "Renaissance *episteme*") for the old one. We must maintain our sense of competing and fragmentary world pictures in the period. And this competition must not be seen as merely between high and low or courtly and popular—though these are, of course, rich topics. Two homogenized competing world pictures are better than a single monolithic one, but a socially stratified "dual-picture" picture is still much too neat. In replacing that model with a more accurate one, we could profit from looking more closely at contemporary history and historiography. While Foucault and some of the members of the *Annales* school in their different ways considered very broad time periods, many other historians define periodization in far smaller units; some, indeed, focus on distinctions among or between decades. Literary critics, however, have tended either to generalize about the English Renaissance as a whole, emphasizing the discontinuities that separate it from other periods, or, alternatively, to posit a sharp divide between Elizabethan and Jacobean England. At the very least we would profit from interrogating and justifying such notions of periodization, and we might find that our insights about broader time periods would be enriched by looking at smaller ones as well. Historians are also typically concerned to establish whether or not a given case is paradigmatic, a problem that, as many scholars have noted, we sometimes neglect in our own work. Literary critics, especially new historicists, too often merely assume that a striking anecdote is representative or revelatory; on this as so many other issues, we could benefit from looking more closely at our sister discipline.

Yet another lesson contemporary historiography could and should teach us is the importance of giving more than token attention to the lower classes, an aim that now characterizes a range of different historians. This perspective is, needless to say, easier to espouse in theory than in practice: for obvious reasons the social groups in question have left few records. Such difficulties may help to explain why, for all its covert and at times overt Marxism, the new historicism has thus far devoted comparatively little attention to the lower classes. Yet much as the familial relationships that Stone finds in the gentry and aristocracy may not reflect the behavior of the middle and lower classes, so responses to, say, the manifestations of royal power during a courtly pageant or even to self-fashioning itself are likely to vary from one social group to another. And gender differences, as well as the regional differences that we emphasized earlier, interact with and complicate these class distinctions—demonstrating yet again the limitations of binary models that merely distinguish the dominant and the subversive.

Anthropology, too, could enrich study of our period even more than it has done so far. Literary critics have tended to rely on a small handful of anthropologists. We might do well to consider other practitioners of that discipline. For example, adopting and adapting Geertz's insights, James Fernandez has developed a distinction between symbolic and social consensus; the former involves shared assumptions about what a social interaction or ritual means, while social consensus, in contrast, consists merely of an agreement that the interaction is necessary.[15] These concepts could perhaps provide a useful framework for the range between acquiescence and dissent in Renaissance culture. This study is only an example, one of the many directions our work could take if we widened our awareness of contemporary historians and anthropologists. It would, indeed, be useful to extend our formal and informal professional contacts as well as our readings in these fields. One of the most encouraging products of the contemporary ferment in historicist Renaissance (and other) studies is the impetus it has given to inter- and multidisciplinary work. We must devise new channels for continuing these contacts and projects, even new institutional channels in our often fragmented colleges and universities. More volumes like this one, including historians as well as literary scholars, might help.[16]

Whatever future developments may be generated by the studies of literature, history, and politics represented in this volume, the scope and the significance of our current investigations are apparent. The courtship of Clio is as fraught and as challenging an enterprise as the other types of courtship analyzed in this book—and the intellectual benefits it promises are far surer than the material benefits sought in vain by so many Renaissance courtiers.

Notes

1. Compare J. Hillis Miller, "Presidential Address, 1986: The Triumph of Theory, the Resistance to Reading, and the Question of the Material Base," *PMLA* 102 (1987): 290: "There is no crisis in the humanities. Quite the opposite. There is, rather, a tremendous vitality, a multiform intellectual energy and healthy diversity in all the fields and modes of our disciplines."

2. For an influential statement of this distinction, see René Wellek and Austin Warren, *Theory of Literature,* 3d ed. (New York: Harcourt, Brace, 1962), esp. pp. 73–74.

3. For some excellent caveats on the distinction between Burckhardt's actual project in *The Civilization of the Renaissance in Italy* and the usual understanding of Burckhardt's views, see Gordon Braden, "It's Not the Years, It's the Mileage," *NLH* 14 (1983): 672–75.

4. See, for instance, A. P. Rossiter's *Angel with Horns,* ed. Graham Storey (London: Longmans, Green, 1961).

5. For a "poetics of culture" see the introduction to Stephen Greenblatt, *Renaissance Self-Fashioning: From More to Shakespeare* (Chicago: University of Chicago Press, 1980), pp. 4–5. For a "new historicism" see Greenblatt's introduction to *The Forms of Power and the Power of Forms in the Renaissance, Genre* 15 (1982): 3–6. Occasionally, Greenblatt allows the latter term to lead him into polemics (see, for instance, "Shakespeare and the Exorcists," in *Shakespeare and the Question of Theory,* ed. Patricia Parker and Geoffrey Hartman [New York and London: Methuen, 1985], p. 165).

6. For the importance of Geertz to Greenblatt, see Richard Strier, "Identity and Power in Tudor England: Stephen Greenblatt's *Renaissance Self-Fashioning,*" *Boundary* 2 (1982): 384.

7. See Roland Barthes, "From Work to Text," in *Image, Music, Text,* tr. Ste-

phen Heath (New York: Hill & Wang, 1977), pp. 155–64; and Michel Foucault, "What Is an Author?" in *Textual Strategies: Perspectives in Post-Structuralist Criticism,* ed. Josué V. Harari (Ithaca: Cornell University Press, 1979), pp. 141–60.

8. See, for instance, the work of Natalie Zemon Davis, especially "Women on Top," in *Society and Culture in Early Modern France* (Stanford: Stanford University Press, 1975), pp. 124–51, and "Boundaries and the Sense of Self in Sixteenth-Century France," in *Reconstructing Individualism: Autonomy, Individuality, and the Self in Western Thought,* ed. Thomas C. Heller, Morton Sosna, and David E. Wellbery (Stanford: Stanford University Press, 1986), pp. 53–63.

9. Jean Howard, "The New Historicism in Renaissance Studies," *ELR* 16 (1986): 25. For some important queries about whether the new historicism escapes "reflection theory," see Edward Pechter, "The New Historicism and Its Discontents: Politicizing Renaissance Drama," *PMLA* 102 (1987): 293–94. Pechter's remarks about "fear of the text" in new historicism, however, seem misguided.

10. Louis Althusser, "Ideology and Ideological State Apparatuses" and "A Letter on Art in Reply to André Daspre," in *Lenin and Philosophy and Other Essays,* tr. Ben Brewster (New York and London: Monthly Review Press, 1978), pp. 127–86, 221–27.

11. See Louis A. Montrose, "Renaissance Literary Studies and the Subject of History," *ELR* 16 (1986): 6–7.

12. Jonathan Dollimore, "Introduction," *Political Shakespeare: New Essays in Cultural Materialism,* ed. Dollimore and Alan Sinfield (Ithaca: Cornell University Press, 1985), p. 12.

13. J. H. Hexter, *Doing History* (Bloomington: Indiana University Press, 1971), p. 68.

14. See Ralph A. Houlbrooke, *The English Family, 1450–1700* (London: Longmans, Green, 1984); Alan Macfarlane, *Marriage and Love in England: Modes of Reproduction, 1300–1840* (New York: Oxford University Press, 1986); and Keith Wrightson, *English Society, 1580–1680* (London: Hutchinson, 1982).

15. James Fernandez, "Symbolic Consensus in a Fang Reformative Cult," *American Anthropologist* 67 (1965): 902–29.

16. We happily acknowledge the existence of the volume edited by Kevin Sharpe and Steven N. Zwicker, *The Politics of Discourse: The Literature and History of Seventeenth-Century England* (Berkeley: University of California Press, 1987).

Part One
The Mid-Tudor Scene

A Tudor Queen Finds Voice:
Katherine Parr's
Lamentation of a Sinner

Did women have a Renaissance? Arguing for gender as one crucial factor in the differential cultural advances shown by historical eras, Joan Kelly followed up her question a decade ago with negative evidence drawn mainly from literary texts.[1] In their depictions of Renaissance court life, women fall gracefully silent as they accede to the place and roles allotted them in men's discourse. But perhaps Kelly's secular outlook was inadequate to address the complex of social facts. For Renaissance England there is another—even an arguably prior—question. Did women have a Reformation? A collection of essays recently edited by Margaret Hannay attests that they did, and yet the issues of female self-affirmation and self-expression remain vexed.[2] A gender differential shows just as clearly in the religious area of literary production. When they promote the faith of Protestantism, learned sixteenth-century Englishwomen almost exclusively play the facilitating roles of patrons, translators, and compilers; they do not author works of their own. As far as I know, if private letters and transcripts of legal testimony are discounted, Reformation England can claim nothing over late medieval England on the score of original female authorship in prose. Against Julian of Norwich's *Showings* or *Revelations of Divine Love* (short text in 1373, long text after 1393) and the dictated *Book of Margery Kempe* (1436–38), English Protestantism might at best hope to set the *First* and *Latter Examinations of Anne Askewe* (1545–47) as redacted by John Bale, were it not for one notable exception.

The two concluding years of Henry VIII's reign (1545–46) saw Katherine Parr, his sixth and last queen, at work on her prose treatise entitled *Lamentation of a Sinner,* an unfolding of the momentous significance she discerned in her Protestant conversion and a publication circulating under her own name within months of Henry's death. In this essay on the text and context of Parr's *Lamentation* I have set myself a twofold aim. First, I characterize in some specificity the achievement registered by this all-but-forgotten work. Second, I inquire into the conditions of its origination and its discourse. Such an inquiry necessarily raises a linked pair of questions about gender and authorship, questions that focus the feature of sexual difference taken, in this case, to its limit in uniqueness. How was Parr as a woman—specifically, a Tudor queen and wife—able to find voice in her *Lamentation* at all? To what extent and in what connections does the voice of the *Lamentation* become an identifiably feminine one?

In John Foxe's pages Katherine Parr receives a spirited portrayal as the Protestant heroine who angled nearest and best with Henry VIII to ensure the future of the Reformation in England.[3] But from anything Foxe records, one would never know that Parr had to her credit two publications as well as her canny exercise of power behind the throne: *Prayers or Medytacions, . . . Collected . . . by . . . Katherine quene of Englande* (1st ed. 1545, six more eds. by 1553) and *The Lamentacion of a sinner, made by the moste vertuous Ladie, Quene Caterin, bewayling the ignoraunce of her blind life* (1st ed. 5 November 1547; 2d ed. 1548; 3d ed. 1563).[4] Since the appearance of a survey article on Parr as a "woman of letters" just over a quarter century ago,[5] the handful of studies aimed at rescuing her from obscurity have, however, reinforced Foxe's view of Parr as ancilla rather than author.[6] These studies attribute to her influence the family harmony and godly erudition in which Edward VI and Elizabeth were nurtured. They present Parr equally as a skilled patron at court, sustaining Cranmer's and Latimer's importance during Henry's conservative last years while advancing several younger Protestant humanists who later attained public prominence, notably Ascham, Cheke, Grindal, and Parkhurst. They credit her with concurrent success in spearheading the project of making Erasmus's scriptural *Paraphrases* accessible in English together with the vernacular Bible in every church in the land.

When these studies reckon at all explicitly with gender, they salute Parr as an outstanding exemplar of female piety and female learning in a Tudor royal tradition that spanned four generations, beginning with Margaret Beaufort, continuing with Catherine of Aragon, redoubling strength with two representatives from the same generation, Catherine's daughter, Mary, and Katherine Parr, and ending with Elizabeth I. Yet recognition of such salient contextual facts has failed to address an equally important factor of uniqueness.[7] As an original composition, Parr's *Lamentation* is without parallel among the religious works in the literary remains of Tudor royal women. Their works are translations and compilations like her own earlier *Prayers*.[8] When Parr's *Lamentation* is set alongside the pious translations produced by other Englishwomen in the sixteenth century, further aspects of uniqueness emerge. In the fullest study we have of this body of work, Mary Ellen Lamb observes that, by century's end, translations of *ars moriendi* works had become an approved outlet for "a female literary strategy through which women could be represented as heroic without challenging beliefs of the patriarchal culture of Elizabethan England."[9] Over against this body of translations, Parr's *Lamentation* stands out for its surprisingly early date and its female author's emphasis on how to live rather than how to die as a Christian. How did Katherine Parr uniquely find the authorial voice that brought her *Lamentation* into being?

I consider the question of authorial voice central to any understanding of this work, although the matter has gone unaddressed in the general neglect of Parr as an author. In the fullest discussion of the *Lamentation* to date, a mere three pages, William Haugaard pays respect to the work as "a variation of the classic religious 'confession'" and "the witness of one lay Christian," but he cannot conceal his regret at Katherine's meager use of individuating touches.[10] She makes just two brief references to Henry VIII; in the first he is "such a godlie and learned king," and only in the second is he "my most soveraigne favorable lorde and housband."[11] She tells us nothing circumstantial about her conversion to the new Protestant faith. As a result of Parr's characteristic reticence in strictly autobiographical matters, her text has been shortchanged in critical discussion. Haugaard concludes, with James McConica, that the queen as author must be assimilated to the Erasmian strain that predominated in the Protestantism of the English court in the 1540s. Haugaard concludes this even though he is well aware that the *Lamentation* diverges sharply from Erasmus in one of its major emphases: Katherine's prolonged reflections on justification by faith as the authenticating mark of her conversion experience.[12]

In my view, an analysis of Parr's authorial voice in the *Lamentation* must begin by attending closely—not just approximately—to the content, organization, and style of what she is saying, in order to assess the adequacy of any putative models for her composition. But gender difference also keeps supervening on the question of models for religious prose, highlighting a complication grave enough to have almost muted female authorship in Parr's day. This is the fact that the available English models were entirely male authors.[13] How was Parr nevertheless able to work her way beyond her earlier borrowed speech of translation (in the *Prayers*) and voice herself as an author (in the *Lamentation*)? To this difficult but vital question there is neither a single nor a uniform answer.

There is not even a single or uniform way to go about seeking an answer. Natalie Davis, for example, has construed the question solely in contextual terms. Her essay on European women who wrote histories between 1400 and 1820 opens by listing four enabling conditions as requisites for female authorship: (1) access to historical materials and to public life, providing opportunities to observe and to ask questions; (2) access to genres of historiography, affording knowledge of rules for ordering and expressing materials; (3) a deep personal sense of connection and involvement with the areas of public life considered appropriate for writing history—termed "especially important" by Davis; and (4) sufficient assurance that the work would find an audience to take its author seriously.[14] At relevant points in the ensuing discussion I too will acknowledge the presence of one or another of Davis's contextual requisites. But my emphasis is deliberately much less contextual than Davis's. I work from the premise—and thus, in effect, argue—that enablement is not merely a product of circumstances. It is also a process that the woman author makes readable in the very production of her text. She reveals both the force and the limits of this process in how she, as author, handles her compositional models. I consider it extremely significant that Parr utilized multiple models in writing her *Lamentation,* and I try to construe the significance of this multiplicity. On the one hand, this fact of textual production bespeaks her relative confidence and independence in working with her models, as well as the support these males lend to her efforts. On the other, it highlights junctures where Parr cannot assimilate her female difference even to these composite resources, and she is compelled to speak otherwise than the males do. At such junctures, as a subject both held by and holding in suspension a yet-incomplete discourse, what Parr intimates is just so much of the woman in the author as her times and her purposes will bear.

In what follows I argue first that the case for relegating the *Lamentation* to an Erasmian model crumbles when Parr's essential divergences from Erasmus in formal structure, major themes, and prose style are duly clarified. I then propose an alternative model, wholly English but eclectic, that builds on Tyndalian foundations with local resources derived from Thomas Cranmer and more comprehensive ones derived from Hugh Latimer. Besides textual evidence, what we know of Parr's biography increases the likelihood that Cranmer and Latimer influenced her at first hand during the period when she was working on the *Lamentation.* Yet, as I have just suggested, even my eclectic English Protestant model will not finally explain every identifying feature of Parr's authorial voice. In calculating the influence of Cranmer and Latimer there are registrations of gender and reverberations from the political context to be added in also. Once this woman's precarious position as a Henrician queen is taken into account, we can better understand why she appears both peculiarly powerful and peculiarly constrained in giving voice to her concerns for her own and England's godliness. In the course of discussion I try to suggest how both work and author can be located within the context of early English Protestantism and how Parr's characteristically oblique self-representation in the *Lamentation* relates to her sense of her gender and status.

I

We know from a surviving inventory that Katherine Parr owned copies of two works by Erasmus, his magisterial *Enchiridion militis Christiani* (written 1501, published 1503; 1st enlarged ed., 1518) and his more minor *De praeparatione ad mortem* (1534).[15] From the fact of ownership we infer her direct acquaintance with Erasmus's central articulation of his "philosophy of Christ" in the *Enchiridion*.[16] Parr's *Lamentation* does exhibit certain Erasmian connections: most notably, the stress on Christian community, social solidarity, and ethical commitment as well as on the necessity of taking the message of Scripture to one's heart. In the 1540s, however, certain key issues were widening the nascent split between Catholics and Protestants, and on these issues Parr explicitly sets herself against Erasmus.

She repudiates his Aristotelian notion of virtue as a habit of the will based on knowledge; for Parr, human nature is inherently reprobate, and any goodness it has is "imputed" through justifying faith in the merits of "Christ crucifyed." Whereas Erasmus appropriates Plato's definition of knowledge to characterize faith as rationally grounded true belief, Parr distinguishes sharply between "dead, humayn, historicall fayth, & knowlege, gotten by humane industrie, . . . whiche may be had with all sinne" and the "true infused fayth and knowlege of Christe," which comes by divine gift when the soul trusts what God "promiseth, and bindeth him selfe by hys worde, to geve . . . to all them that aske hym with true fayth: without whiche, nothing can be doen acceptable or pleasing to God" (*Lamentacion,* sigs. Cii^v–Ciii^r, Biii^v–Biiii^r; *HM,* pp 294–95). She conceives of charity analogously, as the soul's divinely prompted response to the gift of justifying faith. Parr cannot even envisage as a possibility the Erasmian pattern in which the soul acquires charity and other virtues by emulating the example of Christ's life. Consequently, there is nothing in the *Lamentation* to compare with the continuous stress on spiritual effort that grounds Erasmus's use of the Pauline image of the armor of the Spirit as the controlling metaphor of the *Enchiridion*. Parr interprets the armor of the Spirit quite differently. To her this armor is not an array of weapons that every Christian can employ at will (*Enchiridion*, chap. 3), but the peculiar possession of the crucified Christ, by which he conquered the devil on behalf of humankind.

> The princes of the worlde, never did fight with-
> out the strengthe of the worlde. Christ contrary,   David and Christ
> . . . would fight, as David did with Golias, un-   compared in fight.
> armed of all humaine wisdom, and policy, and   Sapi. xvii.
> withoute al worldlie power and strength. Never-
> theles he was fullye replenished, & armed with
> the whole armour of the spirite. . . . Therfore
> when I loke upon the sonne of God . . . so un-   Spirituall Armure.
> armed, naked, geven up, and alone with humili-   Eph. vi.
> tie, pacience, liberalitie, modestie, gentlenes, and
> with all other hys divine vertues, beating downe
> to the grounde al goddes enemies . . . , I am
> forced to saye, that his victorie and triumphe,
> was merveylouse. And therfore Christ deserved   Jesus title.
> to have this noble title, JESUS OF NAZARETH, KING   Mat. xxvii.
> OF THE JEWES.
> (*Lamentacion*, sigs. Cii^v–Ciii^v; *HM*, p. 297)

Just as a soldier dons greaves, breastplate, sandals, helmet, and shield in a prescribed order, so Erasmus lays out his *Enchiridion* for his reader in a sequence of thirty-nine chapters, twenty-two of which are numbered "rules" for progress in the Christian life. This is as unlike Parr's handling of form as could be imagined. By and large, the *Lamentation* unfolds through discrete reflections on topics and Bible verses, keyed for the reader by marginal headings. In one typical run these go as follows: "Man of hys owne proude nature is easely made a Pharisey. Children lerne to be thankeful to your father. Rom. v. Harde hartes receyve no print. i. Cor. ii. Two yoke felowes, Blindnes & hardnes of harte. Profession in baptisme. Christ innocent. Esa. liii. Man sinful. Philip. ii. Christ obedient. Man stubburne. Math. ix. Christ humble. Man proud. John viii. Math. iiii. Christe hevenly. Man worldly. John xiii. John vi. Ma. xviii. Ma. viii. ii Cor. viii. Christ pore. Man riche. Lu. xiii. Lu. xxiii." (*Lamentacion*, sigs. Avi^v–Aviii^r; *HM*, p. 291). Although some antithetical patterning can be discerned here, the larger progression from topic to topic—say, from Pharisees to children to blindness and hardness of heart to baptism—remains unpredictable. This loose stringing together, offset somewhat by devices that locally heighten a sense of form, exemplifies how Parr works with images as well as with topics. A few of her more spiritually charged topics are inseparable from certain images. These topic-image pairings may recur at irregular intervals in combination with other topics, to form new thought complexes. For example, envisaging one's relation to God as that of a loving child, not that of a bond servant working for wages, appears first as a sheer impossibility for an unregenerate soul, next as the focus of a prayer Parr makes for all Christians, and finally as a sustaining element in the faith with which the godly confront the world (*Lamentacion,* sigs. Avi^v, Diii^v, Fiii^v; *HM,* pp. 291, 301, 310). Likewise, stonyheartedness is the condition Parr first reprehends in herself, later pinpoints as the source of the world's disregard of Christ, and still later makes the focus of a prayer for the efficacy of true ministers of the Word (*Lamentacion,* sigs. Aii^r, Avii^r, Dv^r; *HM,* pp. 289, 291, 302).

Except for scattered local antitheses, a few topic-image pairings, and the gradual replacement of private and individual concerns by more general and social ones, the overall sense of structure conveyed by the *Lamentation* is that of serialism. One thing simply follows another. In comparison with the *Enchiridion*'s scalar movement, the *Lamentation* may seem uncontrolled, rhetorically inept. Yet if we project Barbara Lewalski's account of the defining features of "Protestant emblematics" backwards a century, Katherine Parr will show as a formative Protestant writer both in the larger assemblage of her work and in her handling of such topic-image pairings as that of the stony heart. Regarding "larger structural features," Lewalski notes that Protestant revisions of Catholic sequences work "in the direction of randomness" to provide a model of the Christian life "as an irregular, episodic sequence of graces and temptations, successes and failures, rather than an ordered progress by set stages to spiritual perfection." In Protestant representations of the heart, "the special feature," says Lewalski, "is that God acts powerfully *upon* the heart—not located within it . . . , and not in conjunction" with the efforts of the human subject. "The implication is (in accordance with Protestant doctrine) that the renovation of the heart is entirely the work of grace and not a cooperative venture."[17] This implication is exactly the one Parr reaches in the last of her three uses of the image of the stony heart in the *Lamentation.*

The theological divide between Parr and Erasmus also produces marked differences of expression at the level of the sentence. According to Erasmus, the supreme value of Scripture is attested in two mutually reinforcing domains. In the human realm, Scripture draws validation from the weight of the Church's witness over centuries. In the natural realm, Scripture evinces a truth and wisdom that are fully consonant with nature and finally superior to it. This cumulative sense—of the plenitude of divine revelation, of so great a cloud of witnesses—finds cumulative form in the balances and suspensions of a single Latin period, which Coverdale sensitively rendered as follows in his vernacular abridgment of the *Enchiridion:*

> The first rule must be, that we so judge both of Christ and of his holy scripture, that we be sure, how that it greatly perteyneth to oure health, and that though al the world be against it, yet nothing that we perceave with oure natural senses is or can be so true, as it that is red in the scripture, enspyred of god himselfe, brought forth by so many prophetes, approved with the bloude of so many martirs, with the consent of all good men so many hundredth yeares, with the doctryne and life of Christ himself, with so many miracles, &c.: Which scripture is so agreable to the equite of nature, and every where so like it selfe, so raviseth, moveth, and altreth the myndes of them that take hede therunto, yea, and telleth of so many great, wonderful and true thinges, that yf we oft considre the same, it shall stere us up unto more ferventnesse both of faith, praier, and vertue, beyng sure, that as the rewarde of vice and of these momentany pleasures is both vexacion of mynde and eternall punishment, so unto good men shalbe geven an hundred folde joye of a pure conscience, and finally everlasting life.[18]

By contrast, Parr's scripturalism manifests itself as an immediate and subjective response, the first impulsion of her soul under justifying faith. Accordingly, she couches her testimony to the supreme value of Scripture in the ejaculatory, antithetical, and parallel constructions whose chief precedents lie in the Pauline epistles. As in Paul, so too in Parr, ejaculation and antithesis register the oscillations of gospel and law, of divine grace and human effort, that confound the sinner. Then, stabilizing the movement of the prose with their formal responsions, the parallelisms herald the assurance that accompanies true faith.

I knowe O my lorde, thy eyes looke upon my fayth: Saynt Paule sayeth, we be justified by the fayth in Christe, and not by the deades of the lawe. For, if rightwisenes cum by the lawe, then Christ died in vayne. S. Paule meaneth not here, a dead, humain, historicall fayth, gotten by humain industrie, but a supernall livelye fayth, which worketh by charitie, as he himselfe plainlye expresseth.	Justification by a Christian faythe. Roma. iii. Galat. ii. Galat. v.
. . . .	
By this fayth I am assured: and by thys assurance, I fele the remission of my sinnes: this it is that maketh me bold, this it is that conforteth me, this it is that quencheth all dispayre.	Lerne what true fayth doth in man. Ose. ii. Ephe. ii. Rom. v. Galat. iii

(*Lamentacion,* Biii^{r-v}, Bv^r; *HM,* pp. 293–95)

II

Since close examination shows Parr's *Lamentation* diverging markedly
from basic Erasmian features of thought and composition, a search for
possible models must turn elsewhere. Given the very close thematic and
tonal consonances between the reflections on justifying faith in the opening section of the *Lamentation* and Tyndale's repeated treatments of the
same subject, it is not surprising to find other stylistic and formal corre-
spondences between the two. It may, however, seem surprising that Henry's last queen would show any authorial affinities to a man who had been
arrested and burned as a heretic with Henry's complicity. Events in the
intervening decade—1536–46—indicate how this could come about.
Within months of Tyndale's burning in 1536, Cromwell and Cranmer
persuaded the king to confirm his independence of Rome and to bolster
his popularity in the realm by reversing his previous stand and authorizing a vernacular English Bible (mostly Tyndale's work, although this fact
was downplayed with Henry for obvious tactical reasons).[19] Henry's authorization opened the way for cautious maneuvering to credit Tyndale
as the chief exponent of the earliest phase of English Protestantism, and
by 1545 these maneuvers were on their way to success. Thus it is that
Parr's distinction between "a dead, humain, historicall fayth" and "a su-
pernall livelye fayth" leads clearly back toward Galatians by way of Tyndale's excursus on "historical" versus "feeling" faith in his *Answer to
More*.[20] Parr's preferences, moreover, in her profuse citations from Scripture reveal a systematic likeness to Tyndale's: the Pauline epistles and the
Gospels generally; more particularly, Matthew and the first epistle of
John, two texts for which Tyndale had provided detailed expositions.
Together with the fundamental Pauline content of Protestantism, Parr
assimilated the dynamics of Tyndalian style. I have discussed in detail
elsewhere the nervous, antithetical rhythms and the recursions that produce the clausal parallelisms and heaping catalogs so characteristic of
Tyndale's prose.[21] I shall not repeat myself, but instead offer a typical
instance of how similarly Tyndale and Parr could style their writing on a
shared theme. More than any other, the theme in question for them
here—the relation of faith and works in the true reception of the Gospel—would continue to engross the constructive efforts of English theologians throughout the era of the Reformation. Here, first, is Tyndale in
his *Prologue to Romans:*

Where the worde of God is preached purely, and received in the hart, there is faith, the spirit of God, & there also good workes of necessitie, whensoever occasion is geven. Where Gods	Where true fayth is, there are good workes.

word is not purely preached, but mens
dreames, traditions, imaginations, inventions,
ceremonies, & superstition, there is no faith,
and consequently no spirite that commeth of
GOD. And where Gods spirite is not, there can
bee no good workes, even as where an apple
tree is not, there can grow no apples, but there
is unbeliefe, the divels sprite, and evill workes.
Of this, Gods sprite and hys fruites, have our
holy hipocrites not once knowen, neither yet
tasted how swete they are, though they fayne
many good workes of their own imagination to
be justified withal, in which is not one cromme
of true fayth, of spiritual love, or of inward joy,
peace, and quietnes of conscience: for as much
as they have not the worde of GOD for them,
that such workes please GOD, but they are even
the rotten fruites of a rotten tree.[22]

Where fayth lacketh,
there is all evill
workes.

And here is Parr, in one of the socially oriented passages late in the *Lamentation:*

It may be seene how the worde of GOD is evill spoken
of through licencious and evil living: and yet the
worde of God is all holye, pure, sincere, and godlye,
beyng the doctryne and occasion of al holie and pure
living: It is the wicked that perverteth all good
thinges, into evill, for an evil tree can not bring furth
good fruite. And when good seed is sowen in a bar-
reyne and evil grounde, it yeldeth no good corne,
and so it fareth by the word of god: For when it is
heard, and knowen of wicked men, it bringeth furth
no good fruit: but when it is sowen in good ground,
I meane the hartes of good people, it bringeth furthe
good fruite aboundantlye: so that the want & faute
is in men, and not in the worde of god. I praye god
al men & women may have grace to becum meete
tillage for the fruites of the gospell, and to leave one-
lye the jangling of it. . . . For onlye speaking of the
gospel maketh not men good christians, but good
talkers, except theyr factes and workes agree with
the same: so then theyr speche is good, because
theyre hertes be good.

Evil lyving
slaundereth the
best profession.
Psal. xii.

Math. vii.
A similitude.
Math. xiii.
Applicacion.

Prayer.

Math. xii.

(*Lamentacion*, sigs. Fiᵛ–Fiiᵛ; *HM*, p. 308)

At the level of overall form, it is historically as well as literarily suggestive that Parr's *Lamentation* bears more resemblance to Tyndale's *Obedi-*

ence of a Christian Man (1528) than to any other prose tract I know from the period. The *Obedience* was the one work of Tyndale's that reportedly "delighted" Henry VIII when he read the first edition at Anne Boleyn's prompting.[23] The *Obedience* opens with a long, personal, urgently affective preface in which Tyndale exhorts his readers to be steadfast and ready to suffer for free access to the Word of life, the promises of the Gospel, in their own tongue. A much briefer prologue then modulates between personal and social concerns by reflecting that God turns the abuse of temporal power to his own ends, trying the constancy of true believers and exposing hypocrites. The extended body of the work follows. Deploying the categories of the Pauline epistles—rulers and people, clergy and laity, husbands and wives, parents and children, masters and servants—across the spectrum of Tudor society, Tyndale purports to develop a full account of Christian social obligation. The account becomes all the fuller as polemical and theological digressions swell the the main discussion.

A fluid tripartite movement also characterizes Parr's *Lamentation*. The work opens with an account of her conversion experience which is at once highly analytical and yet devoid of autobiographical specificity. Moralized commonplaces of faculty psychology—blind reason, wayward will, vain imaginations—lend a generic cast to Parr's evocation of her own subjectivity. At this precarious point, the inception of discourse, the genderlessness of the self-presentation bespeaks neither cowardice nor cooptation by male norms. Instead, the combination of universalism and personalism that energized early Protestants—the conviction that all souls are equal before God and that every soul is individually accountable to God—empowers Katherine to conceive herself as a subject for discourse on these common grounds. Such (as mine is), she implies, is the human soul. First she reprehends and confesses her sinfulness; then she evokes her struggles with justifying faith, which came home to her at last through her personal apprehension of the theology of the Passion. The middle section of the *Lamentation* expatiates on this theology, which is central to her religious outlook. Parr daringly appropriates devotional terminology for doctrinal purposes as she focuses on what she calls "the booke of the crucifixe." As she works her way toward the introduction of this term, she makes clear that her "crucifix" is not a physical object. Rather, it is a lively image which the inward eye of the Christian is enabled to see through knowledge of the Gospel as characterized by Paul in I Corinthians 2:2: "I determined not to know any thing among you, save Jesus Christ, and him crucified." Echoing the early Reformers' optimism about Bible reading by the laity, Parr outgoes Paul in her reiterated "booke" metaphor, her means for impressing upon her reader the accessibility of this knowledge of Christ. But like Tyndale, she ultimately returns her emphasis to Paul and to the feeling faith without which even the book of Scripture will remain a dead letter.

> Inwardlie to beholde Christ crucified upon the crosse, is the best and goodliest meditacion that can be. . . . Then we shall see our owne crueltie, when we feele hys mercy: our owne unrightwisenes and iniquitie, when we see his rightwisenes and holynes. Therefore to learne to knowe truly our owne sinnes, is to study in the booke of the crucifixe by continuall conversacion in fayth.
>
> *A christian mans booke.*
>
> . . . .
>
> This crucifix is the booke, wherein God hathe included all thinges, & hath most compendiously written therein all truth profitable and necessarye for our salvacion.
>
> *Lessons of the Crucifixe.*
> *i. Cor. ii.*
>
> . . . .
>
> And that this is true, is evident and cleare, bicause the verie true Christian is a Christian by Christe. And the true Christian feeleth inwardlye, by Christ. . . . The true Christian, by Christe, is disburdened from the servitude of the lawe, having the lawe of grace (graven by the Spirite) inhabiting his hart.
>
> *ii. Cor. iiii.*
>
> *Rom. vii.*
>
> (*Lamentacion,* sigs. Bvii^v–Bviii^r, Ci^r, Cii^{r-v}, Diii^r; *HM,* pp. 295–96, 297, 300)

The *Lamentation's* final section extends the lessons and truths of the "booke" of the crucifix into the domain of communal Christian behavior and daily social life. Parr's treatment here reflects the social optimism that characterizes early English Reformers until the accession of Mary Tudor: the polity itself is sound in its order, but occupants of specific positions within it stand in need of moral renewal, a livelier sense of responsibility for the welfare of fellow subjects and souls. Two categories of persons come in for Parr's reprehension, but she interestingly specifies no social positions for them: they are denominated only in Tyndalian terms as "wekelinges" and "carnall gospellers," timid or time-serving souls who deter the establishment of true Protestantism in the realm. By contrast, those whom she commends are "children," "servauntes," "housbandes," and "wyves" who attend to their respective callings. This final section ends with a summons to general amendment of life, reinforced with a sobering, heavily scriptural evocation of the Second Coming.

The affinities displayed in the tripartite structure of Tyndale's *Obedience* and Parr's *Lamentation* are reinforced by others at the local level of composition. The largely unpredictable serialism of both works marks them with the distinctively Protestant irregularity of design that Lewalski has identified for a later period. To organize smaller units of discourse within this open design, Parr employs strategies that Tyndale had adapted to English Protestant use from scholastic methods for disputation and scriptural exposition. Amid the welter of scriptural citations and the runs of miscellaneous headings in the margins of both works, a class of rubrics serves to point up discursive tactics and sectarian implications from time to time.[24] Examples in Tyndale include "An apte similitude," "Contrary preachyng, contrary Doctours," "A compendious rehearsall of that which goeth before" (*Whole Workes,* fols. 102, 109, 178; PS 43:149, 174, 331). Comparable headings in Parr read: "A similitude. Applicacion of the similitude," "Good latinistes and evil divines," "A conclusion with an answere to objections" (*Lamentacion,* sigs. Biiii^{r-v}, Ciiii^v–Cv^r, Fiiii^r, Giii^r; HM, pp. 298, 309, 312).

III

While considerably more pertinent than Erasmus's *Enchiridion,* Tyndale's *Obedience* proves far from an exhaustive model of composition for Parr. Time and again her *Lamentation* takes leave of Tyndalian disputation and scriptural exposition to range into doctrinal articulation, prayer, self-reprehension, moral fervor, and formal complaint. Parr's polyphony makes her voice much more varied than Tyndale's. If certain twentieth-century feminist theorists are correct, the best achievements of women writers will assume the form of "antiphonal, many-voiced works," a form that resists the demure silence or the male-dominant norms of expression to which female gender and authorship have historically been assimilated.[25] Yet Parr's case itself resists easy accommodation either to this contemporary feminist outlook or to Harold Bloom's widely espoused theory of literary history since the Renaissance as a (male) succession in which predecessors and models repeatedly trigger among later writers "the anxiety of influence" and a conflictual stance.[26] In the late Henrician court where the *Lamentation* emerges as a unique production by a female author, such polyphony as Parr achieved appears to have been fostered rather than hindered by close association with two authoritative and authoring males—the leading Protestant clerics Cranmer and Latimer. At this point, before considering textual ramifications of Parr's personal acquaintance with these two men, it is useful to follow Natalie Davis in noting contextual factors that bear upon Parr's authorship.

Although the *Lamentation* was first published nine months after Henry

VIII's death, in November of 1547, it seems that the queen circulated her manuscript earlier among some members of the innermost court circle. Anthony Martienssen, Parr's recent biographer, notes an ostensible reference to a copy of the *Lamentation* that Sir William Paget, one of Henry's two principal secretaries, sent to Stephen Gardiner, bishop of Winchester, the ranking exponent of the old faith in England.[27] Always alert to outspoken Protestantism—especially when it issued in "lamentation" critical of the established order—Paget made up a scandalous parcel for Gardiner, who was in Belgium conducting an embassy for the king. In the parcel, it seems, were a manuscript copy of Parr's *Lamentation of a Sinner* and a copy of Henry Brinkelow's newly printed *Lamentation of a Christian against the City of London, made by Roderigo Mors.* Gardiner's response to Paget, his coreligionist, in a letter dated 5 November 1545, vents his indignation against Brinkelow's book at some length. He promises to write an invective of his own to answer this invective against the London aldermen for failing to demand that the king do away with bishops. In his remarks on the queen's manuscript, Gardiner's heavy-handed repetitions betray his shock: "Mary, to the booke of Lamentacion which youe sent me, I wyl oonly answer lamentably to youe, and, lamentyng with youe, counforte myself; digesting in thiese letters so moch displeasour as I receyved in reding of this most abhominable booke."[28] Parr's book must indeed have been "abhominable" to Gardiner not only for its credo of justifying faith but also for the scorn it poured on "learned men" who "perswade to the credite and beliefe of certeyne unwritten verities, (as they call theym) whiche be not in scripture expressed, and yet taught as doctryne apostolike, and necessary too be beleved" (*Lamentacion,* sig. Fiiii[r]; *HM,* p. 309)—the gist of her passage labeled "Good latinistes and evill divines." Unwritten verities figured centrally in the defense of transubstantiation that preoccupied Gardiner in the late 1540s and set him in ever more bitter opposition to Cranmer.[29] The queen's disparagement declares her no traditionalist but a scripturalist, one of the archbishop's party.

Although we do not know when Katherine Parr underwent the conversion experience on which she reflects to open her *Lamentation,* situational considerations combine with textual ones to indicate that Cranmer's agency was probably crucial. We know that the queen and the archbishop were brought into close contact after the king decided to conduct the French war in person. Henry appointed Katherine regent during his absence—12 July to 1 October 1544—and Cranmer was assigned to attend constantly upon her (Martienssen, pp. 174, 180, 184). The third contextual factor identified by Davis—"a sense of connection, through some activity or deep concern of her own, with the areas of public life" in question, "namely, the political and the religious"—appears as germane to Parr as to Davis's four early modern women historians. So does Davis's fourth factor, an extension of the third. "This 'connectedness' with the issues of public life" gives the prospective woman author confidence to write, confidence that she can find "an audience who will take seriously her publications on these topics."[30] Wielding royal authority in Henry's place must have greatly increased Katherine's self-confidence while also engaging her to the hilt in public life. Her ten-week regency thus appears an important precondition for her finding of authorial voice.

Yet the queen by no means exercised her authorship as compliantly as she did the regency. Henry correctly chose Katherine as the safe vessel of his political concerns. She showed herself able thereafter to steer her own course in religious concerns, to embrace and express convictions opposed to his own (though not to publish them until after Henry's death). Chief among these is the tenet of justifying faith, so dear to the earliest English Protestants. One notable textual link with the queen's personal contacts during the period when she was at work on the *Lamentation* can be traced in her excursus on justifying faith, a passage that bears the stamp of Cranmer's thought and style alike. Here is Cranmer in the Homily of Salvation, which first appeared in print in July 1547:

> Thys sentence: that we be justifyed by faythe onely, is not so meant . . . that we shoulde or myghte . . . be justified wythoute our good workes, that we should do noo good woorks at all. . . . Trueth it is, that our owne workes do not justifye us, to speake properlye of our justifycation. . . . Nevertheles, because fayth doth directly send us to Chryst for remission of our synnes, and that by fayth geven us of GOD we embrase the promyse of gods mercy, and of the remission of our synnes (whyche thing none other of oure vertues or workes properly doeth): therefore Scripture useth to say, that faith . . . doeth justyfye. . . . But that we be justifyed by faith onelye, freely and without workes: is spoken for to take away clearly all meryte of our workes, . . . and therby wholly to ascribe the merite and deserving of our justification, unto Christ onely, and his most precious bloud shedynge.[31]
>
> Fayth alone, howe it is to be understand.

As Cranmer's thought threads its way through antitheses laden with predicate complements ("not so meant . . . that we shoulde or myghte . . . be justified wythoute our good workes," "do not justifye us, to speake properlye of our justifycation," "But that . . . is spoken for to take away clearely all meryte of our workes"), he locates the domain of justifying faith between two extremes: antinomianism, with its disdain for good works, and the works-religion that Protestants decried in Catholic doctrine and practice. In addition Cranmer's procedure is punctiliously analytic—that is, definitional—with respect to basic terms: faith, justification, remission, merit. When Parr in her *Lamentation* likewise undertakes to articulate justifying faith, her predicates evince the antithetical weighting of Cranmer's as they thread their way between the same extremes of antinomianism and works-religion ("is no dirogacion . . . for oute of this fayth springeth . . . yet we may not impute . . . : but ascribe and geve"). Her technical vocabulary and her penchant for doublings ("ascribe and geve," "referre and attrybute," "knowlege and perceyvyng," "very true onlye propertie") also reflect Cranmer's characteristic means for exact and exhaustive expression. His sonorous redundancies find an echo here in Parr's prose:

This dignitie of fayth is no dirogacion to good workes, for oute of this fayth springeth all good workes, yet we may not impute to the worthines of fayth or workes, our Justificacion before god: but ascribe and geve the worthynes of it, wholy to the merites of Christes passion, and referre and attrybute the knowlege and perceyvyng therof, onely to fayth: whose very true onlye propertie, is to take, apprehende and holde fast the promyses of goddes mercie, the whiche maketh us rightwise.	Dignitie of fayth hurteth no workes. Marke diligently without offence. Roma. iii. Roma. v.

(*Lamentacion*, sig. Biiii^{r-v}; *HM*, p. 294)

Apart from this crucial excursus, however, Parr's voice in the *Lamentation* owes more to the liturgical than the doctrinal Cranmer. Each of the collectlike prayers inserted at intervals in her text recalls Cranmer's mastery in this form.[32] Parr works with sureness in assembling the various elements—a vocative or "naming" noun phrase, followed by verb phrases of petition or thanksgiving with their associated complements and then by a final ascription or "renaming"—that fill the "subject" and "predicate" positions of a collect sentence. She also proves an attentive student of the chief syntactic devices used by Cranmer to spread and endow with nuance the capacious single sentence that compromises a collect. Thus in the example below, she emulates Cranmer's characteristic circularity of form and reference ("I shall pray to the lorde . . . that we may serve the lorde"). At the same time Parr's "that" clauses sustain the rich ambiguities between purpose and result on which Cranmer often plays to evoke the conformity of human will and action with the divine:

> I shall praye to the lorde, to take all contencion, & strife away,   Prayer.
> that the sowers of sedition, may have mynde to cease their
> labour, or to sowe it amongst the stones: & to have grace, to
> sowe gratious vertues, where they may both roote and bring
> furth fruite: with sending also of a godlie unitie, and concord   Luke i.
> amongest al Chrystens, that we may serve the lorde, in trewe
> holynes of life.
>
>   (*Lamentacion*, sig. Dv^r; *HM*, p. 302)

IV

If Katherine Parr took Cranmer as a model for certain formulary dimensions—both doctrinal and liturgical—in her work, she found something quite different and even more essential to her authorial purposes in the homiletics of Latimer. As a vocal and highly respected public figure, he provided an illustrious contemporary precedent for the strains of introspection and social morality that mingle in the *Lamentation*. We know that Latimer served as one of the Lenten instructors retained by Katherine in 1546 to expound the Gospels to her and her ladies-in-waiting every afternoon (Martienssen, p. 208). Perhaps she had become personally acquainted with him at an earlier point, for one of her closest friends since girlhood—Catherine Brandon, the intrepidly Protestant duchess of Suffolk—was Latimer's chief patron. Although it makes no mention of Latimer, the title page of the first edition of the *Lamentation* carries an aura of Latimerian association in its reference to "the instaunt desire of the righte gracious ladie Caterin Duchesse of Suffolke" to see this text "set furth and put in print."

Parr's text bears out Latimer's precedent more than anyone else's at crucial junctures of its production. She appears to draw much of her initial warrant as well as her ongoing stimulus for authorship from the self-referential mode so conspicuous in his preaching. Consciously universalizing in its terms and appeal, this Latimerian strategy aims to project the speaker's Protestant identity through avowals of personal failings and personal commitments which are figured, in turn, as responses to the impact of Scripture on experience. Here, for example, are the reflections that open Latimer's best known work, the Sermon of the Plough: "This is one of the places that hath bene racked, as I told you of rackyng scriptures. And I have bene one of them my self, that hath racked, I cry God mercy for it."[33] Elsewhere, in the third of the famous series of sermons delivered at court in 1549 before the boy king Edward, Latimer jestingly repels charges, old and new, that he has been guilty of seditious preaching. Then, suddenly striking a serious note, he confesses that he has been guilty in the past with regard to his calling in a very different way: "I remember how scrupulous I was in my time of blindnes and ignorauncie, when I should say Masse, I have put in water twise or thrise . . . , fearyng that I had not put in water inough." The marginal heading reinforces the self-accusation: "M. Latimer was somthyng scrupulous, when hee was a Masse sayer" (*Frutefull Sermons,* fol. 43^{r-v}; PS 27:138).

Latimer's penchant for reproaching himself before reprehending others finds a continuing analogue in Parr's *Lamentation.* This self-effacing path to authorship, while ultimately Pauline, also allowed for contemporary access by a woman as well as a man, when both, in "feeling faith" as Protestants, knew themselves sinners personally accountable to God. In the opening section Parr's efforts to establish her subject and herself as the speaker of her text move toward expression through self-reprehension. Before that point is reached, however, a suggestive grammatical detail intervenes. Parr's access to self-reference and self-representation, the "I" of her text, is specified as opening by way of another human, some generic "he," who sets an example for her. "Who is he," she asks, "that is not forced to confesse . . . if he consyder what he hath receyved of god, and dothe dayly receyve?" She then continues,

Trulye I am constrayned & forced to speake & write thereof to mine own confusion and shame: but to the greate glorye, and prayse of god.

. . . .

I woulde not cum unto him, but hyd my selfe out of his sight, seking many crooked & bye wayes, wherin I walked so longe, that I had cleane loste his sight. And noo marvayle or woundre, for I had a blynde guide called Ignoraunce, who dimmed so mine eyes, that . . . I coulde not thinke, but that I walked in the perfect and right way.

A blind guide for a blind way.

. . . .

I woulde not learne to knowe the lord and hys wayes. But loved darkenes better then light: yea, darknes semed to me, light. I embraced ignorance, as perfecte knowlege, & knowlege seemed to me superfluous & vayne. I regarded little goddes worde, . . . & followed the vayne folishe imaginacions of my hert. I would have covered my sinnes with the pretence of holynes: I called supersticion godlye meaning, and true holynes, erroure.

Jhon iii.

The jugement of man is corrupt in all thinges.

(*Lamentacion,* sigs. Aii^r–Aiii^v; *HM,* pp. 289–90)

This vocabulary of superstition, crooked byways, blindness, and ignorance as well as the capsule allegory of a blind guide called Ignorance
strongly point toward Latimer as the author who sets the course for Parr
in voicing her *Lamentation*. Yet it is not long before limitations on the
usability of a Latimerian model also begin to show in Parr's text. These
lead us back to manifest social and gender differences. Certain of Latimer's most characteristic strains—his indulgence in autobiographical
digressions, his frank delight in his reputation for earthy utterance, his
topical innuendos regarding the mighty of the realm, his sharp assertions
of his pastoral authority[34]—have no analogue whatever in Parr's voice.
Largely because of his outspokenness, in the plainest English, about Gospel imperatives for England in the here and now, Latimer became the
most famous preacher of his age. For him, it proved feasible if intermit-
tently risky to be a *succès de scandale*. Even when he opposed the Six
Articles in the turbulent 1540s, he met no worse fate than revocation of
his preaching license and confinement to private life in Warwickshire on
a comfortable pension from the crown. Nor was Latimer the only male
author to give voice in outspoken Protestantism during Henry's last
years. Brinkelow—the author paired with Parr in Paget's parcel—was
concurrently employing Tyndalian rhetoric to denounce Gardiner and
other public figures by name as corrupt wordlings, in *The Complaint of
Roderick Mors* (after 1542) and *The Lamentacion of a Christian against the
City of London, made by Roderigo Mors* (1545).[35] By contrast, when she
undertook to write her *Lamentation of a Sinner,* Queen Katherine Parr
held a position so much more contingent and precarious than these men
that the question of how she was able to sustain her voice as a Protestant
author at all returns with new force.

V

At no point in her life or authorship, least of all between 1545 and 1547,
were the prerogatives of a ranking male cleric open to Katherine, either
for denouncing prominent sins and sinners or for braving down a charge
of sedition with a jest. A fuller glance at her situation in the spring of
1546, when Latimer was instructing her in the Gospel, will confirm the
point. This same spring saw the beginning of a plot to dethrone Katherine, which Gardiner masterminded, playing on certain signs of the king's
exasperation with his intelligent and now zealously Protestant wife. The
queen was to be discredited with Henry. She would be exposed as a pre-
sumptuous meddler with his authority and, worse yet, an adherent of a
religion that "did not onely disallow and dissolve the policie and politicke governement of Princes, but also taught the people that all thynges

ought to be in common."[36] To this end, the Gardiner faction engineered the second arrest and interrogation of another longtime friend of Parr's, the brilliantly self-possessed Anne Askew. Renegade enough in having left her two children and her uncongenial husband, Askew had also studied on her own and become learned in the Bible. Her studies led her to repudiate transubstantiation as unscriptural and to express openly memorialist beliefs about Holy Communion. Since she had been in trouble with the authorities about her religious convictions only a year before, Anne fell under suspicion as the likely purveyor of incriminating books found in the queen's chamber. Perhaps she could be made to confess things that would bring down Queen Katherine. Anne was accordingly taken back into custody, where highly placed officials racked her with their own hands. All was to no avail so far as evidence for Gardiner's plot against Katherine went. What Anne did say, however, ensured that she would shortly die at the stake as a heretic.[37] For her part, the quick-witted Katherine reingratiated herself with Henry by volunteering her utter submission to his will before she was ever formally accused.[38]

Here context throws light on a differentiation that cuts across gender to distinguish Anne from Katherine, the defiant from the compliant female, the silenced woman from the one who somehow sustained voice. Parr's text renders that "somehow" historically specific and readable. As the *Lamentation* gains momentum after its launching in Latimerian self-reproach, Parr undertakes by degrees, at selected junctures, to feminize her voice in keeping with her position as Henry's queen. In so doing, she marks her distance from the species of inflammatory Protestant rhetoric practiced by Brinkelow and Askew, and she also sets limits on Latimer's usefulness to her as a model. Unlike "Roderick Mors," Parr will not name names in seeking to advance the Gospel by her mode of lamentation. Nor will she arrogate final authority to herself under her new faith, as Anne had done. A probable allusion to Anne begins in sympathy for those who are "moste cruellie persecuted" when they set themselves "contrarie" to "pastoures . . . so blynded wyth the love of theymselves, and the worlde, that they extol mens invencions and doctrines, before the doctrine of the gospell" although "they be not able to maintayne theyr owne invencions and doctrines, with any jot of the scrypture." "Is not this miserable state," asks Parr, "muche to be lamented of all good christians?" But she proceeds to distance herself from the derisive exposing of error that Askew takes satisfaction in practicing in her *Examinations*. "Yet I can not allow, neyther prayse al kynd of lamentacion," says Parr, "but suche as maye stande with Christian charitie" (*Lamentacion*, sigs. Ei^v–Eii^r; *HM*, p. 304). The conception Katherine voices of her own primary "vocacyon" even as queen—that of "women maryed"—is as conformably Pauline in its content as in its style: "Not beyng accusers, or detractours, . . . they teache honest thinges, to make the yong women sobre minded, to love theyr housbandes, to love theyr children, to be discrete, chast, huswiflye, good, & obedient unto theyr housbandes, that the worde of god be not evil spoken of" (*Lamentacion,* sig. Giiʳ; *HM,* p. 311).

As a result of Parr's distinct if subtle feminization of her voice, ongoing connections between Latimer's homiletics and the *Lamentation* focus the question of how the factor of gender will be accommodated. Her text, in fact, shows gender to be a variable: a difference that may or may not figure within the universalism and personalism of early English Protestantism. Thus, the prayers with which Parr recurrently climaxes and off-sets the plaintive movements of the *Lamentation* can draw validation, if they need to, from Latimer's pronouncement on the "sacrifice of prayer": "this sacrifice a woman can offer as well as a man" (*Frutefull Sermons,* fol. 57ᵛ; PS 27:167). But what Latimer says in the passage that follows this pronouncement is even more comprehensively suggestive regarding Parr's disposition of tones and themes in the *Lamentation.* He declares of prayer, "So, to make an end: This must be done with a constant fayth, and a sure confidence in Christ," and then appends this characteristic capsule allegory:

This fayth is a great state, a lady, a Dutches, a great woman, and she hath ever a great company and traine about her (as a noble estate ought to have). First, she hath a gentleman Usher that goeth before her, and where he is not, there is not Lady fayth. This gentleman Usher is called *Agnitio peccatorum,* knowledge of sinne, when we enter into our hart, and acknowledge our faultes, and stand not about to defend them. . . . Now, as the Gentleman Usher goeth before her, so she hath a traine that commeth behinde her, and yet though they come behinde, they be all of Faythes company, . . . and those be the workes . . . when every man considereth what vocation he is in, . . . and doth the workes of the same, as to be good to his neighbour, to obey God, &c. This is the trayne that foloweth Lady Fayth: as for an example: A faythfull Judge hath first an heavy reckoning of hys fault, repenting him self of his wickednes, & then forsaketh his iniquitie, his impiety, feareth no man, walkes upright, and

> Faith is a great
> state and a
> Dutches.
>
> Knowledge of sinne
> is gentleman Usher
> to Lady Fayth.

he that doth not thus, hath not Lady Fayth,
but rather a boldnes of sinne, and abusing of
Christes passion.
(*Frutefull Sermons,* fol. 58ʳ; PS 27:168–69)

Admittedly, the historical personage evoked and complimented in Latimer's allegory of Lady Faith is not Katherine Parr but, rather, her close
friend Catherine Brandon, Latimer's patron. Yet, thanks to the modula-
tions of Latimer's imagery to include both genders, the authorial Katherine Parr can be identified with the "faythfull Judge," one who follows
or has Lady Faith. Such a one "hath first an heavy reckoning of hys fault,
repenting him self of his wickednes, & then forsaketh his iniquitie, his
impiety, feareth no man, walkes upright." It is remarkable how exactly
this sequence—from faith through repentance to upright works—patterns the overall movement and scope of Parr's *Lamentation.*

As her title and subtitle declare and reinforce, the genre of her work is
a "lamentacion or complaynte" (*Lamentacion,* sig. Aiʳ).[39] The text confirms this generic assignment at the repeated junctures where Parr at
once renews her voice and takes a new subject. Thus her transition from
confession of sin to repentance in faith is signaled by the marginal rubric,
"Lamentacion," and begins thus: "What cause nowe have I to lament,
mourne, sigh, & wepe for my life, & tyme so evil spent?" (*Lamentacion,*
sig. Aviiiᵛ; *HM,* p. 292). Later, striving to give force to the theology of
the Passion which occupies her "booke of the crucifixe" section, Parr
renews her mode of lamentation through another recourse to Latimerian
self-reproach. All the while, however, she sustains a measure of distance
from Latimer in her characteristically unspecific first-person utterances
and in the recognizably feminine connotations that she draws from biblical imagery to attach to herself (here, the pliable clay being molded into
a vessel by the potter's hand).

I certeynlye never knewe myne owne miser-ies, and wretchednes so wel, by booke, ad-monicion, or learnynge, as I have doen by lokyng into the spirituall booke of the cruci-fix. I lamente muche I have passed so manye yeares, not regardyng that divine booke. . . . I never knew myne owne wy-ckednes, neyther lamented for my synnes truly, untill the tyme God inspired me with his grace, that I looked in this booke. Then I beganne to see perfectly, that . . . I was in the Lordes hande, even as the cleye, is in the pot-	The booke of the crucifixe. The first lesson in the booke. Hie. xviii. A christien complaynt.

ters hande: then I began to crye, and saye:
Alas lorde.
    (*Lamentacion,* sigs. Dii^v–Diii^v; *HM,* p. 301)

As noted earlier, this central section, which elaborates the metaphor of the "booke of the crucifixe," is one of the most striking in the *Lamentation.* Here we are brought to the heart of Katherine Parr's theology. Especially notable is the avoidance of any reference to liturgical images, the roods and crucifixes to which Henry had so deep an attachment, or to the Sacrament of the Body and Blood, a prescribed understanding of which in those years was literally a burning issue. While Katherine was working on her *Lamentation,* the martyrdom of Anne Askew came as a horrific reminder of the consequences of declaring publicly against the corporeal real presence in the Sacrament. The queen rejected for herself the voice and authorship of sorts that Anne found through defiance and revolt. Yet Katherine did not pass in silence over the currently dangerous subject of how the faithful receive Christ to themselves. For her, the Passion becomes the vital meeting point of private religious feeling and public enactment, or, more simply, of the faith and works that English Protestants remained so intent on uniting. Drawing on Pauline sources, Parr urges that the mystery of receiving and being received into Christ's body be taken to signify affective incorporation in the community of true Christians. The transitivity of her syntax in a key passage enacts what she seeks to elicit, a sense of divine love made so apprehensible in human form as to inspire humans to embody that love in their lives and institutions.

> The sincere, and pure lovers of god, doo embrace   True christians.
> Christe, with such fervencie of spirit, that . . . they   Ro. xii.
> knowe by their fayth they are members al of one   i. Cor. xii.
> bodie, and that they have possessed al one God, one   Eph. iiii.
> fayth, one baptisme, one joie, and one salvacion.
>   (*Lamentacion,* sig. Dv^r; *HM,* p. 302)

To crown her presentation of a nonliturgical, nonsacramental, yet fully scriptural theology of the Passion as the core of her understanding of true Christianity, Parr proposes to identify communion with Christ as the communion of those who have become "members al of one bodie" by embracing Christ through justifying faith. In 1545–46, when eucharistic controversy abounded, this was a constructive achievement without analogue among English writers. Its singularity may be the result of universalism and personalism conceived specifically by a woman—that is, from a necessarily lay perspective on the institutionalizing of participatory religion. In Parr's conception of Christian communion, the private domain of affectivity and the one public domain—worship—open equally to men and women merge in a spiritual vision of the harmonious English body politic and ecclesiastic that finds more earthbound expression in the social programs and preaching of Latimer and other so-called commonwealth men.[40]

VI

At the transition from the "booke of the crucifixe" section to the socially oriented final section of the *Lamentation,* Parr's vocabulary of lament again takes an expressly Latimerian turn: "It is muche to be lamented, the . . . contencions, and disputacions, that have ben, and are in the worlde aboute Christen religion, & no agremente, nor concord of the same, amongest the learned men. Treuly the devell hath ben the sower of the seede of sedicion, and shalbe the maynteyner of it, even tyl Gods wyll be fulfylled" (*Lamentacion,* sig. Dvii^{r-v}; *HM,* p. 303). At this point also, reverberations arise from the historical context to reinforce the continuity, within Parr's text, both of her concerns as queen and author and of her relations with Latimer. Early in the Lenten season in which Latimer instructed her, the queen received a letter from Sir Thomas Smith, Regius Professor of Civil Law, on behalf of Cambridge University. Smith appealed to the queen for help in preventing the king and his agents from exercising newly legislated powers of confiscation against the university's buildings and lands. Katherine's letter of reply (26 February 1546) urges her view that Cambridge must use its "sundry gifts, arts, and studies . . . as means and apt degrees to the attaining and setting forth the better Christ's reverend and most sacred doctrine, that it may not be laid in evidence against you at the tribunal seat of God how ye were ashamed of Christ's doctrine. For this Latin lesson I am taught to say by Saint Paul, *Non me pudet evangelii.*" Only after stressing that human learning exists to serve and advance knowledge of the Gospel does Katherine announce the results of her intercession with Henry. The king has, she reports, reaffirmed his intention of being "a patron of good learning" who "will rather advance and erect new occasion therefor, than confound those your colleges."[41] The absolute priority set by Parr, in this letter and in the final section of the *Lamentation,* on the use of human learning to disseminate the Gospel is likely to owe its force if not its exact formulation to the teaching of Latimer.

One of the most persistent concerns in Latimer's extant sermons is the need for doctrinally sound, personally committed ministers of the Gospel to combat superstition, ignorance, and a host of social abuses in England. This need not only figures centrally in the Sermon of the Plough, but was a major theme as early as his two-part Convocation sermon of 1538 on a portion of Luke 16:8: "The children of darkness are wiser in their generation than the children of light." In this sermon to the clergy themselves, Latimer spoke with characteristic plainness.

> Nay, this greeved Christ, that the children of this world should be of more pollicye then the children of light; which thing was true in Christes time, and now in our time is most true. . . . Among the Lay people the world ceaseth not to bring to passe, that as they be called worldly, so they are worldly in-deede, driven hedlong by worldly desires. . . . In the Clergy, the world also hath learned a way, to make of men spirituall, worldlinges, . . . where with great pretence of holiness, and crafty colour of religion, they utterly desire to hyde and cloke the name of the world.
>
> *The children of this world ar of more pollicy, then the children of light.*
>
> (*Frutefull Sermons,* fols. 4ᵛ, 5ᵛ; PS 27:41, 43)

This Latimerian topicality, which construes Luke 16:8 as an indictment of England's worldly and otherwise unreformed clergy, is picked up and reechoed by Parr in the last section of the *Lamentation*. But she stops short of proposals for institutional reform, contenting herself with de-crying abuses and promoting godly uses of learning. Since Latimer's po-sition as a cleric admonishing fellow clerics is barred to her, her own reprehensions remain more general and oblique than his while nonethe-less developing out of the very text of his Convocation sermon:

> I suppose there was never more nede of good doctryne to be set furth in the worlde, then nowe in thys age: for the carnall children of Adam be so wise in theyr generacion that, yf it were pos-sible, they would deceyve the chyldren of lyght.
>
> *This age requyreth lernyng. Worldly children.*
>
> . . . .
>
> It wer al our partes and duties, to procure and seeke all the wayes and meanes possyble, to have more knowlege of goddes wordes, set furthe abrode in the worlde, and not allowe Igno-raunce, and discommende knowledge of gods woorde, stopping the mouthes of the unlearned, with suttle and crafty perswasions of Philoso-phie, and Sophistrie, wherof commeth no fruite, but a greate perturbacion of the mynde, to the simple & ignoraunt, not knowing whiche waye to turne theym.
>
> *Knowlege wished against ignoraunce.*

. . . .

The fleshly children of Adam bee so politicke,
subtil, craftie, and wise in theyr kynde, that the
electe shoulde be illuded if it were possible: for
they are clothed with Christes garment, in utter
apperaunce, with a fayer shewe of al godlines,
and holines in theyre wordes.

(*Lamentacion,* sigs. Fiiiʳ–Fvᵛ;
HM, pp. 308, 309–10)

This critique of abuses of human learning by enemies of true religion
modulates into the passage, already noted, where Parr appears to distinguish Askew's self-expression from her own, in terms of an unwarranted
and a warranted "kynd of lamentacion, . . . suche as maye stande with
Christian charite" (*Lamentacion,* sig. Eiiʳ, *HM,* p. 304). But it is her conclusion that supplies the lengthiest demonstration of how inseparable for
Parr were the rightness of her lamentation and the writing of her *Lamentation.* While she as a woman can neither legislate nor preach reform, she
can make an example of herself as a regenerate sinner through her authorship. By this means, in turn, her voice can and does entreat a serious
hearing from others:

God knoweth of what intent and minde I have lamented mine owne sinnes, & fautes to the worlde.
I trust no bodye will judge I have doon it for prayse,
or thanke of any creature, since rather I might be
ashamed then rejoyce, in rehersall therof. For, yf
they knewe how little I esteme, and wey the prayse
of the worlde, that opinion were soone removed &
taken awaie: . . . for I seeke not the prayses of the
same, neither to satisfie it, none other wise, then I
am taught by Christ to dooe, according to Christen   Godly wish.
charitie. I woulde to god we would al (when occa-
sion doth serve) confesse oure faultes to the world,
al respectes to oure owne commoditie laied aparte.

. . . .

Yf any man shalbe offended, at thys my lamenting   A conclusion
the fautes of men, whiche be in the worlde, fanta-   with an answere
sying with theym selves, that I do it eyther of ha-   to objections.
tred, or of malice, to any sort of kynde of people:
verely, in so doing, they shall dooe me greate
wrong: for, I thanke God by hys grace I hate no
creature: yea, I woulde saye more to geve witnes of
my conscience, that nether life, honour, riches,
neyther what soever I possesse here, whiche apper-

teyneth unto myne owne private commoditie, be it
never so deerlie beloved of me, but moste willinglie
and gladly I woulde leave it, to winne any manne to
Christ, of what degre or sorte, soever he were. And
yet is this no thing in comparison to the charitie that
God hath shewed me, in sendinge Christe to dye for
me: no, yf I had all the charitie of Aungels, and
apostles, it shoulde be but like a sparke of fyer compared to a great heape of burning coles.
(*Lamentacion,* sigs. Giii^r–Giiii^v; *HM,* p. 312)

Manifold implications regarding social, religious, and literary aspects
of early English Protestantism arise from the play of contraries in Parr's
self-representation and self-realization as an author. On the one hand, her
brief early references to her relation to Henry VIII and her later Pauline
excursus on wifehood mark her gender and position as conformably
feminine. On the other hand, the process of composition also bespeaks a
gradually intensifying sense of spiritual authority in the work, however
much Parr hedges this in with disclaimers. Thus, in the third and final
section, a sentence may begin modestly enough: "Truly in my simple,
and unlearned judgement . . ." But it continues in ringing tones that cast
self-effacement behind: "no mannes doctryne is to be estemed or preferred lyke unto Christes and the Apostles, nor to be taughte as a perfect
and true doctrine, but even as it doth accorde and agree with the doctrine
of the gospell" (*Lamentacion,* sig. Ei^{r-v}; *HM,* p. 304). As the *Lamentation*
draws to a close, Parr's increased self-assurance bespeaks her sense of the
measure of power to be wielded in the larger religious and social domains
of her time, specifically through authorship.

Yet Parr herself insists that any spiritual authority attaching to her
words has no further design or objectification than the book she is writing. "I have, certeynly," she says, "no curious learning to defende . . . ,
but a simple zele, and earnest love to the truth, inspired of god, who
promiseth to powre his spirite upon al flesshe: whiche I have by the grace
of god (whome I moste humblye honour) felt in my selfe to be true"
Lamentacion, sig. Bviii^{r-v}; *HM,* p. 295). Here the egalitarian tendencies
in early English Protestantism, a strain deeply involved with its scripturalism ("the truth, inspired of god, who promiseth to powre his spirite
upon al flesshe"), clearly register their contribution to Katherine Parr's
authorship as an effect of God's spirit: "felt in my selfe to be true."[42] No
less clearly, however, she herself is careful to refer her authorship to a
realm where the single, ultimate relation of the soul to God transcends
and sets at naught both gender and every other mark of human difference. Overlaying its subtly feminine tones with a prevailing generality

and near anonymity of expression, Parr's *Lamentation* does nothing to impede the program of defusing Protestantism of its radical social potentialities, which was in full career in the England of her day.

However muted the femininity of Parr's voice through long stretches of the *Lamentation,* her gender does operate authorially nonetheless. At midcentury no less than at the end of it, a low voice was ever an excellent thing in women. It was surely obligatory for keeping one's head as a Henrician queen. As I have shown, femininity circumscribes the public domain within Parr's discourse and screens topicality, polemic, and personality from her text. Only the factor of gender, as conditioned by her experience and activated in her text, is adequate to account for the consistent measure of literary distance between Parr's voice and some of the most characteristic strains in Latimer's preaching, as well as the greater distance of her work from the invective of reformers like Tyndale, Brinkelow, Bale, and others. Paget was seriously mistaken, after all, in thinking to make one parcel for Gardiner of this *Lamentation* and the *Lamentation of a Christian against the City of London.* If we are willing to attend with greater sensitivity both to its shared and to its individuating features, we may eventually come to recognize in Parr's *Lamentation* one of the rarer literary achievements of early English Protestantism.[43]

Notes

1. Joan Kelly, "Did Women Have a Renaissance?" in *Women, History, and Theory: The Essays of Joan Kelly* (Chicago and London: University of Chicago Press, 1984), pp. 19–49, reprinted from *Becoming Visible: Women in European History,* ed. Renate Bridenthal and Claudia Koontz (New York: Houghton Mifflin, 1977), pp. 137–64.

2. Margaret Patterson Hannay, ed., *Silent but for the Word: Tudor Women as Patrons, Translators, and Writers of Religious Works* (Kent, Ohio: Kent State University Press, 1985).

3. See *The Acts and Monuments of John Foxe,* ed. Stephen Reed Cattley (London: Seeley & Burnside, 1846), 5:553–61.

4. Both works are in Pollard and Redgrave's *Short Title Catalogue (STC),* nos. 4818 and 4827 (first editions).

5. C. Fenno Hoffman, Jr., "Catherine Parr as a Woman of Letters," *HLQ* 23 (1959): 349–67.

6. See James Kelsey McConica, *English Humanists and Reformation Politics under Henry VIII and Edward VI* (Oxford: Clarendon Press, 1965), pp. 200–234; William P. Haugaard, "Katherine Parr: The Religious Convictions of a Renaissance Queen," *RQ* 22 (1979): 346–59; E. J. Devereux, "The Publication of the English Paraphrases of Erasmus," *BJRL* 51 (1968–69): 348–67, esp. pp. 354–60; Anthony Martienssen, *Queen Katherine Parr* (London: Secker & Warburg; New York: McGraw-Hill, 1973), pp. 1–28, 144–225; and John N. King, "Patronage

and Piety: The Influence of Catherine Parr," in *Silent but for the Word,* Hannay, pp. 43–60. Elizabeth H. Hageman provides a helpful annotated bibliography as "Part 1: Women Writers, 1485–1603" of "Recent Studies in Women Writers of Tudor England," *ELR* 14 (1984): 409–25, esp. p. 414.

7. Laudatory generalities have characterized the small critical notice taken of Parr's *Lamentation* to date. Conyers Read, in *Mr. Secretary Cecil and Queen Elizabeth* (London: Jonathan Cape, 1955), p. 40, apparently issued the first call for recognition of the work's interest and merit. Roland H. Bainton, "Catherine Parr," in *Women of the Reformation in France and England* (Minneapolis: Augsburg Publishing House, 1973), pp. 161–81, took the further step of hailing the *Lamentation* as "one of the gems of Tudor devotional literature," comparable in quality to Marguerite de Navarre's *Chansons spirituelles* or Vittoria Colonna's *Rime religiose.*

8. Margaret Beaufort, Henry VII's mother, englished the fourth book of *The Imitation of Christ* (see *The Earliest English Translation . . . of De Imitatione Christi,* ed. John K. Ingram, Early English Text Society, extra ser. 63 [London: Kegan Paul, Trench, Trübner, 1893], as well as the *Speculum aureum peccatorum,* which Wynkyn de Worde printed under the title *The miroure of Golde to the synful Soule* in 1522. Mary Tudor, Catherine of Aragon's erudite daughter, contributed to the project of englishing Erasmus's *Paraphrases* at Katherine Parr's behest (see Devereux, "The Publication of the English Paraphrases of Erasmus"). The eleven-year-old Elizabeth Tudor presented her stepmother, Katherine Parr, with an English prose version of Marguerite de Navarre's poem *Le Miroir de l'âme pécheresse* as a New Year's gift in 1544: for the text, see Percy W. Ames, ed., *The Mirror of the Sinful Soule: A Prose Translation . . . by the Princess (Afterwards Queen) Elizabeth* (London: Asher and Co., 1897); for discussion, see Anne Lake Prescott, "The Pearl of the Valois and Elizabeth I: Marguerite de Navarre's *Miroir* and Tudor England," in *Silent but for the Word,* Hannay, pp. 61–76. Elizabeth's other religious translations—from Boethius, Calvin, and others—are listed, along with pertinent studies, in Hageman's bibliography, *ELR* 14:416–18. As Hoffman discovered ("Catherine Parr as a Woman of Letters," p. 354), Katherine Parr's own *Prayers or Medytacions* (1545) is almost wholly comprised of an abridgment of the third book of *De imitatione Christi* in Richard Whytford's translation (published ca. 1530).

9. Mary Ellen Lamb, "The Countess of Pembroke and the Art of Dying," in *Women in the Middle Ages and the Renaissance: Literary and Historical Perspectives,* ed. Mary Beth Rose (Syracuse: Syracuse University Press, 1985), p. 209.

10. Haugaard, "Katherine Parr," pp. 356, 358.

11. Katherine Parr, *The Lamentacion of a sinner, made by the most vertuous Ladie, Quene Caterin, bewayling the Ignoraunce of her blind life: set furth and put in print at the instaunt desire of the righte gracious ladie Caterin Duchesse of Suffolke & the earnest requeste of the right honourable Lord, William Parre, Marquesse of North Hampton* (London, 1547), sig. Dvʳ. In the reprint of the *Lamentation* in *The Harleian Miscellany* (London: Robert Dutton, 1808), 1:286–313, these quotations occur on p. 302. Subsequent references to these two editions of 1547 and 1808 are abbreviated *Lamentacion* and *HM* respectively, and are incorporated in my text.

Throughout this essay, when I cite Parr and other sixteenth-century authors, I normalize *i* and *j*, *u* and *v*. I also silently expand all printers' contractions except the ampersand.

12. Haugaard, "Katherine Parr," pp. 349, 357–58.

13. For a sensitive assessment of the conditions that silenced Tudor women writers—one, however, limited to the situation for poetry writing—see Gary F. Waller, "Struggling into Discourse: The Emergence of Renaissance Women's Writing," in *Silent but for the Word*, ed. Hannay, pp. 238–56, esp. pp. 245–49.

14. Natalie Zemon Davis, "Gender and Genre: Women as Historical Writers, 1400–1820," in *Beyond Their Sex: Learned Women of the European Past*, ed. Patricia H. LaBalme (New York and London: New York University Press, 1980), pp. 153–82; quotation from p. 154.

15. F. Rose-Troup, "Two Book Bills of Katherine Parr," *The Library*, 3d ser., 2 (1911): 40–48. Parr's copies were both English translations: the *Enchiridion* a John Byddell imprint in one of several years (1533, 1534, 1538, or 1544, when it was "newly corrected and amended"), the *Preparation to Death* a Thomas Berthelet imprint in 1543 (pp. 42–43).

16. On the importance of the *Enchiridion* as the best single source for Erasmus's conception of the Christian life, see Preserved Smith, *Erasmus: A Study of His Life, Ideals, and Place in History* (New York: Harper & Bros., 1923), pp. 55, 58; John Joseph Mangan, *Life, Character, and Influence of Desiderius Erasmus of Rotterdam* (New York: Macmillan, 1927), 1:174; and Johan Huizinga, *Erasmus and the Age of Reformation*, tr. F. Hopman (New York: Charles Scribner's Sons, 1924; New York: Harper & Bros., Torchbooks, 1957), p. 54.

17. Barbara Kiefer Lewalski, *Protestant Poetics and the Seventeenth-Century Lyric* (Princeton: Princeton University Press, 1979), pp. 195–96. The motif of the stony heart is also a staple of Tyndale's, Latimer's, and Becon's prose.

18. *A shorte Recapitulacion or abrigement of Erasmus Enchiridion, brefely comprehendinge the summe and contentes thereof. Very Profitable and necessary to be rede of all trew Christen men. Drawne out by M. Coverdale Anno. 1545*, STC 10488, sigs. Ci^v–Cii^r; modern-spelling version in *Writings and Translations of Bishop Coverdale*, ed. George Pearson, Parker Society 13 (Cambridge: Cambridge University Press, 1844), pp. 506–7. For the Latin original, see Desiderius Erasmus Roterodamus, *Ausgewählte Werke*, ed. Annemarie and Hajo Holborn (Munich: C. H. Beck, 1933), p. 57.

19. Accounts of the maneuverings between 1536 and 1538 that eventuated in the Great (first royally authorized English) Bible can be found in Charles C. Butterworth, *The Lineage of the King James Bible, 1340–1611* (Philadelphia: University of Pennsylvania Press, 1940), pp. 91–101; and F. F. Bruce, *The English Bible: A History of Translations*, rev. ed. (London: Lutterworth Press, 1970), pp. 50–59.

20. William Tyndale, *An Aunswere unto Syr Thomas Mores Dialogue*, in *The Whole Workes of William Tyndall, John Frith, and Doctor Barnes* (London: John Daye, 1573), fols. 266–68; modern-spelling version in Tyndale, *An Answer to Sir Thomas More's Dialogue*, ed. Henry Walter, Parker Society 45 (Cambridge: Cambridge University Press, 1850), pp. 50–52, 55–56.

21. For references and discussion, see Janel M. Mueller, *The Native Tongue and the Word: Developments in English Prose Style, 1380–1580* (Chicago: University of Chicago Press, 1984), pp. 188–201.

22. "A Prologue upon the Epistle of S. Paule to the Romaines, by M. William Tyndall," in *Whole Workes*, fols. 45–46; modern-spelling version in Tyndale, *Doctrinal Treatises and Introductions to Different Portions of the Holy Scripture*, ed. Henry Walter, Parker Society 43 (Cambridge: Cambridge University Press, 1848), pp. 499–500. Subsequent references to these two editions of Tyndale will be abbreviated *Whole Workes* and PS, respectively, and will be incorporated in my text.

23. The narrative is transcribed from John Foxe's manuscripts by John Strype in *Ecclesiastical Memorials . . . under King Henry VIII*, vol. 1, pt. 1 (Oxford: Clarendon Press, 1822), pp. 172–73.

24. In the wake of Elizabeth L. Eisenstein's massive argument for the press as the most radical force for change in the early modern era (*The Printing Press as an Agent of Change: Communications and Cultural Transformations in Early Modern Europe*, 2 vols. [Cambridge: Cambridge University Press, 1979]), studies of the ideological associations and impact of various typographical conventions are beginning to appear. Arthur J. Slavin discusses the form for payments received that the last Catholic bishop of London devised on the model of papal letters of indulgence and the shunning of this device by early Protestant administrators, in "The Tudor Revolution and the Devil's Art: Bishop Bonner's Printed Forms," in *Tudor Rule and Revolution: Essays for G. R. Elton from His American Friends*, ed. Delloyd J. Guth and John W. McKenna (Cambridge: Cambridge University Press, 1982), pp. 3–23. The early English Protestant marginalia that reached one climax in the famous tendentious glosses of the Geneva Bible (1560) are another undoubtedly important topic of this kind. Suggestive leads for discussion in studies of the later modern period include Lawrence Lipking's "The Marginal Gloss," *Critical Inquiry* 3 (1977): 609–55; and John Dixon Hunt's "Oeuvre and Footnote" in *The Ruskin Polygon: Essays on the Imagination of John Ruskin*, ed. Hunt and Frith M. Holland (Manchester: Manchester University Press, 1982), pp. 1–20.

25. Rachel Blau DuPlessis and Members of Workshop 9, "For the Etruscans: Sexual Difference and Artistic Production—The Debate over a Female Aesthetic," in *The Future of Difference*, ed. Hester Eisenstein and Alice Jardine (Boston: G. K. Hall, 1980), pp. 128–56; quotation from p. 131. See, further, Hélène Cixous's 1975 essay, "The Laugh of the Medusa," in *New French Feminisms*, ed. Elaine Marks and Isabelle de Courtivron (New York: Schocken Books, 1981), pp. 245–64.

26. Harold Bloom, *The Anxiety of Influence: A Theory of Poetry* (New York: Oxford University Press, 1973).

27. Martienssen, *Queen Katherine Parr*, p. 201. Subsequent references to this biography will be incorporated in my text following the author's name.

28. *The Letters of Stephen Gardiner*, ed. James Arthur Muller (Cambridge: Cambridge University Press, 1933), p. 163.

29. See, further, Cranmer's *A Confutation of Unwritten Verities*, first published ca. 1547. There is a modern-spelling edition in John Edmund Cox, ed., *Miscel-*

laneous Writings and Letters of Thomas Cranmer, Parker Society 16 (Cambridge: Cambridge University Press, 1836), pp. 1–82.

30. Davis, "Gender and Genre," pp. 155–56.

31. [Thomas Cranmer,] "A Sermon of the salvation of mankynd, by onely Chryst our Saviour," in *Certaine Sermons appoynted . . . to be declared and read, by al Parsons, Vicars, and Curates, everi Sunday and holi day, in their Churches* (London, 1563), *STC* 13651, sigs. Ei^v–Eii^r, Eiiii^r; modern-spelling version in PS 16:131–32.

32. Mueller, *Native Tongue and the Word,* pp. 226–43, analyzes the stylistic achievement of Cranmer's Prayer Book collects.

33. *Frutefull Sermons preached by . . . M. Hugh Latymer* (London: John Daye, 1571), fol. 12^v; modern-spelling version in George Elwes Corrie, ed., *Sermons by Hugh Latimer,* Parker Society 27 (Cambridge: Cambridge University Press, 1844), p. 59. Subsequent reference to these two editions of Latimer will be abbreviated *Frutefull Sermons* and PS, respectively, and will be incorporated in my text.

35. For an excellent discussion of these traits as consciously cultivated aspects of Latimer's public persona, see Robert L. Kelly, "Hugh Latimer as Piers Plowman," *SEL* 17 (1977): 13–26.

35. See the old-spelling edition of both works, J. Meadows Cowper, ed., *Henry Brinklow's Complaynt of Roderyck Mors . . . and The Lamentacyon of a Christen Agaynst the Cytye of London, made by Roderigo Mors,* Early English Text Society, extra ser., 22 (London: N. Trübner & Co., 1874).

36. John Foxe, *The . . . Ecclesiasticall History . . . contaynyng the Actes and Monuments* (London: John Daye, 1570), fol. 1213; modern-spelling version in Foxe, *Acts and Monuments* 5:556. It is noteworthy that even a queen was not safe from a potential tarring with the brush of Anabaptist primitive communism.

37. For a sensitive discussion, see Elaine V. Belin, "Anne Askew's Self-Portrait in *The Examinations,*" in *Silent but for the Word,* Hannay, pp. 61–80.

38. See Martienssen, pp. 190–94, building on Foxe, *Acts and Monuments,* 5:553–60; Robert Parsons, *A Treatise of Three Conversions of England* (St. Omer, 1603), fol. 593, cited in McConica, *English Humanists,* pp. 226–27; and John Strype's excerpts from Foxe's manuscripts in *Ecclesiastical Memorials,* vol. 1, pt. 1, pp. 598–600. In all this danger and turmoil, one specific in Anne Askew's written account of her *Latter Examination* assumes special significance with regard to the company Katherine Parr was keeping. Anne says that she asked to speak with Latimer at the end of one of her interrogation sessions in the spring of 1546, but the request was denied (*The Latter Examination of Anne Askewe,* in *Select Works of John Bale,* ed. Henry Christmas, Parker Society 1 [Cambridge: Cambridge University Press, 1849], p. 206). Latimer clearly had some special standing, not only with Katherine Parr and Catherine Brandon but also with other women in their extended circle who were serious adherents of the new faith.

39. In "The Female Complaint" (forthcoming in *Social Text*) Lauren Berlant notes the gravitation of female expression toward the genre of complaint. Among conventionalized modes of first-person utterance, this one looks

uniquely amenable to the complainer's insistence on selfhood and her wariness about appropriation. Berlant's contemporary black songwriter is potentially Anywoman who finds voice by defining herself against some aspect of her cultural experience.

40. For relevant discussion, see Helen C. White, *Social Criticism in Popular Religious Literature of the Sixteenth Century* (New York: Macmillan, 1944); Charles M. Gray, *Hugh Latimer and the Sixteenth Century* (Cambridge: Harvard University Press, 1950); Allan G. Chester, *Hugh Latimer: Apostle to the English* (Philadelphia: University of Pennsylvania Press, 1954); A. G. Dickens, *Thomas Cromwell and the English Reformation* (London: English Universities Press, 1959); Mary T. Austin, "The Political, Economic, and Social Aspects of Edward VI's Reign as Viewed through the Sermons and Letters of Hugh Latimer" (Ph.D. diss., Michigan State University, East Lansing, 1961); Mary Dewar, *Sir Thomas Smith: A Tudor Intellectual in Office* (London: Athlone Press, 1964); and Arthur B. Ferguson, *The Articulate Citizen and the English Renaissance* (Durham, N.C.: Duke University Press, 1965).

41. Martienssen, pp. 206–7, citing Strype, *Ecclesiastical Memorials* (no reference given).

42. On the next English Protestant instance (1641–58) of female empowerment afforded by the egalitarian strain that periodically surfaces in Christian spirituality, see Keith Thomas, "Women and the Civil War Sects," *Past and Present* 13 (1958): 42–62, esp. pp. 44–47, 50.

43. Working drafts of this essay received incisive criticisms from Julie Carlson, Mary Beth Rose, Joshua Scodel, and, most especially, Richard Strier. A late version also underwent airings before the students and faculty in the Renaissance Workshop at the University of Chicago in May 1987 and at Purdue University's English Renaissance Prose Conference in October 1987. At Purdue, Arnold Stein's remarks proved especially helpful. I am grateful for all the assistance I have received, and I hope that colleagues will recognize improvements brought about by their questions and comments.

Ideas of Resistance
before Elizabeth

In this discussion we are on the margins of literature. The subject is a phenomenon of language, expression, and publicity that displays, dramatizes, denounces, fantasizes about, and otherwise represents or misrepresents a new world of experience, expressed in the behavior, reactions, and suffering of religious minorities in the tumultuous society of the sixteenth century. A fundamental explosion of human protest and aspiration resounded, over several generations, throughout the oral and print culture of western Europe. For present purposes it is the smoke of ideological dissension rather than the fires of religious war that constitutes the primary target and, arguably, provides the most direct and human access into the lost world of Tudor thought, belief, and action—and, as far as we are concerned, "reality."

The languages not only of "political theory" but also of social protest and action in the Reformation drew upon many sources, but none more effectively and enduringly than that of evangelical dissent, especially as represented by Luther and his kerygmatic epigones and of course by vernacular Scriptures.[1] For the Reformation was directed at the purification of language as well as of doctrine and Christian life in general. Law, Liberty, Authority, Tradition—these totemic concepts were all purged and redefined; and history was rewritten according to a new, or at least renewed, set of values and of names. Legitimacy was sought in conformity to the standards of a old Christian myth, which was the vision of the Primitive Church. As always large social conflicts were accompanied by struggles for language, and so the process of "politicization" exemplified by the Reformation was implied from the beginning in the arguments of theologians and scholars.

The literary strategies of confessional, and eventually political, protest began with processes of recognition and definition, especially recognizing the enemies and defining one's own nature. Find the Devil and fight him; look for God and serve him; formulate the issues and publicize them. In this effort literary energies were directed to the threefold task of self-purification, self-justification, and self-advertisement; and in this enterprise all the resources of language, its elegance and its vulgarities, its beauties and its obscenities, were summoned. Call things by their right names, or find a new terminology: Holy Mother Church was a whore, the pope antichrist, the priesthood an imposture, the Mass an act of defilement and cannibalism; the true church was the "congregation of the faithful" or "community of the saints," the true leader was Christ, the minister of God's word the preacher, the sacrament of the mass a spiritual commemoration. And all of this was to be set down in a credo, or rather a credimus, a confession that had to be made public—proclaimed "to all nations" and in this way, too, politicized.

The political extension of these confessional impulses and strategies shifted criticism to the secular arm, which defended and enforced popery, but fundamentally different tactics were called for, since the divine origin of political (unlike ecclesiastical) power was never questioned. For political argument the results were rhetorical ploys of apparent duplicity, perhaps dissimulation: not religious innovation but the most traditional of beliefs was the basis of protest; not the ruler but his evil advisors were the target of religious protest; not rebellion but peace was the goal of religious protesters. For language the results were an extraordinary ambivalence of terminology: the law (Romanist and Judaic) was a vile human creation, yet the law (Christian, internalized) was righteousness itself; liberty (free will and human indulgence) was a measure of sinfulness, yet liberty (Christian) was the condition of salvation; authority (secular, ecclesiastical) was grounded in sin, yet authority (scriptural) was absolute and divine; tradition (human) was degenerate, yet tradition (spiritual) was eternal and perfect.

In the politicized language of sixteenth-century protest there were many voices and many messages: thundering denunciations and insidious threats, shrill complaints and reasoned arguments, naive appeals and outrageous demands, brave exhortations and pitiful lamentations. In the literature of that age there were many genres overlooked by chronicles of the "good letters" of humanist tradition and vernacular innovation: official attacks on and spontaneous defenses of religious unorthodoxy, anecdotal history and atrocity literature, sermons and jeremiads, satires and allegories, displays of erudition and carnivalesque invention, confessions and credos. In the wake of this literature one can infer continuities between verbal excess, fanaticism, and violence—not only in the inclination toward iconoclasm but also in official repression and persecution. "One begins by burning books and ends by burning men," Erasmus remarked—knowing well that one of Luther's initial acts of protest, a "holy" act he regarded it, was burning the books of canon law.[2]

The politico-religious discourse of Edwardian and Marian England marks a conspicuous intersection between literature and history, and it poses the old question of how to relate the two spheres of experience.[3] For a historian the answer to this must resist simplistic assumptions either of old-fashioned (vulgar Marxist?) theory of ideology or of newer-fashioned (vulgar Derridean?) textuality; must avoid the extremes, that is, of a social-history metaphysics that regards printed works as "reflecting" a prior material reality, and of a text-fetishism that locates that reality between the lines of writings that happen to have been preserved in printed form.

Yet the historian cannot (in Gadamer's words) get "behind the back of language."[4] On the contrary he and she must try to sort out the languages—the ideological dialects, vocabularies, verbal conventions, linguistic and literary resources—of the past; and to this extent the aim must be lexicographical rather than merely exegetical. Language expresses power, but it also may express powerlessness: in a society of deference and corporatism the notion of a single "dominant discourse" may not be appropriate except on the highest and official, but superficial, level. Nor is it sufficient to attend simply to the major philosophical, literary, or even political statements, which in fact may be located better in traditions and genres transcending the social context of the age (not all *livres* are *de circonstance,* and even contemporaries misread La Boétie's *Servitude volontaire* as a political tract). We must listen for all the voices that, in the surviving written texts, echo out of various intellectual traditions as well as religious commitments, social contexts, and political predicaments.

As for the sixteenth century, it must be recalled, and kept in mind, that it was an age of an extraordinary resurgence of rhetoric and (in a modern sense) politicized language. First implicitly and then (in the work of Valla and Ramus) explicitly, Renaissance humanists carried on the subversion of school philosophy and in the process changed attitudes toward—and indeed, as a recent historian has argued, conceptions of—language.[5] The "art of rhetoric" was commonly regarded as a threat to stable government and suitable rather to a republic catering to the rabble (as, among others, Montaigne suggested) than to monarchy.[6] The methods, habits, and eristic inclinations of the profession of law, long associated with the worst as well as the best in rhetorical tradition, reinforced the impact and the public threat of "civil discourse." Even more inflammatory than these secular modes of communication, of course, were the forms of religious expression, above all the sermon and the staged public disputation (institutionalized as the colloquy); and this consideration brings us back to the subject of this essay, which is the literature of protest in mid-sixteenth-century England.[7]

I

In his *Short Treatise of Politike Power,* published in Strasbourg in 1556, ex-bishop and Marian exile John Ponet chose a text from the Old Testament prophet Isaiah: "Wo be unto you (sayeth he) that maketh unryghteous lawes." And then Ponet drew his political lesson from the text: "this terrible wo of everlasting damnation was spoken not only to Jerusalem, but to Germanie, Italie, Fraunce, Spayne, Englande, Scotlande and all other countreyes and nacions."[8] Here is a major premise of what has come to be called resistance theory, and for once English opinion seems to have been in advance of that of the Continent, to the extent at least that Ponet's book was the first comprehensive treatment of the question. In a longer perspective English ideas of resistance were intellectually derivative and abortive—derivative in terms of Lutheran, sacramentarian, and Calvinist argumentation; abortive in the sense that the Elizabethan settlement made Marian speculation a dead letter, at least until the civil wars of the next century. Yet in human and political terms the Marians seem to have been pioneers and innovators, if only because of the novelty of their predicament; and the significance of their political thinking has too often, and unreasonably, been overshadowed by that of Continental Protestants.

In general and in a "Protestant" context English resistance thought began in the Henrician period with a religious commitment to what Luther and other evangelical authors called "Christian liberty"; it advanced to a more socialized conception of "liberty of conscience" in the reign of Edward VI; and it culminated in overt political opposition to the rule of Mary Tudor. These increasingly subversive views, inspired and informed by Continental Protestant attitudes and arguments and disseminated by a relatively small group of dissenters and exiles, were expressed in poetry and drama as well as more prosaic religious and political propaganda; and they reached fever heat in the two or three years before the accession of Elizabeth, leaving a substantial legacy for the more directly revolutionary activities of Puritans in the next century.

Undeniably, there were patterns common to English and Continental resistance movements.[9] This was due not only to common intellectual traditions but also to similarities and even interconnections between English and Continental social and political situations. Both sides of the Channel experienced a confluence of urgent religious and social pressures and various traditions of political ideas offering comfort and perhaps remedies. This can be seen both in the reformation of various Swiss cities and in the political dilemma of the Holy Roman Empire. Yet there were significant differences. The first instance involved a much smaller scale phenomenon, resembling various anticlerical movements of medieval Italian communes (from Arnold of Brescia to Savonarola), while the second was tied to the peculiar constitutional issue dividing the emperor and the German principalities, which could in effect and eventually in principle claim sovereign status. Only in England was the question of resistance posed in the context of a state religion and what seems to us a modern national state, which in itself may bring the Marians more closely in line with modern experience.

There has been a large and lively discussion of resistance thought in recent years, much of it carried out on a fairly high level of abstraction according to standards of a more rational and secular age. Explicitly or implicitly, the discussion has usually been tied to assessments of the priority, rationality, and degree of radicalness of ideas. Lutherans, Calvinists, sacramentarians, Anabaptists, even Catholics—which confessional group went furthest (furthest in anticipation of Locke?) in justifying disobedience to oppressive government? Put differently, which authors have committed themselves most deliberately to the human right of resistance? Or rather, which published texts have declared most unmistakably, and most modernly, the idea of revolution *avant la lettre?* The modern consensus has inclined toward Calvinism (the case having been argued most sharply by Michael Walzer), though Quentin Skinner has recently urged the priority of the Lutherans as the pioneers of resistance, and others have pointed out the significance of apocalyptic writings, [10] while sixteenth-century opinion (not to speak of modern Marxism) would certainly have pointed to the Anabaptists.

Is it possible that this question, like that of the French Reformation in years past (as Lucien Febvre lamented), has also been badly posed? There was a common heritage, or heritages, of resistance thought; and the form of expression had to do largely with political and social context— whence the many embarrassing contradictions and turnabouts not only of particular authors but also of particular parties, depending on whether they were in or out of power. The point is that the history of political thought, at least practical political thought on this level, cannot usefully be written simply as a phase of the history of ideas in the way that topics in, say, the history of science or of literature may be treated (which must to some extent be teleological and "internalist"). In the former case the

"Whig fallacy" seems particularly obstructive. While it may make sense for modern philososophers of science to honor Galileo as a founder of their tradition, it is hardly appropriate, except in the most mechanical way, for modern political philosophers, whatever their ideological persuasion, to look back in the same way upon Calvinists, who in one context had demanded liberation from, even vengeance upon, "tyranny" and in another context had wanted to put their "idolatrous" enemies to the sword, as Calvin once advised a Protestant ruler.[11] On this very complex question, suffice it here to suggest that ideas of resistance can only be appreciated as part of the social history of ideas in a most fundamental sense.

What further complicates this question of resistance is the eclectic character of sixteenth-century political discourse, especially on sensitive issues of individual obedience to public authority. There were a number of competing, yet overlapping, traditions with distinct vocabularies, conventions, styles of argumentation, and intended audiences.[12] No less than six types, it seems to me, may be distinguished in sixteenth-century writings: (1) the classical, which introduces Roman formulas of self-defense and popular sovereignty; (2) the feudal, which offers contractual ideas of mutual obligation and notorious precedence for disobedience; (3) the communal, which recalls the rebelliousness and hard-won "liberties," religious as well as secular, of the medieval communes; (4) the ecclesiastical, covering the spiritual *libertas ecclesiae* of Gregorian reform and attendant defiance of imperial authority; (5) the conciliar, which recalled resistance to and deposition of popes; and (6) the fundamentalist, which refers both to the Pauline attack on the "law" and more radical apocalyptic views that sixteenth-century evangelicals derived from Joachimite tradition (not to speak of Old Testament precedents for active resistance). Each of these forms of discourse at least echo in sixteenth-century resistance literature.

Modern ideas of political resistance, formed (or reformed) in the maelstrom of sixteenth-century religious controversy, were from the start ambiguous and often logically unstable; and it is essential to attend to the language and style of evangelical discourse. Protestant political thought was formulated in a tradition not of philosophy but of Renaissance and Reformation rhetoric, whose "topical" method followed not Aristotelian dialectic but rather the authoritarian and mnemonic procedure of the humanist logic designed by Agricola, Melanchthon, Petrus Ramus, Thomas Wilson, and other theorists of persuasion and predication.[13] The basis of this method, ideal for preaching and propaganda, was argument from concrete but more or less indiscriminate examples, whether classical, biblical, or historical; and this was in itself a condition of the logically confused eclecticism characteristic of Protestant political discourse, for which the sermon always remained the model.

The root ambiguity can be seen in Ponet's characteristic phrase, "unrighteous laws." For Luther (as for Saint Paul) there was a permanent tension between "law" in the sense of social order and "law" in the sense of Jewish or Romanist "bondage." Both were binding, but the first as a necessary protection against anarchy, the second as a set of chains to be cast off. The conflicting connotations are suggested by a contemporary dictionary's definition of the Latin *ius:* "Law: right: authoritie: libertie: power."[14] Consider, too, the contrast between Melanchthon's humanist oration in praise of the "dignity of the laws" and his rejection of the mere "human traditions" of orthodox ecclesiology. This was also in keeping with the Pauline paradox, which on the one hand (Rom. 13) celebrated the divine origin of human authority and on the other hand (passim) rejected the loathsome Judaic law. And of course there was an obverse, symmetrical ambivalence in the notion of "liberty," which referred alternately to the *libertas christianae* idealized by Luther and to arrogant human freedom—whether the "free will" of which Luther was so contemptuous or political license of which he was so suspicious. Both had been indelibly marked by sin, as were all the customs and "positive laws" of man's making.

Most fundamentally, these paradoxes arose from the classical distinction between the private and the public spheres—a kind of moral variation on the medieval problem of universals, expressed in the sixteenth century as the differences between the "internal forum" of conscience and the "external forum" of legal or social norms. They also reflect the divergence between what Guy Swanson has called the "transcendent" doctrine of Protestantism (which posits a "high" God aloof from human concerns) and the "immanent" assumptions of Catholicism (which claimed divine support of and "presence" in the human institution of the earthly church); and they define the basic condition of debates over civil resistance.[15] In the wake of Reformation, resistance was ineluctably dualistic, torn between respect for civil order and contempt for secularized religion, desire for personal salvation and the charge to carry the word to all nations. In a sense this tension has never been overcome.

The exiles from Marian England during the 1550s found themselves in just such a theoretical quandary. Though beneficiaries of "Christian liberty," they were persecuted, imprisoned, or chased from the kingdom; though confident of the justice of their cause, they were outlaws.[16] As a result they were convinced that, as Christopher Goodman wrote in his tract, *How Superior Powers Ougt to be Obeyed,* published in Geneva in

1558, "it is both Lawful and necessarie some tymes to disobeye and also to resist Vngodly magistrates."[17] Therefore, as Goodman went on to say, "this is no doctrine of Rebellion, but only doctrine of peace." Yet at the same time many of the Marian exiles favored and even participated in active resistance to the "Jezabel" Mary. Goodman in particular defended the justice of what he referred to as the "enterprise" and the "cause"— but what most others called the "rebellion"—of Thomas Wyatt and his supporters, including perhaps John Ponet. In such terms, which included the virtuous use of euphemisms and dysphemisms on both sides, there seemed small hope of agreement between reformers and Romanists. This illustrates the linguistic and logical predicament of sixteenth-century debates over resistance.[18]

The ambiguity, if not confusion, concerning the concept of "law" was strikingly dramatized by a work published by John Bale in 1538 and called *The Three Laws of Nature, Moses, and Christ.*[19] According to his "divine comedy," as he called it (*de legibus divinae comoedia*), law was ideally the highest form of wisdom—"the knowledge of things divine and human," in the famous formula he recalled from Roman law—but the Fall had fragmented and weakened it. Things divine had become contaminated by things human. Thereafter law was the product either of nature, of bondage, or of grace; and in more recent times each of these forms had been overthrown—the law of nature by idolatry and sodomy, that of Moses by avarice and ambition, and that of grace by hypocrisy and error ("pseudodoctrine"). "Let Idolatry be dressed like an olde wytche," ran Bale's stage directions, "Sodomy like a monk of all sectes, Ambition bishop, covetousness lawyer, hypocrisy gray friar" and others, including himself ("Baleus Prolucutor" appeared occasionally to comment), as might be appropriate. Return to "Christian liberty" and "pure doctrine" was the only remedy; and as historian and propagandist, "bilious Bale" devoted himself both to the analysis of the disease and to a prescription for its cure.

The dualism of sixteenth-century resistance theory is reflected also in its twofold medieval heritage: first a secular radicalism of the traditional *Widerstandsrecht* based on the mutual right of dissolving a violated feudal compact; and second the ecclesiastical radicalism of the Hildebrandine church based on declaration of spiritual independence (*libertas ecclesiae* was the battle cry of Gregorian reform), which likewise had its roots in Pauline thought.[20] Or put more bluntly, on the one hand was a right of private justice (*Faustrecht*) and on the other hand a kind of political fundamentalism taking its inspiration from the Bible. However indirectly, sixteenth-century resistance movements drew extensively and eclectically on these two ideological traditions, and Marian ideas in particular represent a significant effort of synthesis and reformulation of political thinking from a private rather than a public point of view, based on the principle of individual conscience rather than political authority.

What encouraged Edwardian reformers to their rashness and gave poignancy and direction to Marian political thought was the brief but euphoric period of the Protectorate, when the light of true religion seemed to be dawning in England—when the evangelical superstructure, as it were, seemed to be finding a material base. In this golden age, according to a contemporary jingle by William Baldwin,

> The magistrate was playnly told his fault.
> The man of law was warned not to halt.
>
> . . . .
>
> All Papistrie with fruteles gospel boast,
> Was cryed against and damnde as wicked most.
>
> . . . .
>
> And to be briefe, fro the lowest to the hyest,
> All were desired to live the law of Christ.[21]

The ground for this Edwardian enlightenment had been prepared not only by Erasmian humanism and Cranmer's ecumenism but also by hot gospellers like William Turner, John Bale, and John Hooper, whose anti-Romanist polemic reached heights of hysteria and incitement to iconoclasm beyond the efforts and aspirations of magisterial reformers like Luther. Turner began the hunt for the "Romish fox" and the remnants of canon law still lurking in English society.[22] Bale followed this chase and raged against the new Babylon of Rome, the antichrist, the "horrible monsters" boasting descent from Peter but in fact aping the Jews, and what he called the "booryshe buggerye" of monasticism (which he, like Luther, had experienced).[23] Hooper declared that England had been rid of the pope but not of popery, and in 1546 he became a premature exile in Germany, where he established important contacts, most notably with Bullinger.[24] Under Somerset and Northumberland evangelical preaching flourished, and the repeal of censorship laws opened the doors to an unprecedented flood of printed propaganda—not to speak to active dissent—that seemed to signify, in the phrase of James Gairdner, "Lollardy in power."[25] Continental reformers like Bucer and Martyr wrote congratulatory pieces in celebration of this auspicious "change of religion," and Johann Sledian (who had dedicated two of his earlier publications to Edward VI) chronicled the progress of religion in England in his great history of the Reformation (1556), as did the continuator of Cario's Protestant chronicle, published in English translation in 1550.[26]

II

Despite "Loller" elements, however, the new form of English protest was not homegrown. By midcentury a series of European reformers, preceded by their reputations and translations of their writings, came to teach in English universities, among them Bucer, Peter Martyr, and Bernardo Ochino. For a time England seemed to be in the vanguard of that "evangelical revolution" begun a quarter of a century earlier by French and Swiss exiles, and seemed even to be establishing a political base. Yet the Roman wolf still threatened, especially in the form of the Council of Trent and the notorious "Interim" imposed on Lutherans by Charles V and resisted by Bucer, Melanchthon, and others.[27] In 1548 Calvin sent Somerset one of his characteristic letters of encouragement and exhortation, denouncing among other things the "malice and rebellion" (*seditiones et turbae*) of their mutual enemies and urging the Lord Protector both to promote preaching of the word and "to resist by authority the licentiousness of wicked men."[28] Nevertheless, the horizons of English political as well as religious thinking were considerably widened during the Edwardian period. This was another essential condition of the formation of resistance theories, especially since English reformers habitually looked to Bullinger, Calvin, and other pastors of the scattered Christian flock for encouragement, advice, and often material assistance.

In various ways the experience of Continental reformers formed an ideological paradigm for English reformers, and from the 1530s it was well publicized through translations of and commentaries on the works of Luther, Melanchthon, François Lambert, Zwingli, and Bullinger.[29] Lutheran defenses of the Augsburg Confession and especially attacks on the hated Interim were followed by English publicists and applied to their own circumstances. To Melanchthon and Bucer the Interim of 1548 meant the "return of idolatry,' and it was the immediate cause of the Protestant emigration to England of Bucer, Martyr, and others. In Germany it provoked the strongest statements of political protest from a number of Lutheran cities, including Strasbourg and especially Magdeburg, whose "confession" of 1550 was a model for the later political program of the French and Dutch Huguenots.[30] Elsewhere, too, it was a difficult time for Protestants. As Johann Sleidan wrote of the year 1548, "At this time throughout France, but chiefly at Paris, was burning a persecution renewed for Lutheranisme, where contrariwise in Englande they consulted utterly to abolishe the Popish masse"; and Sleidan had himself been a visitor at that time.[31] No wonder that for a time England seemed to be the new Jerusalem, the last best hope for a purified doctrine and a holy community based thereon.

Before the social predicament created by repression and exile, religious protest was only marginally political, and for the most part it focused on what might be called, from the standpoint of political thought, surrogate questions, which were again drawn from Lutheran precedent. The source of much discussion on both sides of the Channel was questions of costume and ritual; and Hooper, invoking the opinions of Bucer, Calvin, Bullinger, and Martyr, took this as his special target. "Our saviour Jesus Christ," according to a pamphlet of 1548 , "hath not overburdened his churche with many ceremonies."[32] Another of the offspring of monkery and popery was the unnatural practice of celibacy, and Ponet, who had recently taken a wife, campaigned enthusiastically for what he called "godly marriage."[33] By far the most inflammatory issue, however, was the eucharist, central symbol both of papal supremacy and of ecclesiastical error and corruption. As preachers like Ponet and Thomas Lever argued, the soul certainly had a deep spiritual hunger, but it was not the carnal lust of the popish mass. As Ponet declared in a Lenten sermon given before King Edward and his council, "It is an irreverentc and an ungodly opinion, and voyd of all Godlye religion to saye or thynke, that we must eate and chawe with our corporall teeth, or that we must swallow with our corporal throte Christes blessed fleshe and bones, after so grosse a sort, as we eat other kyndes of meat."[34]

But disparate as they may seem, each of these issues showed a particular facet of the many-sided and very problematic conflict between immanent and transcendent religion—of the Protestant effort, that is, to keep the divine uncorrupted by the human. It was antichrist, according to a tract of Rodolph Gualter, englished during the Marian period, that "forged such a kynde of religion, as hath more twitle twatle tores in it, that the levitical law, and all the supersticion that ever gentiles used."[35] So evangelicals could be urged to the "imitation" not only of Christ but also, and more feasibly, of Paul. As Luther's attack on penance led inexorably to an assault on papal authority in general, so the Protestant attack on the principal of immanence represented by the eucharist led to a critique of the secular institutions supporting it. This was another version of that process of "politicization" underlying the religious persecution and civil wars of the sixteenth century.

What gave an edge of radicalism and an evangelical sort of black humor to English anti-Romanism was the apocalyptic influence of Joachimite prophecy. In 1548 Walter Lynn published an English translation of Andreas Osiander's treatise "declaring the beginning and ending of all Poperie and the Popish Kingdome," replete with the satirical and sensationalist cartoons of Hans Sachs, representing the pope in all sorts of uncomplimentary postures—receiving the keys of power from Satan (instead of Peter), for example, consorting with the (Roman) wolf, and running his sword through the Lamb of God.[36] Appearing a year later was Ponet's translation of Ochino, *A Tragoedie or Dialoge of the Iniuste Usurped Primacie of the Bishop of Rome,* which associated the pope with Lucifer and antichrist in similarly prophetic style.[37] As Paul Christianson has recently said, the effects of such apocalyptic visions were to offer a polarized view of the world, to urge catastrophic explanations, and to cast these attitudes in a prophetic mold.[38]

Another result was to intensify the fascination of Protestant theologians, starting with Luther and Melanchthon, with historical assaults on ecclesiastical tradition and justifications of "true religion." In this connection historical writing was given extraordinary force as a weapon of propaganda, not only in analyses of the evils of popery but also, and often concomitantly, in the revived genre of martyrology, begun on a small scale by Bale and carried on massively by John Foxe's *Acts and Monuments.*[39] For Foxe history was not only the elegant and instructive narrative of humanists; it was also a moving tragedy, a description of crimes that cried out for vengeance, a record of Christian deeds and sufferings, and a demonstration of the values and goals of Christian life. In fiery language he identified the heros and villains of the story of "the true and universal congregation of Christ's universal church."

Although Edwardian dissent was theoretically spiritual, it could not avoid associations with more active protest, including and going beyond iconoclasm. As Randall Hurleston wrote in 1550, "there be certain rude feloes which when they heare mention of libertie in sermones, straightwayes with out iudgement despise all maners, lawes and honestie."[40] Although English historians have generally played down direct connections with contemporary conspiracies, "Protestants" certainly participated in the uprisings by Wyatt, among others, very much as the so-called "Huguenots of religion" later joined the "Huguenots of politics" in France in the conspiracy of Amboise in 1560 on the eve of the civil wars.[41] Aside from this, ad hominem argument was a legacy both of Lutheran and of humanist invective, and when directed against powerful men like Gardiner could have dangerous political consequences. Frequently, the language of propagandists like Bale and Hooper was in itself an incitement to violence, and indeed iconoclasm—pulling down the "altars of Baal" and destroying idolatrous symbols—was a logical extension of the rhetoric attacking that "synagogue of Satan" and "stinking Babylon" of Rome.[42] The level of vituperation was sharply raised, of course, when directed at that "Jesabel" Mary and her unspeakable consort, Philip of Spain. At that point, shifting the target from Roman popery to English majesty, religious protest crossed over into rebellion and treason—as many of its propagandists crossed over from the English Babylon to various Continental places of refuge.

The pre-Marian period of euphoric hopes and unchecked polemic was short-lived, and the downfall and subsequent imprisonment of Somerset in 1549 threatened popish reaction, as his execution two years later insured it. Nor was the threat merely doctrinal. In 1550 Thomas Lever preached a sermon at Saint Paul's in the presence of the king and his council, lamenting, while yet acknowledging, that "experience declareth howe here in England pore men have been rebels, and ryche men have not done their duetie."[43] Like Colet before Henry VIII and the lords of convocation a generation earlier, the reverend Lever literally shook his finger under the nose of authority: "and learne ye rulers if ye intende by onely suppression to kepe under rebellion, be ye sure if ye thrust it downe in one place it wyll blaste out with more vyolence and greater daunger in ten other places." Bale reported a remark dropped in December of 1551 by a "frantike papist of Hamshire," who launched into a tirade about current religious turmoil.[44] "Alas poore chylde," he continued, noticing one of his host's children, "unknowne it is to hym, what actes are made now adayes. But whan he cometh ones of age, he wyll se an other rule, and hange up an hondred of such heretyke knaves. Meaning [Bale adds] the preachers of our tyme and their maynteyners."

The accession of Mary a little more than a year later made these remarks prophetic and demanded hard choices from dissenters, including not only those who had participated in rebellions but also those who had committed themselves to "pure doctrine," which, less than by the late king Edward VI, had been protected by Somerset. A number were thrown into prison and carried on their defiance from there. John Bradford, for example, wrote letters to Mary and her Spanish consort "requiring" them "to repent for the unplacing of laws for true religion."[45] Kings and queens "need to know," he added, that "they are God's ministers." With Hooper, Philpot, and others he signed a "supplication" to their majesties to the same purpose. It had little more than rhetorical effect, however, as did Bradford's "farewells" to London, Cambridge, and other beloved communities, written in anticipation of his martyrdom. Philpot's more secular defense of his religious views, claiming privilege of Parliament, was no more effective in saving him from the stake.[46] Under these conditions, in any case, resistance was no longer a merely theoretical matter.

III

Mid-sixteenth-century reformers in general looked with a kind of fascinated horror on the idea and the experience of "rebellion," so near and yet so far from Christian "resistance." Sir John Cheke, himself a victim of the Marian reaction, warned against "the hurt of sedition how greveous it is to a Commune welth," with reference both to the Norfolk rebels and potential uprisings because of religious discontent.[47] The example which almost everyone kept in mind was the Anabaptist threat, especially in the sensational events of Munster, described in lurid detail by Sleidan. This was the motive underlying the various attacks by Calvin and the work of Bullinger, englished in 1551 as *A most necessary & fruitful Dialogue between ye seditious Libertin or rebel Anabaptist and a true obedient Christian*.[48] It was above all the Anabaptist example that led reformers like Calvin, Beza, and Bullinger to exalt and to exaggerate the power of the magistrate to punish "heresy" at just the time that "true Christians" were being persecuted on the same grounds.[49] Hence Marian propagandists like John Proctor found themselves in nominal agreement with Cheke and his Continental colleagues, though his specific target was the "abominable treason" of Wyatt's rebellion, which he had no doubt originated in religious disaffection—"rebellion" being, as he concluded, "the only refuge of heretikes."[50]

As Calvin taught and as many English reformers believed, the worst of all religious offenses was hypocrisy. In 1550 there appeared a translation of a work of Matteo Gribaldi, graced with a preface by Calvin, telling the story of a certain Francis Spera, his denial of Christ, and the terrible punishment wrought by God on his conscience.[51] "And therefore these Nicodemites that will visit Christ only in ye dark and by night and not so openly before men," Bale wrote in 1558, "the Lord will not acknowledge before his Heavenly father."[52] In 1555 there appeared another translation, this one of a dialogue by Wolfgang Musculus, dealing with a so-called "temporizer," prefaced by an epistle lamenting the horrible state of England under Mary.[53] The "temporisour" himself had just come from a fancy (popish) university service with "blowers and organ players," and his conscience was troubled. That was not only folly, remarked the conformist "Mondayne," but unworthy of a good subject; for it was wrong to place the "dreams of theologians" above the authority of the ruler, who sanctioned religious forms. The third speaker, Eusebius, agreed with Temporisour but was dismissed by Mondayne as a "simple superstitious idiot" who read too many books. Eventually, however, the wise Eusebius demonstrated the conviction of Edwardian evangelicals that God had to be obeyed before man, whatever the consequences.

What was the answer to this dilemma of conscience? Must one obey laws requiring attendance at "the masse of the papistes"? Bullinger and Calvin were applied to for advice on this question. "Many do ask me Counsell oftentymes," wrote Calvin in a work translated in 1548, "how they shuld behave them selves among ye papistes where it is not lawful for them to worshyppe God purely: But every man is constrained to use many ceremonies which have bene invented against ye worde of god, an be full of superstition."[54] After a long sermon about the need to avoid religious dissimulation and hypocrisy and if necessary to "follow the way of many thousands of martyrs," Calvin gave the same practical advice he had been offering for some years to French, Dutch, and Italian followers, which was "that he should get him from thence if he can." Almost a decade later an anonymous work posed the same question and concluded with an exhortation to "come out of Egypt and serve God bothe with tongue and harte and with saying and doing, with the outwarde man and inwarde man."[55] This was also the advice given by Bullinger, who had written a masterly survey of the "origin" and progress of such errors.

This prohibition of "Nicodemitism," preached incessantly by Calvin and others, entailed not only public practice of a pure form of religion but the requirement of "bearing witness" to the faith; and this led directly to the time-honored commitment to the role of "martyr," a Greek word which indeed referred to one who testified. But modern technology allowed Protestants to carry on the act of bearing witness in a way, and with repercussions, far beyond what the ancient Christian models could have imagined. "God hath opened the Presse to preach," remarked Foxe, "whose voice the Pope is never able to stop with all the puissance of his triple crowne."[56] Foxe managed to combine ancient martyrology with the modern invention of printing to achieve an unprecedented success as propagandist. From the 1550s there was a flood of such works by himself, Jean Crespin, Ludwig Rabe, Mathias Flacius Illyricus, and Johann Sleidan, all of them based on a common pool of scholarship. What Foxe offered was a true history, "as in a mirror" and after the fashion of book 3 of Calvin's *Institutes;* but going beyond Calvin his book taught two further lessons of more immediate importance. The first was how, in the most concrete way, to imitate the saintly fortitude of the early Christians and indeed Christ himself. The second, less passive, was the expected result of his bloody chronicle. "Did you ever see any murder," he asked the papists in the sort of veiled threat characteristically made by passive resisters, "which came not out and was not repaid?"[57]

The only permissible alternative to martyrdom was exile, and for many this "civic death" was even more frightening, involving as it did the loss of property and inheritance. Of the over eight hundred English persons who made this choice between 1553 and 1558, many took this risk, although others were living outside the law in any case.[58] They sought refuge, most of them, in a few havens of pure religion, notably Zurich, Strasbourg, Frankfurt, Basel, Emden, and what Bale called the "wonderful miracle" of Geneva. "What is exile?" Ponet asked Bullinger in 1556. "A thing which, provided you have the wherewithal to exist, is painful only in imagination. I know that it is the scourge of the Lord; but with what mildness and fatherly affection he deals with me, I can readily learn even from this, that he has afforded me for his comforters Bullinger, Melanchthon, Martyr and other most shining lights of his church." [59] In terms of emotional impact, martyrdom was more impressive, especially as material for the propaganda of Foxe; but exile had certain obvious practical advantages in the formation of a protesting community. It also brought English reformers into direct contact with their Continental brethren. Strasbourg, for example, not only placed its printing presses at the service of English authors like Ponet but established a virtual "seminary of learning," where Ponet could discuss political questions with the likes of Sleidan, who was just then finishing his great history, and François Hotman, who was about to begin his own assault on the Guises. [60] Above all the exile condition permitted direct cross-fertilization with European ideas and the mature and unconstrained formulations of resistance theory by Ponet, Goodman, Foxe, and John Knox, to name only the major authors.

In human terms resistance theory was largely a product of the "exile mentality," which Continental evangelicals had earlier experienced but not in quite so collective a fashion as the pilgrims from Marian England. The theory of resistance was altogether familiar to Luther and the other magisterial reformers. An English translation of an opinion of Melanchthon dealt with the question "whether it be mortall sinne to transgresse civil lawes, which be the commaundement of civill Magistrates"; and his response, like those of Luther, Bullinger, Martyr, and others known to the English, was based on a literal reading of Romans 13, which prescribed damnation for civil resistance. [61] Yet the experience of persecution caused most reformers to shift their position, to begin to interpret the words of Saint Paul, for example, through the distinction between "superior" and "inferior" magistrates, though almost always stopping short of recommending active resistance. [62]

From the 1540s, however, the proselytizing advice of Continental reformers uniformly called for obedience to conscience and even flight from impure and idolatrous society, which was potentially a treasonable act. Bullinger and especially Calvin had lured dozens of young, and not-so-young, believers from the Babylon of Valois France, especially under Henry II, who had renewed systematic persecutions in 1547; and now the English were following paths already well trodden. The "humble, wandering, dispersed . . . members of the church" begged help from their coreligionists, especially from old friends like Calvin and Bullinger.[63] They lamented the Catholic preachers, "spewing out the abominable poison of antichrist," as John Old wrote,[64] and even more bitterly the heretical and tyrannical rule of Mary and her wicked Spanish consort, who (as Lever reported to Bullinger in 1555) not only rejected, but treated with contempt, three petitions preferred by the magistrates (members of Parliament) "that he should restore the true religion . . . , make peace with France . . . and not admit into his counsels any one born out of England."[65] Various anonymous pamphlets deplored the return of antichrist to England and chronicled the course of secular tyranny, including imposition of excessive taxes and intrusion of foreigners into administrative offices, which portended a virtual Spanish "conquest" of England.[66]

"Wherever they go," as the Venetian ambassador Michieli wrote of the exiles, "whether in Italy, Germany or France they licentiously disseminate many things against the English government and the present religion."[67] At least eighty pamphlets were published during the Marian period. Generally, the more articulate exiles sublimated their resentments into mature theories of resistance, drawing on the rich materials and experience of the Reformation as well as medieval, ancient, and biblical precedents. As usual their point of departure was the authority and spiritual antinomianism of their Continental patrons and pastors. As the French Huguenots appealed to Calvin in their own constitutional crisis of 1559 following the death of Henry II, so John Knox, after the death of Edward VI, submitted questions to Bullinger concerning the limits of obedience to godless tyrants who imposed idolatry on Christian subjects.[68] Like Calvin and Luther, Bullinger treated the problem in gingerly fashion, recommending martyrdom if need be but stopping short of suggesting active resistance by private persons. Like Calvin and Luther, too, he ended by shifting the burden of proof to the experts, which meant the lawyers, who could better judge specific circumstances and the secular limitations imposed by legal and constitutional theory.

Among the English it was Bale, whose first exile came in the early 1540s, who opened the question of resistance; and he did so, characteristically, in the context of pope-baiting, starting as early as his second "course at the Romish fox," published in 1543. He began with the familiar scriptural principle, that "the lawes of menne are to be allowed, so long as they agree to the lawes of God. For els are they no lawes, but vyolence and tyrannye."[69] With respect to secular government Bale applied a famous civilian distinction. "Prynces and magistrates beying the mynysters of god, ought to make no lawes for their private commoditie," he continued, "but for the publyque welthe of ther commons. Neyther ought they to decre any thynge against Gods honor. If they do, then the rewle of the lorde must be observed. Necessarye yt ys rather to obey God than manne." Though not specific in their political conse-quences, Bale's qualifications certainly went beyond the simple advice of Saint Paul to obey the higher powers under penalty of damnation.

Further steps were taken by later exiles, most prominently perhaps by John Knox, who brought practical experience with "rebellion" and who introduced the Old Testament notion of a covenant between ruler and subjects.[70] Equally incisive and perhaps more radical was John Ponet, though surely he was only publishing what others were thinking, and saying, privately. Ponet had been chaplain to Cranmer, then bishop of Winchester, with Bale as his chaplain, and had published, among other pamphlets, a translation of Ochino's abusive dialogue against "the iniuste usurped primacie of the Bishop of Rome," which deplored and histori-cally surveyed the "darkness, ignorance, heresie, error, fraude and lyes" of those spokesmen for antichrist who taught that the pope was the suc-cessor of Saint Peter (who had himself, some recalled, been guilty of Nicodemitism in his denials of Christ).[71] In 1555 Ponet settled in Stras-bourg and published his *Short Treatise of Politike Power,* which is perhaps the most comprehensive statement of Marian resistance ideas, yet which (as Ponet himself characteristically protested, well knowing that such would be the charge) contained neither felony nor treason, but only nec-essary admonition and faithful instruction.

Ponet thundered against modern tyranny in the fashion of an Old Tes-tament prophet but also celebrated the grand tradition of Christian mar-tyrs from the time of Nero to the present. For Ponet "politike power" was the product not merely of reason and natural law but of the Al-mighty himself, who, after the fall, authorized it for the good of the people. Did rulers have "absolute power" (referring to the famous civil-ian maxim) over their subjects?[72] Not at all, he answered, since "before Magistrates were, Goddes lawes were." What was more, rulers were sub-ject to the "positive lawes of theyr countreyes"; and by way of further proof, Ponet cited the equally famous civilian formula *digna vox,* which made the *princeps* subordinate to the *populus* and which underlay the au-thority of the parliaments and diets of European states. The final cause of "civile power" was in fact what Ponet called "the libertie of the people" and what, for polemical purposes, he confused or conflated with the evangelical idea of Christian liberty. Playing on the ambiguity of "liberty" as he had on the ambiguity of "law"—both having an external as well as an internal, a public as well as a private, aspect—Ponet en-dowed the key concept of "conscience" with a social dimension and a political significance.

Introducing another sensitive issue, Ponet also cast doubt on some of the secular consequences of tyranny. Does the property of subjects in any sense belong to the ruler? Ponet rejected the extremes of the "Anabaptist madness," endorsing possession in common, and the opposite error leading to the secular tithes, "great taxes," and extortions alien to English, if not Spanish, tradition.[73] Finally, Ponet asked the most fundamental of all political questions. Was it lawful under any circumstances to depose an evil governor, including one who "spoyleth the people of their goddes"? Although there was no "express positive law" for the punishment of tyranny, Ponet found an abundance of evidence and, in effect, justification for such action, drawn from European history as well as the Old Testament. Moreover, popes had not only deposed rulers but had been deposed themselves, and Ponet referred in particular to the canon law remedies applied at the Council of Constance in 1415. Even tyrannicide was not out of the question. Kings were no more immune than private persons from the law, Ponet argued, especially with regard to religion; and so there were laws enough to invoke against self-discrediting tyrants. Such was Ponet's warning, prediction, and perhaps threat (bypassing the crown) to "the Lordes and Commons of Englande."

Two years later (1558) in a book published at the press of the martyrologist Jean Crespin, Christopher Goodman posed the same questions but in a still more fundamental way, quoting the words of Peter and John (Acts 4) when they were banned from preaching by the council of Jerusalem. Their question to the magistrates was simply "whether it be right in the sight of God to obey you rather then God." The question that the apostles asked of the Jews Goodman put to the papists, and his conclusion may be taken as the motto of the Marian resisters—"that rather is God to be obeyed then man," and this "whether he be Kinge, Quene, or Emperour that commandeth or threateneth us."[74] Goodman thus went beyond the common view of Calvin and others that the initiative to disobedience was restricted to the so-called "inferior magistrates" and attributed this authority to all men, "of what state and condicion so ever they be." According to Goodman, "when the Magistrates and other officers cease to do their duety . . . , then God geveth the sworde in to the peoples hande, and he himself is become immediatly their head." It was at this point that Goodman launched into a defense of the cause of "that zelous and godly man Wyat." As for the poor, however, they still, if they lacked the strength to stand in their profession to the death, had the "libertie to flee."

Goodman's position, and that of the English exiles, is summed up memorably, if not elegantly, in a piece of doggerel by William Kethe printed at the end of the treatise.

Rebellion is ill, to resist is not so,
When right through resisting is done to that foo,
Who seeketh, but by ruine, against right to raigne,
Not passinge what perishe, so she spoyle the gayne.
A publick weale wretched, and to farre disgraste,
Where the right head is of cut, and a wrong insteed plaste.[75]

And be sure to heed this advice, he added, or in trying to avoid the coming plague (since you will surely not be welcome in the havens of true religion), you may have to take refuge in New Spain.

This is about as far as the Marian exiles went in their ideas of political resistance. With the accession of Elizabeth such notions became unfashionable virtually overnight, and so for example John Aylmer was led to respond to Knox's notorious blast "against the Monstruous Regiment of Women," which became irrelevant, impolitic, and indeed offensive after Mary's death.[76] Thereafter reformers and returning exiles had an investment, at least of hope, in the Elizabethan settlement. Because Elizabeth had consorted with Protestants like Nicholas Throckmorton, she was perhaps as vulnerable to resistance as Mary had been, and indeed the next generation saw the emergence of a Catholic resistance movement based on principles borrowed for the most part from Protestant publicists. Under these conditions preachers once again turned "against Disobedience and wilful Rebelion," in the words of a contemporary homily.[77]

Protestant resistance thought persisted on the Continent and flourished in just those urban centers, above all Strasbourg and Geneva, that had given refuge to the Marian exiles. In France the death of Henry II produced a political crisis that provoked the same line of thought among the French exiles in these same headquarters of civic independence. Once again Calvin was asked about the legitimacy of resistance, this time to the idolatry and "tyranny" of the party of the Guises; and once again, as Luther had done a generation earlier, he suggested that the question be submitted to the experts, which was to say the lawyers. One of these was Ponet's former neighbor in Strasbourg, François Hotman, who took up precisely the line of argument of the English exiles, though ultimately he pursued it much further—from ad hominem attacks on the Guise family (the cardinal of Lorraine playing the same diabolical role as Philip of Spain, and eventually Catherine de Médicis, as Mary) to a historically based defense of political resistance. This was reinforced by the work of his old friend Beza, who succeeded Calvin as leader of the Genevan church in 1564 and who, during the civil wars in France, finally and explicitly made the shift from passive and martyrly to active and political resistance—at least temporarily, until the Catholic party was thrown into

political opposition. In a very direct sense the French debate—first the
Huguenot and then the Catholic phase—represents the culmination of
Marian arguments, though as John Salmon has shown, resistance ideas
in this radical mode would cross back over the Channel again to rejoin
the English civil wars of the next century—and what is more, would be
preserved for later beneficiaries in the larger movements of the later eighteenth century.[78]

IV

The genesis of resistance ideas, then, has followed a pattern that is only
indirectly dependent on the sources and logic of political theory as scholars have reconstructed and construed it, reading back as it were from
Lockean (if not Rousseauean) models and the natural-law devices of social contract and modern property. Although these notions are not absent, the basic ideas of sixteenth-century resistance cannot be extricated
from religious consciousness and that explosive concept, or behavior
pattern, that Luther called (and gave new meaning to) "liberty of conscience." The context of resistance was tied to what Erich Fromm identified long ago as an essentially "negative" sort of freedom, which acted
at least for a time to dissolve traditional ties and to form new ones.[79] In
the effort to justify this transformation of values, champions of resistance
seized upon texts and arguments from every side, interpreting them and
arguing away contrary views, to provide a foundation for new values
and a new community conforming to these values. In keeping both with
Reanissance rhetoric and Reformation preaching, propagandists like Ponet, Goodman, and Foxe were in any case less concerned with logical
consistency than with consolation, exhortation, and (one may infer) in-
flammation. The more allegations the better, Hotman once recommended, for who knew what arguments might succeed in persuading
some people?

Here, in conclusion, are the principal stages in the ideological and so-
ciological process underlying the emergence of modern "resistance
theory."[80] First, a fundamentalist religious protest, founded on private
"conscience" and opposed to old values—the "law" of the ecclesiastical
establishment of Western Christendom, whose secular head was the Roman papacy and whose spiritual symbol was the "abomination of the
mass." Second, a civic protest against the political authority which supported the old ecclesiastical system and imposed its values on dissidents.
Third, the socialization of protest produced by the need of adherents of
the Protestant "cause" to bear witness and to disseminate—hence, to
"publicize"—their dissenting views. Fourth, the politicization of pro-

test, which was unavoidable in view of the circumstances that a separation could not in reality be made between church and state, nor consequently between heresy and treason, so that a confrontation was set up, and indeed conditions for civil war. Fifth and concomitant with these phenomena, were the assembling of authorities and arguments, the construction of a new perspective, and thereby the creation of a system of values giving legitimacy and political identity to the new confessional community.[81]

The process does not end here, of course, since (short of permanent exile or mass conversion) some sort of accommodation has always to be made with the established society, government as well as church. The point is that resistance ideas, in a most fundamental sense, are not quite the creation of theories developed within an intellectual community. Rather, they are produced by the interaction between irreconcilable views of conflicting communities—ideologies—and only later absorbed into a common tradition, as the idea (if not the reality) of "revolution," for example, has been absorbed and domesticated in Western tradition. This is no doubt a natural process, but historical (distinguished from logical) understanding must penetrate further and try to appreciate the human predicament as well as the political discourse. For this purpose a page or two of Foxe's martyrology may serve better than Locke's *Second Treatise,* certainly for the "social history of ideas" which this question invites.

Various questions remain, various lines of inquiry beckon. One recent issue in the interpretation of the English Reformation has been posed in terms deriving from the "new" social history—reformation from the top down, as traditional historians like Geoffrey Elton assume, or from the bottom up, as devotees of local history have wondered? It does not seem likely that resistance ideas were disseminated very widely, certainly not outside the towns; yet the sort of literature discussed here, an offspring of the vernacular sermon, must come closer to popular culture than the "classical texts" selected for examination by historians of political thought like Skinner and Pocock (although this remains to be proved).

More important, since the subject here is the history of thought and ideology rather than public opinion or "mentality," is the nature of the political discourse in which resistance ideas have been formulated. Inspired in part by the new typographic art, sixteenth-century publicists combined medieval and ancient traditions—joining political and legal theology with imperial, national, civic, and naturalistic ideas—and in so doing developed an extraordinary "language of power." What the Marians developed, on the other hand, was a language of powerlessness, an ideology of the victim and the exile. To the celebration of political authority, in other words, the literature of protest, disobedience, and resistance, as a kind of mirror for rebels, forms a logical complement, whether it was created by opposition and contradiction or by an independent "populist" tradition (in the words of Walter Ullmann), not always in touch with the classics and not necessarily most usefully understood as a milestone on the "high road to revolution." The answers to these questions lie not in our twentieth-century arguments, however, but in "their" sixteenth-century texts, if we can only find them: *tolle lege, tolle lege.*

Notes

1. There has been much recent discussion of the problem of language in history, e.g., Anthony Pagden, ed., *The Languages of Political Theory in Early-Modern Europe* (Cambridge: Cambridge University Press, 1987), with discussions by myself, J. G. A. Pocock, Quentin Skinner, Nicolai Rubinstein, Richard Tuck, Judith Shklar, and others; and also of the crucial question of rhetoric, e.g., James J. Murphy, *Renaissance Eloquence* (Berkeley: University of California Press, 1983), and Brian Vickers, ed., *Rhetoric Revalued*. The basic work is still C. Perelman and L. Obrechts-Tyteca, *The New Rhetoric,* tr. J. Wilkinson and P. Weaver (Notre Dame, Ind.: Indiana University Press, 1969); see also W. J. T. Mitchell, ed., *The Politics of Interpretation* (Chicago: University of Chicago Press, 1983), based on articles from *Critical Inquiry* (1982–83).

2. All this is pursued further in my *Beginning of Ideology: Consciousness and Society in the French Reformation* (Cambridge: Cambridge University Press, 1981), with additional references; and see Carlos M. M. Eire, *War against the Idols* (Cambridge: Cambridge University Press, 1986); as well as the remarks of Stephen Greenblatt, *Renaissance Self-Fashioning from More to Shakespeare* (Chicago: University of Chicago Press, 1980), chap. 2, "The Word of God in the Age of Mechanical Reproduction."

3. This old problem has recently been confronted by literary scholars under the banner of a so-called "new historicism," and in England of "cultural materialism"; see esp. Jonathan Dollimore and Alan Sinfield, eds., *Political Shakespeare: New Essays in Cultural Materialism* (Manchester: Manchester University Press, 1985). For comments by historians on this important literature, see David Sacks "History in Literature: The Renaissance," *Journal of British Studies* 26 (1987): 107–23; Kevin Sharpe, "The Politics of Literature in Renaissance England," *History* 71 (1986): 235–47; and Donald R. Kelley, "Horizons of Intellectual History," *Journal of the History of Ideas* 48 (1987): 143–69, esp. p. 163. But the "old historicism"—"naive and unreflective," as Gadamer calls it; "monological," says Greenblatt (*The Power of Forms in the English Renaissance* [Norman: University of Oklahoma Press, 1982], p. 5)—has long (at least since Dilthey) been superseded, at least in philosophical circles; see, e.g., Hans-Georg Gadamer, "Hermeneutics and Historicism," in *Truth and Method,* tr. G. Barden and J. Cumming (New York: Seabury Press, 1975), pp. 460–91.

4. Hans-Georg Gadamer, *Philosophical Hermeneutics,* tr. David E. Linge (Berkeley: University of California Press, 1976), p. 35.

5. Richard Waswo, *Language and Meaning in the Renaissance* (Princeton: Princeton University Press, 1987).

6. Marc Fumaroli, "Rhetoric, Politics, and Society," in *Renaissance Eloquence,* Murphy, pp. 253–73.

7. A version of this paper was offered at the Folger Shakespeare Library in January 1985 for the seminar on Elizabethan political thought. For comments on that occasion, thanks to John Pocock, Gordon Schocket, Lois Schwoerer, and other members of the seminar and, more recently, to Richard Strier.

8. John Ponet, *Short Treatise of Politike Power* (Strasbourg, 1556), photo-reproduction in Winthrop S. Hudson, *John Ponet, Advocate of Limited Monarchy* (Chicago: University of Chicago Press, 1942), p. 16, citing "Esias" (Isa. 10:1–3).

9. Best discussion now is in Quentin Skinner, *The Foundations of Modern Political Thought,* vol. 2 (Cambridge: University of Cambridge Press, 1978), superseding the older books of J. N. Figgis, J. W. Allen, Christopher Norris, and P. Mesnard; but also see Michael Walzer, *The Revolution of the Saints* (Cambridge, Mass.: Harvard University Press, 1965), as well as the criticism of this work by C. H. George in *Past and Present,* no. 41 (1968): 99. I omit the large secondary bibliography on the question of resistance, but see the works cited in Donald R. Kelley, *The Beginning of Ideology,* pp. 33, 35, 115, 119, 233, 307; I also omit references to standard historical authorities, most notably A. W. Pollard, M. M. Knappen, W. K. Jordan, M. L. Bush, and D. M. Loades.

10. Katharine R. Firth, *The Apocalyptic Tradition in Reformation Britain, 1530–1645* (Oxford: Oxford University Press, 1979); Paul Christianson, *Reformation and Babylon* (Toronto: University of Toronto Press, 1978); and Richard Bauckham, *Tudor Apocalypse* (Oxford: Oxford University Press, 1978), as well as the work of Marjorie Reeves. A dimension of resistance literature unfortunately not pursued here is that of pictorial propaganda, which often served to enhance and even to sensationalize literary polemic, often "for the sake of the simple folk": see especially Marie-Helene Davies, *Reflections of Renaissance England: Life, Thought and Religion Mirrored in Illustrated Pamphlets, 1535–1640* (Allison Park, Pa., 1986).

11. See below, n. 28.

12. An excellent survey and introduction is John N. King, *English Reformation Literature* (Princeton: Princeton University Press, 1982), with full bibliography; and see also Smythe, *Cranmer and the English Reformation* (Cambridge: Cambridge University Press, 1926).

13. Most relevant here is the *Arte of Rhetorique* by the Marian exile Thomas Wilson, ed. G. H. Maire (Oxford: Oxford University Press, 1909). The best introduction is still Walter Ong, *Ramus, Method, and the Decay of Dialogue* (Cambridge, Mass.: Harvard University Press, 1958). On the problem of the language of politics see J. G. A. Pocock, *Politics, Language, and Time* (London: Athenaeum, 1972); and Keith Baker, "On the Problem of the Ideological Origin of the French Revolution," in *Modern Intellectual History,* ed. D. La Capra and S. Kaplan (Ithaca: Cornell University Press, 1982), pp. 197–219; also the remarks

in Jonathan Goldberg, *James I and the Politics of Literature* (Baltimore: Johns Hopkins University Press, 1983).

14. Thomas Cooper, *Thesaurus linguae Romanae et Brittanicae* (London, 1584).

15. Guy Swanson, *Religion and Regime* (Ann Arbor: University of Michigan Press, 1967).

16. Still essential is Christina Garrett, *The Marian Exiles* (Cambridge: Cambridge University Press, 1938), with penciled corrections (indicated by the author) in the Folger Library copy, but see also the rather hypercritical review by J. R. Neale in *EHR* (1939). See also the standard source collections, especially H. Robinson, ed., *Original Letters Relative to the English Reformation* (London: Parker Society, 1846–47); John Strype's *Ecclesiastical Memorials . . . under King Henry VIII* (Oxford: Bagster, 1822); Johann Sleidan, *De Statu Religionis et Reipublicae Carlo Quinto Caesare commentarii*, ed. J. Boemius and C. am Ende (Frankfurt, 1785–86), English tr. 1560; John Foxe, *Actes and Monuments*, ed. G. Townsend, 8 vols. (London, 1843–49); and above all the resources of Pollard and Redgrave's *Short Title Catalogue* (*STC*), which may profitably be supplemented through the Folger's chronological card file.

17. Christopher Goodman, *How Superior Powers Ought to be Obeyed*, (New York: Facsimile Text Society, 1931), p. 8, with a note by C. H. McIlwain.

18. The Marian resistance literature was surveyed by Cardinal Allen, *A True, Sincere, and Modest Defense of English Catholics*, ed. Robert M. Kingdon (Ithaca: Cornell University Press, 1965); and by Milton in *The Tenure of Kings and Magistrates*, ed. W. T. Allison (New York: H. Holt, 1911), pp. 46–49. The most complete listing is Edward J. Baskerville, *A Chronological Bibliography of Propaganda and Polemic Published in England between 1553 and 1558 from the Death of Edward VI to the Death of Mary I*, in *Memoirs*, vol. 136, American Philosophical Society (Philadelphia, 1979).

19. John Bale, *The Three Laws of Nature, Moses, and Christ*, photoreproduction (London, Tudor Facsimile ed.: 1908); and see Leslie P. Fairfield, *John Bale: Mythmaker of the English Reformation* (West Lafayette, Ind., 1976).

20. See Harold J. Berman, *Law and Revolution* (Cambridge, Mass.: Harvard University Press, 1983); and the classic works by Fritz Kern and Gerd Tellenbach.

21. William Baldwin, *The Funerals of King Edward the Sixth* (London, 1560) *STC* 1243.

22. William Turner, *The Huntyng and Fyndyng out of the Romish Fox* ("Basel" [Bonn], 1543 reprint, Cambridge, 1851). Turner's book was one of a series of antipapal tracts published by a certain "Hans Hitprick"; cf. also [W. Copeland?], *The dysclosyng of the Canon of the popysh Masse* (n.p., 1548?) *STC* 17626.

23. John Bale, *A dysclosynge or openynge of the Manne of synne* ([Antwerp], 1543), *STC* 1309, called also "Yet a course at the Romyshe foxe"; Bale, *The Epistle exhortatorye . . . unto his derelye beloved contreye of Englande against the pompouse popyshe Byschoppes thereof* ([Antwerp], 1544), *STC* 129; and Bale, *The Apology . . . agaynste a rank Papyst* (n.p., 1550), *STC* 1275, dedicated to Edward VI.

24. John Hooper, in *Original Letters*, ed. Robinson, 1:21 (letter of January 1546).

25. James Gairdner, *Lollardy and the Reformation* (London: Macmillan, 1911), 3:246.

26. Martin Bucer, *The gratulation . . . unto the churche of Englande for the restitution of Christes religion,* ([London, 1549]) *STC* 3963; Peter Martyr, *An epistle unto . . . the Duke of Somerset* (London, 1550); Sleidan, *De Statu Religionis,* book 21; and Johann Cario, *The thre bokes of Cronicles* (London, 1550), *STC* 4626.

27. Philipp Melanchthon, *A waying and considering of the Interim* (London, 1548), *STC* 17799.

28. John Calvin, *Lettres,* ed. J. Bonnett (Paris: Meyrueis, 1851), 1:261 (22 October 1548). Calvin's dedication to his commentary on Timothy, a scriptural text that, significantly, attacks hypocrisy, points out the irrelevance of law to the "righteous man" and celebrates the "good fight of faith."

29. See F. de Schickler, *Les Eglises du refuge en Angleterre* (Paris: Fischbacher, 1892). It may be noted that the flourishing vocation and business of translation during the Reformation is a subject that needs further, and more expert, study.

30. English translation of Latin and German texts (13 April 1550) in Lowell H. Zuck, ed., *Christianity and Revolution* (Philadelphia: Temple University Press, 1975), p. 137. The Interim of 1548 technically tolerated Protestantism but recognized no Protestant demands and was rejected by various members of the Schmalkaldic League, most notably in the *Magdeburg Confession* (1550), a seminal resistance tract.

31. Sleidan, *De Statu Religionis,* book 20. See Inge Vogelstein, *Johann Sleidan's Commentaries* (Lanham, Md.: University Presses of America, 1986).

32. John Hooper, *Our saviour Jesus Christ hath not overcharged his chirche with many ceremonies* ([Antwerp], Zurich, 1548), *STC* 14556; and [Hooper], *A brief examination for the tyme* (n.p., n.d.), *STC* 10387, including judgments by both Bucer and Calvin.

33. John Ponet, *An Apologie,* ([Strasbourg], 1555), *STC* 20175; and cf. Heinrich Bullinger, *The Christen State of matrimony* (London, 1543), *STC* 4047.

34. John Ponet, *A notable sermon concerninge the right of the lordes supper* (Westminster, 14 March 1550), *STC* 20177, sig. Ciii.

35. Rodolph Gaulter, *Antichrist,* tr. J. D. ("Southwarke," 1556), *STC* 25009, fol. 7v.

36. Andreas Osiander, *A most necessarie treatise . . . ,* tr. Walter Lynn (1548), *STC* 17116; and see the discussion by King, *English Reformation Literature,* pp. 197–200. The woodcuts are also reproduced in R. Scribner, *For the Sake of Simple Folk* (Cambridge, 1981).

37. Bernardo Ochino, *A tragoedie or dialoge . . . ,* tr. John Ponet (1549), *STC* 18771.

38. Christianson, *Reformation and Babylon,* p. 5.

39. Bale's account of the fourteenth-century martyr John Oldcastle appeared in 1544 (*STC* 1276). In general see Donald R. Kelley, "Martyrs, Myths, and the Massacre," *American Historical Review* 77 (1972): 1323–42, and literature there cited; also William Haller, *Foxe's Book of Martyrs and the Elect Nation* (New York, Harper & Rowe: 1963), although his view of the apocalyptic tradition has been severely criticized.

40. Randall Hurleston, *Newes from Rome concerning the blasphemous sacrifice of the papisticall Masse* (Canterbury, ca. 1550), *STC* 14006, sig. Gi.

41. Donald R. Kelley, *François Hotman: A Revolutionary's Ordeal* (Princeton: Princeton University Press, 1973), pp. 105 ff.

42. Cf. C. M. Dent, *Protestant Reformers in Elizabethan Oxford* (Oxford: Oxford University, 1983), p. 5. The "synagogue of Satan" was a favorite phrase of reformers; e.g., François Lambert, *The Summe of christianitie* . . . (n.p., 1536), *STC* 15179; John Knox, *Works,* ed. D. Laing (Edinburgh, 1895), 4:299; and the works of Bale.

43. Thomas Lever, *Sermons, 1550* (London: English Reprints, 1870), p. 26.

44. John Bale, *The Epistle exhortatorye of an Englyshe Christiane unto his derelye beloved contrye of Englande against the pompouse popyshe Byschoppes thereof* (n.p., 1544) *STC* 1294, sig. Bi.

45. John Bradford, *Writings,* ed. A. Townsend (Cambridge: Cambridge University Press, 1848), pp. 385, 403.

46. John Philpot, *The Trew report* . . . (London, 1550), *STC* 19890.

47. [John Cheke], *The hurt of sedition howe greveous it is to a commune wealth* (London, 1549), *STC* 5109.2—unrecorded in Pollard and Redgrave, 1st ed.. Cf. on the Marian side, John Christopherson, *An exhortation to all menne to take hede and beware of rebellion* (London, 1554), *STC* 5207.

48. Heinrich Bullinger, *A most necessary & fruitfull Dialoguee betwene ye seditious Libertin or rebel Anabaptiste & a true obedient Christian* (n.p., 1551), *STC* 3552.5.

49. See Robert M. Kingdon, "The First Expression of Theodore Beza's Political Ideas," *Archiv für Reformationsgeschichte* 46 (1955): 88–100.

50. John Proctor, *The historie of Wyates rebellion* (London, 1554), *STC* 20407, sig. Ai. See also William B. Robison, "The National and Local Significance of Waytt's Rebellion in Surrey," *Historical Journal* 30 (1987): 769–90.

51. Matteo Gribaldi, *A notable and marvalous epistle* . . . *concerning the terible iudgement of God, upon him that for feare of man, denyeth Christ* (n.p., 1556), *STC* 12365.

52. John Bale, *The Pageant of Popes* (London, 1574 [1558]), dedication to the earl of Sussex.

53. Wolfgang Musculus, *The Temporisour* (n.p., 1555), *STC* 18313.

54. John Calvin, *The Mynde of the Godly and excellent lerned man M. John Calvyne,* tr. R. G. (Ipswich, 1548), *STC* 4435; Kelley, *François Hotman,* p. 114.

55. John Calvin, *An answer to a certain godly mannes lettres desiring his frends iudgement whether it be lawful for a christian man to be present at the popish Masse* ([Strasbourg], 1551), *STC* 658; *Two Epistles, one of Henry Bullinger of Tigury* . . . , *another of John Calvyne* . . . , *whether it be lawful for a chrysten man to communicate or be partaken of the masse of the papysts, without offending God and hys neyghbor or not* (London, 1548), *STC* 4080; also [anon.], *A treatise of the cohabitaciyon of the faithfull with the unfaithfull* ([Strasbourg], 1555) *STC* 24246; also Bullinger, *De origine erroris* (Zurich, 1548). In general see Carlo Ginzburg, *Il Nicodemitismo* (Turin: G. Einaudi, 1970); and Mario Turchetti, *Concordia o toleranza?* (Geneva: Librairie Droz, 1984). This essential question will be reviewed

in a forthcoming book by Perez Zagorin, the theory and practice of "dissimulation."

56. John Foxe, *Book of the Martyrs*, 3:702. Besides the much-discussed work of Elizabeth Eisenstein, see D. M. Loades, "The Press under the Early Tudors," *Transactions of the Cambridge Bibliographical Society* 4 (1964): 29–50; and Jennifer Loach, "Pamphlets and Politics, 1553–1558," *Bulletin of the Institute for Historical Research* 48 (1975): 31–44.

57. Foxe, *Book of the Martyrs* 1:508.

58. On exile experience and mentality, see F. A. Norwood, *Strangers and Exiles* (Nashville: Abingdon Press, 1969); and Randolph Starn, *Contrary Commonwealth: The Theme of Exile in Renaissance Italy* (Berkeley: University of California Press, 1982).

59. John Ponet, in *Original Letters*, Robinson, 1:116 (to Bullinger, 14 April 1556); and see E. J. Baskerville, "John Ponet in Exile: A Ponet Letter to John Bale," *Journal of Ecclesiastical History* 37 (1986): 442–47.

60. Marvin Walter Anderson, *Peter Martyr: A Reformer in Exile (1542–1562)* (Nieuwkoop: De Graaf, 1975), p. 117; and cf. Hudson, *John Ponet*, introduction.

61. Philipp Melanchthon, *Whether it be mortall sinne to transgresse civil lawes* (London, 1566), *STC* 22572.

62. See Robert M. Kingdon, ed., *The Political Thought of Peter Martyr Vermigli* (Geneva: Librairie Droz, 1980), especially the commentary on Romans 13.

63. Richard Horn and Richard Chambers, in Robinson, *Original Letters*, 1:127, to the Senate of Zurich, 1556.

64. John Old, *The acquital or purgation of the most catholyke Christen Prince, Edwarde the VI.* (n.p., n.d.), *STC* 18797.

65. Thomas Lever, in *Original Letters*, Robinson, 159.

66. John Scory, *An Epistle . . . unto all the faythfull that be in pryson in England, or in any other trouble for the defense of Goddes truth* ([Emdem] 1555); *STC* 21854; Thomas Becon, *An humble supplicacion* ([Wesel ?], 1554) *STC* 1730; *The Lamentacion of England* (n.p., 1557), *STC* 10014; [John Olde], *A short description of Antichrist unto the nobilitye of Englande* ([Emden, 1555]) *STC* 673.

67. Giovanni Michieli, *Calendar of State Papers, Venetian*, 6:243.

68. Knox, *Works* 3:221.

69. Bale, *A dysclosynge*, sig. Kviii.

70. On this large question see Richard C. Greaves, *Theology and Revolution in the Scottish Reformation* (Grand Rapids, Mich.: Christian University Press, 1980), pp. 116 ff.

71. Bernardo Ochino, *A tragoedie or dialogue . . .* , tr. John Ponet (n.p., 1549), *STC* 18771.

72. John Ponet, *Short Treatise*, pp. 35, 43, passim. In general see David H. Wollman, "The Biblical Justification for Resistance to Authority in Ponet's and Goodman's Polemics," *Sixteenth Century Journal* 13 (1982): 29–41.

73. Ponet, *Short Treatise*, pp. 81, 103.

74. Christopher Goodman, *Superior Powers*, pp. 41, 44, 73, 185.

75. Ibid., p. 235.

76. John Aylmer, *An harborowe for faithfull and trew subjects against the late blowne blastwe concerning the gouvernment of wemen* (Strasbourg, 1559), *STC* 1005.

77. *Sermones or homilies appointed to be read in churches in the time of Queen Elizabeth* (Oxford, 1816), pp. 468–516.

78. John H. M. Salmon, *The French Religious Wars in English Political Thought* (Oxford: Oxford University Press, 1959).

79. Erich Fromm, *Escape from Freedom* (New York: Farrar, 1941).

80. Kelley, *Beginning of Ideology*, chaps. 1 and 8.

81. Christopher Haigh, "Some Aspects of the Recent Historiography of the English Reformation," in *Stadtbürgertum und Adel in der Reformation,* ed. W. Mommsen (Stuttgart: Klett-Cotta, 1979), pp. 88–100.

Part Two
Shakespeare, Politics, and History

Descanting on Deformity: Richard III and the Shape of History

And thus having resoved all the doubts, so farre as I can imagine, may be moued against this Treatise; it onely rests to pray thee (charitable Reader) to interprete fauorably this birth of mine, according to the integritie of the author, and not looking for perfection in the worke it selfe. As for my part, I onely glory thereof in this point, that I trust no sort of vertue is condemned, nor any degree of vice allowed in it: and that (though it not be perhaps so gorgeously decked, and richly attired as it ought to be) it is at the least rightly proportioned in all the members, without any monstrous deformitie in any of them.

James I, Basilikon Doron

Upon a time when Burbidge played Richard III there was a citizen grew so far in liking with him that, before she went from the play, she appointed him to come that night unto her by the name of Richard the Third. Shakespeare, overhearing their conclusion, went before, was entertained and at his game ere Burbidge came. Then, message being brought that Richard the Third was at the door, Shakespeare caused return to be made that William the Conqueror was before Richard the Third.

John Manningham's Diary, 13 March 1601

How does the logic of ghostly authorship inform—or deform—not only the writing of literature but also the writing of history? As a way of approaching this question, I begin with a passage from *The Comedy of Errors*:

> O! grief hath chang'd me since you saw me last,
> And careful hours with time's deformed hand
> Have written strange defeatures in my face:
> But tell me yet, dost thou not know my voice?
> (5.1.298–301)[1]

A complex interrelationship between time and deformation is clearly outlined in Egeon's plea for recognition. For time's hand is already deformed as well as deforming, and it is, explicitly, a writing hand. Be-

This essay was previously published in Marjorie Garber, *Shakespeare's Ghost Writers* (New York: Methuen & Co., 1987) and is published here by permission of Methuen & Co.

tween the "deformed hand" and the still recognizable speaking voice comes, as always, the shadow. Hand/voice; written/spoken. Here, though, that which is *written* is deformed, twisted out of shape, imbued with "strange defeatures." The wonderful word *defeature* means both "undoing, ruin" and "disfigurement; defacement; marring of features" (*OED*). In *The Comedy of Errors* it is twice used to describe the change of appearance wrought by age upon the face, both in Egeon's speech given above and in Adriana's lament for her lost beauty, its loss hastened, she thinks, by her husband's neglect: "then is he the ground / Of my defeatures" (2.1.97–98). It is unfortunate that "defeature" has become, as the *OED* points out, "obsolete," "archaic," "now chiefly an echo of the Shakespearean use," because it offers a superbly concrete picture of the *effects* of ruin, the visible, readable consequences of being—or coming—undone.

I would like to arrive, in this essay, at a consideration of the way in which "time's deformed hand" writes, and thus defaces, history. The concept of defeature is a useful place to start from, since the visible marks of political defeat are often written, or characterized, in what one age will call history writing and another, propaganda. My subject, the "defeatured" player in this exemplum, will be Richard III, an especially interesting case not only because of the fascination that his story has exercised on both admirers and detractors, but also because, like Oxford and Bacon in the Shakespeare authorship controversy, Richard III has been the occasion for much amateur detective work and for the foundation of both English and American societies to clear his name. The Richard III Society, originally known as the Fellowship of the White Boar, was founded in England in 1924; the Friends of Richard III Incorporated, the Society's American counterpart, included among its founding members the actresses Helen Hayes and Tallulah Bankhead.

The most recent full-length study of Richard, by Charles Ross,[2] while in most ways apparently an extremely careful and balanced account, shows the usual pique at this "amateur" espousal of Richard's cause, which has led in turn to the unwelcome development of amateurs writing history: "an Oxford professor of English law, a headmaster at Eton, several peers of the realm and a number of historical novelists and writers of detective stories," prominent among them women. Ross cites Josephine Tey, Rosemary Hawley Jarman, and "a number of others, nearly all women writers, for whom the rehabilitation of the reputation of a long-dead king holds a strange and unexplained fascination" (p. 11). By implication these women are following the self-deluded path of the Lady Anne, whose "strange and unexplained" capitulation to Richard's suit in Shakespeare's play demonstrates female folly and a slightly sentimental belief that a bad man can be reformed or redeemed by the love of a good woman.

Ross's view of Richard is fact-oriented, balanced but binary. He concludes that Richard "does not appear to have been a complex man," and that "any contrarity of 'character' of Richard III stems not from what we know about him but from what we do not know about him" (p. 229). It is the historian's job to disover the facts, and thus to dispel mystery, fantasy, undecidability. With this decidedly "professional" (p. li), male, and hegemonic view of the use and abuse of history writing, set forth in an introductory chapter that is designed to articulate "The Historical Reputation of Richard III: Fact and Fiction," we may begin our consideration of a dramatic character who is self-described as both deformed and defeatured, himself compact of fact *and* fiction: "cheated of feature . . . deformed, unfinished . . . scarce half made up" (*Richard III,* 1.1.19–21).

I

Shakespeare's use and abuse of history in the *Henry VI* plays, and particularly in *Richard III,* is often viewed as a consequence, deliberate or adventitious, of the move by Tudor historians to classify Richard III as self-evidently a villain, his deformed body a readable text. Shakespeare, in such interpretations, emerges as either an unwitting dupe of More, Hall, and Holinshed, or as a coconspirator, complicit in their design, seizing the opportunity to present the Plantagenet king defeated by Elizabeth's grandfather as unworthy of the throne, as unhandsome in person as in personality. Either the dramatist was himself shaping the facts for political purposes, or he was taken in by the Tudor revisionist desire to inscribe a Richard "shap'd" and "stamp'd" for villainy.

In either case, the persuasive power of the portrait has endured. As recently as 1984, for example, René Girard could assert confidently that "when Shakespeare wrote the play, the king's identity as a 'villain' was well-established. The dramatist goes along with the popular view, especially at the beginning. Richard's deformed body is a mirror for the self-confessed ugliness in his soul."[3]

It is clear, however, that no account of Shakespeare's literary or political motivations in foregrounding his protagonist's deformity is adequate to explain the power and seductiveness of Richard's presence in the plays. Indeed, the very fascination exerted by the historical Richard III seems to grow in direct proportion to an increase in emphasis on his deformity.

It may be useful here to document briefly the ways in which the vagaries of transmission, like a game of historical telephone, succeeded in instating Richard's deformity as the party line. The story of Richard's prolonged gestation, "held for two years in his mother's womb, emerging with teeth, and with hair down to his shoulders," like the picture of the hunchback, "small of stature, having a short figure, uneven shoulders, the right being higher than the left," is first told in the *Historia Regium Angliae* of Warwickshire antiquary John Rous, who died in 1491.[4] Polydore Vergil, Henry VII's Italian humanist historian, situated Richard in the scheme of providential history as the antagonist of Tudor ascendancy. Thomas More's *History of Richard III* established the enduring popular image of the villainous king as monster, in an account that artfully ascribes some of the more lurid details to rumor while passing them on.

> Richarde the third sonne, of whom we nowe entreate, was in witte and courage egall with either of them, in bodye and prowesse farre vnder them bothe, little of stature, ill fetured of limmes, croke backed, his left shoulder much higher then his right, hard fauoured of visage, and suche as in states called warlye, in other menne other wise. He was malicious, wrathfull, enuious, and from afore his birth, euer frowarde. It is for trouth reported, that the Duches his mother had so muche a doe in her trauaile, that shee coulde not bee deliuered of hym vncutte: and that hee came into the worlde with the feete forwarde, as menne bee borne outwarde, and (as the fame runneth) also not vntothed, whither menne of hatred reporte aboue the trouthe, or elles that nature chaunged her course in hys beginninge, whiche in the course of his lyfe many thinges vnnaturallye committed.[5]

More's account was borrowed by both Hall and Holinshed, and survives substantially unchanged in Shakespeare's *Richard III*. We might note that there is already a disparity between Rous's "history" and More's. Rous describes Richard's right shoulder as being higher than his left. More, with equal particularity, asserts that "his left shoulder [was] much higher than his right." The augmentation "much" puts a spin on the reversal; More grounds his own authority in rhetorical emphasis and in doing so further distorts the figure of Richard—and the rhetorical figure for which he will come to stand. Both the change of shoulder—toward the sinister—and the emphasis implied by "much" suggest the pattern of amplification and embellishment characteristic of the Richard story throughout its history.[6]

   In the first tetralogy, unusual stress is placed on Richard's physical deformity, which is repeatedly anatomized and cataloged. King Henry calls him "an indigested and deformed lump" (*3 Henry VI* 5.6.51), Clifford a "foul indigested lump, / As crooked in thy manners as thy shape!" (*2 Henry VI* 5.1.157–58), and the Lady Anne a "lump of foul deformity" (*Richard III* 1.2.57). Significantly, he is at once "misshap'd," unshaped, and preshaped. Born in a sense prematurely ("sent before my time"), feet first, and with teeth already in his mouth, to the wonderment of the midwife and waiting women (*3 Henry VI* 5.6.52, 75–76), he is disproportioned and deformed, but at the same time unfinished, incomplete, as his own testimony makes plain. Nature, he says in *3 Henry VI,* conspired with love

> To shrink mine arm up like a wither'd shrub,
> To make an envious mountain on my back
> Where sits deformity to mock my body;
> To shape my legs of an unequal size,
> To disproportion me in every part,
> Like to a chaos, or an unlick'd bear-whelp
> That carries no impression like the dam.
> (3.2.156–62)

In the opening soliloquy of *Richard III,* he recurs to this description, again placing the blame on nature and love.

> I, that am rudely stamp'd, and want love's majesty
> To strut before a wanton ambling nymph;
> I, that am curtail'd of this fair proportion,
> Cheated of feature by dissembling nature,
> Deformed, unfinished, sent before my time,
> Into this breathing world scarce half made up,
> And that so lamely and unfashionable
> That dogs bark at me as I halt by them—
> Why I, in this weak piping time of peace,
> Have no delight to pass away the time,
> Unless to spy my shadow in the sun,
> And descant on mine own deformity.
> (1.1.16–27)

Generations of readers have been strongly affected by this relation between the deformity and the moral or psychological character of Richard. One such reader was Sigmund Freud, who turned to the example of Richard's deformity to characterize patients who think of themselves as "exceptions" to normal rules. Such patients, Freud says, claim that "they have renounced enough and suffered enough, and have a claim to be spared any further exactions; they will submit no longer to disagreeable necessity, for they are *exceptions* and intend to remain so too."[7] This claim seems apt enough for Richard's opening soliloquy, which Freud goes on to quote: "that figure in the creative work of the greatest of poets in whose character the claim to be an exception is closely bound up with and motivated by the circumstance of congenital injury" (p. 160). But when Freud comes to discuss the passage, he finds it to signify not Richard's desire to deflect his energies from love (for which his deformity renders him unsuitable) to intrigue and murder, but rather a more sympathetic message for which the resolution to "prove a villain" acts as a "screen." The "something much more serious" (p. 161) that Freud descries behind the screen is, essentially, a variation on the theme of the family romance. His Richard declares,

> Nature has done me a grievous wrong in denying me that beauty of form which wins human love. . . . I have a right to be an exception, to overstep those bounds by which others let themselves be circumscribed. I may do wrong myself, since wrong has been done to me— and now [says Freud] we feel that we ourselves could be like Richard, nay, that we are already a little like him. Richard is an enormously magnified representation of something we can all discover in ourselves. We all think we have reason to reproach nature and our destiny for congenital and infantile disadvantages; we all demand reparation for early wounds to our narcissism, our self-love. . . . Why were we born in a middle-class dwelling instead of a royal palace? (p. 161)

For Freud, then, Shakespeare's Richard III represents not so much a particular aberrant personality warped by the accident of congenital deformation, as the general psychological fact of deformation at birth and by birth, the congenital deformation that results "in ourselves," in "all" of us, because we are born to certain parents and in certain circumstances, incurring, inevitably, certain narcissistic wounds. Thus for Freud the character of Shakespeare's Richard marks the fact of deformation in the register of the psychological, just as we shall see the same character mark the inevitability of deformation in the registers of the political and the historiographical.

Moreover, in Freud's narrative the political is also explicitly present, though it is signified by a lacuna, a lapse in the progress of his exposition. "For reasons which will be easily understood, I cannot communicate very much about these . . . case-histories. Nor do I propose to go into the obvious analogy between deformities of character resulting from protracted sickliness in childhood and the behaviour of whole nations whose past history has been full of suffering. Instead, however, I will take the opportunity of pointing to that figure" (p. 160), and so on to Shakespeare and Richard III. What is the "obvious analogy" he resists? It seems reasonable to associate the "deformities of character resulting from protracted sickliness in childhood" and, indeed, the "behavior of whole nations whose past history has been full of suffering" with some specific rather than merely general referent. And if we consider the year in which this essay was first published, in *Imago* 1915–16, we may be reminded of the circumstances of Germany in the First World War and, most directly, of the personal circumstances of Kaiser Wilhelm. For Wilhelm II of Prussia was born with a withered arm, a congenital defect that made him the target of gibes from his childhood playmates, including his cousin, who would become Czar Nicholas of Russia. As a recent historical study describes him, Wilhelm II "was a complicated man of painful insecurity—his left arm was withered and useless—who sought in pomp and bluster, in vulgar displays of virility, to mask his handicap and to assert what he devoutly believed in: his divine right to rule. But he craved confirmation of that right and yearned to be loved and idolized. Beyond the flawed character was a man of intelligence and vision."[8]

Wilhelm II, then, is also considered—or considered to have considered himself—an "exception" to normal rules. Freud takes exception to mentioning him—or even, perhaps, to consciously identifying him—and instead displaces his analysis onto the safely "literary" character of Shakespeare's Richard. And Richard's opening soliloquy, descanting on deformity, provides a revealing narrative of the ways in which the line between the "psychological" and the "historical" is blurred.

"Unlick'd," "unfinished," "indigested"—"not shaped" for sportive tricks, "scarce half made up." The natal circumstances and intrapsychic discourse of Shakespeare's Richard, who ironically resolves, despite his initial disclaimers, to "court an amorous looking-glass" (*Richard III* 1.1.15, 1.2.255, 262), uncannily anticipate the language of Jacques Lacan's description of the "mirror stage." Lacan writes of

> the view I have formulated as the fact of a real specific prematurity of birth in man. . . . This development is experienced as a temporal dialect that decisively projects the formation of the individual into history. The *mirror stage* is a drama whose internal thrust is precipitated from insufficiency to anticipation—and which manufactures *for the subject, caught up in the lure of spatial identification, the succession of phantasies that extends from a fragmented body-image to a form of its totality that I shall call orthopaedic*—and, lastly, to the assumption of the armour of an alienating identity, which will mark with its rigid stricture the subject's entire mental development.[9]

Characteristically, Richard turns this chaotic physical condition into a rhetorical benefit, suggesting that he can "change shapes with Proteus for advantages" (*3 Henry VI* 3.2.192), be his own parent and his own author, lick himself into shape—whatever shape the occasion requires. Queen Elizabeth tells him that he cannot win her daughter "Unless thou couldst put on some other shape" (*Richard III* 4.4.286). But the shape in which we encounter him is already a deformed one—the natural deformity of historical record.

Peter Saccio gives a highly useful account of the evolution of Richard the monster in his study of Shakespeare's English kings.

> This lurid king, hunchbacked, clad in blood-spattered black velvet, forever gnawing his nether lip or grasping for his dagger, has an enduring place in English mythology. He owes something to the facts about the historical Richard III. He owes far more to rumor and to the political bias, credulity and especially the literary talent of Tudor writers. . . .
>
> As myth, the Tudor Richard is indestructible. . . . As history, however, the Tudor Richard is unacceptable. Some of the legend is incredible, some is known to be false, and much is uncertain or unproved. The physical deformity, for example, is quite unlikely. No contemporary portrait or document attests to it and the fact that he permitted himself to be stripped to the waist for anointing at his own coronation suggests that his torso could bear public inspection.[10]

In fact, when we come to examine the portrait evidence, we find that it is of considerable interest for evaluating Richard's alleged deformity. A portrait now in the Society of Antiquaries of London, painted about 1505, shows a Richard with straight shoulders. But a second portrait, possibly of earlier date, in the Royal Collection, seems to emblematize the whole controversy, for in it, X-ray examination reveals an original straight shoulder line, which was subsequently painted over to present the raised right shoulder silhouette so often copied by later portraitists.[11]

Richard is not only deformed, his deformity is itself a deformation. His twisted and misshapen body encodes the whole strategy of history as a necessary deforming and *un*forming—with the object of *re*forming—the past. Shakespeare exemplifies this strategy with precision in a remarkable moment in *Much Ado about Nothing,* when the vigilant and well-intentioned Watch overhears a comment by Borachio: "Seest thou not what a deformed thief this fashion is?" "I know that Deformed," remarks the Second Watch wisely to himself, "'a has been a vile thief this seven years; 'a goes up and down like a gentleman. I remember his name" (3.3.125–27). Like Falstaff's eleven buckram men grown out of two, this personified concretion takes on an uncanny life of its own in the scene. When Borachio and Conrade are confronted with their perfidy, Deformed is identified as a coconspirator: "And one Deformed is one of them; I know him, 'a wears a lock" (lines 169–70), and again, "You'll be made bring Deformed forth, I warrant you" (lines 172–73). This is precisely what happens to the reinvented historical figure of Richard III.

Created by a similar process of ideological and polemical distortion, Richard's deformity is a figment of rhetoric, a figure of abuse, a catachresis masquerading as a metaphor. In a viciously circular manifestation of Neoplatonic determinism, Richard is made villainous in appearance to match the desired villainy of his reputation and then is given a personality warped and bent to compensate for his physical shape.

For Shakespeare's play, in fact, encodes what we might call a supposititious presupposition. Richard's deformity is not claimed, but rather presupposed, given as fact in service of the question, "Was his villainy the result of his deformity?"—a question not unlike "Have you stopped beating your wife?" Jonathan Culler has shown that the presuppositions that govern literary discourse are mistakenly designed as givens, as "moments of authority and points of origin," when in fact they are only "retrospectively designated as origins and . . . therefore, can be shown to derive from the series for which they are constituted as origin." As with literary conventions, so also with historical presuppositions that constitute the ground of a discursive continuum—here the "History" of Richard III. To adapt Culler's argument about speech acts, "None of these [claims of historical veracity] is a point of origin or moment of authority. They are simply the constituents of a discursive space from which one tries to derive conventions."[13]

Richard's deformity, itself transmitted not genetically but generically through both historiography and dramaturgy, becomes the psychological and dramatic focus of the play's dynamic. Shakespeare has written history backward, taking Hall's and More's objective correlative (he looked the way he was; he should have looked this way because he was in fact this way; he should have been this way, so he must have looked this way) and then presupposed it. Richard's own claim that he can "change shapes with Proteus for advantages" is a metahistorical comment on his Lamarckian evolution as villainous prototype, every misshaped part an overdetermined text to be interpreted and moralized, descanting on his own deformity. Shakespeare's play brings "Deformed forth" as an embodiment of the historical process that it both charts and epitomizes.

History is indeed shown by the play to be a story that is deformed from the outset, by its very nature. The figure of Hastings, for instance, seems predestined to bring out particularly uncanny modes of deformation through the ghostly doublings of the Scrivener and the Pursuivant. The Pursuivant (an official empowered to serve warrants) who accosts Lord Hastings in *Richard III,* act 3, scene 2, is also named Hastings and appears by that name not only in the Quarto text but also in Hall's *Union of the Two Families of Lancaster and York.* The absence of his name from the Folio has caused some editorial speculation, and the Arden editor's long discussion of this absent name emphasizes the strangeness of the figure: "The entire episode as it appears in F seems pointless: it merely repeats what has already been said by Hastings, adds a superfluous character, and would probably be cut by an economy-minded producer. The fact that it was not cut in Q suggests that someone felt strongly enough about it to retain it, and that the identity of the pursuivant served to make an ironical point."[13]

According to both Hall and Shakespeare, Hastings receives a number of warnings of the fate that is to befall him. His horse stumbles, Stanley dreams that the boar will rase their helms and sends a cautionary word to Hastings, and still Hastings remains adamantly blind to his danger.

At this point, in a remarkable scene reported by Hall and dramatized by Shakespeare, Hastings encounters the pursuivant who bears his own name. He greets him warmly, reminiscing about the last time they met, when Hastings was fearful for his life. Now, ironically feeling more secure, he rejoices to note that his former enemies, the queen's allies, have been put to death, and he himself is "in better state than ere I was" (3.2.104). Hall moralizes with some satisfaction on this latest ironic twist: "O lorde God, the blyndnesse of our mortal nature, when he most feared, he was in moste surety, and when he reconed his selfe most surest, he lost his lyfe, and that within two houres after."[14] Shakespeare makes the same point more subtly and forcefully by prefacing this encounter with Richard's decision to "chop off his head" if Hastings will not agree to their "complots" (3.1.192–93) and then following it with a knowing aside from Buckingham to the audience. The encounter with the pursuivant (literally, a "follower") named Hastings is an example of the uncanny in one of its most direct forms, recognizable and strange at once. The action itself is doubled, as Hastings meets "Hastings" coming and going and does not understand what he sees. Hastings's own name functions in a subdued allegorical way throughout this scene, which could be emblematized as *festina lente,* making Hastings slowly.[15]

Another example of doubling and displacement within a historical event is provided by the odd little scene with the Scrivener (3.6). Borrowed by the playwright from his chronicle sources, this scene becomes in its dramatic embodiment a model of history as a kind of ghostwriting, since it encodes and "engross[es]" the fashioning of a rival text. The Scrivener complains that he has spent eleven hours copying the indictment of Hastings "in a set hand," or legal script. The first draft, or "precedent," "was full as long a-doing, / And yet within these five hours Hastings liv'd / Untainted, unexamin'd, free, at liberty" (lines 7–9). The Scrivener laments the duplicity of the times—"Who is so gross/That cannot see this palpable device" (lines 10–11), "engross'd" by his own set hand—and yet who dares to say he sees it?

This packed little scene demonstrates at once the play's preoccupation with writing and the preemptive—indeed pre*scrip*tive—nature of its political design. The Scrivener's indignation is both moral and professional, for his task of scriptwriting had begun before the incident that was to occasion it and ended too late to authorize—although it will retrospectively "legitimize"—the death of Hastings. Since the previous scene has already presented the spectacle of Hastings's decapitated head, displayed by Lovell and Ratcliffe to the London populace and an apparently grief-stricken Richard, the existence, belatedly revealed, of a meticulously crafted indictment undercuts the idea of historical accident or spontaneous action. History is not only deformed but also preformed. Hall recounts the story with particular attention to the length of time the drawing of the indictment would take.

> Nowe was thys proclamacion made within two houres after he was beheaded, and it was so curiously endyted and so fayre writen in Parchement in a fayre hande, and therewith of it selfe so long a processe, that every chyld might perceyve that it was prepared and studyed before (and as some men thought, by Catesby) for all the tyme betwene hys death and the proclamacion proclaimyng, coulde skant have suffyced unto the bare wrytyng alone, albeit that it had bene in paper and scribeled furthe in haste at adventure.[16]

Like the disparity between the "truth" of Shakespeare's play and the historical figure it encodes, the "palpable device" of the long-prepared indictment and the apparent hasting of Hastings's demise opens the question of authority. Which comes first, the event or the ghostwriter?

So far is Richard from being merely the passive psychological victim of his deformity, he early on becomes deformity's theorist and manipulator, not only "descanting" upon it, but projecting and displacing its characteristics onto others. The death of Clarence is a good example of how this works in the play. Clarence is imprisoned at Edward's order, but at the instigation of Richard. The two murderers who go to the Tower to carry out the execution bear Richard's warrant for entry. And Edward is nonplussed when, at the worst possible time from a political standpoint, Clarence's death is announced. "Is Clarence dead?" he asks. "The order was reversed." "But he, poor man, by your first order died," says Richard. "And that a winged Mercury did bear; / Some tardy cripple bare the countermand, / That came too lag to see him buried" (2.1.87–91).

The phrase "tardy cripple" spoken by the crippled Richard is doubly ironic. He himself is represented in this account not by the cripple, but by "winged Mercury," fleet of foot, who bears the message of execution—here, in fact, made possible by Richard's forged warrant. The "tardy cripple," coming "too lag" to save Clarence, is Richard's displacement of deformity onto the foiled intentions of his well-formed brother the king.

An even more striking instance of this crippling or deforming of the world outside Richard occurs in the scene at Baynard's Castle (3.7), in which Richard enters aloft between two bishops, "divinely bent to meditation" (line 62), and Buckingham stages a public entreaty to persuade him to accept the throne. Buckingham describes Richard as the rightful heir, with "due of birth" and "lineal glory" (lines 120–21), able to prevent the resigning of the crown "to the corruption of a blemish'd stock" (line 122). But his description of the present state of governance is oddly pertinent (and impertinent) to the man he is apparently addressing.

> The noble isle doth want her proper limbs;
> Her face defac'd with scars of infamy,
> Her royal stock graft with ignoble plants,
> And almost should'red in the swallowing gulf
> Of dark forgetfulness and deep oblivion.
> (3.7.125–29)

Here the cripple is England, wanting "proper limbs" (compare Richard's own ironic description of "me that halts and am misshapen thus" as "a marv'llous proper man" in the eyes of the Lady Anne [1.2.250–54]). "Defac'd" and especially "should'red" make the transferred anatomical references unmistakable.

In the final scene of *3 Henry VI* an ambitious and disgruntled Richard had murmured aside, "Yet I am not look'd on in the world. / This shoulder was ordain'd so thick to heave, / And heave it shall some weight, or break my back" (5.7.22–24). In the scene of the wooing of Anne, Richard protests that Queen Margaret's slanderous tongue "laid their guilt upon my guiltless shoulders" (*Richard III* 1.2.98), again mischievously calling attention to his own physical deformity; later he is twitted by young York to the same effect ("Because that I am little like an ape / He thinks that you should bear me on your shoulders" [3.1.130–31]). Richard's deformed shoulder is what "shoulders" the noble isle of England into near oblivion, but in Buckingham's anatomy of the deformed state the "proper man" is the well-derived Richard, who will restore the kingdom to its wonted shape. In both of these cases a condition of deformity is transferred, to the hypothetical messenger or the diseased polity.

Deformity as a self-augmenting textual effect, contaminating the telling of Richard's story as well as Richard's story itself, has been associated with his literary presence almost from the first. More's account of the notorious sermon of Dr. Shaa is a good example. Dr. Shaa had been persuaded to preach a sermon in which he would impute the bastardy of Edward's sons and point out Richard's physical resemblance to his father, the Duke of York. He was to have intoned these sentiments, comparing Richard's visage and behavior to those of the admired duke, at the point when Richard himself appeared in the congregation. Richard, however, was late, and the key passage already past when he did turn up. Seeing him enter, Dr. Shaa, in a flurry of discomfiture, began to repeat his point-for-point comparison, but "out of al order, and out of al frame," [17] to the consternation of the audience. The "shamefull sermon" having backfired, Shaa fled to his house and was forced to "kepe him out of sight lyke an owl," and soon "withered away" of shame.

In this little story Dr. Shaa sees himself as a writer of predictive history, predicating the future on a repetition of the past (the second Richard an image of the first). But his narrative, out of all order and out of all frame, like Richard's own misshapen body, becomes in More's retelling the perversion and distortion of its intended form and design. Moreover, Dr. Shaa himself is contaminated by the rhetorical force of the prevailing mythology about Richard. In the course of More's account Shaa himself becomes deformed, or "withered," as if by the disseminated agency of his ignoble association with Richard, whose own arm is "like a wither'd shrub" (*3 Henry VI* 3.2.156), "like a blasted sapling, wither'd up" (*Richard III* 3.4.69). The figure of Richard keeps escaping its own boundaries, to appear uncannily replicative in the authors of his twisted history.

Other putative sources for Shakespeare's play have suffered the same suggestive narrative contamination. Francis Seager's complaint, *Richard Plantagenet, Duke of Gloucester,* one of the tragedies published in the 1563 *Mirror for Magistrates,* is described by a prose commentator in the volume as appropriate to its subject. The roughness of the meter was suitable, since "kyng Rychard never kept measure in any of his doings. . . . it were agaynst the *decorum* of his personage, to use eyther good Meter or order." [18] The "decorum of his personage" seems also to have affected the Arden editor, Antony Hammond, who describes this same poem as "a dull, lame piece of verse." [19]

Such observations reflect the powerful ghostly presence of the lame and halting Richard. E. M. W. Tillyard, writing of the first tetralogy, remarks upon "the *special shape* in which the age of Elizabeth saw its own immediate past and its present political problems," and again of "the *shape* in which the War of the Roses appeared to Shakespeare's contemporaries." [20]

That "special shape" is Richard's. Images of "the beauty of virtue and the deformity of vice" were commonplace in Tudor writings (this particular phrase comes from the second preface to Grafton's *Chronicle at Large* (1569), probably written by Thomas Norton, the author of *Gorboduc*); but when the subject turned explicitly to Richard, the correspondence of physical, moral, and poetic or stylistic deformity seems particularly overdetermined.

Bacon's essay "Of Deformity" reads like a description of Richard III, though it may have been provoked more directly by Robert Cecil.

> Deformed persons are commonly even with nature; for as nature hath done ill by them, so do they by nature; being for the most part, as the Scripture saith, "Void of natural affection," and so they have their revenge of nature. Certain there is a consent between the body and the mind, and where nature erreth in the one, she ventureth in the other. . . . Whosoever has anything fixed in his person that doth induce contempt, hath also a perpetual spur in himself, to rescue and deliver himself from scorn; therefore all deformed persons are extreme bold. . . . Also it stireth in them industry, . . . to watch and observe the weakness of others that they may have somewhat to repay. Again, in their superiors it quencheth jealousy and it layeth their competitors and emulators asleep; as never believing they should be in possibility of advancement, till they see them in possession. So that, upon the matter, in a great wit deformity is an advantage to rising. . . . they will, if they be of spirit, seek to free themselves from scorn, which must be either by virtue or malice.[21]

Samuel Johnson cites these sentiments with approbation in his notes on *3 Henry VI,* making explicit their relevance to Richard ("Bacon remarks that the deformed are commonly daring, and it is almost proverbially observed that they are ill-natured. The truth is, that the deformed, like all other men, are displeased with inferiority, and endeavour to gain ground by good or bad means, as they are virtuous or corrupt").[22] And, indeed, this too may be an instance of overdetermined contamination. Dr. Johnson's stress on "deformities" reflects his own self-consciousness of deformation. Suffering from scrofula as an infant, Johnson was marked throughout life by "scars on the lower part of the face and on the neck,"[23] which he sought to conceal in his portraits by presenting the better side of his face to the painter's view. Until the age of six he bore on his arm an open, running sore, or "issue," cut and left open with the idea of draining infection. This, and the partial blindness also induced by tuberculosis in infancy, produced in him a "situation so appalling," writes Walter Jackson Bate, that "we are naturally tempted to speculate on the psychological results" (p. 7).

But Johnson's most striking observations about deformity in Shakespeare occur in another connection. "We fix our eyes upon his graces, and turn them from his deformities, and endure in him what we should in another loathe or despise." The subject of these comments, astonishingly, is not Richard III, but Shakespeare himself—and the "deformities" are those of literary and dramatic creation. "I have seen," he continues, "in the book of some modern critic, a collection of anomalies, which shew that he has corrupted language by every model of depravation, but which his admirer has accumulated as a monument of honour."[24] "Anomalies," "corrupted language," "model of depravation"—all this sounds very like Richard III as he is received by a reluctantly admiring audience. Not only does Richard theorize his own deformity, he generates and theorizes deformity as a form of power.

II

In a response to a recent collection of essays entitled *"Race," Writing, and Difference*, Houston A. Baker, Jr., discusses Shakespeare's Caliban as an example of what he calls "the deformation of mastery," the way in which a representative of the indigenous population finds a voice within the colonialist discourse of the master, Prospero.[25] Caliban, the "hooting deformed of Shakespeare's *The Tempest*," provides for Baker an opportunity to describe "a drama of deformation" as it is articulated by the indigenous Other that advertises itself through a phaneric mask of display. Caliban's metacurses, his deployment of language against language, are a result of his conscription by Western culture, his "willingness to barter his signs for the white magician's language" (p. 392). His physical deformity and his curses are alike indices of this double bind. What Baker proposes—and he is here troping the present-day Afro-American scholar's discourse on Caliban's—is a "'vernacular' invasion and transcendence of fields of colonizing discourse in order to destroy whitemale hegemony" (p. 382). Unable to go back to a prelapsarian or pre-Prosperian innocence (another impossible and hypothetical origin only fantasized in retrospect by the play), Caliban and his twentieth-century heirs must find a solution to the double bind in a "triple play" of what Baker calls "supraliteracy," the deployment of the vernacular, "hooting" phaneric deformities that are the sign of the slipped noose, of the freed, independent, and victorious subject.

What Baker is here calling for, in an elegant phaneric display of his own, is essentially a rhetoric and a politics of deformation. His word "hoot," which he takes from an ethological description of gorilla display, nowhere appears in *The Tempest*, but it suggests the "mimic hootings" of Wordsworth's Boy of Winander, and even the phaneric "hoos" of Stevens's Chieftain Iffucan of Azcan.

The "deformed slave" who is Caliban has lately been taken as the site of deformation for a number of contemporary debates. Thus we might consider Caliban not only as a figure for the colonized subject, but also as a figure for mixed genre, as Paul Howe has suggested,[26] or (on the model of Frankenstein's monster) as a figure for woman. And this kind of deformation, too, has potential relevance for Richard III. In the course of Shakespeare's play Richard himself develops what is in effect a rhetoric of deformation, calling attention to the novelties of his physical shape and the ways in which that shape liberates him from the constraints of conventional courtly deportment. "Cheated of feature by dissembling nature," Richard himself feels free to cheat and dissemble; "deformed, unfinished," he freely descants on his own deformity.

"Man," writes Nietzsche in his essay "The Use and Abuse of History," "braces himself against the great and ever greater pressure of what is past: it pushes him down or bends him sideways, it encumbers his steps as a dark invisible burden which he would like to disown."[27] So Richard "Crook-back" (*3 Henry VI* 1.4.75; 2.2.96; 5.5.30) is bent not only by specific historical distortions but by the intrinsic distortion of history, which Richard bears, like an ape, on his shoulders. Again, as *Titus Andronicus* particularizes in its decapitations and cutting off of hands the dismembering of historiographical writing, so *Richard III* anatomizes the dangers of re-membering, of history as an artifact of memory.

Writing of what he describes as "monumental history," Nietzsche argues that

> as long as the soul of historiography lies in the great stimuli that a man of power derives from it, as long as the past has to be described as worthy of imitation, as imitable and possible for a second time, it of course incurs the danger of becoming *somewhat distorted*. . . . there have been ages, indeed, which were quite incapable of distinguishing between a monumentalized past and a mythical fiction. . . . Monumental history deceives by analogies: with seductive similarities it inspires to fanaticism; and when we go on to think of this kind of history in the hands of gifted egoists and visionary scoundrels, then we see empires destroyed, princes murdered, wars and revolutions launched and the number of historical "effects in themselves," that is to say, effects without sufficient cause, again augmented. (Pp. 70–71)

"Gifted egoists and visionary scoundrels," "wars and revolutions launched," "princes murdered," the past "somewhat distorted" in the direction of mythical fiction—Nietzsche is uncannily describing not only monumental history but also Richard III—and *Richard III*. Moreover, Richard himself in his opening soliloquy articulates the process of monumental history.

> Now are our brows bound with victorious wreaths,
> Our bruised arms hung up for monuments,
> Our stern alarums chang'd to merry meetings,
> Our dreadful marches to delightful measures.
>
> (1.1.5–8)

This is the description of something completed and assimilated, something finished—against which Richard remains defiantly incomplete and imperfect: "curtail'd of this fair proportion, / Cheated of feature by dissembling nature, / Deform'd, unfinish'd, sent before my time / Into this breathing world scarce half made up" (lines 18–21). Yet Nietzsche, too, writes of the consciousness of history as something that reminds man of "what his existence fundamentally is—an imperfect tense that can never become a perfect one" (p. 61). So the imperfect and unperfected Richard stands over against "the phrase 'it was'" (p. 70).

It is in the multiple narratives of birth that Richard comes most clearly to stand as an embodiment of the paradoxical temporality of history. On the one hand, he is premature: "deform'd, unfinish'd, sent before [his] time." Yet on the other, he is born too late, "held for two years in his mother's womb, emerging with teeth," overdeveloped and overarmed. Both Robert N. Watson and Janet Adelman[28] have identified, in psychoanalytic terms, another birth scene, a fantasized one in which the "unlick'd bear-whelp" carves his own way out of the womb, making a birth canal where none exists.

> Seeking a way, and straying from the way,
> Not knowing how to find the open air,
> But toiling desperately to find it out—
> Torment myself to catch the English crown;
> And from that torment I will free myself,
> Or hew my way out with a bloody axe.
>
> (*3 Henry VI* 3.2.176–81)

Figuratively, this may be seen as a process of violently willful biological birth; politically, it presents itself as a birth of historical process. Premature, Protean, fully and functionally toothed, Richard here hews out an historical path, the way to the crown (and to the chronicles). The violence of his act is inseparable and indistinguishable from that act itself. His use of history is simultaneously and necessarily its abuse.

There is another retelling of the birth story in *Richard III,* this one by the Lady Anne:

If ever he have child, abortive be it,
Prodigious, and untimely brought to light,
Whose ugly and unnatural aspect
May fright the hopeful mother at the view,
And that be heir to his unhappiness!
(1.2.21–25)

This passage, too, can be conceived as a description of autogenesis. The fantasy child who is to be the only offspring of Richard and Anne is Richard himself.[29] A different construction, or reconstruction, of Anne's speech, however, might read this predictive curse as the birth of history. History—the historical subject and the synthetic Shakespearean history play—is the prodigious and untimely result of the union of chronicle and drama. Anne's imagined scene of the mother's dismay (she does not, of course, envisage *herself* as the "hopeful mother" of his child) strongly recalls King Henry VI's account of the birth of Richard: "Thy mother felt more than a mother's pain, / And yet brought forth less than a mother's hope" (*3 Henry VI* 5.6.49–50).

As I have argued elsewhere,[30] recent critical displacements of the once-fashionable notion of "providential history" by a politically self-conscious, ideologically determined reshaping of historical "fact" have foregrounded the degree of belatedness intrinsic to and implicit in Elizabethan history plays. The "now" of these plays is always preeminently the "now" of the time of their literary genesis—the time is manifestly out of joint, and the retrospective reconstruction of history ("to tell my story," to pursue Hamlet's own chronicling of the process) is the only means of shaping time at either the protagonist's or the dramatist's command. "May not an ass know when the cart draws the horse?" asks Lear's Fool (*King Lear* 1.4.223), but the cart, or tumbril, of historical events inevitably draws the hero's charger in its wake. Thus the repudiation of the fiction of historical accuracy or "objectivity," the self-delusive and far-from-benign assumption that the past can be recaptured without contamination from the present, has become a crucial starting point of both the Foucaldian and the deconstructive projects. For history is always in the process of deconstructing itself—of becoming, as it always was, "history," the story that the teller imposes upon the reconstructed events of the past.

This is not new news to the chroniclers of chroniclers. Sidney's famous description of the historian in his *Apologie for Poetrie* characterizes him as "loaden with old mouse-eaten records, authorizing himself (for the most part) upon other histories, whose greatest authorities, are built upon the notable foundation of hearsay, having much ado to accord differing writers, and to pick truth out of partiality."[31] The historian is constrained by his burden of facts; "many times he must tell events, whereof he can yield no cause; or if he do, it must be poetical" (p. 233)—must, that is, make the move from "fact" to fiction, "for that a feigned example, hath as much force to teach, as a true example." One of the best known passages in the *Apologie* addresses the question of theatrical fictions, mimesis, and allegoresis.

> What child is there, that coming to a play, and seeing Thebes written in great letters upon an old door, doth believe that it is Thebes? If then a man can arrive, at that child's age, to know that the poet's persons and doings, are but pictures what should be, and not stories what have been, they will never give the lie, to things not affirmatively, but allegorically, and figuratively written. And therefore, as in history, looking for truth, they go away full fraught with falsehood; so in poesy, looking for fiction, they shall use the narration, but as an imaginative ground-plot of a profitable invention. (P. 249)

This quotation, often cited, is frequently truncated by the omission of the last sentence. Its sense seems to be that poesy—which here includes drama—is less culpable of distortion than history, because it does not pretend to objectivity. Or, to put the position somewhat differently, its distortion is the product of design. A very similar position is adumbrated in "The Use and Abuse of History," in Nietzsche's argument that the only possible "objectivity" in the framing of history comes in the work of the dramatist, who alone writes history as an expression of the "artistic drive" rather than as a putatively authoritative and objective record of *what was*. For drama, in Nietzsche's terms, offers

> an artistically true painting but not an historically true one. To think of history objectively in this fashion is the silent work of the dramatist; that is to say, to think of all things in relation to all others and to weave the isolated event into the whole: always with the presupposition that if a unity of plan does not already reside in things it must be implanted into them. Thus man spins his web over the past and subdues it, thus he gives expression to his artistic drive—but not to his drive towards truth or justice. Objectivity and justice have nothing to do with one another. (P. 91)

By contrast to drama all other modes of historical writing are fundamentally unsatisfactory, constructive in some ways but destructive in others. Since they are written by historical subjects in effect created by the very history they seek to document, there can be no objective or authoritative vantage point for their observations. And this point is oddly but firmly insisted upon by both Sidney and Nietzsche. Thus Sidney claims that "the best of the historian is subject to the poet; for whatsoever action, or faction, whatsoever counsel, policy, or war stratagem, the historian is bound to recite, that may the poet (if he list) with his imitation make his own" (p. 234). And Nietzsche writes that the human subject must situate himself or herself "*against history*" (p. 106); "if you want biographies, do not desire those which bear the legend 'Herr So-and-So and his age,' but those upon whose title-page there would stand 'a fighter against his age'" (p. 95).

The title page of biographies; "the history of great men" (p. 95). It is often asked about Shakespeare's *Richard III*, as about other pivotal works in the Shakespeare canon (e.g., *Julius Caesar*): Is it a tragedy or is it a history? Is it, as both Quarto and Folio title pages call it, "the tragedy of Richard III," or, as the Folio classifies it, generically to be listed under the histories? Nietzsche has here uncannily provided an answer to the question of *why* this is a question: the birth of history can only be presented as the birth of tragedy.

"The Use and Abuse of History" (1874) is indeed in some sense a coda or extrapolation of Nietzsche's great study of the rise and fall of the tragic vision in ancient Greece, *The Birth of Tragedy* (1871). In that work, as Hayden White has noted, Nietzsche "lamented the decline and fall of ancient tragedy, and named the modern historical consciousness as its antitype."[32] "The Use and Abuse of History" continues this exploration of what has gone wrong, of what has been lost with the loss of the classical tragic vision.

But Nietzsche's remarks are not confined to the Greeks alone. There is another dramatist who haunts Nietzsche's text, and that dramatist, perhaps unsurprisingly, is Shakespeare. Twice he takes as his starting point what someone else has said about Shakespeare's intersection with the modern historical world. Quoting Franz Grillparzer, Nietzsche critiques the contemporary German's sensibility, developed, so he says, "from his experience in the theater. 'We feel in abstractions,' [Grillparzer] says, 'we hardly know any longer how feeling really expresses itself with our contemporaries; we show them performing actions such as they no longer perform nowadays. Shakespeare has ruined all of us moderns'" (p. 81). Shortly thereafter, Nietzsche quotes Goethe: "Goethe once said of Shakespeare: 'No one despised outward costume more than he; he knew very well the inner human costume, and here all are alike. They say he hit off the Romans admirably; but I don't find it so, they are all nothing but flesh-and-blood Englishmen, but they are certainly human beings, human from head to foot, and the Roman toga sits on them perfectly well.'" Nietzsche takes this opportunity to condemn present-day literati and officials, who could not be portrayed as Romans because they are not human beings but only flesh-and-blood compendia and as it were abstractions made concrete. . . . creations of historical culture, wholly structure, image, form without demonstrable content and, unhappily, *ill-designed form* and, what is more, *uniform*. And so let my proposition be understood and pondered: *history can be borne only by strong personalities, weak ones are utterly extinguished by it* . . . He who no longer dares to trust himself but involuntarily asks of history "How ought I to feel about this?" finds that his timidity gradually turns him into an actor and that he is playing a role, usually indeed many roles and therefore playing them badly and superficially. (pp. 85–86)

"*Ill-designed form* and, what is more, *uniform.*" For Nietzsche the modern politician's failure lies precisely in his conformity to unthinking standards of political correctness, what Nietzsche scornfully calls "objective" standards, as if any strong personality, in his view, could be "objective" or subscribe to an "objective" reading of history. "Ill-design" for Nietzsche is thus the obverse of what it is for *Richard III*. In Shakespeare's play Richard's physical appearance, his ill-design, perversely glories in its difference from the usual, the uniform, the fully formed.

The famous scene in which he woos and wins the Lady Anne ("and will she yet abase her eyes on me. . . . On me, that halts and am misshapen thus / My dukedom to a beggarly denier, / I do mistake my person all this while! / Upon my life she finds (although I cannot) / Myself to be a marv'llous proper man. / I'll be at charges for a looking glass" [1.2.246–55]) displays a Richard whose narcissistic posturing translates ill-design ("misshapen thus") into "proper" or handsome appearance—and thus to *proprietary* and *appropriative* behavior, made possible by his flouting of the conventional *proprieties.*

Shakespeare appears a third time in this relatively short essay, when Nietzsche is offering a critique of the "philosophy of the unconscious" of Eduard von Hartmann (p. 115). Von Hartmann's description of the "manhood of man" is ironically disparaged by a citation from Jaques's celebrated speech in *As You Like It,* on the seven ages of man—a citation that not surprisingly encodes the word "history":

Last scene of all,
That ends this strange, eventful history,
Is second childishness, and mere oblivion,
Sans teeth, sans eyes, sans taste, sans every thing.
(2.7.163–66)

The Richard who comes into the world already provided with teeth is an apt counterimage to this toothless historical deterioration. Yet, as these citations make clear, the power of drama as a historical force can be enfeebling as well as enabling, reducing men to actors in the very act of raising history to drama. "Overproud European," writes Nietzsche in an apostrophe that neatly deconstructs Pico's *De dignitate hominis,*

> you are raving! Your knowledge does not perfect nature, it only destroys your own nature. Compare for once the heights of your capacity for knowledge with the depths of your capacity for action. It is true you climb upon the sunbeams of knowledge up to Heaven, but you also climb down to chaos. Your manner of moving, that of climbing upon knowledge, is your fatality; the ground sinks away from you into the unknown; there is no longer any support for your life, only spider's threads which every new grasp of knowledge tears apart.—But enough of this seriousness, since it is also possible to view the matter more cheerfully.
>
> The madly thoughtless shattering and dismantling of all foundations, their dissolution into a continual evolving that flows ceaselessly away, the tireless unspinning and historicizing of all there has ever been by modern man, the great cross-spider at the node of the cosmic web—all this may concern and dismay moralists, artists, the pious, even statesmen; *we* shall for once let it cheer us by looking at it in the glittering magic mirror of a *philosophical parodist* in whose head the age has come to an ironical awareness of itself. (P. 108)

Self-irony, proclaimed by a philosophical parodist eying history (and the construction of the human subject) in a glittering magic mirror. It is a stunning evocation of Richard III. "Shine out, fair sun, till I have bought a glass, / That I may see my shadow as I pass" (*Richard III* 1.2.262–63). Over and over again, Shakespeare's Richard Crook-back is compared to a spider, spinning plots. Queen Margaret refers to him as a "bottled spider, / Whose deadly web ensnareth thee about" (1.3.241–42), and the hapless Queen Elizabeth recalls her warning when it is too late: "O, thou didst prophesy the time would come / That I should wish for thee to help me curse / That bottled spider, that foul bunch back'd toad!" (4.4.80–81). The Lady Anne likewise classes him with "spiders, toads, / Or any creeping venom'd thing that lives" (1.2.19–20)—even as she succumbs to his designs. Indeed Richard's father, the duke of York, his predecessor in vengeful soliloquy, had claimed for himself the same identification: "My brain, more busy than the laboring spider / Weaves tedious snare to trap mine enemies" (*2 Henry VI* 3.1.339–40).

Is the present afflicted or instructed by the power of tragedy to "weave the isolated event into the whole?" Can the "tireless unspinning and historicizing of all there has ever been by modern man, the great cross-spider at the node of the cosmic web"—occupied with weaving "spider's threads which every new grasp of knowledge tears apart"—be seen as that which cripples as well as empowers the observer who would profit from historical models, historical example, historical textualizations? This is perhaps the question Shakespeare forces us to ask of our own ambivalent fascination with "that bottled spider / Whose deadly web ensnareth [us] about": Richard III—and *Richard III*—as the dramatization of the power of deformity inherent in both tragedy and history.

Notes

1. *The Riverside Shakespeare,* ed. G. Blakemore Evans et al. (Boston: Houghton Mifflin, 1974). All citations from the plays are to this edition unless noted in the text.

2. Charles Ross, *Richard III* (Berkeley: University of California Press, 1981).

3. René Girard, "Hamlet's Dull Revenge," *Stanford Literary Review* 1 (Fall 1984): 159.

4. Geoffrey Bullough, ed., *Narrative and Dramatic Sources of Shakespeare* (London: Routledge and Kegan Paul, 1975), 3:223.

5. *The Yale Edition of the Complete Works of St. Thomas More,* vol. 2 *The History of King Richard III,* ed. Richard Sylvester (New Haven and London: Yale University Press, 1963), p. 7. Sir Horace Walpole, one of the earliest defenders of Richard's reputation, characterized More as "an historian who is capable of employing truth only as cement in a fabric of fiction" (*Historic Doubts on the Life and Reign of Richard III* [London: J. Dodsley, 1768; reprint, 1965], p. 116), and recent scholars have explicitly identified the kind of "fiction" More is writing as *drama.* Thus A. R. Myers asserts that "his history is much more like a drama, unfolded in magnificent prose, for which fidelity to historical fact is scarcely relevant" ("The Character of Richard III," originally published in *History Today* 4 (1954), reprinted in *English Society and Government in the Fifteenth Century,* ed. C. M. D. Crowder (Edinburgh and London: 1967), p. 119, cited in Ross, *Richard III;* and Alison Hanham argues that the *History* is really a "satirical drama" meant to display More's own cleverness rather than his command of fact (*Richard III and His Early Historians* [Oxford: Clarendon Press, 1975], pp. 152–90).

6. I am indebted to Richard Strier for this observation.

7. Sigmund Freud, "Some Character-Types Met With in Psychoanalytic Work," in *Character and Culture,* ed. Philip Rieff (New York: Collier Books, 1961), p. 159.

8. Fritz Stern, *Gold and Iron* (New York: Vintage Books, 1979), p. 437.

9. Jacques Lacan, "The Mirror Stage as Formative of the Function of the I," in *Ecrits,* tr. Alan Sheridan (New York: W. W. Norton, 1977), p. 4.

10. Peter Saccio, *Shakespeare's English Kings* (New York: Oxford University Press, 1978), pp. 158–59. In a recent study of biography and fiction in Tudor-Stuart history writing (*Biographical Truth: The Representation of Historical Persons in Tudor-Stuart Writing* [New Haven: Yale University Press, 1984]) Judith H. An-

derson notes that historians regularly impeach Shakespeare's play for its lack of fidelity to historical fact and points out accurately that the play would lose its power if it did not convince the audience that it was "somehow real history" (p. 111)—"despite ourselves, we believe it" (p. 123). Yet Anderson's view of Richard's deformity is a relatively conventional one. Citing Freud, and reasserting the humanistic commonplace that suffering creates art, she describes Richard as "the misshapen product of his nature and time and also, as we watch him in the play, the product of his own making" (p. 117). Whether self-fashioned or twisted by his own deformity, Richard is seen as compensating for a disability, rather than seizing that disability as the occasion for a theoretical exploration of the nature of deformation.

11. Pamela Tudor-Craig, *Richard III* (1973), cited in Ross, *Richard III,* pp. 80, 92–93.

12. Jonathan Culler, "Presupposition and Intertextuality," in *The Pursuit of Signs* (Ithaca: Cornell University Press, 1981), p. 177.

13. Antony Hammond, ed., *King Richard III,* The Arden Shakespeare (London and New York: Methuen, 1981), p. 338.

14. Edward Hall, *The Union of the Two Noble . . . Families of Lancaster and York* (1548), cited in Hammond, *King Richard III,* 353.

15. See Sigmund Freud, "The Uncanny" (1919), in *Studies in Parapsychology,* ed. Philip Rieff (New York: Macmillan, 1963), pp. 19–60, especially pp. 38–42 on "the double" and the repetition compulsion.

16. Hall, cited in Hammond, *King Richard III,* p. 354.

17. More, *History of King Richard III,* p. 68.

18. Bullough, *Sources* 3:232.

19. Hammond, *King Richard III,* p. 87.

20. E. M. W. Tillyard, *Shakespeare's History Plays* (New York: Collier Books, 1962), p. 72, emphasis added.

21. Francis Bacon, *Essays Civil and Moral* (London: Ward, Lock, 1910), pp. 69–70.

22. Arthur Sherbo, ed., *Johnson on Shakespeare* (New Haven and London: Yale University Press, 1968), 7:605.

23. Walter Jackson Bate, *Samuel Johnson* (New York: Harcourt Brace Jovanovich, 1979), p. 7. See Bate's sensitive treatment of these physical deformities and Johnson's apparent repression of their origins, esp. p. 9. My thanks to Joseph Bartolomeo for reminding me of the relevance of Johnson's own physical disabilities.

24. Samuel Johnson, "Preface to Shakespeare," in *Johnson on Shakespeare,* Sherbo, 7:91.

25. Houston A. Baker, Jr., "Caliban's Triple Play," in *"Race," Writing, and Difference,* ed. Henry Louis Gates, Jr. (Chicago: University of Chicago Press, 1986), p. 390.

26. Paul Howe, personal communication, January 1987.

27. Friedrich Nietzsche, "The Use and Abuse of History," in *Untimely Meditations,* tr. R. J. Hollingdale (Cambridge: Cambridge University Press, 1983), p. 61. Hollingdale translates this famous essay as "On the Uses and Disadvantages

of History for Life." I use his translation, as being the most accurate modern version, but take the liberty of retaining the title by which the piece is best known to English readers—and, I think, most suggestively rendered for argumentation. Page references of this essay are hereafter included in the text.

28. Robert N. Watson, *Shakespeare and the Hazards of Ambition* (Cambridge: Harvard University Press, 1984), p. 20; and Janet Adelman, "Born of Woman: Fantasies of Maternal Power in *Macbeth*," in *Cannibals, Witches, and Divorce: Estranging the Renaissance*, ed. Marjorie Garber (Baltimore: Johns Hopkins University Press, 1986). pp. 91–93.

29. See Watson, *Shakespeare and the Hazards of Ambition*, p. 26.

30. Marjorie Garber, "What's Past Is Prologue: Temporality and Prophecy in Shakespeare's History Plays," in *Renaissance Literary Genres: Essays on Theory, History, and Interpretation*, ed. Barbara Lewalski, Harvard English Studies 14 (Cambridge: Harvard University Press, 1986), pp. 301–31.

31. "An Apology for Poetry," in *Sir Philip Sidney: Selected Poetry and Prose*, ed. David Kalstone (New York: Signet Classic, 1970), p. 227. Page references of this essay are hereafter included in the text.

32. Hayden White, *Metahistory: The Historical Imagination in Nineteenth-Century Europe* (Baltimore and London: Johns Hopkins University Press, 1973), p. 356.

Faithful Servants:
Shakespeare's Praise
of Disobedience

Unto thee, O King, I have done no hurt.

Daniel 6:22 (Geneva Bible)

I

Sartre saw his early thinking about ethical matters as having been powerfully shaped by the experience of occupied France in World War II. He was imbued with the conviction, appropriate to those special circumstances, that the essential challenge of the moral life was having the courage to do what was right, not the difficulty of knowing what to do.[1] The basic choice, for the ordinary citizen of occupied France, was between collaboration and resistance. In this essay, I will argue that Shakespeare sets up similar special circumstances in *King Lear,* and that the play can be seen, in part, as an extended meditation on the kinds of situation in which resistance to legally constituted authority becomes a moral necessity, and in which neutrality is not a viable possibility. Maynard Mack sounds like Sartre on occupied France when he observes that in *Lear,* "the will is agonizingly free" and that almost every character "is impelled, sooner or later, to take some sort of stand."[2] My perspective has also been partly anticipated by the justly celebrated essay on "'Service' in *King Lear*" by Jonas Barish and Marshall Waingrow.[3] I will extend the emphasis of Mack, Barish and Waingrow, and others on "the circumstantial sociality of the *Lear* world,"[4] but I will treat the theme of proper disobedience in a more strictly *political* context than these critics do.

Whether there were limits to the obedience that inferiors owed their social and political superiors was one of the great questions of Renaissance and Reformation political thinking. It was not an issue on which a stable consensus or even, in many cases, stable individual positions existed.[5] Both the humanist and the Reformation traditions were ambiguous and self-contradictory on the matter. A crucial moment for the entire

humanist tradition occurs in the second book of *The Courtier.* Federico
Fregoso, in attempting to sum up the view of the ideal courtier that he
has been expounding, describes the courtier as turning "all his thoughts
. . . to love, and (as it were) to reverence the prince hee serveth, and . . .
to be altogether plyable to please him." Pietro da Napoli interrupts with
the bitter remark that such a "plyable" courtier is not an ideal but a reality ("of these . . . now adayes ye shal finde ynow"), since what Federico
has described is "a joly [*jolie*] flatterer."[6] Federico distinguishes the courtier from his wicked shadow first by an appeal to motives (flatterers do
not truly love their lords) and then by insisting that when he speaks of
the courtier's obedience to his prince, he means obedience only to "commandements that are reasonable and honest" (p. 106).

This is clearly a momentous assertion, but Federico does not pursue it.
He goes on instead to define and exemplify a category of morally neutral
commands; the issue of wicked commands is dropped. The question of
limits to obedience, however, returns with the discussion of how the
courtier is to advance himself. Vincentio Calmeta denies Federico's claim
that courtiers can rely on virtue to succeed and can eschew "any naughtie
way" or "subtill practise." Federico asserts (with, presumably, un-
intended satire) that it is not totally impossible to find a prince who rewards virtue but that, if the courtier finds himself serving a prince who
only values "naughtie" practices, "as soone as he knoweth it, let him
forsake him" (p. 112). Calmeta dissents from this as well, arguing that
wicked princes are not only normal but must be endured: "wee must
take them with all their faultes." He appeals to "infinite respectes" that
"constraine a gentleman after he is once entred into service with a Lord,
not to forsake him." When Federico continues to insist on the absolute
priority of moral duties, the question again arises "whether a gentleman
be bound or no, while he is in a princes service, to obey him in all things
which he shall commaund, though they were dishonest and shameful
matters." Federico stoutly maintains that "in dishonest matters we are
not bound to obey any bodie," and another interlocutor (Ludovico Pio)
bursts in to register the full shockingness of the view Federico has articulated. The terms in which the question of obedience is now posed are
brutally realistic: "and what? . . . if I be in service with a prince who
handleth me wel, and hopeth that I will doe any thing for him that may
bee done, and he happen to command me to kill a man, or any other like
matter, ought I to refuse to doe it?" (p. 112). Federico insists that a prince
is to be obeyed only in "thinges that tend to his profit and honour"
(which are, presumably, virtuous things) and that he must be disobeyed
in things that do not so tend. This immediately raises the issue of private

judgment, from which Federico weakly backs off with the obfuscatory remark that it is often hard to distinguish ill from good things, especially with regard to killing.

In the course of this dialogue, a clear sense of moral imperative has been muddied by the "infinite respectes," presumably prudential and practical, that would recommend loyalty regardless of the situation, and by the sudden and highly unsettling emergence of the issue of epistemological uncertainty.[7] Lauro Martines has argued that while "the relation between the prince and the courtier" is at the conceptual center of *The Courtier,* from the political point of view, "Castiglione, who insists on this relationship, has no clear view of it."[8] The humanist tradition did not offer a clear mandate. Neither the philosophically explicit fourth book of *The Courtier* nor the similar dialogue in book 1 of More's *Utopia* moved beyond the impasse in which Castiglione's Federico left the question of service to the wicked. The fourth book of *The Courtier* extends the distinction between the courtier and the flatterer (the former is a truth-teller, the latter a liar) and sees all the courtier's accomplishments as means of establishing a context of affection in which he can speak truth, but it returns to Federico's view that if the prince's nature is utterly unredeemable, the courtier must flee—lest he feel, in words repeated from book 2, "the hartgriefe that all good men have which serve the wicked" (p. 301; in book 2, p. 112).[9] Tyrannicide is highly praised in passing (pp. 289–90), but not mentioned in the practical context.

In More, the issue of "pliability" versus moral rigor is equally vexed. The alternative to moral rigor is not endurance but active accommodation, making the best of every bad situation, the all-purpose advice that "whatever play is being performed, perform it as best you can."[10] This "other philosophy, more practical for statesmen" put forth by "Morus" is then subjected to a devastating critique by the traveler and Platonist, Raphael Hythlodaeus. To be a "pliable" moralist at a wicked (that is, normal) court, would not merely cause the courtier or counselor "hartgriefe" but would also be dangerous to him ("he would be counted a spy and almost a traitor who gives only faint praise to evil counsels") and morally disastrous. Such a courtier would either be forced into wickedness himself or "made a screen" for the wickedness of others (p. 52). At this point the topic is dropped.[11]

The Protestant tradition was equally unresolved on the question of obedience to the wicked. On the one hand, the Reformers extolled (over against the papacy) the God-given legitimacy of secular rulers; on the other, they insisted on the God-given legitimacy and inviolability of individual conscience. In the first decade of the Reformation, this tension was resolved by a strict distinction between nonobedience and resistance.

To the question, "When a prince is wrong, are his people bound to follow him then too?" Luther answered, "No, for it is no one's duty to do wrong," and cited Acts 5:29 ("we ought to obey God rather than men")—always a potentially explosive text.[12] Ultimately, for Luther, the decision whether to obey or not was a matter for the individual conscience enlightened by the Word, but he distinguished sharply between dis- (that is, non-) obedience and active resistance. In the case of immoral commands, he as strongly deprecated resistance as he insisted upon nonobedience. Nonobedience led to the glory of martyrdom; resistance to the sin of rebellion. In *The Obedience of a Christian Man,* Tyndale followed Luther closely, emphasizing nonresistance even more strongly than Luther did—"neither may the inferior person avenge himself on the superior, or violently resist him, for whatsoever wrong it be."[13] In the summary at the end of his treatise, however, Tyndale added a crucial reservation: "[princes] may not be resisted: do they never so evil. . . . Neverthelater, if they command to do evil, we must then disobey, and say, 'We are otherwise commanded of God.'" We are still, however, "not to rise against them" (p. 332).[14]

The Edwardine homily on "Good Order and Obedience to Rulers" echoes Tyndale. After its famous opening paragraph on cosmological order and degree as a metaphysical principle, the homily goes on to argue, solely on the basis of biblical citation, that "it is not lawful for inferiors and subjects in any case to resist" the superior powers.[15] Christ taught that even wicked rulers have their power from God; Peter "bringeth in the patience of our Saviour, to persuade obedience to governors, yea, although they be wicked." In the example analyzed at greatest length, David "did know that he was but king Saul's subject, though he [David] were in great favour with God, and his enemy king Saul out of God's favour" (pp. 109–11). The homily also includes, however, a very strong exhortation to nonobedience, an exhortation even stronger than Tyndale's: "yet let us believe undoubtedly, good Christian people, that we may not obey kings, magistrates, or any other, though they be our own fathers, if they would command us to do any thing contrary to God's commandments." But nevertheless "in that case we may not in any way resist violently" (pp. 112–13). The tension here between nonobedience and nonresistance is at its highest.

The later homily "Against Disobedience" rather than on obedience eliminates the tension. Written in 1570, immediately in the aftermath of the rebellion of the northern earls, it takes us all the way from Tyndale to Hobbes. Centrally acknowledging the existence of wicked as well as virtuous rulers, it asks the vital question, "What shall subjects do then? Shall they obey . . . wise and good princes and contemn, disobey, and rebel against . . . undiscreet and evil governors?"[16] God forbid, it responds, and its first move is to deny the validity of that dangerous thing, individual conscience—"what a perilous thing were it to commit unto the subjects judgment, which prince is wise and godly . . . and which otherwise." As in Hobbes, private judgment is seen as leading to perpetual unrest.[17] Every prince is thought to be ungodly by some subjects, and "if therefore all subjects that mislike of their prince should rebel, no realm should ever be without rebellion" (p. 556). This homily is a brilliant piece of writing, and it faces the obvious next question directly—what if there is no epistemological problem: "What if the prince be undiscreet and evil indeed, and it [is] also evident to all men's eyes that he is so?" The answer is unequivocal even in this case—"let us patiently suffer" (p. 557). As in the earlier homily, David is invoked as an especially edifying model, an example of the irrelevance of either superior virtue or specific divine favor in justifying rebellion against the obviously wicked. A good man is an obedient subject. There is no possible tension. David was "so good a subject that he obeyed so evil a king" (p. 566). Conscientious nonobedience vanishes as either an option or an obligation.

There is, however, a strand within the Protestant tradition that expanded rather than withdrew the doctrine of conscience, that intensified nonobedience into resistance rather than diminishing it into endurance. To locate this strand, we must turn to the English Protestant writers who faced what was to them genuinely the equivalent of the Nazi occupation of France, the reign in England of a Catholic queen married to the king of Spain. The Marian exiles John Ponet and Christopher Goodman, along with the Scots John Knox and George Buchanan, were the most radical political theorists of the century. By 1530, Luther had renounced his earlier opinion that resistance to an established secular ruler was always wrong. He argued that certain kinds of immoral magistrates (i.e., Catholic crusaders against Protestants) are themselves rebels, and that therefore opposition to them is not rebellion.[18] Melanchthon argued similarly, yet within the Lutheran and later the Calvinist theory of proper and mandated resistance, there remained an unwillingness to assign the duty of resistance to every member of a society ruled by an immoral and ungodly prince.[19] Most of the major Protestant thinkers of the midcentury, like the Huguenots later, located the duty of active resistance in "lesser magistrates" to the exclusion of private individuals.[20] Ponet, Goodman, and Buchanan did not so limit their justification of resistance.[21]

A striking and little-remarked feature of the political thought of Ponet and Goodman is their conception of collective responsibility. They insisted that the passive allowance of wickedness was itself wickedness.

Ponet is particularly emphatic that not only "the doers" but also "the consentours to evil" shall be punished.[22] Ponet recognized that, as Hannah Arendt puts it, "politics is not like the nursery," that "in politics obedience and support are the same."[23] Of Nero's crimes, Ponet asks, "Who were to be blamed for these cruell actes? He for doing them, or others for flattring him, or the senate ād people of Rome in suffring him? Surely there is none to be excused, but all to be blamed." Ponet concedes that "he is a good citezin that dothe none evil" but insists that "he is a better that letteth [prevents] others, that they [the others] shall not doo hurt nor uniustice." The blood of innocents will be demanded of those who consent to or even passively allow atrocities—on the part of their political "head" as well as others. Ponet has no patience with prudence ("O faynte heartes" [Biiʳ]), equivocation (Eviiiᵛ), or with Morus-like adapting to the play at hand (he parodies one of his contemporaries as saying "if the Turke ruled in Englād, I wold frame mi selfe to live according" [Lviᵛ–viiʳ]). In a striking moment of direct address, Goodman warns those who merely follow orders that it is not only the commanders of evil who shall feel "Gods heavy wrathe," but "so shalt thou, being made an instrument of their impietie."[24] Ignorance is no excuse in moral contexts (p. 167); nor are examples of the great (p. 180) or the teachings of conservative political theory—"comon and symple people" think that they must be obedient "because their doinges are counted tumultes and rebellion" and therefore they "suffer themselves like brute beastes rather than reasonable creatures, to be led and drawen where so ever their Princes commandementes have called" (pp. 145–46). The doctrine of conscience is paramount. "Thou thy self must answer for thy self," says Ponet (Diiiʳ)—and for those around and above you, too.[25]

An example Ponet treats at length is Saul's commandment to "his owne household wayters and familiar servantes" to kill Ahimelech (1 Sam. 22:17). With typical verve and dramatic imagination, Ponet presents the servants as having had the option of saying to Saul, "we wilbe your true obedient servauntes, we will believe as the king believeth, we will doo as the king biddeth us." Instead, however, having recognized God as the supreme power and having used their own judgment regarding Ahimelech's guilt, they "playnly and utterly" refused to obey "the kinges unlawfull commaundement." In acting thus, Ponet insists, they were "yet the kinges true servauntes and subjectes" (Dvʳ). On the question of whether Christians are as free as "Ethnicks" to kill malefactors, "yea, though they were magistrates," Ponet at first asserts that "in som cases" Christians are equally free (as "when a governour shall sodainly with his sword rune upon an innocent"), then seems to espouse a conservative general principle which denies such freedom ("all things . . .

according to ordre"), and then lists five kinds of exceptions to this apparently absolute principle (Gviii^{r-v}).[26] Later on in the *Treatise,* Ponet tells the story of one of these exceptions (Ehud killing Eglon in Judges 3) at length and notes that the deed is specially commended in Scripture even though Ehud was "a private person" authorized "only by the spirite of God" (Hvi^r). From Ehud, Ponet moves to the case of Matathias, the first leader of the Maccabean revolt (1 Macc. 2:17–28), who not only refused to obey Antiochus's commandment to commit idolatry but also slew a coreligionist he saw obeying the law and then fell upon "the ordinary commissioners" sent from Antiochus to announce the law (Hvi^r). "These examples," Ponet rather coyly says, "need no further exposition."

Goodman provides the "further exposition" that Ponet pretends to think superfluous. Goodman notes that it might seem "a strange doctrine" and "a great disorder" that "the people" should "take unto them the punishment of transgression" (pp. 185, 191), but nonetheless, he assures the reader, it is the true doctrine of Scripture polity. This is the line that Buchanan develops. In *De Jure Regni apud Scotos,* many of the positions of Ponet and Goodman attain their most lucid and perhaps most radical exposition. Classical and scriptural views are fully identical for Buchanan (as for they will be for Milton later). Buchanan joins what he sees as the injunction of Scripture "to cut off wickedness and wicked Men, without any exception of rank or degree" to a classical conception of tyrannicide: "a Tyrant is a publick Enemy, with whom all good men have a perpetual warfare."[27] Buchanan sees God as "many times" stirring up "from amongst the lowest of the people some very mean, and obscure man to revenge Tyrannical Pride" (p. 54). Most important, Buchanan develops the hint in Ponet on the way in which disobedience is true loyalty to the immoral commander. "Doth he seem to respect the Good of a mad Man," Buchanan asks, "who looseth his Bonds?" He develops the analogy—"they who are restored to Health do render thanks to their Physitian, whom before they hated, because he would not grant their Desires whilst they were sick"—and then applies it: "if Kings continue in their Madness, whoever doth most obey them, is to be judged their greatest Enemy." The disobedient servant is the true physician; the obedient cherish the disease (pp. 57–58). Buchanan returns to the physician conceit at the end of the dialogue. "B's" interlocutor, "M," is worried, like Castiglione's Calmeta, over the "hazards and inconveniences" that attend on such radical views. B is serenely untroubled by prudence and timidity. The good physician, says B, knows when and how to administer his medicines (p. 68).

Kenneth Muir has noted a possible imagistic and conceptual borrowing from Ponet's *Shorte Treatise* in *Lear,* and there is a striking and fairly unusual phrase ("court holy-water") common to both works, but the aim of this survey is not to establish sources for *Lear* but rather to show the range of ideas about "how superior powers ought to be obeyed" that were readily available to Shakespeare.[28] My analysis will try to demonstrate that in *Lear* Shakespeare consistently dramatized and espoused the most radical of these ideas and placed them in a purely secular context. Following Muir, I would argue that *Lear* is the culmination of a development in Shakespeare's political thinking from a concern with the maintenance of order to a concern with corrupt and corruption-inducing authority.[29] *Hamlet* marks the turn, though Shakespeare had touched on some of the issues earlier. The most interesting of the earlier treatments are in *Richard III* and *King John*. In *Richard III*, the murderers of Clarence present their "commission" to a jailor who "will not reason what is meant thereby," and the murderers see themselves as "loyal," dutiful, and absolved of responsibility because "What we will do, we do upon command."[30] Later in the play, Sir James Tyrrel, who supervises the murder of the young princes in the tower, presents himself as Richard's "most obedient subject" (4.2.66). In *King John,* Hubert must weigh his "warrant" and oath ("I have sworn to do it") against the human meaning of blinding the young prince on whom he has attended (4.2.38–124). The case of Rosencrantz and Guildenstern is perhaps closest to that of Sir James Tyrrel, but they do not seem (like Tyrrel) "discontented"—merely and utterly venal and obsequious. As Guildenstern says, they obey and give themselves "in the full bent" to lay their service freely at Claudius's feet to be commanded (*Hamlet* 2.2.29–32). I think that we are meant fully to share Hamlet's disgust at Rosencrantz's and Guildenstern's making love to their employment—even if this does not fully justify Hamlet's treatment of them. With Emilia's refusal to be an obedient wife to Iago— "'Tis proper I obey him, but not now" (5.2.197)—we come to the very threshold of *Lear*. After *Lear,* in the Romances, as I will show in a brief epilogue, the distinction between virtuous disobedience and improper loyalty becomes axiomatic for Shakespeare.

II

The opening scene of *Lear* raises the issue of proper and improper obedience almost immediately, but before turning to this aspect of the scene a larger issue about the political orientation of the play should be faced. If the spring of the whole tragic action, or at least of the Lear plot, is seen to be the division of the kingdom, then the entire play would seem to be oriented in a conservative direction, toward the ideology of order and degree—"The specialty of rule hath been neglected." If, however, Lear's initial plan for a three-way division with Cordelia having the middle was a sensible and politically astute one given that he had no male heir and that his two elder daughters were married to powerful and potentially antagonistic dukes—a problem the Folio version emphasizes—what we witness in the opening scene is not a disastrous plan being made yet worse, but a true crisis—a set of spontaneous bad decisions on Lear's part supervening on a plan that might well have been workable.[31] Reading the scene in this way helps us better understand Shakespeare's presentation of the behavior of both Cordelia and Kent. They are both to be seen as caught by surprise. Cordelia was not planning to disappoint Lear in public, nor was Kent planning to protest the arrangements Lear was making. The love test was not part of the initial design since, as the opening prose exchanges make clear, the shares to go to each of the sisters had already been carefully worked out and minutely discussed with the participants and with the king's chief counselors. Kent's concern for Lear's "safety" (line 156) is a response to the *revised* plan.

In Shakespeare's play, unlike the old play of *Leir,* the love test is a kind of game that Lear is playing—"Which of you *shall we say* doth love us most" (line 56)—while waiting for Gloucester to return with Cordelia's suitors. The official business of the scene is to ratify the division of the kingdom through public proclamation, and the one piece of actual business is to declare which of Cordelia's suitors has succeeded (lines 44–47). The love test is purely ceremonial, and the suggestion that it is part of the division merely a flourish. As Stanley Cavell has argued, all three of the daughters understand perfectly what is being asked of them.[32] Goneril participates in the ceremony brilliantly. She realizes that Lear is calling more for "word" than "matter" and makes inspired use of inexpressibility topoi to fulfill her ceremonial role and free herself from "matter." Regan can only echo Goneril (lines 68–70), and Cordelia commits herself to matter rather than to words (lines 76–77). Her initial act is mere refusal, nonobedience ("Nothing, my Lord"). She insists on distinguishing herself from her sisters and from the terms of the ceremony. When drawn into speech, she fills in the content of her present and future relations to her father, while the occasion calls only for form. She commits herself to a "plain" rhetoric of concrete enumeration, rather than to a ceremonial rhetoric of comparatives and superlatives. Her behavior might not seem to us to fall within the terms of the political, but in Renaissance social and political discourse the relation of a child to a parent was an essential part of the general nexus of hierarchical subordination as well as a vital source for more strictly political analogies.[33] It is crucial to the value structure of *King Lear* that, from the point of view of conservative moral and political thinking, Goneril is entirely correct in saying to Cordelia, "you have obedience scanted" (line 277).[34] "Prescribe not us our duty," says Regan (line 274). Goneril and Regan are mouth-pieces for "duty" and "obedience" straightforwardly conceived.[35]

We recall that the Homily on Obedience reminded us that, although we may not "in any wise" resist violently, we must believe undoubtedly that there are circumstances in which we "may not obey kings, magistrates, or any other, *though they be our own fathers.*" Yet we cannot help wondering whether Cordelia's situation was truly one of these special circumstances (whose existence the later homily will deny). Goneril's condemnation is not enough, at this point in the play, to lead us to approve wholeheartedly of Cordelia's behavior. Perhaps some honorable form of compliance would have been possible.[36] "Duty" and "obedience" are rendered problematic by the contrasting actions—that is, speeches—of Cordelia and her sisters, but disobedience is not fully valorized by Cordelia's behavior. For this, we must turn to Kent. It is in Kent's behavior that the theme of virtuous, morally mandated disobedience, even interference, is fully articulated.

Kent is normally thought of as a feudal retainer, and while this captures some central elements of his characterization, it obscures his identity as a Renaissance courtier. In scene 1, Kent attempts exactly what the revised "schoolmaster" courtier of Castiglione's fourth book is supposed to do: to use his personal skills and the relationship to the ruler that these skills have brought him to tell his prince an unpalatable truth. Another function of the opening prose interlude is to give us some sense of Kent's normal behavior as a courtier. He is not by nature or habit boorish or even plainspoken. From this point of view, what is striking about the opening encounter is how exquisitely Kent handles the almost impossible social situation in which Gloucester's crudely jocular introduction of Edmund-as-bastard places him.[37] Kent's initial addresses to Lear are both courtly. "Good my Liege," he begins, after the astounding curse on Cordelia (line 119). Lear immediately shuts him up with a threat and announces the new division and abdication plan. Kent tries the courtly mode again (though subtly echoing Cordelia's rhetoric of concrete enumeration): "Royal Lear / Whom I have ever honour'd as my King, / Lov'd as my father . . . As my great patron" (lines 139–41). Only when Lear again cuts him off with a threat does Kent alter his style (his counterpart in *Leir* falls silent at this point). Shakespeare has him know exactly what he is doing and has him explicitly call attention to the relation between the extremity of the situation and the abandonment of decorum. "Be Kent unmannerly, / When Lear is mad," he announces, and he pro-

ceeds to address Lear as unceremoniously as possible—without a prologue, in the familiar form, and with a generic, nonhonorific description:
"What wouldst thou do, old man?"

Kent's rudeness is chosen, under pressure, as a moral stance. The
world that he is occupying here is at a borderline where that of Castiglione merges into that of Ponet (Annabel Patterson has suggested that it
is the world of Parliamentary privilege).[38] Again "thouing" Lear, Kent
explains that in speaking out, he is acting out of faithfulness: "Think'st
thou that duty shall have dread to speak / When power to flattery bows?"
His anticourtly style—like Cordelia's, he implies—is not an option but a
moral obligation: "to plainness honour's bound / When majesty falls to
folly" (lines 147–48). Kent is acting like Buchanan's "physician" in refusing to acknowledge as legitimate the wishes of the king-as-madman. He
is attempting to recall Lear to reason—"in thy best consideration, check
/ This hideous rashness"—and to recollection—"Thy youngest daughter
doth not love thee least." Yet he keeps speaking long after it is clear that
Lear is only being incensed by his resistance; he ignores two direct commands and then interrupts Lear midoath. This final move produces, in
the Folio only, a small act of resistance by Albany and, if Beth Goldring
is right, Cordelia, in checking Lear from physical violence to Kent.[39]
Kent's attempt at schoolmaster courtiership receives precisely the "reward" (line 171) that Hythlodaeus or Castiglione's Calmeta would have
predicted, and in the final speech before his banishment, Kent combines
Buchanan's image with Ponet's prophetic stance, presenting himself
more clearly as bearing witness than as advising.

> Kill thy Physician, and thy fee bestow
> Upon the foul disease, revoke thy gift,
> Or whil'st I can vent clamour from my throat,
> I'll tell thee thou dost evil.
>
> (lines 162–65)

The structure of values established in the first scene continues
throughout the play. Plain speech and conscientious breaches of decorum
remain touchstones of value and are richly developed as such. Kent reenters the play in act 1, scene 4, manifesting his characteristic awareness
of style ("I other accents borrow"), now in the role of non-"gentle" servant, a menial who is incapable of courtly speech (he can only "mar a
curious tale in telling it" [lines 32–33]).[40] The introduction of Kent as
Caius is immediately followed by a brief and haughty appearance by a
gentlemanly serving-man, Oswald, Goneril's steward, and by a brief interjection by one of Lear's retainers. This figure, raised from servant to
knight in the Folio, takes it on himself to comment to Lear on the devel-

oping situation—"to my judgment, your Highness is not entertain'd with that ceremonious affection as you were wont" (1.4.55–57). The quality captured in this wonderful phrase, "ceremonious affection," the quality of normative or ideal courtliness, is entirely missing from the world of this play. Given its lack, loving plainspokenness is the only alternative. In the face of Lear's anger at his presumption, the Knight explains his behavior thus: "I beseech you pardon me, my Lord, if I be mistaken; for my duty cannot be silent when I think your Highness wrong'd." Again, as in scene 1, in unusually negative or perilous situations, "duty cannot be silent"—even at the risk of breaching decorum.

Oswald reenters at this point, dutifully following the instructions that (in the Folio) we have seen Goneril issuing to him in the previous scene ("put on what weary negligence you please" [1.3.13–14]), and Kent intervenes. Shakespeare now introduces the last of the lovingly rude truthspeakers in the play, the Fool, whose first action is to identify with Kent (or to identify Kent with himself). The construction of this scene is clear. Shakespeare is lining up the characters—Kent, the Fool, and the nameless Knight on the one hand, Oswald and Goneril on the other. As in the equivalent scene in *Twelfth Night,* willingness to tolerate the Fool is one way of making the division.[41] The Fool, a licensed plainspeaker, presents an utterly cynical, Hythlodaeus-like view of court life—"Truth's a dog must to kennel; he must be whipp'd out when Lady Brach may stand by th' fire and stink" (lines 109–10)—and shortly after, in the great dramatic moment of the scene, Goneril, Lady Brach herself, enters.[42] Here, as throughout, Goneril speaks for decorum. She begins her reproof of Lear with an attack on the Fool's license as typical of the "rank and not to be endured riot" with which Lear's retinue threatens to infect the manners of her sober court (lines 198–201, 239–43). She does not appreciate it when Lear adopts something like the Fool's "pranks" to make a point (lines 233–35).[43] Her elaborately suspended and complexly subordinated syntax allows her to present her own desires as objective necessities— "the shame itself doth speak / For instant remedy." Lear reacts to the iron fist behind the abstract rhetoric, and at this point Albany enters. The question becomes where Albany stands. "Is it your will? Speak, Sir," Lear demands (line 256). Albany pleads ignorance (line 271), is horrified at the excess of Lear's curse (line 288), and then, after Lear rushes out, begins a weak protest. Goneril cuts him off, appealing (in the Folio) to political prudence[44] and tasking Albany for foolishness, or at least "want of wisdom" (line 342). Albany weakly accepts the possibility of Goneril's superior politic prudence, weakly recommends leaving well enough alone, and, when Goneril is about to counter, exits with "Well, well, th' event." At this point, we are surely meant to see Albany as, in Buchanan's words, one of "those who, albeit they are not ignorant what is lawful and just or right, yet prefer a quiet sloathfulness to honest hazards, and hesitating in their minds, do frame their consultation on the expectation of the Event."[45]

Throughout her conversation with Albany, Goneril is constantly calling for Oswald (this is intensified in the Folio). Goneril relies on Oswald to be totally instrumental to her purposes: Oswald is not only to warn Regan about Lear's knights, but "thereto [to] add such reasons of [his] own / As may compact it more" (1.4.336–38). Kent is sent to Regan by Lear, and in act 2, scene 2, the inevitable confrontation takes place. As Barish and Waingrow note, in the structure of the play, Kent and Oswald are *systematically* contrasted.[46] The sight of Oswald sends Kent into a Fool-like aria of virtuoso prose imprecation. The thematically central insult—present only in the Folio—is the description of Oswald as a "super-serviceable" rogue;[47] Oswald would "be a bawd in way of good service" (2.2.16–18). The essential picture is of a man who would do anything on command, "in way of good service."[48] In explaining his anger at Oswald to Cornwall, Kent expounds on the point, now in high verse. He is incensed that "such a slave as this should wear a sword"; "such smiling rogues" as Oswald

> smooth every passion
> That in the natures of their lords rebel,
> Being oil to fire, snow to the colder moods;
> Renege, affirm, and turn their halcyon beaks
> With every gale and vary of their masters,
> Knowing naught (like dogs) but following.
> (2.2.69–77)[49]

This is the figure Pietro da Napoli discerned in Federico Fregoso's "altogether plyable" courtier; it is the smiling client in Juvenal's Third Satire and in Jonson's *Sejanus*.[50] Such a figure encourages rather than, as Kent did in scene 1, stands against irrational passions. Shakespeare's treatment of this figure suggests the dialectic of Luther and Buchanan in which the improperly obedient participate more fully in "the name and quality which is termed rebellion" than do the nonobedient, since submissive servants aid and abet a rebellion "in the natures of their lords."[51] The culminating dog-image suggests an essential distinction between brute and "reasonable service," between those who are capable of loyal disobedience and those who, in Goodman's words, "suffer themselves like brute beastes rather than reasonable creatures, to be led and drawn where so ever their Princes commandements have called." The metaphysical "antipathy" Kent posits between himself and Oswald is between two con-

ceptions of obedience, one conscientious and limited, the other "naught
. . . but following."

In the scene between Kent and Oswald, Cornwall stands as the voice
of propriety. "Know you no reverence," he asks the railing Kent (2.2.66).
"Yes, sir," Kent politely answers, but appeals, first, to the "privilege" of
righteous anger (line 67) and then to something like the Fool's licensed
parrhesia—"Sir," he says, "'tis my occupation to be plain" (line 89).[52]
Cornwall's response to this is extremely interesting. He detects the element of willfullness in Kent's behavior and offers a brilliant, Astrophil-
like parody of affected plainness—"he cannot flatter, he, / An honest
mind and plain, he must speak truth; / And they will like it, so; if not,
he's plain" (lines 95–97). Parody then turns into moral critique. Cornwall
recognizes the contrast between Kent and Oswald but he sees Kent as
worse, as one of "these kinds of knaves . . .[who], in this plainness /
Harbour more craft and more corrupter ends / Than twenty silly-
ducking observants" (lines 98–100). The moral moorings of the play
threaten to come loose here. Yet while it is generally true that, as Zitner
puts it, "no verbal style is self-validating,"[53] the ethic of *Lear* is so deeply
anticourtly that there is no plain knave in the play. For the figure Cornwall describes, we must look to *Othello,* not to *Lear.* As is the case with
Lear's association of plainness with pride in scene 1 (line 128), the play
does not support the possible critique. The plain style remains a locus of
value. Significantly, Kent defends his "dialect" and his sincerity by asserting his willingness to disobey Cornwall on moral grounds—"he that
beguil'd you in a plain accent was a plain knave; which for my part I will
not be, though I should win your displeasure to entreat me to't" (lines
107–10).

In the name of the thin conception of propriety and decorum that
Cornwall shares with Goneril and Regan, he commands the deeply indecorous step of putting Kent, the king's messenger, in the stocks. At
this point, the moral pressure falls on Gloucester. He was offstage during
the great explosion of scene 1; the pressure was all on Kent there, as it
was on Albany in act 1, scene 4.[54] In acts 2 and 3, the pressure, as Mack
puts it, "to take some sort of stand" is on Gloucester. Gloucester's first
protest is polite but nonetheless real—"Let me beseech your Grace not
to do so" (2.2.136).[55] He disobeys a direct command (from Cornwall, in
the Folio) in staying with Kent, and he does not palliate or equivocate in
his judgment—"The Duke's to blame in this" (2.2.155).[56] Yet when Lear
enters the scene, Gloucester finds himself bearing messages back and
forth between Lear and his daughter and son-in-law. As the purposeful
quality of the behavior of Cornwall and Regan begins to dawn fully on
Lear, Gloucester utters one of the great cries of the appeaser—"I would

have all well betwixt you" (2.4.117)—but the rest of the scene makes it clear that there is no middle position in this world. Gloucester says nothing further during the entire interchange between Lear and Cornwall, Regan, and finally, Goneril, yet follows Lear out into the storm. The same line in which Gloucester's desertion is noted, however, also announces his return (2.4.293). Gloucester is still temporizing. Despite his compassionate evocation of Lear's situation (2.4.298–300), he seems prepared to obey the command that he has received from Cornwall: "shut up your doors, my Lord" (2.4.306).

In assessing the moral and political significance of Gloucester's behavior in act 3, it is important to be aware of his exact social status vis-à-vis Cornwall and Regan. To Gloucester, Cornwall is "the noble Duke my master, / My worthy arch and patron" (2.1.57–58); it is only through Cornwall's authority that Gloucester has access to state power and can issue his proclamation against Edgar ("The Duke must grant me that," Gloucester avers [2.2.80]). There is no doubt about the distance in social and political status between Gloucester and Cornwall. Cornwall rules half of England (including the region in which Gloucester has his house); he is Gloucester's acknowledged sovereign, his "master" (recall "Let me beseech *your Grace*").[57] Yet by the time we first see Gloucester in act 3, he has made his choice. Authority and humanity have definitively split apart, and he has lost the former in the name of the latter—"When I desir'd their leave that I might pity him, they took from me the use of mine own house" (3.3.2–3).[58] In true regal idiom, Gloucester is charged, "on pain of perpetual displeasure," not to aid Lear. Charity has become a crime, but Gloucester now feels in the grip of a moral imperative—"If I die for it, as no less is threatened me, the King, my old master, must be reliev'd" (3.3.17–19). It is important to read "old" here as "former" as well as "aged." Gloucester is insisting on a duty that does not depend on the immediate political situation. When he finds Lear on the heath, he reemphasizes the point, speaking the language of morally mandated disobedience to "superior powers," of higher than immediate duty. "Go in with me," he says to Lear, "my duty cannot suffer / T'obey in all your daughters' hard commands." Gloucester means his duty to Lear, but he could also mean his duty to Cornwall and company—as we shall see. In any case, he stresses his disobedience—"Through their injunction be to bar my doors . . . yet have I ventured" (3.5.145–49). As in all the moments of moral courage in the play, "duty" and "obedience" are opposed.[59]

It is important to be clear on Gloucester's political as well as his social situation. In sending Lear to Dover, Gloucester is aiding an invading enemy (and, perhaps, a popular rebellion).[60] The letter that Edmund, in his major act of loyalty, passes on to Cornwall proves Gloucester "an intelligent party to the advantages of France" (3.5.10). Cornwall and company are not misusing language in speaking continually of "the traitor Gloucester."[61] Gloucester cannot, ultimately, deny the charge when it is specifically put to him—"I am tied to the stake," he says, "and I must stand the course" (3.7.53). Yet although Gloucester is indeed a traitor, the scene of his mutilation is not presented as a judicial one. Shakespeare has Cornwall explicitly declare the extrajudicial, purely private nature of his actions—"Though well we may not pass upon his life / Without the form of justice, yet our power / Shall do a court'sy to our wrath" (3.7.24–26). There is no legal or political point to torturing Gloucester.[62] The presentation of a world with its values reversed is made literal in Cornwall's first mutilation of Gloucester—"Upon these eyes of thine, I'll set my foot" (line 66)—and the Regan-Goneril sense of decorum culminates in the rationale Regan provides for fully blinding Gloucester— "One side will mock another; th'other too" (line 60). At this point, one of the most remarkable and politically significant moments in the play occurs. A character designated in both the Quarto and the Folio merely as Servant imperiously interrupts Cornwall, commanding, "Hold your hand, my Lord." Regan and Cornwall are utterly surprised—Regan says, "How now, you dog," and Cornwall exclaims, "My villain," meaning "my menial"—but the servant appeals, as Kent had earlier, to the privilege of righteous anger and fights with Cornwall. Regan takes hold of a sword and (in the Quarto stage direction) stabs the servant in the back, exclaiming, with the full weight of outraged decorum, "A peasant stand up thus!"

Regan is right. The servant's behavior is outrageous. Shakespeare is presenting the most radical possible sociopolitical act in a way that can only be interpreted as calling for his audience's approval. This is Ehud killing Eglon in Ponet; this is Matathias. The servant is obviously not a "public person," and his action is one of outright interference rather than mere nonobedience, since he has not been directly commanded to do anything.[63] The scene is that which Buchanan describes and endorses: "from amongst the lowest of the people some very mean, and obscure" person is stirred up to revenge tyrannical pride and weakness. It is worth noting that, from a technical point of view, the servant, like Gloucester, is committing treason. As Mary Hallowell Perkins points out, "as late as 1728, for a servant to kill his master or mistress was counted a specially heinous crime, far worse than ordinary murder"; it was the crime of Petit Treason and as such was punishable by drawing followed by hanging.[64] Recognizing the political radicalism of this scene (entirely a Shakespearean invention) perhaps helps solve a long-standing puzzle: Why did

Shakespeare have the mutilation take place on stage? Dr. Johnson and most nineteenth-century critics and directors found this scene improper and excessive. Theatrical convention demands that this sort of thing happen offstage. The political helps explain the theatrical radicalism. Shakespeare perhaps felt that only through the extreme moral revulsion brought on by having to witness such a scene could he rely on his audience to approve rather than to recoil when they saw "a peasant stand up thus" and mortally wound a prince. To the question in the Homily against Disobedience—"But what if the prince be undiscreet, and it [is] also evident to all men's eyes that he is so?"—Shakespeare offered an answer very different from that of the homily.[65]

The rationale the servant offers for his act is as remarkable as the act itself. After commanding Cornwall to stop what he is doing, the servant characterizes his own behavior as loyalty rather than rebellion:

> I have serv'd you ever since I was a child,
> But better service have I never done you
> Than now to bid you hold.
> (3.7.71–73)

This is the clearest articulation and the most extreme case in the play of what we might call "Kent's paradox" of service through resistance. Direct interference is presented as an act of service. Again Ponet and Buchanan are relevant. Ponet insists that when Saul's "household wayters and familiar servauntes" rebelled against Saul's unlawful commandment to kill Ahimelech, they were "yet the kinges true servauntes and subjectes." In the Geneva Bible, Daniel tells Darius that, in flouting an official decree, "unto thee, O King, I have done no hurt" (Dan. 6:26). The gloss explains that since Daniel "did disobey the Kings wicked commaundement [in order] to obey God," he "did no injurie to the King."[66] Buchanan would see the Servant as another political "physician." We can begin to appreciate how important this conception was to Shakespeare by reflecting that he could have gotten the same plot effect, but not the paradox, if he had made the interfering servant one of *Gloucester's* rather than one of Cornwall's retinue. The scene takes place, after all, in Gloucester's house (as Gloucester keeps saying). Shakespeare wanted the servant to be Cornwall's in order to make the paradox of "better service" possible.[67]

In a world where atrocities like the blinding of Gloucester occur, there is no room for temporizing. When we next see Albany, "never," as Oswald says, "was man so chang'd" (4.2.3). He and Oswald find each other morally unintelligible—"he call'd me sot, / And told me I had turn'd the wrong side out," Oswald reports; "what most he should dislike seems pleasant to him" (4.2.8–10). In the Folio, which drastically cuts Albany's critique of Goneril's treatment of Lear, the condemnation of Goneril remains strong, but the focus of the scene is Albany's reaction to Gloucester's story rather than to Lear's—or rather, to a messenger's narrative of the scene we have just witnessed. The focus is precisely on the narration and on Albany's reactions, the kinds of reactions that Oswald, in his role as messenger, found so odd. This second messenger is another Oswald. He is entirely concerned with the business at hand (which is perhaps why in the Folio he is Messenger rather than Gentleman, a function rather than a social status). "Oh my good Lord," he begins, "the Duke of Cornwall's dead, / Slain by his servant, going to put out / The other eye of Gloucester" (4.2.70–72). The "news" is the death of Cornwall; what Cornwall was doing at the time is almost irrelevant. The Messenger's casualness about the moral content of his message—"going to put out / The other eye"—is dramatized by Albany's response—"Gloucester's eyes!" The Messenger takes no account of this response; he continues his story of how Cornwall was killed. Albany's response to the description of Cornwall's servant "bending his sword / To his great master" is to see the action as divinely sanctioned, perhaps even inspired—as Ponet saw Ehud or Matathias.[68] He does not worry about the servant's social status. He also does not lose track of the human situation—"But, O poor Gloucester! / Lost he his other eye?" The Messenger clarifies the point and turns immediately to Goneril with his business—"Both, both, my Lord, / This letter, Madam, craves a speedy answer" (4.2.81–82). This messenger remains a "good servant."[69]

The major "good servant" in this sense, however, continues to be Oswald. He was largely absent in act 3—though imagistically present in Lear's reference to "servile ministers" and in "Tom o' Bedlam's" past as a proud serving-man—but Oswald reemerges quite prominently in act 4.[70] Kent's view of him proves true. Oswald is present when Goneril makes her plans for murder and adultery with Edmund, and she assures Edmund that "This trusty servant / Shall pass between us" (4.2.18–19). Having become "a bawd in way of good service," Oswald remains a "trusty servant" to Goneril. In act 4, scene 5, he will not let Regan unseal Goneril's letter. "I may not, Madam," he tells Regan, "My lady charg'd my duty in this business" (lines 17–18). For Bradley (as, more recently, for Marvin Rosenberg), this is a typically Shakespearean humanizing touch, showing that Oswald "is not wholly worthless." Dr. Johnson was frankly puzzled—"I know not well," he wrote, "why Shakespeare gives to Oswald, who is a mere factor of wickedness, so much fidelity."[71] Johnson's puzzlement is more helpful than Bradley's "humanism" or Rosenberg's "tough-mindedness." This is hardly a moment when we are meant to admire Oswald. At the end of the scene, Regan, who has recognized the strategic folly of sparing the blinded Gloucester's life, reminds Oswald that "If you do chance to hear of that blind traitor, / Preferment falls on him that cuts him off" (lines 37–38). "Would I could meet him," says Oswald chillingly, "I should show / What party I do follow."

The next scene provides Oswald with his chance; it is the only moment in the play when we see Oswald acting on his own. We learn that there was more than class snobbery to Kent's anger "That such a slave as this should wear a sword." For Oswald, the blind Gloucester is "a proclaim'd prize," a way to "preferment." He adopts the unctuous impersonality of Goneril and Regan—"the sword is out / That must destroy thee," he tells Gloucester grandly (4.6.226–27). Edgar, disguised now as "a most poor man" (line 218) rather than as Tom o' Bedlam, interposes. Oswald's reaction calls attention to the indecorousness, the illegality, and the imprudence of the (apparent) poor man's intervention: "Wherefore, bold peasant / Dar'st thou support a publish'd traitor? Hence, / Lest that th'infection of his fortune take / Like hold on thee." Edgar suddenly breaks into dialect; Zitner is certainly correct that "what releases Edgar's dialect manner is Oswald's courtly one, his succession of coldly turned phrases, his lofty epithets."[72] Oswald is speaking as a great man here—"Let go, slave, or thou di'st"—and Edgar's dialect is intended as a specifically lower class version of the plain style—"Good gentleman, go your gait, and let poor volk pass . . . Chill be plain with you." They fight, and Edgar's peasant cudgel defeats Oswald's sword.[73] This scene is clearly meant to recall the intervention of the other, actual "bold peasant" of act 3, scene 7. The language—"peasant . . . slave . . . dunghill"—is filled with echoes of the earlier scene. The effect is to reinforce the image of this sort of peasant rebellion as a paradigm of moral action.

Edgar's epitaph for Oswald is worth careful attention. With his dying breath, Oswald attempts to see his duty to Goneril fulfilled, and Edgar comments, "I know thee well: a serviceable villain; / As duteous to the vices of thy mistress / As badness would desire" (lines 249–51). "Duteousness" in the play is not a virtue in itself. It is morally neutral. The question is duteous to whom or to what? Unlike Bradley, the play does not admire mere doglike fidelity. "Serviceableness"—mere instrumentality—is always negative. It is part of Shakespeare's portrayal of what it means, in Johnson's great phrase, to be a "factor of wickedness" that Oswald has "so much fidelity." As Arendt remarks, "total loyalty is possible only when fidelity is emptied of all concrete content."[74] The critique of doglike fidelity is precisely a critique of "good service" literally conceived. It is important to distinguish between Oswald and Edmund as "good servants." Edmund's specialty, as Barish and Waingrow note, is loyal service,[75] but the central dialectic of the play in this regard is not the critique of hypocrisy and opportunism (the Fool's targets), but the critique of dedicated superserviceableness (Kent's target).

In the act 5, we are given a final example of both opportunism and superserviceableness. We get to witness how a dog's obeyed in office. After Lear and Cordelia are captured, Edmund enlists an unnamed "captain" into his service. Edmund offers preferment, gives a lesson on smiling as the wind sits ("know thou this, that men / Are as the time is"), and then describes the essential feature of the service he is asking—"thy great employment / Will not bear question; either say thou'lt do't, / Or thrive by other means" (5.3.33–35). No thought about the content of the command is acceptable. The Captain must agree to "do't" before he knows what "it" is. The Folio version of this interchange omits the Captain's ironic claim to humanity: "I cannot draw a cart nor eat dried oats; / If it be man's work, I'll do't."[76] The omission has the effect of dramatizing what it means for a human being to make himself into a mere instrument. The Folio Captain allows himself to be entirely Edmund's "creature." He has no independent consciousness. His only words are to say what Edmund tells him to—respectfully: "either say thou'lt do't, / Or thrive by other means." "I'l do't, my Lord," is his entire speaking part. He is not given an exit line. He goes off silently and obediently, like a proper dog, suffering himself like a brute beast rather than a reasonable creature to be led and drawn wheresoever his master commands.[77] Through this moment we realize that the mad Lear's Fool-like or Hythlodaean view of his society is true only under certain conditions: a dog's obeyed in office only when its followers are also dogs.

As Barish and Waingrow observe, the final speech of the play "reiterates the note of service."[78] What they do not recognize is the paradoxical nature of the obedience the lines recommend:

> The weight of this sad time we must obey;
> Speak what we feel, not what we ought to say.

Here, at the final moment of the play, the paradoxical conception of obedience through breaching normal decorum is once again affirmed.[79] We "obey" the "weight" of *Lear* by not doing and saying what, in normal times, "we ought." Integrity is all.[80]

III

If, after *Lear,* Shakespeare never again so clearly espoused active resistance, the distinction between the good servant who disobeys immoral commands and the wicked who will do anything becomes a fundamental axiom. The Romances prior to *The Tempest* are explicit on this point.[81] In *Pericles,* the conversation between Antiochus and Thaliard echoes that between Edmund and the Captain in *Lear.*

> *Ant.:* We hate the prince of Tyre, and thou must kill him:
> It fits thee not to ask the reason why:
> Because we bid it. Say, is it done?
> *Thal.:* My Lord, 'tis done.

(1.1.157–60)

When Thaliard arrives at Tyre to do his job, he explains his conception of duty: "if a king bid a man be a villain, he's bound by the indenture of his oath to be one" (1.3.7–8). These themes are reiterated later in the play. In suborning Leonine to kill Marina, Dionyza admonishes him, "Thy oath remember; thou hast sworn to do it" (4.1.1). In the (would be) murder scene, Leonine keeps returning to this rationale. "I am sworn / To do my work with haste," he tells Marina (4.1.68–69). When she asks quite sensibly, "Why will you kill me?" he responds, in lines that echo Antiochus's charge to Thaliard, "My commission / Is not to reason of the deed, but do't." Leonine seizes Marina with the words, "I am sworn, / And will dispatch" (lines 90–91). The final obedient servant in *Pericles* is worse than "a bawd in way of good service," he is a loyal servant of a bawd. With regard to selling Marina's virginity in the marketplace, the Bawd says, "Get this done as I command you." Boult replies, "Performance shall follow" (4.2.57–59).

In *The Winter's Tale,* Shakespeare's fullest portrayal of a king behaving as a madman, all the virtuous characters adopt Buchanan's, or at least Federico Fregoso's, perspective on such a situation. Camillo, the king's most trusted counselor, is enjoined to murder a man (also a king) whom Camillo believes to be innocent. Shakespeare makes Camillo fully aware that if he were to comply with Leontes' command, he could appeal for justification to orthodox social thinking: "I must be poisoner / Of good Polixenes; and my ground to do't / Is the obedience of a master" (1.2.351–53). Camillo goes on, however, to describe his master (à la Buchanan and Kent) as "one / Who in rebellion with himself will have / All that are his so too." Instead of smoothing this passion that in the nature of his lord rebels, and thereby participating in the rebellion, Camillo decides instead, following the advice of Castiglione's Federico and Ottaviano, to forsake his lord's service. He subverts Leontes and then deserts him in order not to take part in Leontes' self-rebellion.

The Kent-like figure in *The Winter's Tale* is another plain and rude speaker, a shrew transformed into prophetic truth-teller, Paulina. Paulina describes herself to the deranged king as

> your loyal servant, your physician,
> Your most obedient counsellor, yet that dares
> Less appear so in comforting your evils
> Than such as most seem yours.
>
> (2.3.54–57)

She says of the more complaisant court figures, "You that are so tender o'er his follies / Will never do him good" (2.3.127–28). This is exactly Buchanan's perspective: "if Kings continue in their Madness, whoever doth most obey them, is to be judged their greatest Enemy." And, interestingly, in a play that contains (albeit misapplied) a scathing description of a "hovering temporizer, that / Canst with thine eyes at once see good and evil, / Inclining to them both" (1.2.301–3), the figure who attempts to temporize and occupy a middle position—who commits an inhuman act because he is "by oath enjoin'd" (3.3.52)—exits famously pursued by a bear.

In *Cymbeline,* perhaps written immediately following Shakespeare's revision of *Lear,*[82] the theme of virtuous disobedience is almost obsessive. Cloten, the tragicomic villain-prince of the play, expounds at length to Pisanio, a truly virtuous servant, his (Cloten's) view of the obedience that inferiors owe him:

> Sirrah, if thou wouldst not be a villain, but do me true service, undergo those employments wherein I should have cause to use thee with a serious industry—that is, whatever villainy soe'er I bid thee do, to perform it directly and truly—I would think thee an honest man.
>
> (3.5.109–13)

None of the virtuous servants in the play consider acting thus to do "true service" or to be "an honest man." In disobeying the wicked queen's commands and substituting a soporific for poison, Cornelius claims to be "the truer, / So to be false with her" (1.5.43–44). Pisanio, in a situation that parallels Camillo's, is commanded by a master he believes to be acting madly to, in Ludovico Pio's words, "kill a man"—or, in this case, a woman. Speaking of and to his absent master, Pisanio recalls that he has been enjoined obedience "Upon the love and truth and vows which I / Have made to thy command." Pisanio's meditation on his duty to murder on this basis recalls a key word from *Lear:*

> If it be so to do good service, never
> Let me be counted serviceable.
>
> (3.2.14–15)

Shakespeare's firm opinion on this matter is stated by Posthumus at the opening of the fifth act, when he begins to attain moral clarity:

Every good servant does not all commands;
No bond, but to do just ones.

Ponet would certainly have agreed—as, presumably, would Mr. John Bate, the wealthy merchant who, in 1606, refused to pay what he considered an unjust tax.[83]

Notes

1. Jean-Paul Sartre, "The Itinerary of a Thought," *Between Existentialism and Marxism*, tr. John Mathews (New York: Pantheon, 1974), pp. 33–34.
2. Maynard Mack, *King Lear in Our Time* (Berkeley and Los Angeles: University of California Press, 1972), p. 90. The will in *Lear* is, in Luther's terms, "bound" as well as free; as Mack says, while "choice remains in the forefront," action in the play "seems to spring directly out of the bedrock of personality" (p. 93).
3. Jonas A. Barish and Marshall Waingrow, "'Service' in *King Lear*," *SQ* 9 (1958): 347–55.
4. Mack, *King Lear in Our Time*, p. 100.
5. For an excellent historical overview of the whole period, see Quentin Skinner, *The Foundations of Modern Political Thought*, 2 vols. (Cambridge: Cambridge University Press, 1978). For a brief overview of the English context at the end of the sixteenth century, see Richard L. Greaves, "Concepts of Political Obedience in Later Tudor England: Conflicting Perspectives," *Journal of British Studies* 22 (1982): 23–34.
6. Baldassare Castiglione, *The Book of the Courtier*, tr. Sir Thomas Hoby, Everyman's Library (London: J. M. Dent, 1928), p. 106. All further page references to *The Courtier* will appear in the text.
7. On the unsettling quality of this epistemological uncertainty, see Wayne A. Rebhorn, *Courtly Performances: Masking and Festivity in Castiglione's Book of the Courtier* (Detroit: Wayne State University Press, 1978), p. 188.
8. Lauro Martines, "The Gentleman in Renaissance Italy: Strains of Isolation in the Body Politic," in *The Darker Vision of the Renaissance*, ed. Robert S. Kinsman (Berkeley: University of California Press, 1974), p. 89.
9. For an explanation of the tightness of this connection between the fourth book and the second, see Lawrence V. Ryan, "Book 4 of Castiglione's *Courtier*: Climax or Afterthought?" *SRen* 19 (1972): 156–79.
10. Sir Thomas More, *Utopia*, tr. Edward Surtz (New Haven: Yale University Press, 1964), p. 49. Further page references will appear in the text.
11. For an excellent account of the tensions in More (though perhaps overly sympathetic to "Morus"), see Stephen Greenblatt, *Renaissance Self-Fashioning from More to Shakespeare* (Chicago: University of Chicago Press, 1980), chap. 1, esp. pp. 34–36.

12. "Secular Authority: To What Extent it Should be Obeyed," in *Martin Luther: Selections from His Writings,* ed. John Dillenberger (New York: Doubleday, 1961), p. 399.

13. "The Obedience of a Christian Man," in *Doctrinal Treatises and Introductions to Different Portions of the Holy Scriptures by William Tyndale,* ed. Henry Walter (Cambridge: Cambridge University Press, 1848), p. 175. Further page references will appear in the text.

14. This is the passage that led More to refer to Tyndale's "holy book of disobedience." See Sir Thomas More, *The Dialogue concerning Tyndale,* ed. W. E. Campbell (London: Eyre and Spottiswoode, 1927), p. 273. It nicely dramatizes the tensions in Tyndale's position to compare More's characterization with Henry VIII's alleged delight in the "Obedience" as a "book for me, and all kings to read" (quoted from Strype in *Doctrinal Treatises by Tyndale,* p. 10).

15. *The Two Books of Homilies Appointed to Be Read in Churches* (Oxford: Oxford University Press, 1859), p. 109. Further page references in text.

16. "An Homily against Disobedience and Wilful Rebellion," in *Two Books of Homilies,* p. 555.

17. See Thomas Hobbes, *Leviathan,* ed. C. B. Macpherson (New York: Penguin, 1968), p. 365.

18. "Dr. Martin Luther's Warning to His Dear German People," tr. Martin Bertram, in *Luther's Works,* American Edition 47, ed. Franklin Sherman (Philadelphia: Fortress Press, 1971), pp. 18–20.

19. On the change in Luther's views, on Melanchthon's views, and on Bucer's retreat from thses positions, see Skinner, *Foundations,* 2:200–206.

20. For Calvin, see the final two sections of the *Institutes* (4.20.31–32). For a classic Huguenot statement of the distinction between lesser magistrates and private persons (with a very cautious allowance for divinely inspired exceptions to the distinction), see the "Vindiciae contra tyrannos" in *Constitutionalism and Resistance in the Sixteenth Century,* ed. and tr. Julian H. Franklin (New York: Western Publishing Co., 1969), pp. 149–56.

21. On the significance and originality of the Marian exiles as political theorists, see Donald R. Kelley, "Ideas of Resistance before Elizabeth," above.

22. John Ponet, *A Shorte Treatise of Politicke Power* (1556), facsimile (New York: Da Capo Press, 1972), sig. Dvii^r.

23. Hannah Arendt, *Eichmann in Jerusalem,* rev. ed. (New York: Penguin, 1965), p. 279.

24. Christopher Goodman, *How Superior Powers Ought to be Obeyed* (Geneva, 1558), facsimile (New York: Da Capo Press, 1972), p. 167.

25. When, later in the sixteenth century, Catholics took up resistance theory, they did not endorse this conception of conscience. In *A True, Sincere, and Modest Defense of English Catholics,* William Allen cites various Protestant authors, including Knox and Goodman, on justified resistance, but insists that where the Protestants rely on their private consciences ("their private folly and fantasy," their "particular imaginations"), Catholics "do commit the direction of matters so important to the Church" (ed. Robert M. Kingdon [Ithaca: Cornell University Press, 1965], p. 142).

26. For his conception of the "freedom" of "Ethnicks" (pagans) with regard to tyrannicide, Ponet is unquestionably thinking of Cicero's views, especially in the *Oratio pro Milone,* from which Ponet quotes. See Winthrop S. Hudson, *John Ponet: Advocate of Limited Monarchy* (Chicago: University of Chicago Press, 1942), p. 85.

27. George Buchanan, *De Jure Regni apud Scotos; or, A Dialogue, concerning the due Privilege of Government in the Kingdom of Scotland* (London, 1689), pp. 51, 66. Further page references in text.

28. For the possible borrowing, see *King Lear,* ed. Kenneth Muir, The Arden Shakespeare (London: Methuen, 1972), p. 146 (note on 4.2.49–50). For "court holy-water" (meaning flattery), see *Lear* 3.2.10, and Ponet, *Shorte Treatise,* sig. Mii^r ("This is not holy water of the court"). Muir, p. 100, cites other instances of the phrase. In quoting from *King Lear,* I will give line numbers in the Arden edition for convenience of reference, but since I accept the arguments for the two distinct texts of *Lear* and for the Folio version as Shakespeare's own revision of the play, and since—as my analysis will make clear—I believe the Folio version to intensify the themes on which I am focusing, I will (unless specifically indicated) accept substantive readings only from the Folio. I have used *The Norton Facsimile of the First Folio of Shakespeare,* ed. Charlton Hinman (New York: Norton, 1968); and *King Lear 1608 (Pied Bull Quarto),* Shakespeare Quarto Facsimiles 1 (Oxford: Clarendon Press, 1939). All other Shakespeare plays are cited from Alfred Harbage, gen. ed., *William Shakespeare: The Complete Works* (Baltimore: Penguin, 1969). For recent work on the texts of *Lear,* see notes 34 and 60 below.

29. Kenneth Muir, "Shakespeare and Politics," in *Shakespeare in a Changing World,* ed. Arnold Kettle (New York: International Publishers, 1964), p. 72. That corruption at court was a problem that came to the fore in England in the first decade of the seventeenth century is argued in a famous and widely influential essay by J. E. Neale, "The Elizabethan Political Scene," in *Essays in Elizabethan History* (New York: St. Martin's, 1958), pp. 59–84. Neale's conclusions are supported in modified form in Joel Hurstfield, "Political Corruption in Modern England: The Historian's Problem" and "The Political Morality of Early Stuart Statesmen," in *Freedom, Corruption, and Government in Elizabethan England* (Cambridge: Harvard University Press, 1973), pp. 137–62, 183–96.

30. In response to the murderers' appeal to the king's authorization, Clarence does not dispute their loyalty to Richard but points out their indifference to a higher law, offering the standard Protestant justification for disobedience: "Erroneous vassals! the great King of Kings / Hath in his law commanded / That thou shalt do no murder. Will you then / Spurn at his edict, and fulfil a man's?" (*Richard III* 1.4.190–93).

31. For a cogent analysis of Lear's initial plan as politically shrewd and workable, see Harry V. Jaffa, "The Limits of Politics: *King Lear,* Act 1, Scene 1," in *Shakespeare's Politics,* ed. Allan Bloom and Harry V. Jaffa (1964; reprint, Chicago: University of Chicago Press, 1981), pp. 113–45; for the greater and more coherent dramatic effect of reading the scene in this way, see G. R. Elliott, "The Initial Contrast in *Lear,*" *JEGP* 58 (1959): 251–63. Lear's goal "that future strife / May be prevented now" (1.1.43–44) appears only in the Folio. In *The True Chronicle*

Historie of King Leir, there is explicit concern over the issue that God has not granted Leir "an heyre indubitate" (line 44). See Geoffrey Bullough, ed., *Narrative and Dramatic Sources of Shakespeare* (New York: Columbia University Press, 1973), 7:338. Primogeniture did not apply to women (see Joyce Youings, *Sixteenth-Century England,* The Pelican Social History of Britain [New York: Penguin, 1984], p. 113). Rosalie Colie sees the relevance of this in "Reason and Need: *King Lear* and the 'Crisis' of the Aristocracy," in *Some Facets of King Lear: Essays in Prismatic Criticism,* ed. Rosalie L. Colie and F. T. Flahiff (Toronto: University of Toronto Press, 1974), pp. 196–98.

32. Stanley Cavell, "The Avoidance of Love: A Reading of *King Lear,*" in *Must We Mean What We Say?* (New York: Scribner's, 1969), p. 290.

33. For a powerful and (more or less) typical example, see William Gouge, "Of Domesticall Duties," in *The Workes of William Gouge,* rev. ed. (London, 1627). For this type of discourse, see Gordon J. Schochet, *Patriarchalism in Political Thought* (Oxford: Blackwell, 1975).

34. The assignment of this speech to Goneril is a Folio alteration. Randall McLeod is correct in noting that the Folio adds to Goneril's part and that Goneril is "cooler" in the Folio, but I think that he very much misses the nature of cruelty in the play in seeing this coolness as making Goneril milder in the Folio ("'*Gon.* No more, the text is foolish,'" in *The Division of the Kingdoms: Shakespeare's Two Versions of King Lear,* ed. Gary Taylor and Michael Warren [Oxford: Clarendon Press, 1983], pp. 155–93). This volume will henceforth be cited as *Division.*

35. This helps explain why, as Edwin Muir puts it, Goneril and Regan "have a good conscience, even a touch of self-righteousness" ("The Politics of *King Lear,*" in *Essays on Literature and Society,* rev. ed. [Cambridge: Harvard University Press, 1965], p. 40).

36. Bradley states this view strongly. See A. C. Bradley, *Shakespearean Tragedy* (1904; reprint, New York: Meridian, 1955), p. 256.

37. Sheldon P. Zitner has noticed the morally alert courtliness of this initial exchange in "*King Lear* and Its Language" (in *Some Facets of King Lear,* p. 6). Barish and Waingrow note that Edmund "takes Kent as his model in the forms of service" ("'Service' in *King Lear,*" 350).

38. See Annabel Patterson, *Censorship and Interpretation: The Conditions of Writing and Reading in Early Modern England* (Madison: University of Wisconsin Press, 1984), p. 71. Patterson argues for the political indeterminacy of the play, but if *Lear* can be seen as supporting Parliamentary privilege, especially with regard to the king's highly unpopular plan for "Great Britain," then this provides an immediate context in which the division of the kingdom(s) could have been positively rather than negatively conceived. I owe this suggestion to Leah Marcus (for the issue of the unification of the kingdoms, see Marcus, "*Cymbeline* and the Unease of Topicality," below).

39. Beth Goldring, "*Cor.*'s Rescue of Kent," in *Division,* pp. 143–51.

40. For the distinction between menials and "serving-men," see I. M., *A Health to the Gentlemanly Profession of Serving-Men,* Shakespeare Association Facsimiles 3 (London: Oxford University Press, 1931).

41. Goneril's initial complaint against Lear has to do with Lear's defense of the

Fool against one of her "gentlemen" (1.3.1–2). In the Folio, where Goneril is addressing Oswald in this scene, it is unlikely that the "gentleman" against whom Lear defended the Fool is Oswald, but if it is (as is more likely in the Quarto), the situation referred to exactly parallels that in *Twelfth Night* (1.5) of Fool versus Steward.

42. On the class implications of *dog* versus *brach*, see Muir's note on 1.4.110, in the Arden *Lear*, pp. 39–40.

43. See William Empson, "Fool in *Lear*," in *The Structure of Complex Words* (London: Chatto and Windus, 1964), pp. 129–30.

44. Lines 1.4.321–32 (Arden), from "This man hath had good counsel" to "When I have show'd th' unfitness," are a Folio addition.

45. Buchanan, *De Jure Regni apud Scotos*, p. 61.

46. Barish and Waingrow, "'Service' in *King Lear*," p. 353.

47. The substitution of "super-serviceable" for the Quarto's "superfinical" is one of the most telling pieces of evidence for the Folio's greater clarity about the themes that I have been tracing.

48. A word must be said about the social dimension of Kent's attack on Oswald. Jonathan Dollimore has recently objected to its class bias. He sees Kent as having internalized the play's "dominant ideology of property and power" and therefore as insulting Oswald "in terms of the latter's lack of material wealth" and consequent dependence on service (*Radical Tragedy: Religion, Ideology, and Power in the Drama of Shakespeare and His Contemporaries* [Chicago: University of Chicago Press, 1984], p. 201). Dollimore (following Muir's notes) is certainly correct about the social orientation of Kent's language, but his interpretation of this seems to me misguided. Oswald is certainly not to be imagined as poor. To be the steward of a noble household was a very high and respectable position; it could open the way to "gentle" status and to yet further advancement. See, for instance, the biography of William Ffarington, Esq., of Worden, Lancashire, steward until 1594 to Lord Ferdinando Strange, earl of Derby, in *The Stanley Papers*, pt. 2, *The Derby Household Books*, ed. F. R. Raines (Manchester: Chetham Society, 1853), pp. xviii–xcviii. See also Paul V. B. Jones, *The Household of a Tudor Nobleman*, University of Illinois Studies in the Social Sciences 6 (1917); and Mark Girouard, *Life in the English Country House* (New Haven: Yale University Press, 1978), pp. 82–83. Unless Oswald is finely, even ostentatiously, dressed in a very grand version of Goneril's livery, many of Kent's insults make no sense, nor does Lear's remark about Oswald's "borrowed pride" (2.4.183). Kent's descriptions of Oswald as "beggarly," and so on, are ironic, meant to call attention to the fact (of service) that Oswald's manner and dress seek to deny. For Oswald as an "ordinary courtier" (as opposed to extraordinary types like Kent or Sidney), see Frank Whigham, *Ambition and Privilege: The Social Tropes of Elizabethan Courtesy Theory* (Berkeley: University of California Press, 1984), pp. 20–21.

49. I have largely followed the First Folio here but have accepted from the Quarto "renege" for "revenge" in line 75, and "gale" for "gall" in line 76. The Folio version of line 74, reading "being" rather than "bring" (Q), is grammatically slightly rougher but conceptually more powerful. To read "naught" instead

of "nought" (Q) in line 77 creates (or recaptures from the stage) a highly significant pun: "knowing nothing" and "knowing wickedness."

50. See *Sejanus, his Fall*, act 1, lines 34–41, in *Ben Jonson*, ed. C. H. Herford and Percy and Evelyn Simpson (Oxford: Clarendon Press, 1932), 4:356, and see 9:598 for the Juvenalian source. The passage in *Lear* is closer to Jonson than to Juvenal. Muir, Arden *Lear*, p. xxi, notes the connection.

51. For the quotation, see Luther, *Warning to His Dear German People*, p. 20. Jonson's treatment does not suggest this dialectic.

52. It is relevant to the political meaning of the defense of "folly" and plain-speaking in the play that in the *Shorte Treatise*, Ponet presents himself as a kind of Fool, speaking "not so finely as som others can, but boisteously after my rude maner" (Kiiᵛ). Luther adopted the persona of "a Court-fool" in the preface to the *Appeal to the Ruling Class [of Germany]*, (*Selections*, Dillenberger, p. 404). For a powerful meditation on the function of this persona, see Robert Weimann, "History and the Issue of Authority in Representation: The Elizabethan Theater and the Reformation," *NLH* 17 (1986): 456.

53. Zitner, "*Lear* and Its Language," in *Some Facets of King Lear*, p. 9.

54. In "The Diminution of Kent," Michael Warren suggests that Kent and Gloucester are dramatic counterpoises—when one is in focus, the other is not (*Division*, pp. 59–73).

55. The Folio perhaps weakens Gloucester's protest at this point by cutting lines 137–41a. The acknowledgment of Kent's "fault," however, is also cut.

56. David Bevington has pointed out to me that Gloucester's not following Cornwall offstage could easily be played as dithering, rather than as defiant non-compliance. In either case, however, he does not comply.

57. Muir's assertion (Arden *Lear*, p. 63) that Cornwall is "subordinate" to Regan is based on a very dubious reading of Regan's "interruption" of Cornwall at 2.1.117–18. Lear twice speaks of "the Duke of Cornwall and his wife" (2.4.94, 113), and it should also perhaps be noted (as Elliott, "Initial Contrast," p. 261, does) that in act 1, scene 1, after the disinheriting of Cordelia, Lear seems to see himself as dividing the kingdom between Cornwall and Albany (1.1.126–27), his "beloved sons" (1.1.137).

58. For a very similar discussion of the opposition between authority and humanity in the play, see Weimann, "History and the Issue of Authority," p. 473.

59. A striking feature of the way in which moral obligations are conceived of in the play is that they are always put in terms of "duty," never in terms of "conscience." This perhaps reflects the play's stress on concrete human relations as the source of morality, and it perhaps also reflects the thoroughgoing secularism of the play. "Conscience" appears both in Holinshed (Bullough, *Sources*, 7:317), and in *Leir* (line 880; Bullough, *Sources*, 7:359).

60. Elimination of references to a French invasion is one of the most consistent departures of the Folio from the Quarto. Steven Urkowitz has argued that in the Folio substitution of "a power already *footed*" for "a power already *landed*" in 3.5.13, rebellion rather than invasion is suggested (*Shakespeare's Revision of King Lear* [Princeton: Princeton University Press, 1980], p. 73). Gary Taylor sees the

Folio alterations to the latter part of the play as systematically emphasizing rebellion rather than invasion, and he notes that, with regard to Jacobean politics, this
made the Folio more rather than less radical ("Monopolies, Show Trials, Disas-
ter, and Invasion: *King Lear* and Censorship," in *Division,* p. 80).

61. This is emphasized in the Folio, in which Gloucester is called a "traitor" or
"treacherous" twice more than in the Quarto.

62. For the theory of judicial torture, see John H. Langbein, *Torture and the
Law of Proof* (Chicago: University of Chicago Press, 1977).

63. In performance, a director would have to decide whether or not to make
this servant one of those holding the chair in which Gloucester is bound.

64. Mary Hallowell Perkins, *The Servant Problem in English Literature* (Boston:
R. G. Badger, 1928), p. 75.

65. Compare Sidney Shanker, *Shakespeare and the Uses of Ideology* (The Hague:
Mouton, 1975): "passivity could be no response desired for *Lear*" (p. 144).

66. *The Geneva Bible,* a facsimile of the 1560 edition, introduction by Lloyd E.
Berry (Madison: University of Wisconsin Press, 1969), p. 361a. According to
Peter Heylyn, King James not only found this translation extremely unsatisfactory but held that "the Notes upon the same in many places savour of Sedition"
(quoted in Hudson, *John Ponet,* p. 185). In the Authorized Version, the verse is
translated "*before thee,* O king, I have done no hurt."

67. In their extremely interesting essay, "The Language of Social Order: Individual, Society, and Historical Process in *King Lear*" (in *Literature, Language, and
Society in England 1580–1680,* ed. David Aers, Bob Hodge, and Gunther Kress
[Totowa, N.J.: Barnes and Noble, 1981]), David Aers and Gunther Kress see the
servant here (like Cordelia in scene 1) taking "the traditional ideology" so literally that "it becomes a subversive force in itself" (p. 87). This is of a piece with
taking Kent as a feudal retainer. Again, I feel the force of this suggestion but
would point to more contemporary ideological formations.

68. Albany's response is metaphysical and pagan—"this shows you are above,
/ You Justices" (F)—rather than biblical. This serves to defuse or cushion somewhat the potential radicalism of his comment (compare note 59 above, on the
absence of "conscience" as a term in the play). For the systematic quality of the
paganism of *Lear,* see William R. Elton, *King Lear and the Gods* (San Marino,
Calif.: Huntington Library, 1968). It is also worth noting that the Messenger's
account differs slightly from what we saw. The Messenger emphasizes the purely
affective side of the servant's intervention, seeing him as acting only out of a
private feeling—"thrill'd with remorse"—rather than out of the complex understanding of conscientiously limited duty that the servant articulates.

69. In the Quarto, this Gentleman's "neutral" narrative is clearly meant to
contrast with that of the compassionate Gentleman in the following scene (4.3),
which the Folio cuts. In the Folio, the Messenger's account of Gloucester's blinding is the only extended narration in the play.

70. Oswald does appear, in propria persona, in act 3. At the beginning of scene
7, he makes a brief appearance with some "intelligence" and then goes off with
Goneril and Edmund, who also make brief appearances. Shakespeare seems to
want all the wicked characters to appear in this scene.

71. Bradley, *Shakespearean Tragedy,* p. 238 (including the Johnson quote); Marvin Rosenberg, *The Masks of King Lear* (Berkeley and Los Angeles: University of California Press, 1972), p. 93.

72. Zitner, "*Lear* and Its Language," p. 10.

73. On the class implications of the weapons, see Mack, *King Lear in Our Time,* pp. 53–54.

74. Hannah Arendt, *The Origins of Totalitarianism,* expanded ed. (New York: Harcourt, Brace, 1968), p. 324.

75. Barish and Waingrow, "'Service' in *King Lear,*" p. 350.

76. Urkowitz seems to me mistaken in characterizing the Captain's exit lines in the Quarto as rationalization or self-justification (*Shakespeare's Revision of King Lear,* p. 104). The lines are an expression of determination to duty. They are perhaps based on some lines in *Leir,* in which a very eager-to-serve Messenger tells Gonorill, "Use me, trust me, commaund me: if I fayle in anything, tye me to a dung cart, and make a Scavenger's horse of me" (lines 1014–16; Bullough, *Sources,* 7:362). This figure from *Leir* lies somewhere behind the Captain and Oswald, but the *Leir* Messenger is a comic-melodramatic villain ("A purse of gold giv'n for a paltry stabbe!").

77. Aers and Hodge suggest that the Captain here is to be seen as an "employee" in the newly modern (capitalist) sense ("Language of Social Order," p. 88). I do not think the economic framework is relevant here. "Employment" is not being used in the modern sense.

78. Barish and Waingrow, "'Service' in *King Lear,*" p. 355.

79. For the speech as a rationale for the anticonventional, see Zitner, "*Lear* and Its Language," p. 4.

80. Lauro Martines, who characterizes the Renaissance as a period in which "the thrust of political power [was] such that it afforded men few choices," notes that "personal integrity must have been doubly rare then" ("The Gentleman in Renaissance Italy," p. 77).

81. *The Tempest* is more conservative than the plays, from *Hamlet* on, which precede it. There is a hint of the proper disobedience theme in Ariel's refusal to do Sycorax's "abhorred commands" (1.2.273), but the stress of the play, nevertheless, is on proper obedience rather than on proper disobedience. The explanation for the conservatism of *The Tempest* is probably to be found in its colonial context (for which see, *inter alia,* Paul Brown, "'This thing of darkness I acknowledge mine': *The Tempest* and the Discourse of Colonialism," in *Political Shakespeare: New Essays in Cultural Materialism,* ed. Jonathan Dollimore and Alan Sinfield [Ithaca: Cornell University Press, 1985], pp. 48–71).

82. For this hypothesis, see Gary Taylor, "*King Lear:* The Date and Authorship of the Folio Version," *Division,* p. 386.

83. For helpful comments on earlier drafts of this essay, I am grateful to Louis Montrose, Leonard Tennenhouse, David Bevington, Richard Helgerson, Tom Stillinger, and Lauren Berlant. I am also grateful to lively audiences at the Newberry Library, the 5-College Renaissance Seminar at Smith College, the University of Texas at Austin, and the University of Washington, St. Louis.

Cymbeline and the Unease of Topicality

In the third year of his reign, James I more than once descended upon Parliament like Jove with his "thunderbolts" to chide its members for their sluggishness with a pet project of his, the creation of Great Britain through the union of England and Scotland. He had expected his coronation in England and the Union of the Kingdoms to "grow up together" as a matter of course; instead, he had encountered "many crossings, long disputations, strange questions, and nothing done." The image of James as Jove swooping down with his thunder became a leitmotif of the parliamentary session. If the king were at distance from that legislative body, they would be safe from his blasts: "Procull a Iove, procul a Fulmine." But the king was at hand, attending closely to the debates, threatening to loose his blasts against the lawmakers if his project were not expedited.[1]

In the most important masque of the same year, Ben Jonson's *Hymenaei*, the Union of the Kingdoms was effected symbolically through the marriage of two young aristocrats from very different backgrounds. At least some contemporaries took note of the political allegory: they were able to read its essential elements as part of the Stuart project. Juno presided over the masque's marriage ritual, her name Iuno anagramatized as Unio to represent the union of England and Scotland. Far above in the heavens stood Jove her spouse with his thunderbolts, again a representation of James, who liked to describe himself as a Jove figure and as a loving husband to the nation, with Unio, a united Britain, as his wife.[2] Here, however, Jove appeared in milder aspect, his menacing thunder silenced, because in the masque, at least, the "marriage" of the kingdoms had finally taken place.

This essay is an abridged version of chapter 3 in Leah Marcus, *Puzzling Shakespeare: Local Reading and Its Discontents* (Berkeley and Los Angeles: University of California Press, 1989) and is published here by permission of the Regents of the University of California.

In Shakespeare's *Cymbeline,* written and performed perhaps two years later, at the very latest in 1610, Jove appears yet again in connection with the theme of the Union of the Kingdoms.[3] Jupiter descends, straddling an eagle, spouting fire, hurling his bolts, to castigate the mourning ghosts who "Accuse the Thunderer" of faithlessness toward the sleeping prisoner Posthumus. The god proclaims his continuing favor, promises to "uplift" the unfortunate man, and leaves upon his chest a riddling tablet that, when interpreted at the end of the play, turns out to presage the Union of the Kingdoms.[4] In terms of the play's contemporary context, Jove is clearly to be identified with King James I, the creator of Great Britain, who had a similar habit of intruding upon his subjects to lecture them when his plans for the nation went unheeded or misunderstood.

The topical identification is usually suppressed or overlooked. In *Cymbeline,* as quite regularly in Shakespeare, topical meaning has registered with generations of editors and critics as intolerable textual turbulence. The play's most obviously topical passages have been rejected as "not Shakespeare." In particular, editors have branded the mysterious tablet left for Posthumus by Jupiter as spurious: its "ludicrous" heavy-handed message is all too easy to interpret in terms of the guiding myths of the Stuart monarchy. Forty years ago, G. Wilson Knight set out to rehabilitate the prophecy as "true" Shakespeare, and his effort led him—uncharacteristically for Knight but not surprisingly, given the material he was dealing with—straight into a reading of the play as political allegory. Some editors still argue that the prophecy cannot be Shakespeare. They base their claim partly on stylistic evidence, since the passage is awkwardly at odds with other portions of the text, but even more on the grounds that it represents a political "intrusion," links the universal Shakespeare far too closely with a specific and not altogether laudable seventeenth-century cause.[5] It is as though when Jacobean ideology is at issue, Shakespeare cannot be allowed any stylistic heterogeneity, even though accepting the prophecy as Shakespeare opens up new possibilities for interpretation. Traditionally for editors and critics of the play, textual palimpsest has been preferable to the specter of a Shakespeare who could be interpreted as celebrating a Stuart political cause.

Cymbeline seems to demand that we read it as part of the milieu of the Stuart court, rather as we might explicate the exquisitely detailed and sustained political allegory of a masque by Ben Jonson. In his own formulation, it was the "nature and propertie" of such entertainments to "present alwayes some one entire bodie, or figure, consisting of distinct members, and each of those expressing it selfe, in the[ir] owne active spheare, yet all, with that generall harmonie so connexed, and disposed, as no one little part can be missing to the illustration of the whole." In these "magnificent Inventions," "the garments and ensignes deliver the nature of the person [James I] and the word the present office" of the king.[6] If we immerse ourselves in the Jacobean materials to which *Cymbeline* seems persistently to allude, we will discover that the play, like a Jonsonian court entertainment, is far more deeply and pervasively topical than even its most avid political "lock-pickers" have found it to be. But in some of its episodes, the play stubbornly refuses to make sense at the level of Stuart interpretation. Those episodes will be of particular interest to us here. If the most obviously topical materials appear intrusive in *Cymbeline,* that is in part because they are presented *as* intrusions—they are curiously static emblems or mysterious written texts which arrest the play's theatrical momentum. To undertake topical reading of *Cymbeline* is to enter a labyrinth in which political meanings are simultaneously generated and stalemated, in which the political "authorship" of James I is put forward in a series of arresting, even jarring, visitations which impose a relentless textuality upon the flow of events and which, through their resistance to assimilation in the action, undermine the very political message they seem designed to communicate.

The play's resistance to political "reading" according to the constraints of an authored document would not have the destabilizing effect it does in terms of the play's Stuart interpretation if James I had been a different type of monarch. Unlike Elizabeth, who had usually made a point of mystifying her political purposes, James insisted upon the "crystal" clarity and availability of his; he demanded that his policy utterances be "read" as his own authored documents. At least as he characteristically portrayed them, royal texts, like the policy behind them, had to be self-consistent and "legible." And he offered his subjects a plethora of texts to read. When he came down from Scotland, he brought his most illustrious book with him. *Basilikon Doron* was hastily published in a London edition in 1603 so that it could be admired by his new subjects at the same time that the new kind offered himself for their "reading." His other major books were published in England in 1604. Given James's predilection for authorship, it was perhaps not mere happenstance that some of his major policy declarations became known as *Books*—the *Book of Sports,* the *Book of Bounty.* He made a point of claiming personal proprietorship over the subject matter and style of his royal proclamations: "Most of them myself doth dictate every word. Never any proclamation of state and weight which I did not direct." In a similar way, through his sponsorship of the King James Bible, he established himself even as a "principle mover and author" behind Holy Writ, at least as it was promulgated in England. At the Hampton Court Conference of 1604, admiring bishops called him "a Living Library and a walking Study."[7]

In Scotland, King James had actually composed court entertainments. In England, he also "authored" masques in that he promoted (or at least rewarded) a new attention to architectonics and to the laws of visual perspective, so that entertainments at court not devoted to celebrating some other member of the royal family regularly centered on the king himself and his most significant policy initiatives: all lines converged upon the Jacobean "line." For better or for worse, through his own authorship, James provided would-be panegyrists with a wealth of texts which could be mimetically recapitulated in entertainments at court. The masque licensed deviations from the Jacobean political "line" but typically ended up containing them within a broader assertion of royal power and authority.[8] In proclamations, speeches, and entertainments, even (at times catastrophically) in his attempts at practical politics, James insisted on his own governing line of interpretation and political action, a line emanating from the royal wisdom, the clear "sincerity" of his heart.

The editor of *The Workes of the Most High and Mighty Prince, Iames* complained in his preface that James's subjects scattered words and jangling criticism of the king's métier of author as fast as he could gather the royal texts together, as though "Since that Booke-writing is growen into a Trade; It is as dishonorable for a *King* to write bookes; as it is for him to be a Practitioner in a *Profession*."[9] Behind the complaint are some of the new assertions about authorship or the "author-function" that have been discussed by Michel Foucault.[10] The assertion of authorship provided a way for lowborn self-made people to aspire beyond their origins. It was associated with the setting of limits upon the uncontrolled proliferation of meaning. Like his editorial assistants, King James saw himself as performing the patient authorial task of collecting meaning, arranging it, beating back the political and moral chaos of unregulated signification in order to forge diverse materials into "one Body" (Preface, B2ᵛ). It is the paradigmatic situation of authorial prerogative, whether bookish or political: the "imposition of a conclusive, self-identical meaning that transcends the seriality of displacement," and translates politically into the imposed order of absolutism.[11] James's kingship was an absolutism of the text.

The king encountered considerable resistance to his novel ideas about royal authorship and authority. According to the editor of his *Workes,* many of his subjects complained, "It had been better his Maiestie had neuer written any Bookes at all; and being written, better they had perished with the present like *Proclamations,* then haue remayned to *Posterity:* For say these Men, Little it befitts the Maiesty of a *King* to turne Clerke, and to make a warre with the penne, that were fitter to be fought with the Pike; to spend the powers of his so exquisite an vnderstanding upon papers, which had they beene spent on powder, could not but have preuayled ere this for the conquest of a Kingdome" (Preface, B2ᵛ). When James scolded his own son Prince Henry for his inattention to learning, threatening to disinherit him in favor of his brother Charles, "who was far quicker at learning and studied more earnestly," Henry answered back indirectly through his tutor, "I know what becomes a Prince. It is not necessary for me to be a professor, but a soldier and a man of the world. If my brother is as learned as they say, we'll make him Archbishop of Canterbury." His father took the retort "in no good part." [12]

Some of the same resistance to royal "authorship" is visible in *Cymbeline*, with its awkward, intrusive royal texts. In part, of course, we find such resistance because we want to find it—pursuing *différance* is usually more congenial for new historicists and other postmodernist critics than constructing idealized visions of harmony. Yet there is reason to suppose that contemporary audiences might have felt a similar discomfort with the play's call for unity under the name of Great Britain. Along with an array of relatively commonplace Stuart motifs, *Cymbeline* displays a number of specific mechanisms that work against the communication of its Stuart message, engendering an "unease of topicality" specific to this play. We might call it an "unease with Jacobean textuality." Inevitably, our sense of the relative strength of the play's Stuart message as opposed to its modes of evasion will depend on our own critical (and political) stance. And yet, in the interpretation of *Cymbeline*, as very frequently in the decipherment of the Stuart masque, we have to follow the "authorized" line of political allegory in order to discover the gaps, the devices by which, to repeat King James's own complaint about how his subjects evaded his intended meanings, the clear text is "rent asunder in contrary sences like the old Oracles of the Pagan Gods." [13] It is not enough to say that the play deconstructs its own dominant mode of signification. That can be said of every Shakespearean play. Instead, we need to look for the "local" topical meanings of the deconstruction, its particular cultural and political resonances, the specific moments in the dramatic action at which its energies burst forth. To do topical reading of *Cymbeline*, we must play the pedant along with James I, explicating political allegory in a rather straightforward, linear fashion—according to principles of unity like those associated with the rise of authorship in the late Renaissance and displayed in official "spectacles of state" like the Stuart court masque.

I

Cymbeline seductively courts topical reading by presenting its audience with a series of riddles and emblems which arouse a desire for explication. Some of them are interpreted within the play, while others are not. The effect is to make the unsolved puzzles all the more teasingly enticing. Many of the play's riddles are clustered in its final scenes. The Soothsayer twice recounts his vision of the eagle winging its way westward to vanish in the beams of the sun. First he misinterprets it to forecast Roman defeat of Cymbeline and the Britons, then he reinterprets it correctly as a sign of new Roman-British amity,

> which foreshow'd our princely eagle,
> Th' imperial Caesar, should again unite
> His favor with the radiant Cymbeline,
> Which shines here in the west.
>
> (5.5.474–77)

The cryptic tablet placed upon Posthumus's breast by Jupiter is another important riddle. It is read twice during the action—the only text so privileged in all of Shakespeare's plays—and in the Folio it is printed exactly the same way both times like a properly "authored" document.[14] At the end of the play, it is finally deciphered as linking the reunion of Posthumus and Imogen to the discovery of Cymbeline's long-lost sons and the regeneration of Britain.

Even out in remote Wales, far from the world of the court, there are emblematic "texts" to be interpreted, natural lessons in morality imprinted upon the landscape. According to the teachings of Belarius, tutor to the king's exiled sons, a hill signifies dangerous eminence like that won and lost in the courts of princes; the low mouth of their cave teaches the virtue of humble devotion. When Imogen begins breathing the mountain air of Wales, she too starts creating emblems. Her assumed name Fidele is recognized by the end of the play as a sign of her abiding faith in Posthumus despite his rejection of her. When she awakens after her deathlike sleep, she reads the flowers beside her as signifying the false pleasures of the world; the body of Cloten signifies its cares (4.2.297–98).

Shakespeare calls attention to some of the play's riddles through the device of repetition: appearing more than once, they become insistent, demand interpretation. Along with the riddles and emblems deciphered within the play, there are other repeated motifs carrying an aura of hidden significance. "Blessed Milford" Haven is a Welsh port named many times by many different characters in the course of the action; it attracts them from widely scattered places as though by magnetic force. But the almost incantatory power of "Milford" is never satisfactorily explained by any of the characters. The victory of Guiderius, Arviragus, and Belarius over the Roman forces in the narrow lane is another insistent motif that is never quite unraveled. The episode is first enacted on stage, then recounted no fewer than four times, the last in a derisive rhyme by Posthumus that casts scorn upon people who attend overmuch to riddles.

> Nay, do not wonder at it. You are made
> Rather to wonder at the things you hear
> Than to work any. Will you rhyme upon't,
> And vent it for a mock'ry? Here is one:
> "Two boys, an old man twice a boy, a lane,
> Preserv'd the Britons, was the Romans' bane."
> (5.3.53–58)

Posthumus distrusts such marveling, his facile rhyme appearing to parody the play's heavy-handed way with prophetic language. But he himself is the play's most interesting riddle. Not only does he, at the end, bear upon his breast a tablet that demands and receives interpretation, but the other characters refer to him as though he were a text in need of explication, the "catalogue of his endowments . . . tabled by his side" and he, to be perused "by items" (1.4.5–7). Posthumus is Shakespeare's creation. He does not occur in the historical sources.[15] His past contains some mystery. One bystander acknowledges, "I cannot delve him to the root" (1.1.28). He is praised for his "fair outward" and for virtuous "stuff" within; he comes of noble stock and—apparently—prosperous estate, yet appears impoverished, without the power or influence he might be expected to have to combat his sudden banishment.

In the artistic economy of *Cymbeline,* riddles exist to be interpreted—interpreted, as riddles conventionally are, through the finding of a single answer that dissolves their ambiguity into clarity. In fact, all of the play's riddles can be interpreted by reference to the play's contemporary Stuart milieu—even the cryptic "text" that is Posthumus himself. It is a marvelous device for arresting the free proliferation of topical meaning and focusing interpretation upon a single set of motifs. What is accomplished by such revelation of meaning in terms of the texts of James I is another matter, however.

It is, by now, pretty generally accepted by Shakespeareans willing to consider a Stuart *Cymbeline* at all that the play's emphasis on the ideal of a united Britain and its vision of empire—the Roman eagle winging its way westward to vanish into the British sun—can be interpreted in terms of James I's cherished project for creating a new "empire" called Great Britain, a revival of the ancient kingdom of Britain which had, according to popular legend, been founded by Brute, son of Aeneas.[16] Almost as soon as James had arrived from Scotland to claim the English throne in

1603, he had issued his "Proclamation for the uniting of England and Scotland," which called upon the "Subjects of both the Realmes" to consider themselves "one people, brethren and members of one body"; the next year, by proclamation, he assumed the "Stile, of King of Great Britaine." His subjects were blanketed with propaganda for the union. The royal project was lauded in poetry and public pageantry, an organizing motif of his coronation pageant in 1604 and the Lord Mayor's Shows for 1605 and 1609 and of courtly entertainments like Jonson's *Hymenaei;* it was also publicized through treatises and pamphlets, even through the coin of the realm. One of the new gold pieces issued by James I bore the inscription "Faciamus eos in gentem unam."[17]

However, his subjects on both sides of the Anglo-Scottish border were less than enthusiastic about the proposal, muttering patriotic slogans about their nation's safety in isolation, much like Cloten and the wicked queen in the play, displaying distrust, even open hatred, toward their "brethren" across the border or (on a higher level of discourse) stating serious reservations, on grounds of legal and religious principle, about James I's strong identification with Roman ideals and institutions. A visiting foreign dignitary observed, "The little sympathy between the two nations, the difference of their laws, the jealousy of their privileges, the regard of the succession, are the reasons they will never . . . join with another, as the King wishes."[18] But James persisted nonetheless. The political plot of *Cymbeline,* in marked contrast to the prevailing spirit of nationalism in Shakespeare's earlier history plays, culminates in a vision of harmonious internationalism and accommodation that mirrors James's own policy. The British and Roman ensigns wave "Friendly together," the fragmented kingdom of Britain is reunited, and the nation embarks on a new and fertile era of peace.

The romantic plot of *Cymbeline* can be related to the same set of goals. James was an indefatigable matchmaker among his individual subjects, as among nations and peoples. He took particular pride in state marriages that bridged political and religious differences like *Hymenaei*'s union between Lady Frances Howard, from a pro-Catholic, pro-Spanish family, and the earl of Essex, from a line of staunch Calvinists. From *Hymenaei* in 1606 to the masques for the Palsgrave Frederick and the king's daughter Elizabeth in 1613, nearly every court marriage important enough to be celebrated with a wedding masque at all was celebrated as a particular instance of the king's wider project for uniting England and Scotland. One of the new coins he issued in honor of Great Britain even bore an inscription from the marriage service: "Quae Deus conjunxit nemo separet," "Those whom God hath joined together let no man put asunder." A prefatory poem to one of the wedding masques asked, "Who can wonder then / If he, that marries kingdomes, marries men?"[19] The ruptured, then revitalized marriage of Imogen and Posthumus in *Cymbeline,* like the actual marriages engineered by James, can be linked to his higher policy of creating a united Britain out of nations in discord.

So can the barriers to union: the play's constant quibbling with matters of law and ceremony echo the same milieu of controversy. Attending to some of the fine points of the debate will aid us in reading the "text" of Posthumus. When James I left Edinburgh for London in 1603, he left his original subjects without a resident monarch. An integral part of his project for the creation of Great Britain through the union of England and Scotland was the naturalization of the Scots. His motto for the project was "Unus Rex, unus Grex, & una Lex": one king, one flock, one law. But that last phrase posed unexpected difficulties, since England and Scotland operated under very different legal systems. England had its venerable common law and Scotland the civil law, essentially a Roman code. Despite his disclaimers, it seems clear that James I preferred Scots law over the English system and hoped to mold Britain's "one law" in accordance with the Roman model, which he considered clearer, more succinct, and more hospitable to his views on royal absolutism. But that hope was dashed by English parliamentarians and common lawyers, who viewed the import of aliens and the imposition of an alien legal system as tantamount to national extinction. When James descended upon them like Jove with his thunderbolts, the immediate question at hand was the naturalization of the Scots. Despite the attempts of James's supporters to argue for the honor and reasonableness of their brethren to the north, members of Parliament conjured up horrific visions of beggarly Scotsmen swarming across the border and devouring England's prosperity. Parliament refused to naturalize the king's Scottish subjects until the question of law was settled, preferably by bringing Scotland into accordance with England.[20]

Meanwhile, the Scots had their own fears about the union: like the English, Scottish parliamentarians were adamant about preserving their "ancient rights" and liberties. But the Scots were even more adamant about preserving their own reformed Kirk. James's Project for Union called for the creation of a single British church, a ceremonial church upon the Anglican model. When it came to this aspect of the union, it was the Scots who were anti-Roman, worried that their pure Kirk would be corrupted by a union with "popish" Anglicanism and enforced conformity with English canon law, a system also based upon Roman civil law. In Jonson's *Hymenaei,* Anglican ritual is celebrated as a comely descendant of Roman ceremonial and Roman civil law; it is attacked by "untempered humors" and "affections" but successfully defended by

Reason and Order.[21] In actuality, the "humors" of the Scots were less easily overcome. By 1607, James's project for Great Britain was foundering on the rocks of English and Scottish prejudice. He was willing to modify his original proposal for "one law" and create a union that preserved the distinctness of the two legal systems. But both parliaments balked. In England the Scots were scorned as aliens, mercilessly pilloried in plays and satires. Numerous duels were fought between Englishmen and Scotsmen. Scots were barred from holding public office and denied the precedence of rank: on ceremonial occasions, English parvenus would elbow out Scots of the old nobility. Since Parliament refused to remedy the situation, James I went to the courts. Through the famous case of the Post Nati, decided in 1608, he sought to settle the question of the naturalization of the Scots and thereby clear the way for his beloved Project for Union. Never, his advisers warned the nation, would there be a real unity of kingdoms until the "mark of the stranger" had been removed from the Scots.[22]

The Post Nati were all those Scotsmen born after James had ascended the English throne, theoretically uniting the kingdoms. James had proclaimed them citizens of Britain, and according to the Roman code they were already citizens, yet in England they were deprived of any recourse at law. The case of the Post Nati concerned a dispute over land titles and hinged on whether a Scotsman born since the Proclamation of Union had the right to defend his ownership of property held in England in a court of English law. But despite the narrowness of the immediate problem it posed, it was perhaps the most important case of the reign, argued at the King's Bench, then moved on account of its momentous implications into the Exchequer, pondered by every one of England's highest justices. The case established principles about the rights of alien peoples which became fundamental to all later treatments of the same issues, such as the constitutional arguments of the American colonists before 1776. The case of the Post Nati was widely publicized, a matter of alehouse conversation; several of its most important documents were published. By nearly unanimous decision of the judges involved, the Post Nati were declared citizens, entitled to recourse at English law despite their continuing ties to the alien Roman system.[23]

We cannot be sure whether Shakespeare's play was written before or after the case of the Post Nati was settled in 1608; *Cymbeline* is usually dated 1608 or 1609. In any event, the probable outcome of the case was well known in advance. But in the character of Posthumus, the one "born after," a man theoretically married to Imogen in the Temple of Jupiter and therefore "wedded" to her kingdom yet kept in isolation and suspension, deprived of his natural rights, Shakespeare creates a dramatic figure whose alienation and restoration symbolically parallel the fortunes of James's subjects "born after," the Post Nati. *Cymbeline* recasts the faltering national union as a beleaguered marriage between two individuals, Imogen and Posthumus, and thereby invests the legal and political issues bound up with the project for Great Britain with a troubling immediacy, an urgency that seems to quicken toward a concrete political goal— James I's goal of relieving the agony of exile and creating a genuine union.

II

The divided Britain of *Cymbeline* is not to be equated with the wrangling Britain of James I. Rather, it is a partial analogue and prefiguration. In the Britain ruled by Cymbeline, as in the Britain of James I, a "marriage" has produced dislocation. The situation of Posthumus at the beginning of the play is in many ways like that of the Scots after 1603. His surname Leonatus—born of or under the Lion—suggests James's well-known device of the Stuart lion; the king was fond of comparing the Scots to his own heraldic animal. [24] Posthumus is a nobly born beggar, like many of the Scottish aristocrats, at least as they appeared to the more prosperous English. To his humiliation, he cannot reciprocate Imogen's gift of the diamond with a love token of equal value (1.1.121–22). He is an altogether proper gentleman yet held in low esteem. He has until the marriage held the office of gentleman of the bedchamber, a position monopolized by Scotsmen even in James I's court at Whitehall during the early years of the reign. But through the marriage, Posthumus is deprived and exiled, just as the citizens of Scotland were distanced from their king and from the center of government when James assumed the English crown.

Posthumus has gained the respect of most of Cymbeline's courtiers. But like the Scots, he is divided between Britain and Rome and, as a result, held in suspicion, particularly after the outbreak of Cymbeline's war against Rome. His birth under a "Jovial star," his latinate name, his close ancestral ties with the Continent, especially Rome and France, place him in an enemy camp. But in the Britain of the play, unlike the Britain of James I, he has no king to take his part against the local chauvinists. The similarities between James and Cymbeline have often been noted in topical readings of the play: both kings have two sons and a daughter; like James, Cymbeline is associated by the final scenes with a vision of the rebirth of empire. Unlike James, however, and unlike the Cymbeline of Shakespeare's historical sources, who was noted for unfaltering devotion to Rome, the Cymbeline of the play has abandoned his earlier allegiance to Caesar Augustus and is as stubbornly anti-Roman for most of the action as any of his subjects. He lends a sympathetic ear to the patriotic sloganeering of the wicked queen and Cloten, who, like members of the English House of Commons, plead against Roman influence and the "Roman yoke" on grounds of their ancient British liberties. Cloten, in particular, is a fanatic about law. His speech is peppered with idle legalisms: even his wooing of Imogen is a "case" in which her woman will be enlisted as his "lawyer" (3.3.76–77). King Cymbeline himself, like his wife and doltish stepson, is a fervent advocate of native British law—the law of Mulmutius mangled by Caesar's sword. Mulmutius and the "ancient liberties of the House" were similarly prominent in contemporary parliamentary speeches *against* James I and his notions of empire and royal prerogative.[25]

But Posthumus is not only a victim of such prejudice—he nurtures prejudices of his own. He is almost as devoted to legalistic language as Cloten.[26] A much more devastating flaw is his susceptibility to the insinuations of Iachimo, an Italian, who convinces him all too easily that Imogen his wife is unchaste. Shakespeare ingeniously (albeit anachronistically) separates two levels of Roman influence in the play—that of the ancient Rome of Caesar Augustus, associated with the ideals of James I, with peace and a benevolent code of law, and that of the Renaissance Rome of the degenerate Italians, associated rather with perversion, bawdry, and amorality. It is probably not mere happenstance that Shakespeare modeled the romantic plot in accordance with a tale out of the bawdy Italian Boccaccio. Posthumus's easily aroused distrust of the virtuous Imogen recasts into personal terms the Scottish prejudice against the Church of England, that sluttish "Whore of Babylon." He displays a paranoid willingness to doubt Imogen even before the bargain with Iachimo is concluded—a trait that the wily Italian attributes to "some religion" in him (1.4.137–38).

Imogen is far too full and complete a character to be reduced to the level of allegory, but she is associated with images of ceremonial worship throughout the play. Her chamber is likened to a chapel and resembles an elaborately decorated sanctuary, its roof "fretted" with "golden cherubins" (2.4.89). She is several times referred to as a "temple": by a lord of the court ("That temple, thy fair mind," 2.1.64), by Arviragus ("so divine a temple," 4.2.56), and finally, by the repentant Posthumus ("The temple / Of virtue was she; yea, and she herself," 5.5.222–23). She is also associated with the enactment of due ceremony. It is Imogen who observes in Wales that the "breach of custom / Is breach of all" (4.2.10–11), and Guiderius reiterates her attention to decorum when he hears his brother's "solemn music" in lament of her seeming death: "All solemn things / Should answer solemn accidents" (4.2.192–93).

In Wales, Imogen does not recognize her long-lost brothers, nor they her; yet there is an immediate bond of sympathy among them, which is given outward expression through acts of religious propriety. The two princes in exile are, in fact, remarkably liturgically minded for a couple of untutored savages. Their pagan ceremonies curiously resemble the ceremonial Anglicanism advocated by James I and Archbishop Bancroft but distrusted by Puritan elements in the church. They greet the sun with a "morning's holy office," like matins; their dirge over the "dead" Imogen, her body laid with the head toward the east, is spoken antiphonally to music, much like an Anglican liturgy. They have, of course, been guided by Belarius, but he comments on their "invisible instinct" for civility as for valor (4.2.178). Their innate respect for ritual and due ceremony is charged with political significance. It suggests, as James I and his churchmen often argued in defense of the Anglican Church against English Puritans and Scotch Presbyterians, that liturgical worship is not some popish import but a native cultural form, as natural to the British as their valor. Their ceremonialism is pagan, to be sure, but a precursor of Anglican worship, like Cymbeline's thankful feasts and rituals in the Temple of Jove at the end of the play or like the Roman rituals of *Hymenaei*. It would be easy to make too much of the play's frequent allusions to questions of law and ceremony: such passages can be interpreted on many different levels. But taken in the aggregate, they shape a subtle pattern of reference that links the various factions in the Britain of King Cymbeline to analogues in the renascent Britain of King James I, the "parliamentary" xenophobia of Cloten and his mother balanced against Posthumus's hysterical willingness to heed rumors of "popish" Italian defilement.

The one central character who is always true to the union is Imogen herself. Her devotion to Posthumus does not falter even in the face of compelling evidence that he has "forgot Britain." She suffers as much from the enforced separation as those whose narrowness of vision brought it about, yet even she is subject to error and has something to learn about the nature of prejudice. At the beginning of the play, she scornfully rejects Cloten on the grounds that he and Posthumus have nothing at all in common: "I chose an eagle / And did avoid a puttock" (1.1.141–42). Cloten is not worth her husband's "mean'st garment." Even her scornful term "puttock" may appear too kind to Cloten, that dreadful "mass of unhingement." Yet Posthumus is also less than perfect. He and Cloten undergo parallel experiences, like a man and his distorted shadow. Both are step- or foster sons to the king, both woo Imogen, they fight one another, both gamble with Iachimo and lose. As Cloten sets off to rape Imogen, he assumes Posthumus's garments. By act 4, both men have literally or figuratively "lost their heads."[27] When Imogen mistakes the decapitated body of one for the other, their identities are temporarily superimposed. She weeps over the puttock, thinking him an eagle; clothes become the man.

The scene of Imogen's desolate but misguided grief over Cloten is difficult to read without an uncomfortable admixture of levity; it is also difficult to stage effectively. Stephen Booth's suggestion that the two roles be played by a single actor removes the most obvious incongruity,[28] but there remain awkward moments, perilously close to low comedy, like Imogen's reaching out toward what she takes to be Posthumus's "Jovial face" only to find the head unfortunately missing. And yet the scene makes excellent sense as illustration of the "Jacobean line." Imogen's error demonstrates the interchangeability of the two men, considered only in terms of their outward endowments, and therefore serves as a forceful argument against blind prejudice of either the English or the Scottish variety. The political fragmentation of a divided Britain deprived of its Jove-like or "Jovial" head is associated with bizarre images of physical and psychic dissolution.

Throughout the play, prejudice is associated with extinction and dismemberment—a vision of a part, not the whole. When Posthumus is convinced of Imogen's falseness, he vows to "tear her limb-meal"; yet without her, he is "speechless," his name at "last gasp" (1.5.54–55); he has "forgot himself" and his identity becomes increasingly problematic. Imogen unknowingly echoes her husband's wish to destroy her when she discovers his failed trust: "I must be ripp'd. To pieces with me!" (3.4.33); "I am nothing," she declares as she embraces the dismembered body of her "master" (4.2.368). Cloten's actual mutilation parallels Posthumus's loss of identity as a result of his own and others' prejudice. When the seemingly lifeless body of Imogen is laid beside the headless corpse, both partners to the union appear to have become the "nothing" each is without the other. Of course, the extinction is apparent, not real: Posthumus is still alive. But Imogen does not know that. She awakens, mourns her slain "master" and embraces him, only to swoon again like one dead upon the lifeless body as on a "bloody pillow."

Discovering this grisly mockery of the ideal of union, Lucius comments on its unnaturalness: "For nature doth abhor to make his bed / With the defunct, or sleep upon the dead" (4.2.138–39). As a sequence of events, *Cymbeline*'s grotesque tableaux of dismemberment are improbable, even ludicrous. But they can be read as emblems of the political effects of prejudice. Genuine union is organic: one part of it cannot exist without the other. Cloten is a body without a head; so Posthumus has been a subject unnaturally deprived of his "head," the king. In his pub-

lished speeches and proclamations, James I frequently used similar images of dismemberment—a body without a head—to convince his English and Scotch subjects of the bizarre indecorousness of continuing
to thwart the Union of the Kingdoms, a "marriage" suspended as a result of needless exile and alienation like the marriage of Posthumus and
Imogen.[29]

Imogen clings faithfully to the ideal of union, achieving a certain pa-
thos despite the horror of her symbiotic attachment to the mutilated
body. But that lowest point in her fortunes is soon transcended. The
Roman soothsayer and Lucius, the Roman commander, encounter Imogen and the corpse just as the Soothsayer has interpreted his vision of the
eagle winging its way westward into the sun. On stage, the visual image
of a union in extinction is counterpoised against the Soothsayer's words
of prophecy, promising vigor and prosperity to come. Imogen quickly
returns to consciousness. It is almost as though she is roused by the
Soothsayer's vision from the "nothing" she has felt herself to be in symbiotic identification with the corpse. She buries the body and attaches
herself as a page to Lucius, the honorable Roman: the heiress to Britain's
crown adopts the cause of its opposite in war.

As Imogen and the other characters gradually converge upon "blessed"
Milford Haven, the dismembered and alienated fragments of the kingdom are slowly gathered back together and the riddles gradually resolved. Milford Haven, as numerous commentators have noted, was the
Welsh port where James I's ancestor Henry VII had landed when he came
to claim the kingdom in the name of the Tudors. James's descent from
Henry gave him his right to the English throne; his identification with
the first Tudor was so intense that when he died he was, at his own wish,
buried in Henry VII's tomb.[30] As Henry's claim formed the basis of James
I's project for a reunited Britain, so Henry's landing place becomes the
locus for the reunion of the lovers and a healing of the fragmentary vision
that has kept the two apart. All of the play's tangled lines converge upon
the point at which the "Jacobean line" originated. Imogen is more right
than she knows when she exclaims, "Accessible is none but Milford way"
(3.2.82).

Imogen and Posthumus become unknowing precursors of a new era
of peace and accommodation between the warring Rome and Britain
when each of them changes sides. As Imogen becomes "Roman," so
Posthumus, who has been living in Rome and arrives back in Britain
among the "Italian gentry," assumes instead the guise of a British peasant
to fight alongside another group of exiles, Belarius and the king's long-
lost sons. The riddle of the man and two boys in the narrow lane who
save the Britons from the Romans is taken from Scots history and was

an exploit actually performed by three Scotsmen named Hay—the ancestors of James I's favorite Lord Hay,[31] one of the Scots who, like Posthumus in the play, had to contend with insular British prejudice. The
three heroes in the lane, like Posthumus himself, are associated with the
heraldic animal of James: they "grin like lions" as they repel the attack
(5.3.38). The joining of the two lines of "lions" to uphold Britain is a
common motif in contemporary materials supporting the idea of Great
Britain. The emblem of James I in Henry Peacham's popular collection
Minerva Britanna; Or, A Garden of Heroical Devices (London, 1612), for
example, is addressed "To the High and mightie *IAMES*, King of greate
Britaine" (p. 11) and depicts the English and Scottish lions uniting (as
they did in the royal person of the king) to hold up the crown of "famous
Britaine."

Through the battle in the narrow lane, Posthumus proves himself
the equal of the sons of Cymbeline. Even the most narrow-spirited of
James I's English subjects admitted that the Scots were excellent fighters.
By his valorous part in the action Posthumus demonstrates his possession of the proverbial "strength o' the' Leonati" and its value to Cymbeline's side. His association with things Roman and French is no barrier to
his ability to act for the good of Britain. But no one recognizes that yet,
because no one knows who he is. Indeed, he is practically invisible, effaced from accounts of the glorious victory in the lane. Just as James I
and his advisors had claimed that there could be no Act of Union until
the "mark of the stranger" had been removed from the Scots, so the
vision of a united Britain that concludes the play depends on the discovery and reading of the "text" of Posthumus.

Even without a disguise, Posthumus has been an unsolved enigma for
others and "to himself unknown." He shifts his garments and allegiance
with protean speed—he is first Italian, then British, then Roman. Ironically, he makes the final shift out of a suicidal wish to "spend his breath"
to aid the cause of his dead Imogen, unaware that she is still alive and has
also changed sides. His frantic oscillation between the two warring nations must give way to the recognition that his marriage is still intact.
Through it, the two nations have already begun to dissolve into a new
composite entity. To rediscover who he is and what his experiences
mean, Posthumus must go through a symbolic union-in-death with Imogen just as Imogen had earlier with him. In the British prison he hopes
only for reunion beyond the grave; he falls asleep communing silently
with the wife he believes he has destroyed. But as in Imogen's encounter
with Lucius and the Soothsayer, Posthumus's embracing of death is lifted
and transformed by a vision of renewed life. His seeming extinction is
like the political extinction feared by English and Scottish patriots who

opposed the Project for Union—more apparent than real. His noble ancestors appear "as in an apparition" to offer him back his identity and plead for his restoration to the esteem, prosperity, and marriage befitting his noble worth. His mother demands,

> With marriage wherefore was he mock'd,
>   To be exil'd, and thrown
> From Leonati seat, and cast
>   From her his dearest one,
>   Sweet Imogen?
>
> (5.4.58–62)

In pleading for Posthumus, his forebears plead for a restoration of the Union of the Kingdoms. Posthumus's continuing deprivation is a "harsh and potent" injury upon a "valiant race," the race of the Leonati, or the Scots. But Posthumus is not only an analogue of the exiled Scots; he is a more generalized figure whose exile, trial, and restoration take on theological dimensions and assume the pattern of spiritual rejuvenation. Jove descends and announces, in answer to the prayer of the Leonati,

> Whom best I love, I cross; to make my gift,
> The more delay'd, delighted. Be content.
> Your low-laid son our godhead will uplift.
> His comforts thrive, his trials well are spent.
>
> (5.4.101–4)

Exaltavit humiles: as Britain has been saved and ennobled by the valorous deeds of its "low-laid" exiles, so Jove will "uplift" the exiles themselves. The god assents to the prayers of the Leonati, leaving upon Posthumus's breast the riddling tablet that ties the restoration of the kingdom of Britain to the end of his "miseries" and banishment.

The new era of empire, of peace, harmony, and fertility, commences, appropriately enough, with the public reading of Posthumus's "rare" book; "When as a lion's whelp shall, to himself unknown, without seeking find, and be embrac'd by a piece of tender air; and when from a stately cedar shall be lopp'd branches, which, being dead many years, shall after revive, be jointed to the old stock, and freshly grow; then shall Posthumus end his miseries, Britain be fortunate and flourish in peace and plenty" (5.4.138–44). No sooner is the text explicated by the Soothsayer, now called Philharmonus, than Cymbeline announces, "My peace we will begin" (5.5.461). And reading the text of Posthumus provides the necessary keys for the correct interpretation of the vision of the Soothsayer. The eagle of empire will pass from the Rome of Caesar Augustus to a reunited Britain. As King Cymbeline's reconciliation with

Posthumus, the "lion's whelp," presages English acceptance of union with the "alien" Scots, so the king's recovery of his long-lost sons restores another lost limb of his kingdom, the alien territory of Wales. The explication of the riddle of the tablet might almost serve as a model for the reading of the play's "Stuart line."

In the Britain of *Cymbeline,* unlike the Britain of James I, Wales, or Cambria, is a separate country. The Roman ambassador to the court of Cymbeline is escorted only as far as its border at the River Severn; British law is not applicable beyond that point. Belarius, like Posthumus, is a man unfairly cast into exile, accused of overfriendliness toward Rome, reacting to his disentitlement by developing prejudices of his own. But the renewal of peace with Rome rejoins Wales to Britain in the persons of Cymbeline's sons. Shakespeare may have intended a reference to Prince Henry, whose creation as Prince of Wales was imminent and would symbolically reaffirm Wales's part in Great Britain. Entertainments written for the investiture, like Samuel Daniel's *Tethys' Festival,* include references to Milford Haven and the Tudor conquest—some of the same political material evoked in *Cymbeline.*[32]

Through the discovery of the lost children, the ancient kingdom of Brute is finally reunited: England and Scotland at last all under one head, branches of a single tree, as Cymbeline, Posthumus, Imogen, Arviragus, and Guiderius all comprise one line. Imogen has lost her title to the kingdom but gained "two worlds" in exchange. With the exposure of Iachimo, the last vestiges of Posthumus's suspicion of Imogen are dispelled, and the corruption of Italianate Rome is clearly separated from the virtue of its Augustan antecedent. Earlier on, Posthumus's warweary jailor had exclaimed, "I would we were all of one mind, and one mind good" (5.4.203–4). That wish is answered in the play's long final scene of *polyanagnoresis,*[33] when all the characters gather to disentangle the remaining riddles, piece together a common history, and forge one nation out of a heterogeneous mass of individual "liberties" and customs, Roman and British laws. Similar resolutions of the conflicts impeding the creation of Britain were common in contemporary pageants. Peacham's emblem of James also provides a striking analogue: according to the ideal of the Union of the Kingdoms, England and Scotland both uphold the crown of Britain, "And one their Prince, their sea, their land and lawes; / Their loue, their league: whereby they still agree, / In concord firme, and friendly amitie" (p. 11).

The most important action occurring in *Cymbeline* as the peace of Augustus descends upon Britain may well be what happens offstage and unmentioned within the play: the birth of Christ, which took place during the reigns of Cymbeline and Caesar Augustus, bringing a new "gracious season" of love and reconciliation among humankind. But another event associated with the golden reign of Augustus was the redescent of Astraea, goddess of justice, and the birth of the Roman law. Cymbeline freely offers Caesar Augustus the disputed Roman tribute which earlier he had scornfully refused—a sign of amity between nations which demonstrates his new receptivity to the Roman law, the *jus gentium* that governs the relations among nations, a branch of the same law by which the Post Nati would have been granted automatic citizenship in Britain.[34] In the new alliance, the "justice" of Roman tribute and the mercy of peace and reconciliation are not opposed to one another but work together for harmony, just as James I envisioned an empire of Great Britain in which tolerance and respect for the "alien" Roman law would cement, not cancel, union. At the end of the play, legal niceties about whose law and what kind drop out of sight along with the factional interests that had given them such spurious importance. The play ends as James I's reign had begun, with a proclamation of union.

Cymbeline orders that his peace be "published" to all his subjects. But in his Britain, unlike the Britain of 1608, the prejudice and malice that have hindered the Project for Union have either consumed themselves, like the wicked queen who "concluded most cruel to herself," or been conquered through inward transformation. Posthumus and King Cymbeline have undergone a "conversion" to the cause of union. In terms of standard humanist theory and James's own cherished belief about the relationship between texts and actions, reading and "application," Shakespeare can be interpreted as calling for a similar self-searching and self-transformation on the part of his audience. Everyone who kept abreast of Jacobean politics in 1608 and 1609 was aware of the king's Project for Union, acquainted with its proposed benefits for the nation. By coming to know themselves and their own prejudice, the audience would learn to grow beyond the xenophobia of disreputable characters like the queen and Cloten, for whom the "defect of judgment" is the "cause of fear" (4.2.112–13). They would overcome their partial vision and learn to "read" Posthumus aright as the essentially noble figure he is beneath his own equivalent prejudice. One of the chief barriers to the Project for Union would thereby be removed. The play ends in an openness to the winds of change, a zest for expansion and renewal, as though to intimate that such a transformation is possible. Whether the space between texts and action is so readily negotiable is another matter, however. And so, finally, we return to the vision of Jupiter, which is curiously absent from the one contemporary description we have of the play in performance.

III

Cymbeline demands political interpretation. It displays various characters in the act of finding political meaning in cryptic emblems; it offers its audience an expanded set of verbal texts and symbolic visions that cry out for similar explication. But our reading thus far has left one "text" uninterpreted, the image of descending Jupiter. For anyone immersed in the contemporary milieu, an initial identification would be obvious and almost unavoidable: Jupiter is James, who had swooped down upon his Parliament in similar fashion to announce his continuing protection of his despised countrymen the Scots, who was frequently depicted as Jove with his thunderbolts in connection with the Project for Union ("Procull a Iove, procul a Fulmine"), or as Jove with his emblematic animal the Roman eagle. In the coronation pageant, for example, James had been represented as a Roman eagle who had flown westward to London.[35] The dreamlike interlude over which Jupiter presides in *Cymbeline*—rather as the figure of Jupiter had presided over Ben Jonson's *Hymenaei* a little earlier—has some of the quasi-liturgical patterning to "Solemn music" of a masque at court. And like a Stuart masque or pageant, *Cymbeline*'s vision of Jupiter shows forth the royal will "clear" and "without obscuritie." The Leonati beg Jove to open his "crystal window" upon them in much the same way that James I himself had volunteered to open the transparent crystal of his heart to his subjects in several of his published speeches and in his admonitions to the 1606–7 Parliament.[36] According to the Folio stage directions, "Jupiter descends in thunder and lightning, sitting upon an eagle. He throws a thunderbolt. The Ghosts fall on their knees" (5.4.93–95). Perhaps the members of Parliament upon whom James had descended with his "thunder" in 1606 and 1607 had reacted with a similar shocked obeisance.

After chiding the Leonati for their lack of trust, Jupiter reveals his plan, foreordained all along, for relieving the sufferings of the deprived Leonati. Posthumus's birthright and marriage will be restored. Like James as he portrayed himself before the 1606–7 Parliament during the debate over the union, Jove will allow no impediment to come between his will and its execution: "I will not say anything which I will not promise, nor promise any thing which I will not sweare; What I sweare I will signe; and what I signe, I shall with GODS grace euer performe."[37] Jupiter departs, leaving behind him, almost exactly as the bustling pedant-king James I might have done, a written text for his thunderstruck subjects to ponder until they achieve enlightenment. It is a rather stupendous set of images, or at least it can be with the right staging, as several twentieth-century productions have demonstrated. But the descent of Jupiter can also be awkward, intrusive, like James I's sudden, "divine" visitations upon Parliament—as much fulmination as *fulmen*. Either way the vision is performed, it is hard to imagine how it could have been missed by anyone in a contemporary audience who was paying even minimal attention to what was happening on stage.

Simon Forman's 1610–1611 summary of *Cymbeline* shows considerable attention to intricacies of plot but lamentably little interest in political motifs that "might, without cloud, or obscuritie, declare themselves to the sharpe and learned." Both what Forman includes and what he omits are interesting in light of the play's "local" meaning. He picked up some of the incantatory power of "Milford," repeating the name several times, but conflated Posthumus and Cloten for part of the action, or so his confusion of pronouns seems to indicate. It is perhaps evidence that the two roles were performed by a single actor, but also evidence that the play's bizarre emblems of prejudice could easily be misread. In his account, Forman failed to include minor bits like the queen's attempted poisoning, but also major episodes like the vision of Jupiter, unless we are to imagine such a potentially stunning *coup de théâtre* as subsumed under the hasty "&c." with which he concludes his account of the action.[38] Beyond the repeated mention of Milford, Forman's summary shows no evidence that he grasped the play's Jacobean "line." It would perhaps be utopian to expect to find such evidence. Forman took his notes for purposes connected with his medical and magical practice as a London cunning man. The explication of political allegory was not, perhaps, germane to his professional needs, whatever those might have been. To the extent that contemporaries *did* understand topical materials in masques or plays or pamphlets as conveying some specific political message, they tended to note it only fleetingly and in passing, in conversational or epistolary gossip.

Yet there may have been other factors contributing to Forman's seeming oblivion. It is altogether possible that the descent of Jupiter was not performed in the version he saw,[39] or that it was so massively deemphasized that it became less than memorable. Jupiter could have walked on, for example, instead of descending by means of a machine, and the lines describing his descent could have been cut. Or the descent could have been staged in such a problematic way that it was easier to "forget" than to assimilate into a summary of the action. If, to take only one possibility, Jupiter sat awkwardly on his emblematic bird—hardly the usual mount for a being of human form—the grandeur of his visitation could have been massively undercut. Like the episode of Imogen's misguided grief over Cloten's headless body, the descent of Jupiter is perilously balanced between the compelling and the ludicrous. It is "double written" or overwritten in a way that calls special attention to it and invites political decipherment but that also provides a mechanism by which the "authorized" political reading can be dispersed or ridiculed. To use James I's own complaining language for such abuse of the clear royal intent, the descent of Jupiter is contrived in such a way that it can easily be "throwne" or "rent asunder in contrary scenes like the old Oracles of the Pagan Gods." In London, 1610, before an audience for whom the play's political meaning was at least potentially legible, how and whether the episode got "read" according to the Jacobean line would depend in large part on how it was brought to life in the theater.

The same is true of the play as a whole. By imbedding *Cymbeline*'s "Jacobean line" within structures that at least potentially call it into question, Shakespeare partially separates the play from the realm of authorship and "authority," reinfuses its topicality with some of the evanescence and protean, shifting referentiality that was still characteristic of the Renaissance theater in performance as opposed to authored collections of printed *Workes*.[40] If King James I made a practice of beating off the subversive proliferation of meaning in order to communicate his "clear" political intent, Shakespeare in *Cymbeline* can be seen as one of those jangling subjects who scatter language and signification, dispersing the king's painstaking crafting of a unified whole nearly as fast as the royal author can put it together.

Cymbeline repeatedly invites its audience to "reading" and decipherment. If they follow its Jacobean line, they are invited to "apply" the play's message to their personal lives in much the same way that characters within the play repeatedly read moral maxims out of the landscape and events around them. And yet, the play's most important texts never operate according to such an orderly, rational agenda for interpretation. Reading in *Cymbeline* may be enticing, but it is also directly and repeatedly thematized as fraught with dangers, almost inevitably "misreading." Posthumus has to be "read," yet in the play character is seldom legible. "Who is't can read a woman?" Cymbeline complains (5.5.48), and Imogen and the others experience similar difficulties. Since the "scriptures" of Posthumus have "turn'd to heresy," she declares all reading suspect: "To write and read / Be henceforth treacherous" (4.2.317–18); all interpretation is hopelessly "perplex'd." By the end, of course, such misreadings are disentangled and "unperplexed," but not before reading itself—the very integrative process by which the play's Stuart meaning can be collected by its audience—has been shown to be highly fallible.[41]

Cymbeline appears to posit a causal connection between the correct

"reading" of its cryptic Stuart riddles and inner and outward transformation. Yet the translation of interpretation into action is not once effected within the play itself. Symbolic visions are often followed by salutary and revitalizing events. After the Soothsayer's speech, Imogen
awakens and attaches herself to the Romans; after Posthumus's dream,
the prisoner is freed; after the interpretation of the riddling tablet, King
Cymbeline proclaims the *Pax Britannica*. But in each case the relationship
between the emblematic visions which demand reading and the acts that
follow them is indecipherable. It is not clear whether or not Imogen is
moved to action by the Soothsayer. If so, she is inspired by false divining,
since his interpretation is partially mistaken. Posthumus's dream is followed by his release from prison, but there is no clear causal relationship
between one thing and the other beyond Jupiter's declaration that he has
been controlling events all along. Posthumus himself has understood neither his vision nor the mysterious tablet. As often as not in *Cymbeline*,
the riddling follows upon events instead of inspiring them, as in the
maxim about the man, two boys, and the lane, and in Cymbeline's declaration of peace, which does not arise out of the reading and interpretation of the "text" of Posthumus but has already been effected through
the British military victory and the restoration of the exiles. Even as
Cymbeline seems to argue for political action—the effacing of the "mark
of the stranger" from the exiled Scots—the play calls into question the
relationship between texts and action and therefore renders problematic
its own status as a text which can be "read" according to the Jacobean
line as a call for political unity and national renewal.

If *Cymbeline*'s riddling texts fail as pragmatic agents for change
through acts of interpretation, the play leaves open the possibility that
they may still serve, almost sacramentally, as vehicles for irresistible
power, like the Soothsayer's vision of the eagle of empire winging its way
steadily westward—on high, remote, serenely indifferent to the human
unraveling of riddles. That is the way Jupiter portrays himself as operating upon the world of human events. Everything has happened according to his masterplan for Britain. He has allowed the "divorce" of Imogen and Posthumus in order to test and renew them both ("Whom best I
love I cross"); he also claims credit for the sudden reversal of fortune that
reinstates the union. The fact that characters in the play so frequently
evoke "Jove" or "Jupiter" in their oaths and supplications adds to the
sense of the deity's overriding presence in Britain.

Cymbeline's politics is imbedded in a form that is less than hospitable
to the potential for rational human action. In this play, as in Renaissance
tragicomedy generally, human agency regularly dissolves; human beings
are swept along by forces apparently incalculable. The dramatic form is,

however, quite hospitable to the claims of Stuart absolutism, in that the wondrous energies that secretly govern the action can be identified with the "sacred" power of the monarch in his "body politic." Tragicomedy as a distinct, defined dramatic genere in England appeared shortly before the accession of James, and King James associated himself closely with it. He used the generic term himself to describe his marvelous deliverance (as a result of his own astute "reading" of an enigmatic plot) after the Gunpowder Treason in 1605. One of the purposes of that conspiracy had been, according to a chief perpetrator, to destroy the Union of the Kingdoms and blow the Scots back across the border. The deliverance of the nation was, in the king's own formulation, a "Tragedie" for the plotters, a "Tragicomedie" for himself and his "Trew Subiects."[42] Stuart court masques often celebrate a similar overriding destiny that grows out of the royal will and the king's special prescience. In the masque, royal proclamations were often portrayed as transforming the nation as though effortlessly, through the irresistible, divine power of James I—in much the same way that Jupiter claims hidden but absolute "authority" over all the turnings of *Cymbeline*.

In *Cymbeline,* Stuart texts do sometimes evoke wonder among at least some of the characters. Reading, if it works at all in the play, works by inspiring the reader to marvel at the truth he or she has managed to decipher. And yet, here again, discomfort with the interpretive process is overtly thematized. Posthumus ridicules the inane gawking of those who stand marveling at riddles and symbolic visions: "Nay, do not wonder at it. You are made / Rather to wonder at the things you hear / Than to work any" (5.3.53–55). His taunt sounds very much like contemporary complaints against King James himself that he devoted himself too completely to the marvels of the book when he could accomplish far more by the sword. Yet Posthumus is describing a structural mechanism of the play he inhabits. *Cymbeline* plants seeds of impatience with the very riddles out of which it is constructed, an irritation like that expressed by Posthumus as he mockingly dissolves his own heroism into doggerel after his defeat of the Romans.

A prime example is the text offered by the great god Jupiter himself: it is written in very colorless prose (by Shakespearean standards at least)— only slightly more compelling than the doggerel produced by Posthumus. It is so inferior as a text to the marvel Jupiter seemed to promise that many editors have been convinced that it cannot be Shakespeare. And its neoscholastic interpretation by the Soothsayer is heavy-handed in the extreme. Asked, like an oracle, to "Read, and declare the meaning," the Soothsayer infelicitously interprets "The piece of tender air, thy virtuous daughter, / Which we call 'mollis aer,' and 'mollis aer' / We term it 'mulier'; which 'mulier' I divine / Is this most constant wife" (5.5.448–50). This niggling, labored mode of interpretation sounds rather too much like the pedant-king James himself, and can easily be understood as mockery of the play's own process of "wondering" decipherment of riddles and emblems of state. The play's major texts are awkward, apart—they produce disjunction, resist assimilation into the flow of events. Again there is a strong parallel with King James. Like Jupiter in the play, James was forever disconcerting his subjects by producing oracular documents, long speeches, or proclamations which he liked to think of as *Books*—divine, arbitrary texts that heralded magnificent transformations for the nation but were too often relied on by the scholar-king as though they could substitute for the painstaking political maneuvering that actually got things done. Jupiter's texts in *Cymbeline* are equally magical, or purposeless—perhaps evoking wonder, perhaps exposing the ineptitude of their "author." If Jupiter is indeed, as he claims, all powerful, why does he need texts at all? Similar questions could be asked about James I and his vast claims for his own prerogative.

If *Cymbeline* follows the Jacobean line, it also reproduces some of the incongruities in the actual working of Stuart policy that undermined royal claims about the mystical organic "union" of all James's subjects—like members of a single animate body—under his authority as head. In fact, James's political doctrine of essences was one of the major points of contention in the parliamentary debates over the Project for Union. Contemporaries "sharpe and learned" enough to read *Cymbeline*'s Jacobean message at all were perhaps also capable of reading its portrayal of disjunctions between James's theory and his political practice. Upon such a contemporary audience, *Cymbeline* might well have produced dissatisfaction with the "Jacobean line." Or at least, through its critique of the wonders of the almighty authored text, it may have intensified existing dissatisfaction with James, his clerkish political blundering, and his odd notions of kingship.

Much would depend on how the play was staged. To fall back upon the range of political meaning that could have been elicited through different modes of staging is, perhaps, to abrogate the Duty of the Critic to determine the Author's Intent. But I would argue that it was part of Shakespeare's intent in *Cymbeline* to be able to sidestep the "self-sameness" and internal coherence growing out of emerging conventions of authorship. There was no way that he could "author" the play and its political message himself, even if he had wished to (and we have no particular evidence that he did). Following the play's invitation to linear interpretation would lead inevitably to the Jacobean line, to the Jacobean vision of organic political unity, and to James as "author"—"Accessible is none but Milford way." By interweaving the play's "authorized reading" with a subtle critique of ideas about textual authority, Shakespeare gave the play back to the institution of the theater, created a potential for multiplicity and diversity in performance that the Stuart *Cymbeline* did not—by definition, could not—have.

The play may well have taken markedly different forms at different times and in different places. If it was performed at court, it could well have communicated the Jacobean line with almost the same stupendous glorification of James in his "immortal body" as monarch that was characteristic of the Stuart masque. In such a setting or in a theater capable of sophisticated theatrical effects, the play's overlay of uncertainties and questioning could have been overcome through spectacular staging of scenes like the descent of Jupiter—through the creation of visual and auditory wonders marvelous enough to silence all but the most intransigent distrust of theatrical "magic." On the other hand, in a different setting or even in the same setting (since we should not be overly wooden and formulaic about the predictability of performance) the play could have been staged in ways that subtly highlighted its own deconstruction of reading and royal authorship. Forman perhaps saw such a *Cymbeline* in the public theater—a *Cymbeline* in which the play's political symbols were muted or problematized to the point that they became indecipherable.

Theatrical "deconstruction" of *Cymbeline* could have fragmented the Jacobean line by placing special emphasis on the play's barriers to reading, by undercutting its "wonders," and by giving strong credibility to characters like Posthumus who distrust such things. With the right balancing (or, in Stuart terms, the *wrong* balancing) of energies on stage, the play's perceptual and volitional gaps could easily have been made to appear unbridgeable. But given the play's contemporary milieu, there was also a potential for theatrical "cryptonymy," which would arrest the process of deconstruction—for a mode of performance that read beneath and across the play's seemingly unbridgeable fissures and implanted a sense of underlying unity by uncovering an essence called union, identical with the person and power of the monarch.[43]

A theatrical cryptonymy of *Cymbeline* would call attention to the play's disjunctions and difficulties in order to beckon beyond them toward an idealized realm of political essence from which they would be revealed as mere ephemera, surface turbulence upon a political and artistic entity that was indissolubly organic, at one with itself at the level of deep structure. *Mutatis mutandis* the play would then, for all its surface questioning, reaffirm the royal line not so much through King James as in spite of him; it would disperse the pedantic, orderly rituals of reading in order to "decrypt" the sacred immanence of royal power.

In the Renaissance, the two mutually reversing operations were equally possible and available (under different labels than I have been using here) as counters in political debate. Legal and parliamentary "de-constructionists" challenged the doctrine of essences in its particular Ja-cobean form of official "state" organicism associated with the body of the monarch, by pointing toward those elements of the national life that the Jacobean vision of unity had to disallow in order to constitute itself. Cryptonymy—"Platonic politics" might be a more fitting label for it in its English Renaissance form—was a reading of underlying essences which "healed" social rifts and political fragmentation by pointing toward deeper unities already invisibly in place through the fact of James I's kingship. Part of the fascination of considering James I's Project for Union and *Cymbeline's* fragile "unity" together is that both the play and the seething political debate mobilize similar strategies for defending and circumventing the Jacobean line.[44]

In *Cymbeline,* much of the power of the drive toward idealization is generated from the fact that the idealization comes too late. By the time *Cymbeline* was staged in 1608 or 1609 or 1610, James's Project for the Union of the Kingdoms and the creation of Great Britain had reached political stalemate. Parliament was no longer willing to consider the mat-ter. The courts had indirectly endorsed the royal project, but without any way of enforcing it. James continued to rant and bluster but gradually turned his attention to less intractable goals. The mistrust and prejudice continued on both sides of the border. Indeed, on the level of the play's contemporary functioning, *Cymbeline's* discomfort with its own "gov-erning line" can be seen as a symptom of continuing English and Scottish prejudice, continuing refusal to "read" the alien aright. For there was to be no ratification of the Project for Union during that century.

Despite James I's victory in the case of the Post Nati, the "marriage" of England and Scotland was still hanging in "unnatural" suspension in 1633–34, when *Cymbeline* found favor with Charles I in a performance at court. It seems fair to assume that in this performance, the play's "Stuart line" was allowed to shine forth in its full flush of idealism and promise. The revival was almost certainly prompted by Charles I's celebrated pro-gress to Scotland earlier that year to receive the Scottish crown: the head of the Scottish state had been fleetingly restored to his "exiles." It was his first visit as king of England to the northern kingdom. The public cere-mony of his coronation as king of Scotland gave renewed visibility to the idea of the Union of the Kingdoms in the person of Charles, their mutual head. Not only that, but Charles's visit was designed to implement one part of his father's program for Britain, the creation of a unified British church by bringing Scotland into accordance with the Anglican liturgy and Anglican church government.[45] Given the immediate context, *Cymbeline*'s promulgation of official Anglican ideology about the indigenous nature of proper "liturgical" reverence and ceremony would have taken on particular prominence. But despite the renewed efforts on the part of crown and church, the stalemating of union continued. Charles I's attempt at matchmaking between kingdoms was even less successful than his father's. It led eventually to a destructive war with the Scots, a conflict that helped to precipitate the civil war and the execution of the king. Such cataclysmic divisions do not heal overnight. Great Britain was finally created only in 1707. And as recurrent, sometimes violent, separatist movements since then have borne witness, the Union of the Kingdoms has never quite achieved the luminous harmony presaged in the final moments of *Cymbeline*.

Notes

1. For particulars of the parliamentary debate, see Wallace Notestein, *The House of Commons, 1604–1610* (New Haven: Yale University Press, 1971), pp. 250–54; David Harris Willson, ed., *The Parliamentary Diary of Robert Bowyer, 1606–1607* (Minneapolis: University of Minnesota Press, 1931), pp. 257n, 269, 282, 287–88; and for James's published views, C. H. McIlwain, ed., *The Political Works of James I* (Cambridge: Harvard University Press, 1918), p. 291. Comparison of James to the Thunderer had also come up in earlier Commons debates. In 1604, for example, his answer to a parliamentary petition was received by the solemn and amazed MPs like a "thunderbolt." See G. B. Harrison, *A Jacobean Journal: Being a Record of Those Things Most Talked of during the Years 1603–1606* (London: George Routledge and Sons, 1941), p. 131.

The present article is excerpted from chap. 3 of *Puzzling Shakespeare: Local Reading and Its Discontents,* forthcoming from the University of California Press in 1989. For a broader discussion of the "unease of topicality" and related issues, the reader is referred to the book-length study.

2. Stephen Orgel and Roy Strong, *Inigo Jones: The Theatre of the Stuart Court* (Berkeley: University of California Press, 1973), 1:105–14; see also D. J. Gordon, *The Renaissance Imagination,* ed. Stephen Orgel (1975; reprint, Berkeley: University of California Press, 1980), pp. 173–77.

3. For the purposes of this reading, I am taking the (by now) standard position that the Jupiter scene is Shakespearean and was regularly included in the play as performed. Problems with this position will be discussed later on.

4. Quotations from *Cymbeline* will be from *The Complete Works,* ed. David Bevington, 3d ed. (Glenview, Ill.: Scott, Foresman, 1980), and cited in the text. I have checked each against the First Folio version (1623).

5. See G. Wilson Knight, *The Crown of Life,* 2d ed. (London: Methuen, 1948), pp. 129–202; and W. W. Greg's survey of critical opinion in *The Shakespeare First Folio: Its Bibliographical and Textual History* (Oxford: Clarendon Press, 1955), p. 413. As Greg points out, even E. K. Chambers, who opposed most disintegrationism, regarded the descent of Jupiter as a "spectacular theatrical interpolation"; there has, however, been massive disagreement as to precisely where the "interpolation" begins and ends.

6. Cited from Jonson's description of his part in James I's coronation pageant, *Ben Jonson,* ed. C. H. Herford, Percy Simpson, and Evelyn Simpson (Oxford: Clarendon Press, 1925–52), 7:90–91; he followed similar principles in the masques.

7. James is cited from James F. Larkin and Paul L. Hughes, eds., *Stuart Royal Proclamations,* vol. 1, Royal Proclamations of King James I, 1603–1625 (Oxford: Clarendon Press, 1973), pp. v–vi; for the bishops, see William Barlow, *The Svmme and Svbstance of the Conference . . . at Hampton Court, Ianuary 14, 1603* [for 1604] (London: Mathew Law, 1604), p. 84.

8. See Orgel and Strong, *Inigo Jones;* my *The Politics of Mirth: Jonson, Herrick, Milton, Marvell, and the Defense of Old Holiday Pastimes* (Chicago: University of Chicago Press, 1986), which includes several detailed political readings of court masques; and on perspective, Roy Strong, *Art and Power: Renaissance Festivals, 1450–1650* (1973; reprint, Berkeley: University of California Press, 1984), p. 32.

9. *The Workes of the Most High and Mightie Prince, James,* ed. James [Montagu], (London, 1616), sig. B2ᵛ. My discussion of James's authorship is strongly indebted to Richard Helgerson and Michael O'Connell, "Print, Power, and the Performing Self," presented at the Modern Language Association, 1984, which the authors were kind enough to send me in manuscript. For a revised and expanded version of the essay authored by Helgerson alone, see "Milton Reads the King's Book: Print, Performance, and the Making of a Bourgeois Idol," *Criticism* 29 (1987): 1–25.

10. Michel Foucault, "What Is an Author," tr. Josué V. Harari, in *Textual Strategies: Perspectives in Post-Structuralist Criticism,* ed. Harari (Ithaca: Cornell University Press, 1979), pp. 141–60.

11. Michael Ryan, *Marxism and Deconstruction: A Critical Articulation* (Baltimore: Johns Hopkins University Press, 1982), pp. 3–5. As numerous historians have pointed out, however, James's saving grace was his incapacity for consistency in practice and his state's technological incapacity for thorough enforcement of the Jacobean "line."

12. Cited from the *Calendar of State Papers, Venetian Series* in *James I by His Contemporaries,* ed. Robert Ashton (London: Huchinson, 1969), p. 96.

13. For this and other public protests of clarity and sincerity, see McIlwain, *Political Works of James I,* pp. 280, 286, 290, 292, 306. See also Jonathan Goldberg's discussion in *James I and the Politics of Literature* (Baltimore: Johns Hopkins University Press, 1983), which argues for Jacobean opacity as the "outside" of royal absolutism and the demand for clarity. My discussion differs from Goldberg's in that while he presents royal inscrutability as the inevitable accompaniment of James's absolutist ideology, I want to further historicize the idea—high-

light the particular times and conditions under which the internal instability of James's formulations became particularly visible.

14. Warren D. Smith, *Shakespeare's Playhouse Practice: A Handbook* (Hanover, N.H.: University Press of New England, 1975), p. 32n. The exactitude was easily achievable in the printing house, since the same block of type could have been used both times. Nevertheless, it is tempting to see the precise repetition as indicative of reverence—or mock reverence—for the text in question.

15. See Geoffrey of Monmouth, *Histories of the Kings of Britain,* tr. Sebastian Evans (London: Dent, 1904), pp. 99–104; Richard Hosley, ed., *Shakespeare's Holinshed* (New York: Putnam's Sons, 1968), pp. 4–8; and Kenneth Muir, *The Sources of Shakespeare's Plays* (London: Methuen, 1977), pp. 258–66. Of course, the story of Posthumus has fictional analogues in novellas by Boccaccio and others. David Bergeron notes that there is a Posthumus among the Roman analogues to Shakespeare's play and that Augustan Rome stands behind the play as a "kind of paradigm." See his "*Cymbeline;* Shakespeare's Last Roman Play," *Shakespeare Quarterly* 31 (1980): 31–41 (especially note 19). If so, the Roman allusions he cites work against the play's overt idealization of Augustan Rome and contribute to the stalemating that I will discuss later on.

16. The present study is particularly indebted to Knight, *Crown of Life,* pp. 129–202; and to the topical interpretations of Emrys Jones, "Stuart Cymbeline," *Essays in Criticism* 11 (1961): 84–99; Howard Felperin, *Shakespearean Romance* (Princeton: Princeton University Press, 1972), pp. 188–95; and Glynne Wickham, especially *Shakespeare's Dramatic Heritage* (New York: Barnes and Noble, 1969), and "Riddle and Emblem: A Study in the Dramatic Structure of *Cymbeline,*" in *English Renaissance Studies Presented to Dame Helen Gardner,* ed. John Carey (Oxford: Clarendon Press, 1980), pp. 94–113.

In *Shakespeare's Military World* (1956; reprint, Berkeley: University of California Press, 1973), Paul A. Jorgenson sees the play as displaying ambivalence about its own denigration of Elizabethan nationalism in favor of the Jacobean "forest of olives," pp. 202–4. Frances Yates takes a narrower view in *Shakespeare's Last Plays: A New Approach* (London: Routledge and Kegan Paul, 1975), arguing (pp. 28–52) that Shakespeare's play speaks for the strongly Protestant group surrounding Prince Henry and Princess Elizabeth; her interpretation underestimates the importance of empire to James I himself. Recent treatments of the play in its Jacobean political context include D. E. Landry, "Dreams as History: The Strange Unity of *Cymbeline,*" *Shakespeare Quarterly* 33 (1982): 68–79; the discussion building up to *Cymbeline* in Jonathan Goldberg, *James I,* pp. 231–41, 287n; and David Bergeron, *Shakespeare's Romances and the Royal Family* (Lawrence: University Press of Kansas, 1985). See also Hallett Smith's attempt to reduce all topical approaches to the play to absurdity in *Shakespeare's Romances: A Study of Some Ways of the Imagination* (San Marino, Calif.: Huntington Library, 1972), which is a good example of the kind of critical overhostility that my work seeks to come to terms with.

17. See the analysis of the coronation pageant in Graham Parry, *The Golden Age Restor'd: The Culture of the Stuart Court, 1603–1642* (New York: St. Martin's Press, 1981), pp. 1–39; and in the early sections of Jonathan Goldberg's *James I.*

See also Wickham, "Riddle and Emblem," pp. 100–102; and *Dramatic Heritage,* pp. 250–54. For James I's proclamations, see Larkin and Hughes, *Stuart Royal Proclamations,* 1:18–19, 94. For the coin, see Notestein, *House of Commons,* p. 247. The idea of uniting the kingdoms was not a new one but had been brought up on several previous occasions. See G. W. T. Omond, *The Early History of the Scottish Union Question* (Edinburgh: Oliphant, Anderson, and Ferrier, 1897), pp. 9–51; and Gordon Donaldson, "Foundations of Anglo-Scottish Union," in *Elizabethan Government and Society: Essays Presented to Sir John Neale,* ed. S. T. Bindoff, J. Hurstfield, and C. H. Williams (London: Athlone Press, 1961), pp. 282–314. As Donaldson notes, during the sixteenth century in particular there had been a gradual linguistic and cultural amalgamation between the two peoples.

18. The comment was made by the French ambassador (quoted in Notestein, *House of Commons,* pp. 211–12). My discussion is indebted to the general studies of the Project for Union by David Harris Willson, "King James I and Anglo-Scottish Unity," in *Conflict in Stuart England,* ed. W. A. Aiken and B. D. Henning (London: Jonathan Cape, 1960), pp. 43–55; Omond, *Early History of the Scottish Union Question,* pp. 68–83; and Notestein's detailed account of the parliamentary debtes on union, especially pp. 79–80 and 215–54.

19. Thomas Campion, *Lord Hay's Masque,* dedicatory poem to James I, quoted in Wickham, "Riddle and Emblem," p. 112; as Gordon shows (*Renaissance Imagination,* p. 169), contemporaries recognized the political reference. See also the Sibyl's prophecy at the end of Campion's *The Lords' Masque,* in Orgel and Strong, *Inigo Jones,* 1:246; Parry, *The Golden Age Restor'd,* pp. 102–6; and for the theme of union in Ben Jonson's *Hymenaei,* Gordon, pp. 157–84; and the addition to Gordon's argument in my "Masquing Occasions and Masque Structure," *Research Opportunities in Renaissance Drama* 24 (1981): 7–16. For the Union-as-marriage motif on coins, see Omond, *Early History of the Scottish Union Question,* pp. 68–69.

20. This is, of course, a brief summary of a set of complex issues. See Notestein, *House of Commons,* pp. 233–35 and ff.; David Harris Willson, *James VI and I,* (London: Jonathan Cape, 1956), pp. 253–56; Willson's "King James I and Anglo-Scottish Unity," in the collection *Conflict in Stuart England,* Aiken and Henning; McIlwain, *Political Works of James I,* p. 292 and Appendix B, pp. lxxxvii–lxxxix; and especially R. C. Munden's corrective to Willson, "James I and 'the Growth of Mutual Distrust': King, Commons, and Reform, 1603–1604," in *Faction and Parliament: Essays in Early Stuart History,* ed. Kevin Sharpe (Oxford: Clarendon Press, 1978), pp. 43–72; and Brian P. Levack, "The Proposed Union of English Law and Scots Law in the Seventeenth Century," *Juridical Review,* n.s. 20 (1975): 97–115. See also Brian P. Levack, *The Formation of the British State: England, Scotland, and the Union* (Oxford: Clarendon Press, 1987). I regret that this study appeared too late for me to use in my own discussion.

More general aspects of the controversy over law are discussed in J. G. A. Pocock, *The Ancient Constitution and the Feudal Law* (Cambridge: Cambridge University Press, 1957), pp. 20–69; and in C. Brooks and K. Sharpe, "History, English Law, and the Renaissance," *Past and Present* 72 (1976): 333–43.

21. On Scottish resistance to James's ecclesiastical reforms, see Samuel R. Gardiner, *History of England from the Accession of James I to the Outbreak of the Civil War* (London: Longmans, Green, 1884), 1:303–6 and ff.; and Willson, "King James I and Anglo-Scottish Unity," p. 49. On the Roman law in Jonson's masque, see my reading in "Masquing Occasions and Masque Structure," pp. 9–11.

22. Notestein, *House of Commons*, p. 240. Notestein discounts the claim, made by the French ambassador, that Scots were being denied precedence (p. 212) on grounds that it may have come from the Scots themselves and that James I would not have tolerated such behavior. But as the whole debate over union demonstrates, James did not have all that much control over English attitudes and comportment, particularly when he was not present. The hostile climate in England would tend rather to support the claim. See Willson, *King James VI and I*, pp. 252–55; and Willson, "King James I and Anglo-Scottish Unity," pp. 45–48.

23. There is a detailed discussion of the case and the controversy surrounding it in Gardiner, *History of England* 1:301–57. The major documents of the case, including the arguments of Sir Francis Bacon, council for Calvin in the Exchequer, the 1608 report of Sir Edward Coke, and the opinion of James's chancellor Sir Thomas Egerton, are reprinted in T. B. Howell, ed., *A Complete Collection of State Trials*, vol. 2 (London: Hansard and Longman, 1816), cols. 559–696. Egerton's arguments were published at the request of James I in 1609. On some of the contradictions surrounding the case and their effects on the arguments that preceded the American Revolution, see Harvey Wheeler, "Calvin's Case (1608) and the McIlwain-Schuyler Debate," *American Historical Review* 61 (1956): 587–97.

24. For examples of the many public ways in which James I associated himself and the Scots with the lion, see Jones, "Stuart Cymbeline," pp. 88–93; Notestein, *House of Commons*, p. 80; and Wickham, "Riddle and Emblem," pp. 95–106. The lion was also associated with Britain and considered to have been the heraldic animal of King Brute himself.

Frances Yates's argument in *Shakespeare's Last Plays* (pp. 51–59) that *Cymbeline* was revived to celebrate the marriage of the Palsgrave Frederick and Princess Elizabeth is linked to my own, in that Frederick was also an alien, also associated with the heraldic imagery of the lion, his marriage yet another example of James's policy for peace and empire. But otherwise there are few similarities between him and Posthumus. Frederick was not a despised alien, but quite popular in England. His marriage with Elizabeth was eventually torn by strife (the Thirty Years' War) but not until well after the play had been written.

25. See, for example, Notestein, *House of Commons*, p. 251.

26. See, in particular, Posthumus's contract with Iachimo (1.4.143–73), where his language of "covenants" and "articles" seems excessively legalistic for the bargain being concluded. G. Wilson Knight (*Crown of Life*, p. 178) has taken general note of the play's preoccupation with law.

27. See Joan Hartwig, "Cloten, Autolycus, and Caliban: Bearers of Parodic Burdens," in *Shakespeare's Romances Reconsidered*, ed. Carol McGinnis Kay and Henry E. Jacobs (Lincoln: University of Nebraska Press, 1978), pp. 91–103;

LEAH S. MARCUS

James Edward Siemon, "Noble Virtue in *Cymbeline*," *Shakespeare Survey* 29 (1976): 51–61; and for the characterization of Cloten, H. N. Hudson, *Lectures on Shakespeare*, 2d ed. (New York: Scribner, 1857), 2:215.

28. Stephen Booth, "Speculations on Doubling in Shakespeare's Plays" (1979), reprinted in *King Lear, Macbeth, Indefinition, and Tragedy* (New Haven: Yale University Press, 1983), pp. 149–53.) Other critics have made the same suggestion.

29. McIlwain, *Political Works of James I*, pp. 271–73, 292; Larkin and Hughes, *Stuart Royal Proclamations* 1:18–19, 94–98. As D. J. Gordon demonstrates (*Renaissance Imagination*, pp. 162–79), this organic political imagery was not only to be found in the speeches of James; it was endemic to discussions of the union, and indeed, to discussions of the body politic, though far from universally accepted in terms of its Jacobean political implications, as I shall note below. For a study of some of the general political implications of the play's imagery of rape and bodily fragmentation, see Ann Thompson's fine study, "Philomel in *Titus Andronicus* and *Cymbeline*," *Shakespeare Survey* 31 (1978): 23–32.

30. Bergeron, *Shakespeare's Romances and the Royal Family*, p. 41 (citing Antonia Fraser's biography of James).

31. Wickham, "Riddle and Emblem," p. 102.

32. See Glynne Wickham, "Shakespeare's Investiture Play: The Occasion and Subject of *The Winter's Tale*," *Times Literary Supplement*, 18 December 1969, p. 1456; Wickham, "Romance and Emblem: A Study in the Dramatic Structure of *The Winter's Tale*," in *The Elizabethan Theatre*, ed. David Galloway (Waterloo, Ontario: Macmillan Co. of Canada, 1973), 3:82–99; Robert Speaight, *Shakespeare: The Man and His Achievement* (London: Dent and Sons, 1977), p. 337; and for Daniel's masque and the investiture symbolism, John Pitcher's essay in *The Court Masque*, ed. David Lindley (Manchester: Manchester University Press, 1984), pp. 33–46.

33. The hilariously apt term is borrowed from Philip Edwards, *Threshold of a Nation: A Study in English and Irish Drama* (Cambridge: Cambridge University Press, 1979), p. 91.

34. On Augustus and the birth of Roman law, see Yates, *Shakespeare's Last Plays*, especially p. 42; McIlwain, *Political Works of James I*, pp. 271–73 (James's 1603 speech before Parliament); and for the impact of the birth of Christ, especially Northrop Frye, *A Natural Perspective: The Development of Shakespearean Comedy and Romance* (New York: Columbia University Press, 1965), pp. 66–67.

For arguments for the citizenship of the Post Nati on the basis of the *jus gentium*, see Notestein, *House of Commons*, pp. 225–27; and Howell, *State Trials*, vol. 2, cols. 563 and ff. See also Margaret Atwood Judson, *The Crisis of the Constitution* (1949; reprint, New York: Octagon, 1964), pp. 134–35, 165–66. Matters were complicated by the fact that, as Wheeler points out, the antiunion forces also marshalled arguments from the civil law, no doubt to counter the tactics of the king's supporters. Caesar Augustus was, of course, the founder of Roman civil law.

35. Wickham, "Riddle and Emblem," p. 102.

36. See the speeches cited in note 13 above and Jonson's language describing

the impact of court pageantry in Herford, Simpson, and Simpson, *Ben Jonson* 7:90–91.

37. McIlwain, *Political Works of James I,* p. 305; for the immediate context, see Notestein, *House of Commons,* p. 245.

38. For Forman's summary of the play and discussion of it, see E. K. Chambers, *William Shakespeare: A Study of Facts and Problems* (Oxford: Clarendon Press, 1930), 2:338–39. Forman's note leaves the performance date unclear. Chambers argues for 1611 but conjectures that the play would have been written the previous year.

39. Those who hold that the descent is theatrical interpolation can argue that it dates from after the performance in 1610 or 1611. Given its particular reverberation with parliamentary affairs in 1606–8, I find that viewpoint implausible.

40. For a fuller discussion of this distinction, see Stephen Orgel, "What Is a Text," *Research Opportunities in Renaissance Drama* 24 (1981): 3–6; and the fuller discussion of Shakespearean topicality in my *Puzzling Shakespeare.*

41. This point has been emphasized in many recent discussions. See in particular Bergeron, *Shakespeare's Romances and the Royal Family,* pp. 147–56; and Meredith Skura's essay "Interpreting Posthumus' Dream from Above and Below: Families, Psychoanalysis, and Literary Critics," in *Representing Shakespeare: New Psychoanalytic Essays,* ed. Murray M. Schwartz and Coppélia Kahn (Baltimore: Johns Hopkins University Press, 1980), pp. 203–16.

42. See Glynne Wickham, "From Tragedy to Tragi-Comedy: *King Lear* as Prologue," *Shakespeare Survey* 26 (1973): 33–48. On the gulf between the genre of tragicomedy (or romance) and topicality, I am also indebted to Felperin, *Shakespearean Romance,* pp. 194–96; and Fredric Jameson, *The Political Unconscious: Narrative as a Socially Symbolic Act* (1981; reprint, Ithaca: Cornell University Press, 1985), pp. 148–50.

43. I am using the term *cryptonymy* much as it has been used in recent post-Freudian interpretation to describe the process by which a kind of "speech" can be given to gaps and splits that divide one area of the self off from other areas and make it unavailable to the same discursive space. See in particular Nicholas Abraham and Maria Torok, *The Wolf Man's Magic Word: A Cryptonymy,* tr. Nicholas Rand, Theory and History of Literature 37 (Minneapolis: University of Minnesota Press, 1986), and the foreword by Jacques Derrida, which reincrypts the authors' operation of decrypting. The fissures in question are not the same as those created by repression, in that materials on both sides of the split are almost equally available to the self, but not at the same time or along the same perceptual continuum. Naming the word or constellation of words and events that underlies the fissure and constitutes it, at least potentially allows a structural transformation that permits the two discursive spaces, the split-off areas of self, to flow together. The same "healing" process can be invoked for political and artistic discontinuities to the extent that such splits follow a similar morphology and to the extent that they are perceived as pathological, insufferable, urgently requiring repair.

44. On the doctrine of essences as a subject for debate, I am particularly indebted to R. C. Munden, "James I and 'the Growth of Mutual Distrust,'" p. 64.

45. Felperin, *Shakespearean Romance,* p. 195; Chambers, *William Shakespeare* 2:352. For a detailed account of Charles's policies toward the Scottish kirk, see Gardiner, *History of England* 7:274–98; and among many other recent studies of the possible impact of Caroline ecclesiastical policy, Conrad Russell, ed., *The Origins of the English Civil War* (New York: Harper and Row, 1973), especially the introduction (pp. 1–31) and the essays by Michael Hawkins, Nicholas Tyacke, Robin Clifton, and P. W. Thomas.

Part Three
Poets, Courtiers, and the Monarchy

Sidney and His Queen

In 1579—that fateful year when Queen Elizabeth, age forty-six, seemed seriously to be considering marriage to the Catholic duke of Anjou, age twenty-one—Sir Philip Sidney famously clashed with the earl of Oxford on the tennis court. As an episode in Sidney's tragic career, it has pride of place for drama in Sir Fulke Greville's account of his friend's short but heroic life. As an episode that reveals the social dance of Elizabethan society in all its anthropological intricacy, the complex strategies of challenge and riposte it exhibits may help us to situate the social function of another set of strategies in Sidney's life and to retrieve in part the politics involved in his authorship of the first sonnet sequence in the English language. Sidney's use of a self-abasing emphasis on his socially inferior position paradoxically redounds to his greater honor in the challenge to the earl of Oxford; in *Astrophil and Stella,* Sidney gains mastery by a similar strategy of self-abasement, taking control not merely of his text, but of his inferior social situation.

In Greville's prose narration, Sidney is already at play on the courts when

> A Peer of this Realm, born great, greater by alliance, and superlative in the Princes favor, abruptly came into the Tennis-Court, and speaking out of these three paramount authorities, he forgot to entreat that, which he could not legally command. When by the encounter of such a steady object [as Sir Philip], finding unrespectiveness in himself (though a great Lord) not respected by this Princely spirit, he [Oxford] grew to expostulate more roughly. The returns to which stile comming still from an understanding heart that knew what was due to it self, and what it ought to others, seemed (through the mists of my Lords passions, swoln with the winde of his faction then reigning) to provoke in

yeelding. Whereby, the less amazement, or confusion of thoughts he stirred up in Sir Philip, the more shadowes this great Lords own mind was possessed with: till at last with rage (which is ever ill-disciplin'd) he commands them to depart the Court. To this Sir Philip temperately answers; that if his Lordship had been pleased to express desire in milder Characters, perchance he should have led out those, that he should now find would not be driven out with an scourge of fury. This answer (like a Bellows) blowing up the sparks of excess already kindled, made my Lord scornfully call Sir Philip by the name of Puppy. In which progress of heat, as the tempest grew more and more vehement within, so did their hearts breath out their perturbations in more loud and shrill accents.[1]

Sidney's response puts Oxford "in his place"—specifically, by insisting on his position above Sidney in the social scale, a position that requires a "natural" gentility which Oxford's behavior contradicts. Sidney's request for "milder characters" characterizes Oxford's behavior as out of character for his class and hence finally *not* deserving Sidney's due deference. Here then, Sidney's humility—and specifically his sense of his own socially inferior position—becomes a weapon of honor against the very hierarchy that would limit the power of the inferior position.

Anthropologist Pierre Bourdieu may help us to understand the social dynamics of the nuanced moves in such a process as this challenge to honor.[2] According to Bourdieu, "A gift or a challenge is a provocation, a provocation to reply. . . . The receiver of a gift is caught in the toils of an exchange and has to choose a line of conduct which, whatever he does, will be a response (even if only by default) to the provocation of the initial act. . . . If, obedient to the point of honour, he opts for exchange, his choice is identical with his opponent's initial choice: he agrees to play the game, which can go on for ever, for the riposte is in itself a new challenge."[3] Most significantly, "only escalation, challenge answering challenge," signifies the continuation of the game. In Greville's account of the interchange between Sidney and Oxford, one can count at least five separate challenges and ripostes (which are themselves further challenges): first Oxford's "un-legal" command to Sidney to leave the court and Sidney's evidently very deferential refusal to do so. What the notion of legality supplies here is the possibility for an ideal equality in honor, such an equality being the presupposition on which the game of honor depends. Thus, as we see, if an earl *unlawfully* commands a gentleman, he may end up confronting someone "princely"; yet, as Bourdieu notices, "the popular consciousness is nevertheless aware of actual inequalities" (p. 13), and these inequalities provide infinite possibilities for strategies. Greville explains specifically that Sidney most provoked Oxford by "yielding"—presumably saying he would leave, but in such a way as to insult Oxford. Such "yielding," then, supplies a third riposte, itself a challenge. Then comes the second and direct command to depart the court (presumably for a second time), and Sidney's temperate explanation that it is only the earl's bad manners that make him resist.

In a sense, Sidney is here only making use of what is available to any social inferior when challenged by a social superior: according to Bourdieu, "in the case where the offender is clearly superior to the offended, only the fact of avoiding the challenge is held to be blameworthy, and the offended party is not required to triumph over the offender in order to be rehabilitated in the eyes of public opinion. . . . He has only to adopt an attitude of humility which, by emphasizing his weakness, highlights the arbitrary and immoderate character of the offense" (p. 13).

Greville goes on to explain that there was an audience to this quarrel, as there is in all honor challenges. The audience for these interchanges, however, was quite distinct: a group of French ambassadors who were at court for the Anjou marriage negotiations.

> The French Commissioners unfortunately had that day audience, in those private Galleries, whose windows looked into the Tennis-Court. They instantly drew all to this tumult: every sort of quarrels sorting well with their humours, especially this. Which Sir Philip perceiving, and rising with inward strength, by the propspect of a mighty faction against him; asked my Lord, with a loud voice, that which he had heard clearly enough before. Who (like an Echo, that still multiplies by reflexions) repeated this Epithet of Puppy the second time. Sir Philip resolving in one answer to conclude both the attentive hearers, and passionate actor, gave my Lord a Lie, impossible to be retorted, "in respect, all the world knows, Puppies are gotten by Dogs, and Children by men." (Pp. 65–66)

This zoological riposte is not only "unanswerable," it makes clear the issue of class rank and family status at the heart of the conflict on the tennis court. Class, or the social hierarchy which cut across national boundaries and which supported the dynastic politics of the period, underlay the marriage negotiations and had given them the strange urgency they had taken on for Queen Elizabeth in 1579, when her other options in the Netherlands were running out. Sidney's unanswerable report opens a paralyzing fissure; Oxford does not respond, and in Greville's text the Elizabethan hierarchy is, though still functioning, exposed in all its vulnerability to manipulation from below.

> Hereupon those glorious inequalities of Fortune in his Lordship were put to a kind of pause by a precious inequality of nature in this Gentle-

man. So that they both stood silent a while, like a dumb shew in Tragedy; till Sir Philip sensible of his own wrong, the forrain, and factious
spirits that attended; and yet, even in this question between him, and
his superior, tender to his Countries honour; with some words of sharp
accent, led the way abruptly out of the Tennis-Court; as if so unexpected an accident were not fit to be decided any farther in that place.
Whereof the great Lord making another sense, continues his play, without any advantage of reputation; as by the standard of humours in those
times it was conceived. (P. 66)

One might score the game so far: advantage Sir Philip. But, at so politically charged a moment (and indeed following the rules for such interchanges), the fracas could not stop there. Thus, Greville reports that
Sidney, hearing nothing from Oxford for a whole day, sent a gentleman
to him to "awake him out of his trance," for the French would assuredly
think any pause in response "if not a death, yet a lethargy of true honor
in both." As Bourdieu points out, timing in such spontaneous exchanges
is crucial to how they are to be interpreted (pp. 8–9). The visit from the
gentleman stirred Oxford to think of sending Sidney a challenge to a
duel. While Oxford debated within himself, evidently the Privy Council
got wind of the quarrel and commanded a peace between the two participants. What remains to us of this maneuver is a letter from Sidney to Sir
Christopher Hatton: "As for the matter dependinge betwene the Earle of
Oxford and me, certainly, sir, howe soever I mighte have forgeven hym,
I should never have forgeven myself, if I had layne under so proude an
injurye as he would have laide uppon me, neither can any thinge under
the sunn make me repente yt, nor any miserye make me goo one half
worde back from yt: lett him therefore, as hee will, digest itt."[4]

   Given this furious standoff, the Council decided to let the queen handle
it. Her response was to make the issue of rank absolutely explicit. According to Greville, she "like an excellent monarch" put before Sidney
the difference in degree between earls and gentlemen, the respect inferiors owe to their superiors, and the necessity of princes to maintain
their own creations, as degrees descending between the people's licentiousness and the anointed sovereignty of crowns: "the Gentlemens neglect of the Nobility taught the Peasant to insult both" (p. 68). Sidney
responded with his own legal rights as a member of the gentry; he reminded her that she herself was content to cast her own actions into the
same molds her subjects did, and to govern all her rights by their laws.
He even went so far as to remind her that her father had passed an act
that allowed the gentry free appeal to him against the oppression of the
grandees (p. 69). (What Elizabeth responded to this history lesson, Greville does not say.)

Greville's story is worth considering in such detail because, however unreliable its idealizing treatment of Sidney, it aptly demonstrates the strategies and subtle shades of power and ploy available to an Elizabethan player within the complicated, interlinking codes that organized society. As Bourdieu argues, "The differences between the two parties [to a challenge] are never clear cut, so that each can play on the ambiguities and equivocations which this indeterminacy lends to their conduct. The distance between failure to riposte owing to fear and nonreply bespeaking contempt is often infinitesimal, with the result that disdain can always serve as a mask for pusillanimity" (p. 14).

It is clear from Greville's account that the queen's intervention is actually part of Oxford's response to Sidney. She not only was of Oxford's promarriage party, she continued to make his point about social privilege. Her insistence on the absolute necessity for maintaining class and rank on the tennis court also pointed to what had been at the heart of the marriage question all along. Wallace MacCaffrey has persuasively argued that Elizabeth's uncharacteristic eagerness to get a husband, beyond any premenopausal desperation to produce an heir, had to do with her dwindling options in the war in the Netherlands. She was uncomfortable about committing herself to action—as Sidney had wanted her to—on behalf of a group of Protestants who were rebelling against their anointed (if Catholic) sovereign, and she could thus never embrace anti-Spanish action as an ally of the prince of Orange with the same enthusiasm she could have used in support of such a policy on behalf of her own husband, a born royal.[5]

An early and assiduous supporter of England's joining a Protestant league, Sidney had long attempted to forge alliances with German princelings and Dutch rebels.[6] The tennis court challenge, having everything to do with Elizabeth's courtship of her royal Catholic suitor, was marked in its most "spontaneous" details by the realities of that larger courtship, with its own central issue of rank. No king would wish to ally himself with common rebels, of course, but Elizabeth's more precarious position as a *female* prince, unendowed with the gender natural to patriarchal authority, required her to insist on the privileges of birth above all else, for it was only by this instrument that she held her throne.

If we avail ourselves of Bourdieu's view of the repertoire of strategies available to both sides in a series of exchanges, we can readily see that in Elizabethan society, the shifting of the conflict from the tennis court to the Court itself, where Elizabeth held her corrective audience with Sidney, merely shifts the stage upon which the same game is played out. The court for the game is, finally, the whole social organization of the Elizabethan polity, ranked into its appropriate hierarchical orders in support of the ultimate focus of power: royal prerogative. In Greville's text, Sidney has the last word in this larger arena as well. In his terms, Sidney "obeyed not" and in this disobedience left "an authentical president to after ages, that howsoever tyrants allow of no scope, stamp, or standard, but their own will; yet with Princes there is a latitude for subjects to reserve native and legall freedom, by paying humble tribute in manner, though not in matter, to them" (p. 69). Humbling himself in manner, Sidney, according to Greville, reserves a freedom in matter. At the same time, however, Greville uses Sidney's disobedience rather paradoxically to reveal *Elizabeth's* princeliness. Tyrants (like James, under whom Greville wrote the *Life of Sidney*) allow no latitude for play with strategies. Sidney's freedom to disobey the queen proves her a proper prince. In fact, Elizabeth's princely patience in her attempt to settle the honor challenge between him and Oxford, was doubtless due to more than her queenly forbearance. Her gender put real limits on her power, visible not only in her need to marry royally. If Henry VIII's laws granted Sidney certain freedoms in appealing to his daughter Elizabeth, we can see that Sidney was also using some liberties he believed he held by a far older right. By right of his sex.

As Greville tells the story of the tennis court fracas, its general context is not only the Anjou match but more specifically Sidney's famous letter to Elizabeth, in which he directly attempted to dissuade her from marrying the French royal duke. At least as Greville saw it, the tennis match is merely another version of the same conflict. The strategy of the letter to the queen was just as risky as the challenge to her favorite Oxford, though unlike that quarrel, the letter was less spontaneous. Elizabeth had ordered that John Stubbs and his printer Page, who had written and published a pamphlet against the Anjou match, should have their right hands cut off. Sidney's private letter to the queen transgressed far less than the public pamphlet. Greville argues in defense of Sidney's conduct that "this Gentlemans course was not by murmur among equals or inferiors, to detract from Princes; or by a mutinous kind of bemoaning error, to stir up ill affections in their minds, whose best thoughts could do him no good; but by due address of his humble reasons to the Queen herself, to whom the appeal was proper" (p. 61). Again the social inferior may triumph over the superior by stressing the humility of his position: one may play the game of rank and gain power from *any* position.

Humbly indeed, the letter begins. Sidney addressed it to his "Most feared & beloved, move swete and gracious Soveraine . . . carying no other olive branches of intercession, but the lying myself at your feet, nor no other insinuacion . . . but the true vowed sacrifice of unfeined love, I will in simple & direct terms (as hoping they shall only come to your mercifull eyes) sett down . . . my minde in this most important matter."[7] Sidney's personal motives in opposing the match had a great deal to do with his hatred of Catherine de' Medici, the duke of Anjou's mother, who was thought to have arranged the St. Bartholomew's Day massacre. He had been in Paris and had personally witnessed the massacre in 1572, only seven years before a match between the royal houses was being proposed for a second time, in 1579. Thus he reminds Elizabeth that the "common people will know that he is the sonne of that Jezabel of our age: that his brothers made oblacion of their owne sisters marriadge, the easier to make massacres of all sexes" (p. 52). Even given this motive, Sidney's discourse in the letter becomes surprisingly blunt; for example, one of his stated objections to the match, while a clever move against the queen, is emphatically both personal and coarse: "Often have I heard you," he reminds her, "with protestacion say: No private pleasure nor self affection could lead you unto [marriage]. . . . Nothing can it adde unto you but the blisse of children, which I confess were an unspeakable comfort, but yet no more apparteining to him then to any other to whome that height of all good happes were allotted to be your husband. And therfore I think I may assuredly affirm that what good soever can follow mariage is no more his than any bodies" (p. 55). In essence, any man who could impregnate Elizabeth would do as well. Sidney utterly ignores the paramount qualifications possessed by Anjou—his royal rank, which included his direct connection to an anti-Spanish throne. Instead, Sidney reduces marriage to the bare business of biological reproduction, thereby implicitly reducing Elizabeth to that female role.

Years earlier, Sidney's first artistic effort had been to write a masque advising the queen about marriage. In *The Lady of May,* he offered Elizabeth a choice between a do-nothing shepherd and an overactive and—at least in Sidney's text, privileged—woodsman. At the actual performance of the masque, choosing against the advice Sidney offered in the text, Elizabeth selected the sheepish shepherd. Interestingly, the manuscript note recording Elizabeth's refusal to follow Sidney's authorial intentions suppresses her reasons, using a significant strategy to do so: "it pleased her Majesty to judge that Epsilus [the shepherd] did better deserve her [the Lady of May]; but what words, what reasons she used for it, this paper which carieth so based names, is not worthy to containe."[8] Humility and a profound sense of social inferiority allows Sidney not merely to triumph over, but to obliterate, Elizabeth's challenge to his authority; such a move becomes a virtual Sidney signature.

Later, in the question of the real marriage to "Monsieur," of course, Elizabeth ultimately chose as Sidney had advised. She may, in fact, never have seriously intended marrying Anjou in the first place—although the anxiety of Sidney and others suggests that the project was more real than any other match proposed during her long reign. Greville is aware of the risks Sidney took in his strategy of direct confrontation but argues that directness was itself his own best protection. "Although he found a sweet stream of Sovreign humours in that well-tempered Lady, to run against him, yet found he safety in her self, against the selfness which appeared to threaten him in her" (p. 61). Greville's ostensible point here is that Elizabeth royally remained above faction, thus proving her proper princeliness—in implicit contrast to James's lack of it. But his language imposes on Elizabeth a schizoid character. This split in the "selfhood" of his prince, Greville may owe to the traditional notion of the two bodies of the king; but he is undoubtedly indicating as well the problematic fact that one of Elizabeth's bodies was historically female, a state of affairs that introduced constant static into the patriarchal politics of the period.

It is in fact intriguing that Sidney was disposed to be so disobedient to his sovereign in these two particular, and parallel, episodes of challenge and marriage making. For the two are not only linked in Greville's text, they are, anthropologically speaking, analogous. Bourdieu describes the challenge to honor as another version of the challenge implicit in the exchange of gifts. In patriarchal societies, the most precious gift that can be exchanged is a woman, given in marriage from one man or group of men to another, the exchange forming, as many anthropologists agree, the quintessential act of civilization.[9] What also links the two episodes, then, is not only the provocational nature of both social interactions but also the fact that such interactions usually take place only between males. Honor challenges and marriage making are supposed to be gender-specific activities, even in Elizabethan England.

According to Bourdieu, honor "is very closely associated with virility. . . . the point of honor is a permanent disposition, embedded in the agents' very bodies in the form of mental dispositions, schemes of perception and thought, extremely general in their application, such as those which divide up the world in accordance with the oppositions between the male and the female, east and west, future and past, top and bottom, right and left, etc., and also, at a deeper level, in the form of bodily postures and stances, ways of standing, sitting, looking, speaking, or walking."[10] While Elizabeth may have taken herself out of the usual gender dichotomies by insisting on not only her sovereignty but her virginity, thus rising above all categories of woman and subsuming them all—virgin, wife, and mother—into a later goddesslike transcendence, nevertheless, actively considering these roles in reality in 1579, she would have been more vulnerable to traditional gender distinctions than ever

before or since.[11] In refusing to heed her advice about his honor challenge, Sidney is only exercising his right as male against her (female)
interference. In writing to her about her choice of partners, Sidney exercises his male authority to restrict her freedom to bestow herself how she
might wish. As a woman, Elizabeth has no traditional rights in these
specific matters; and if Sidney has few rights as a commoner in both the
challenge to an earl and the advice to a queen on whom she should not
marry, he had many rights in both cases as a sexual male. Sidney pits his
rights as male against Elizabeth's female prerogative and, in both cases,
wins.[12] In both the challenge to honor and in the marriage making, when
Elizabeth's real sex clashed with her figuratively male gender as patriarch, she had no absolute rights.

The pamphleteer Stubbs's attempt to speak for the country in a public
arena had aroused her ire; Sidney's private letter offended less not only
because it was private, but because Sidney's class, while still common,
was distinctly "gentle" (whereas Stubbs, a lawyer, had no birth rank). In
fact, both Stubbs and Sidney were probably speaking for the Council
itself.[13] Hubert Languet, Sidney's Continental humanist friend, forgave
Sidney the risk he had taken in writing the letter because he assumed that
Sidney had been asked to do so by the patriarchs of his group.[14] Otherwise the risk he took would have been unacceptable: he had been a most
promising statesman, one whom Elizabeth had entrusted as a very young
man with an important embassy. In the Anjou affairs, Languet worried
that Sidney's jeopardy was so great he might have to leave the country.
Significantly, this fear derived from Languet's assumption that Sidney
had affronted a male, not a female: that threat came not from the queen
but from Anjou.[15] Such anxiety on Languet's part suggests further that it
was Elizabeth's femaleness that allowed this most primitive resistance,
revealed in Sidney's letter—a gender bias that may have been hinted at as
well in Sidney's reminding her of her father's policies about protecting
the gentry. It could not have been lost on her that a vast number of these
policies were predicated on Henry VIII's passionate desire to avoid female rule. Thus, while it must remain speculative, an anthropological
analysis of Sidney's behavior grants him some cultural authority for his
otherwise self-destructive insistence that the queen not marry where she
apparently wished. Her dynastic, royal (but female) privilege must bow
to his nationalist male principle.

Greville reports that after the letter, Sidney "kept his access to her
Majesty as before," but in fact there was a period of forced—or self-
imposed—rustication when Sidney repaired to his sister's estate in Wilton. Scholars are undecided as to the motive for Sidney's withdrawal
from court.[16] The ambiguity here is one of the more intriguing aspects

of his career—a point where we have lost the matter behind the opacity of a silent manner. Was he summarily sent down? Did he leave of his own choice? His year's absence is the more intriguing because scholars guess that it was during this time that Sidney began his accidental career, as he puts it in the *Apology for Poetry*, of "paper blurrer" and wrote the first version of the *Arcadia* for his sister's amusement. Leonard Tennenhouse has recently argued that the political plot of the *Arcadia* pivots on a conflict between a "strictly patrilineal system of inheritance where power is always embodied in a male, and a bilateral system where power descends through the daughters of the first son." The central question of the plot becomes "under what conditions could a female monarch marry without compromising the power inhering in the Crown."[17] When seen in this light, the *Arcadia* in effect continues Sidney's consideration of the problematic Tudor traffic in women.

When Sidney in his *Apology for Poetry* laments how "idle England has grown so hard a stepmother" to poets that they are impoverished, we realize how poetry itself—the apologetic, defensive practice of it—may be yet another strategy against the queen, its best protection being its indirection. One may, in fact, trace the progress of poesy in the *Apology* from its derogated status at the opening of the treatise to its ultimate reign in the conclusion as "monarch" over all the other arts. In *Young Philip Sidney*, James Osborn suggests a line of reasoning that gives this figurative usurpation at least a possible historical background. Briefly put, Sidney's preeminence at home among his uncle Leicester's radical-activist Protestant faction and his privileged entertainments abroad by Continental defenders of the Protestant cause (such as Languet and his contacts), made him a very powerful opponent to the pacifist Queen Elizabeth. With a political base in the Netherlands, Sidney "could then," Osborn argues, "become the Dudley candidate for Elizabeth's throne."[18] However rash such a speculation seems, it does usefully remind us that Elizabeth's position was always far more precarious *at the time* than her huge retrospective historical success often allows us to realize. She may have had John Stubbs's hand cut off, but all she could do to Sidney was send him down from court (if indeed she did) and deny him lucrative appointments—as she definitely did. That by such deprivations she could also impoverish him was due in part to his familial, dynastic misfortunes, as well as to her royal disfavor.

Sidney's return to court, after the year's retirement following the debacle of the French marriage, occasioned the exchange of New Year's gifts: his present to Elizabeth was a "whip garnished with small diamonds."[19] Such a gift, calling attention to their previous differences, is witty, apologetic, and insistent on their differences. Sidney politicly participated that year in a tournament in which he was a member of the duke of Anjou's entourage. He thus graciously defers in manner—but not in matter. Greville suppresses the year's absence and other such conflictual features of his friend's and his sovereign's relationship, though he does constantly complain that Sidney had no proper stage on which to enact his heroic designs. Writing under James I, Greville's purpose is to make both Sidney and his queen ideal exemplars of both sovereignty and courtship—of self-limiting power and expansive, imperial statesmanship. To this end, the next episode Greville chooses to relate, after the tennis court challenges and Sidney's rebuff of the queen's correction, is Sidney's secret expedition with Sir Francis Drake to the West Indies, "wherein [Sidney] fashioned the whole body with purpose to become head of it himself" (p. 70).

While Sidney's part in the Drake project was kept a secret, it was, in due course, found out, and just as he was on the verge of sailing from Plymouth, he was commanded by royal decree to return to court, the message sent by a peer of the realm "carrying . . . in the one hand grace, the other thunder" (p. 76). The offered "grace" was, at long last, an appointment as governor of Flushing, in the Netherlands. In pursuit of the political line Sidney's party had long been espousing, Elizabeth had finally granted the appointment. In pursuit of chivalric bravado, if not victory for the Dutch rebels, during a skirmish with Spanish troops, Sidney took off his thigh armor before charging the enemy and received the bullet that, entering at the knee and shattering the thigh bone, left the festering wound from which he soon died at the age of thirty-one.[20] Before narrating the story of Sidney's tragic end in 1586, two years before the defeat of the Armada, Greville outlines a map of his hero's imperial imagination in two chapters that encompass a remarkable analysis of the possible strategies open to England in what should have been, according to Greville's account of Sidney's thought, a concerted and strategic war with Spain. After canvassing all the political interconnections between such disparate parts of the map as Poland and the Ottoman Empire (Sidney's imperial politics are global), he settled, so Greville records, on taking the war with Spain to the New World. Sidney's intention was to plant England's empire on the mainland of America, thereby draining England of the excess population that threatened its stability while increasing trade, and hemming in Philip of Spain by cutting off his supply lines from the New World. On Greville's testimony, it would appear that the foundations of the British Empire were laid in Sir Philip Sidney's prophetic imagination.

Specifically, Sidney intended to revive the hazardous enterprise of "Planting upon the Main of America" (p. 117), a "new intended Plantation, not like an Assylum for fugitives . . . but as an Emporium for the confluence of all Nations that love, or profess any kinde of vertue, or Commerce" (pp. 118–19). The word "plant" takes on a special character in Greville's text, serving as a link in his narrative and contrasting the real politics of courtship, which Greville exposes in his analysis of his own, less heroically ideal life, with the heroic politics of his dead friend. Himself a much more successful courtier to Elizabeth than Sir Philip had been, Greville explains how his own success came to be: "I finding the specious fires of youth to prove far more scorching than glorious, called my second thoughts to counsell, and in that Map clearly discerning action and honor to fly with more wings than one; and that it was sufficient for the plant to grow where his Sovereigns hand had planted it; I found reason to contract my thoughts from those larger, but wandring horizons of the world abroad, and bound my prospect within the safe limits of duty, in such homes services, as were acceptable to my Sovereign" (p. 149). Greville would not plant America, but be a homegrown plant well-watered by his sovereign's hand. With his tragic death Sidney escaped such sad and resigned restrictions and sailed into history the most renowned member of his generation, as well as the most popular Elizabethan poet throughout the next century.[21] In this assessment of his and his friend's lives, Greville reverses our usual sense of success and failure in court careers. Judged by the terms of the day, Greville was far more successful because he had been chosen by Elizabeth, whereby, in Sidney's own admission, the queen was always "apt . . . to interpret everything to my disadvantage" (*Works* 3:167); Greville, however, chooses to deprecate himself in relation to Sidney, who was not chosen and who could therefore remain independent, glorious, and heroic. For his own strategic purposes under James, Greville reverses the usual standard for evaluating a courtier's success: Sidney is to be judged not by what he accomplished, but by what he could have done, had his prince chosen him to do it.[22]

It may have been the same strategic purpose that inspired Greville to suppress any mention of Sidney's sonnet sequence—the work through which we of this century have best known him.[23] Greville gives a full list of all of Sidney's other texts, stressing in particular Sidney's politically motivated translation of the Psalms and analyzing his didactic procedures in the revised *Arcadia*. Of course, his suppression of *Astrophil and Stella*—which had spawned innumerable copies, and indeed, on which he himself modeled his own sonnet cycle *Caelica*—may have been due simply to the cycle's precipitous drop from fashion after the death of Elizabeth. And here too Greville shows his sensitivity to strategies. If courtly compliment to a putative female reader had been fashionable at Elizabeth's court, it was distinctly not so under James, who had, not surprisingly, no taste for the form.[24] Accordingly, although the sequence had been published in 1591, Greville neglects to include it in the oeuvre, possibly because it no longer had a recognizable political function.[25] Its intense and circumscribed efflorescence allows us, however, to consider possible analogies in political function among four "court" episodes: a challenge on a tennis court, a conflictual conversation between a sovereign and subject at court, the contextualizing courting negotiations for a marriage match, and a Petrarchan sequence that displays the maneuverings of an attempted erotic seduction, that is, a "courtship." Yet before going on to consider Astrophil's peculiarly Elizabethan politics, we need to ask, what does the reduplication of language in all these various kinds of "courtships" have to say about the relations between language and social practice in Elizabethan England?

In another of his arguments, Bourdieu points to the defensive blindness of structural linguistics about the social context of the object it academically constructs. If language were as polysemous as linguistics would have it, "speech would be," according to Bourdieu, "an endless series of puns."[26] Bourdieu objects to an artificial arena for language, an academic treatment of polysemy which specifically "breaks the organic relation between competence and the field"; such puns "are ungraspable in practice because production is always embedded in a field of reception. . . . One can only speak of the different meanings of a word so long as one bears in mind that their juxtaposition in the simultaneity of learned discourse (the page of the dictionary) is a scholarly artifact and that they never exist simultaneously in practice"—except, as Bourdieu allows, in actual puns (those produced for reception in the field). What such an interesting quarrel with contemporary linguistics points up is that the language of earlier eras was not so highly regulated as it is now and that, lacking dictionaries as we think of them and obviously in love with wordplay (if we are to trust Spenser's practice and Shakespeare's representations of courtly chat), the Elizabethan era is a most interesting one for attending to the practical possibilities of wordplay in the social field. Not only were there no dictionaries in Elizabeth's era, save for books giving English equivalents of Latin words (or other foreign languages) and definitions of technical (or "hard") words, there were also no rules by which to censure the pun as transgressive. The simultaneity of meaning that marks a pun may not have been so odd and out of the ordinary then as now.[27] What this means for a reading of sixteenth-century language is that not only must we attend to the polysemy of its texts—the punning potential of a word whose meaning would probably have been heard and seen by Elizabethan ears and eyes much more readily than by our far differently trained organs of perception—but that we must also attempt to hear the *social* resonance of wordplay as well. The simultaneity of meaning in a pun might provide a social as well as a verbal or poetic strategy. Read in these terms, the sonnet sequence Sidney wrote becomes a social practice that addresses relations of real power and does so through the most ostensibly textual of verbal manipulations: the pun.

In his edition of Sidney's poetry, after reviewing the fascinating biographical and political context of *Astrophil and Stella*, William Ringler summarizes,

> When we compare the known facts of Sidney's life during the years 1581–82 with the sonnets, we are immediately struck with how much of his biography he left out of his poems. He tells us nothing about the disappointment of his hopes in being superseded as the Earl of Leicester's heir, nothing about his trip to Antwerp, nothing about his dominating interest in politics and international affairs . . . and most significant, nothing about his activities in opposition to the proposed marriage of the Duke of Anjou and the Queen. The sonnets concern courtship, and yet they do not contain a single hint of the attempts being made at the time he was writing to marry him to Stella's sister, Dorothy Devereux, or of his own interest in the same time in Frances Walsingham.[28]

In fact, Sidney did ultimately marry Frances Walsingham, and she, after his death, married the earl of Essex, the brother of Penelope Devereux— that is, of Stella. Prior to his marriage, Sidney had been disinherited by the birth of son to his uncle the earl of Leicester and his uncle's new wife, the countess of Essex—that is, Penelope/Stella's mother. Sidney had been expecting to inherit from his uncle should Leicester die childless. It had been in part the cachet of being Leicester's heir—that is, heir to Elizabeth's most powerful favorite—that had made Sidney so welcome on the Continent, where Dutch and German princes wanted to marry him to their daughters.

Arthur Marotti has pointedly stressed the immediate historical context of Sidney's authorship of the sequence: "when Sidney wrote the sonnets (or gathered them into a sequence), he was and *he was known as* a politically, economically and socially disappointed young man."[29] According to Marotti, "love is not love" in *Astrophil and Stella* but rather Sidney's attempted reorganization of his humiliating experience as a failed courtier: the sequence "wittily converts the language of ambition into the language of love" (p. 402). The problem, as Marotti sees it, was that a private courtship finally provides "no compensation for sociopolitical defeat," especially because the sequence merely stages "a painful repetition of the experience in another mode" (p. 405). In this interpretation, Sidney is no more successful as a lover than he was as a courtier: ultimately he is denied his lady's favor.

What such an otherwise brilliant rereading of the sequence as Marotti's leaves out are the strategic possibilities open to Sidney upon his decision to write a *Petrarchan* sequence. A paradoxical strategy of sexual domination is one of the more intriguing interests of Petrarchan poetry; as Ann Jones and Peter Stallybrass summarize it, "although the lover depicts himself as humble suitor to a dominating lady, he actually performs an act of public mastery, demonstrating his virtuosity in the practice of a masculine convention."[30] Thus, while the language of love into which Sidney translates his political frustrations was perfect for the problem, it was not, as they point out, unpolitical to begin with: "the inequality of the servant . . . to his master . . . , the inequality of the subordinated sex . . . to the dominant sex. . . . The blurring of these two discourses is the method by which Astrophil can continue to maneuver without too blunt a naming of unequal positions. He is concerned, indeed, not so much to alter the categories as to manipulate them so as to redistribute power" (p. 60). The overt plot of the sequence in which Stella denies Astrophil any final fulfillment (although the eighth song allows us to guess at more) may repeat Sidney's public defeat in politics, but, by the same token, it is the author's total control over Stella as a (silent) character in his plot which enacts his masculine, social mastery. Such a redistribution of power is at issue in any sonnet sequence (as in any honor challenge). What makes Sidney's sequence different is the remarkable historical specificity with which it attempts this distribution.

The signal point of interconnection between poetic text and cultural context is that Sidney distinctly identifies Stella as Penelope Devereux. He does so, moreover, by punning on her *husband*'s name. To do so is to name Stella specifically in terms of the traffic in women, a procedure that may have carried for Sidney the complicated history of Penelope Devereux's involvement in that quite circumscribed traffic, since she had once earlier been named as a possible bride for him. The certainty of this historical identification makes Sidney's sequence unique: while—*pace* A. L. Rowse—we will never know who Shakespeare's Dark Lady is, or resolve doubts about Rosalind and Elizabeth Boyle in the *Amoretti*, or at this late date discover the identity of Laura, we do know, absolutely, that Stella is Lady Rich.[31] If we pause for a moment to ask why the identification is through her husband's name rather than her own, we can see how the word "Rich" and the meanings it sustains in the sonnets not only names for Sidney his various sociopolitical failures, it offers a strategy for revaluing them. One could imagine a whole series of poems that might have identified Penelope Devereux in other ways just as certainly—to take only one possibility, in terms of her mythically resonant name, Penelope. Having previously named himself Philisides (Philip Sidney) in the character of the Arcadian poet, Sidney here signals a similar identification by the name Astrophil, which is properly spelled with the "i," for it takes a syllable from "Philip." What is, after all, in a name?

Is Stella Lady Rich because Penelope Devereux was the daughter of the woman whose giving birth to a son impoverished (disenriched) Sidney? Is she Lady Rich because her married name is the word for what Sidney thereby lost? Or is it that, by ironizing the name, Sidney avails himself of a poetic strategy that will allow him to claim his title as an autonomous author of his individual destiny, revaluing and enriching his career in his own terms?

> Towards Aurora's Court a Nymph doth dwell,
> Rich in all beauties which man's eye can see:
> . . . .
> Rich in the treasure of deserv'd renowne,
> Rich in the riches of a royall hart,
> Rich in those gifts which give th'eternall crowne;
> Who though most rich in these and everie part,
> Which make the patents of true worldly blisse,
> Hath no misfortune, but that Rich she is.
>
> (Sonnet 37)

The notion of richness contained in Stella's real, historical name, offers Sidney not merely the chance to identify her (and therefore to indicate the dynastic disappointment her mother's bearing a son to his uncle had caused him) but also the chance to query the issue of value itself, as Elizabethan society understood it to work in various social discourses. Stella is "rich" in courtly reputation (achieved value), in her virtually royal nobility of character (class, or ascribed value), in religious spirituality (eternal crowns are better than earthly); she also has "patents," that is, monopolies, on the market in "true worldly bliss." Her only misfortune is that she is married to a dolt.[32] The dolt's name, however, allows Sidney to redefine his own poverty: "now long needy Fame / Doth even grow *rich, naming my Stellas name*" (Sonnet 35). How such a private revaluation of his sense of himself—no longer a defamed courtier, but a poet famously inspired by love—will affect that public career becomes an issue in the poems themselves.

> "Art not asham'd to publish thy disease?"
> Nay, that may breed my fame, it is so rare:

"But will not wise men thinke thy words fond ware?"
Then be they close, and so none shall displease.
"What idler thing, then speake and not be hard?"
What harder thing then smart, and not to speake?
(Sonnet 34)

Sidney's worry about publication here not only alerts us to the problematic position Petrarchan writing occupied at the time Sidney wrote (it would be thought fond ware), but it also makes clear that the privileged audience for the sonnets is not Stella herself, but the "wise men" who would probably find the poems foolish. Not to be heard by them, it appears, is not to be heard at all. The sonnets were in fact kept close, circulated to only the smallest coterie of readers, apparently kept closer than Sidney's other poetry.[33] So it would appear that Sidney held to his decision not to publish; hence any argument that would claim that Sidney expected to make up for his dynastic disappointments and answer the court's murmurings specifically about his ambition (which he denies in sonnets 23, 27, and 30) by stunning them with his exquisitely displayed folly in love is certainly not one that would work for Sidney in his lifetime. In order for him to achieve a display of "public mastery," as Jones and Stallybrass suggest, the poems need to have become public— as, of course, they did after his death. The first audience for the poems was, apparently, only his immediate family, in fact those who would have been most disappointed by his failures and to whom a palliative set of excuses might have been most welcome. Indeed, he may never have intended to publish—that is to circulate in any way—*Astrophil and Stella*. (His brother Robert gave few clues as to the existence of his own poems, which were not published until 1984 from a single autograph manuscript.[34]) However, it is helpful, in evaluating just how useful a strategy the sequence could have been in Sidney's overall career, to remember that he did not live to implement it. He died accidentally only four years after he wrote it. It is therefore a bit hasty to dismiss the sequence as actual social strategy because it made no difference in Sidney's life. As imaginary poetic (and potentially social) strategy it does indeed stage a recuperation of competitive authority among court wits and poetasters and manages a nostalgic recapture of class rank.

Note, for example, that Sidney's address in Sonnet 37, in which he names Stella as Penelope Rich, is "Listen Lordings with good eare to me / For of my life I must a riddle tell." Doubtless an allusion to Chaucer's even then archaic oral stance, such an address asserts the high old, aristocratic rank Sidney ascribes to his poems by way of their imagined audience. Aurora's court, where Sidney enthrones Stella, is like the more valued courts of old. There such lordings are interpreters, as well, who will figure the riddle of the name; sympathetic readers unlike, presumably, the censorious auditors of a present-day court.

Other subjects of address (his fellow poets) are not necessarily high in birth rank, but, as poets, Astrophil can lecture them on the value of their own poetic endeavors. If speaking and not being "hard" is less hard than not speaking, speaking and being heard by an imaginary audience who will be daunted by the value of one's speech is remarkably easy.

> How falles it them, that with so smooth an ease
> My thoughts I speake, and what I speake doth flow
> In verse, and that my verse best wits doth please?
> Guess we the cause: "What, is it thus?" Fie no:
> "Or so?" Much lesse: "How then?" Sure thus it is:
> My lips are sweet inspired, with Stella's kisse.
>
> (Sonnet 74)

In imagining the circulation of his poems, Sidney imagines his own socially recognized mastery. As a textual battleground, the poems compete not only with Spenser, Greville, Dyer, Sidney's own brother Robert, or prior court poets in the English tradition such as Wyatt and Surrey, who had used Petrarch's mode for similar court-serving ends; his rivals extend to all the male Continental practitioners of the sequence. That Oxford was known as a versifier might have some immediate significance; so too, Elizabeth was known to try her hand at poetry. Because Sidney's sequence specifically concerned an adulterous and unidealized passion (as Petrarch's did not), it would have made a commanding scandal in Elizabeth's court. That it was not addressed to the queen, in the midst of a prevailing fashion for courtly compliment of her, may have been its most pointed aggression against her central authority. He would not play politics by her rules but would turn her Petrarchan forms to his own purposes.[35]

Sidney makes a bid for poetic fame by denying such poetic ambition, just as he denies his political ambition: "Stella thinke not that I by verse seeke fame, / Who seeke, who hope, who love, who live but thee"; in this poem, he eschews as well a specific Petrarchan prominence indicated by the pun on Laura/laurel: "Nor so ambitious am I, as to frame / A nest for my yong praise in Lawrell tree." Sidney abjures the very name of poet: "In truth I sweare, I wish not there should be /Graved in mine Epitaph a Poet's name" (Sonnet 90). The name with which he consistently ends his poems is hers, Stella. And she, of course, is—so the historical identification says—more than a mere sign of his poetic fame, as Petrarch's pun on Laura/laurel implies. Unlike other mistresses of that tradition, Stella is real and identified, and Astrophil insists that his passion is no mere motive for verse making. Stella thus is not merely the sign of his poetic originality and authority, but of Sidney's problematical historical situation. He turns his Petrarchan abasement into authority, manipulating a character, Stella, who allows him to woo, conquer, and be rejected, and, by his manipulation of that rejection, discursively to control his own recent misfortunes in his career. His Petrarchan abasement changes his rank, from a vulgarity the muses would never visit ("Muses scorne with vulgar braines to dwell") to a private ease of nobility predicated on a kiss; it grants him, if only in his text, the power to make her say what he wants her to, as in the refrain to the fourth song:

> Take me to thee, and thee to me.
> "No, no, no, no, my Deare, let be."

> Wo to me, and do you sweare
> Me to hate? But I forbeare,
> Cursed be my destines all,
> That brought me so high to fall:
> Soone with my death I will please thee.
> "No, no, no, no my Deare, let be."

Such a strategy turns traditional abasement into one kind of authority, in the process fulfilling the demands Sidney made on his countrymen in the *Apology,* to write as if they really were in love.[36]

Paying tribute, in humble manner though not in matter, to the imperative of erotic desire, Sidney obliquely claims his own political importance. Thus in Sonnet 30, he lists all the thorny diplomatic problems facing the Elizabethan ruling elite: will the Ottoman Empire make another attack on Christian Europe, what of Polish-Russian relations, what will happen in the French wars of religion, how will the prince of Orange's rebellion fare in the Netherlands, how will the Irish rebels take recent victories by his father, what will Scotland do? "These questions busie wits to me do frame; / I, cumbred with good maners, answer do, / But know not how, for still I think of you" (Sonnet 30). As Marotti acutely notes, this is the first time that Stella is directly addressed in the sequence (p. 401). The poem puts her (and privacy) directly in contrast to, and superior in value to, the affairs of court and state that her very important lover finds cumbering his public life. In opting for a different kind of courtship, private erotic suitorship, Sidney chooses a different kind of fame. Hereby rewriting his political frustrations, imposed from above by a queen jealous of the prerogatives he as a courtier had very insistently resisted, Sidney claims that the choice not to be a famous statesman was his own. His strategy here, to make his lack of preferment look like his own choice, by shifting the place of conflict away from the real court into his own psychic battles with honor and duty and desire, has certain costs. It is enslavement not to a queen—as Greville chose, letting himself be planted where his sovereign's hand would place him— but enslavement to Stella, a nineteen-year-old wife of a courtly cipher, whose name played ironically on the riches Sidney had, in any case, already lost.

What was Stella like? Greville consistently calls Sidney the "unattended Cassandra of his age," and—if we understand the underlying politics of the sequence as a subtle resistance to the queen—we may note that Sidney's selection of Penelope Rich for his Stella was not only punningly appropriate to his predicament, it was in time to prove itself prophetically so. Years later, Penelope Devereux was evidently very instrumental in her brother, the earl of Essex's, uprising against Elizabeth. At his interrogation, Essex rather ungallantly blamed his sister for helping to instigate his attack on the queen: "my sister . . . did continually urge me on with telling me how all my friends and followers thought me a coward, & that I had lost all my valour. . . . She must be looked to, for she had a proud spirit."[37] At the time of his uprising, Essex was married to Frances Walsingham, Sidney's widow. Brother of the woman for whom Sidney had famously written he'd given up all, husband to Sidney's wife—Robert Devereux, earl of Essex, may not have done what he did because he inherited Sidney's intransigence along with his wife and sword (which Sidney had willed him). But Essex can stand as emblem of the resistance potentially present in the dynastic faction (cemented by the traffic in women) for whom Sidney had earlier been spokesman. Penelope Devereux is without doubt Astrophil's Stella. She is also without doubt the only woman we know to have urged her brother to rebel against Queen Elizabeth.

At age eighteen, of course, recently departed from a virtuous upbringing at her home with the Huntingtons and married to a rich heir the same year that Elizabeth contemplated marrying the duke of Anjou, Sidney's Penelope Devereux Rich would not have been, when Sidney wrote, the rebel to all propriety and authority she turned out to be. However, only two years after Sidney's death, some six years after the sequence was written, she took up at age twenty-six with a veteran of Zutphen, Sir Charles Blount, with whom she had a total of five illegitimate children.[38] She also showed herself more loyal to Sidney's brother Robert than her own brother was and risked censure to aid him.[39] It is, of course, dangerous to judge how well *Astrophil and Stella* may have served Sidney by how favorably Penelope Rich received its identification with her and how

little she apparently paid for any of her own transgressions against honor
or authority.⁴⁰ Sidney, for his part, counted up his costs:

> My youth doth waste, my knowledge brings forth toyes,
> My wit doth strive those passions to defend,
> Which for reward spoile it with vaine annoyes.
> I see my course to lose my selfe doth bend:
>   I see and yet no greater sorrow take,
>   Then that I lose no more for Stella's sake.
>
> (Sonnet 18)

Sidney died bankrupt and in debt; not until the very end of his life did
he regain that heritage of service to the crown which his father and uncle
had enjoyed. In the meantime, the knowledge he had, he spent on toys
like the *Arcadia* and *Astrophil and Stella*. Sonnet 18 implies that, like some
glorious Anthony, he is happy to destroy himself, a world well-lost for
love. But he also confesses that he wished he had more to lose. He desires
not only Stella but also all the riches, fame, and achievement he would
happily throw away for her.

To see that, in such ambiguous balanced couplets as this last, Sidney
manages to have it both ways is to see the overall strategy of the sequence. If he never, as Greville confessed, "was Magistrate, nor possessed of any fit stage for eminence to act upon," and even if his life was
short and his fortunes private, yet there are—as Greville hopes—"lines
to be drawn, not Astronomicall, or imaginary, but reall lineaments . . .
out of which nature often sparkleth brighter rayes in some, than ordinarily appear in the ripeness of others" (pp. 38–41). If Sir Philip Sidney was
denied his stage not only by the queen's abiding mistrust but by his early
death, he yet left the lines in which he claims he authored his own ruined
career. While Greville obviously felt the sequence needed to be suppressed, preferring an unpreferred statesman to a preeminent poet, Sidney's own legend for himself told a different story. Of course, he did not
die of passion, or of Petrarchan poetics. He died, in fact, of Protestant
politics—and his own, not the queen's (the same Protestant politics that
would harry James, and behead Charles). If we have to work this hard to
retrieve that simple fact about his life, our difficulty is testimony to how
thoroughly Sidney's self-creation as poet-lover has prevailed over Greville's legend of soldier-statesman. We need to read the politics back into
the poetry not only to see that the politics are indeed embedded there but
also to perceive how well Sidney's strategy of mystification succeeded.
While it is not true that he threw over a blossoming career as courtier/
statesman to become a love-struck poet, it *is* true that he did not succeed

at winning either of his ladies' favor, neither Stella's or the queen's, because he refused to play by their rules of "tyran honor."
For finally, the poems are filled with the strategies of such a rich authority that to challenge that authority and give its author, as he did
Oxford, the lie, risks making the critic too much of a cynic. If puppies
are begotten by dogs, and children by men, it is useful to realize that
poets still author, if not the entirety of their political lives, then at least
the most powerful legends about them.[41]

Notes

1. Sir Fulke Greville, *The Life of the Renowned Sir Philip Sidney* (London:
Henry Seile, 1652), pp. 63–65; hereafter cited in the text.

2. Frank Whigham, *Ambition and Privilege: The Social Tropes of Elizabethan
Courtesy Theory* (Berkeley: University of California Press, 1984), pp. 4–5, argues
for the "double adaptation of Bourdieu's formulation" in order to fit it to the
social practices of Elizabethan England. First, honor was a "notion specific to the
ruling elite, not shared by all males" (unlike Bourdieu's undifferentiated societies); and second, honor was no longer merely a question of birth but could be
"achieved as well as ascribed."

3. Pierre Bourdieu, *Outline of a Theory of Practice*, tr. Richard Nice (Cambridge: Cambridge University Press, 1977), p. 12.

4. *The Prose Works of Sir Philip Sidney*, ed. Albert Feuillerat, 4 vols. (Cambridge: Cambridge University Press, 1969), 3:128; hereafter cited as *Works*.

5. Wallace T. MacCaffrey, *Queen Elizabeth and the Making of Policy, 1572–1588*
(Princeton: Princeton University Press, 1981), pp. 295–96.

6. James M. Osborn, *Young Philip Sidney, 1572–1577* (New Haven: Yale University Press, 1972), pp. 475–500.

7. *Works* 3:51.

8. Ibid. 2:216. David Kalstone notes that it is difficult to understand the
queen's rejection of Therion the woodsman (*Sidney's Poetry: Contexts and Interpretations* [New York: W. W. Norton, 1965], p. 46). Sidney may have been counting
too heavily on a completely socialized response from Elizabeth when he asked
her to elect as husband for the Lady, one who, in the Lady's words, "withall . . .
growes to such rages, that sometimes he strikes me." For a discussion of Sidney
at the Elizabethan court see Louis A. Montrose, "Celebration and Insinuation:
Sir Philip Sidney and the Motives of Elizabethan Courtship," *Renaissance Drama*,
n.s., 8 (1972): 3–35, especially p. 22 for comment on *The Lady of May* as Sidney's
attempt to "explore the foundations and limits of royal power, and to promote
the rights and interests of men of his own status vis-á-vis the crown and peer-
age." See also Alan Sinfield, "Power and Ideology: An Outline Theory and Sidney's *Arcadia*," *ELH* 52 (1982): 259–78, for a discussion of Sidney's class position
"at a point of structural confusion."

9. For a critique of Lévi-Strauss's arguments about exogamy, see Gayle
Rubin, "The Traffic in Women: Notes on the 'Political Economy' of Sex," in

Toward an Anthropology of Women, ed. Rayna Reiter (New York and London: Monthly Review Press, 1975).

10. Bourdieu, *Outline*, p. 15. The specific content of the honor challenge, as Greville reports it, would seem to insist upon male virility, in the process somewhat eliding the female function of reproduction in marriage. It is probable that Oxford originally intended the epithet "puppy" to insult Sidney in terms of his own achieved status of masculinity—any family insult ("race of dogs") would have been less important. Sidney's unanswerable riposte—if dogs beget puppies, then *men* beget children—insists that all the world already knows that he, Sidney, is a man (and in so saying proves it); Sidney was higher born on his mother's than on his father's side and so could claim some nobility through his mother. Yet Sidney here—one might say unconsciously—emphasizes the shared biological substratum rather than the class rank he could claim through his mother, who was daughter of a duke.

11. For a discussion of Elizabeth's transcendence, see Louis A. Montrose, "*A Midsummer Night's Dream* and the Shaping Fantasies of Elizabethan Culture," in *Rewriting the Renaissance: The Discourses of Sexual Difference in Early Modern Europe*, ed. Margaret Ferguson, Maureen Quilligan, and Nancy J. Vickers (Chicago: University of Chicago Press, 1986), pp. 65–87.

12. For a discussion of the problems Elizabeth faced as a female prince see Allison Heisch, "Queen Elizabeth and the Persistence of Patriarchy," *Feminist Review* 4 (1980): 45–56.

13. MacCaffrey, *Queen Elizabeth*, pp. 265–66.

14. *The Correspondence of Sir Philip Sidney and Hubert Languet*, tr. Steuart A. Pears (1845; London: William Pickering, 1971), p. 187.

15. Ibid., p. 170.

16. Richard C. McCoy, *Sir Philip Sidney: Rebellion in Acadia* (New Brunswick, N.J.: Rutgers University Press, 1970), chap. 1, outlines the general tensions between Sidney and Queen Elizabeth. See also A. C. Hamilton, *Sir Philip Sidney: A Study of His Life and Works* (Cambridge: Cambridge University Press, 1977), pp. 27–28.

17. Leonard Tennenhouse, *Power on Display: The Politics of Shakespeare's Genres* (New York and London: Methuen, 1986), p. 25.

18. Osborn, *Young Philip Sidney*, p. 497.

19. William A. Ringler, Jr., ed., *The Poems of Sir Philip Sidney* (Oxford: Clarendon Press, 1962), p. 440. Citations of Sidney's poems are to this edition.

20. Sidney placed such Protestant politics, his "love of the caws" [cause], as he put it, above his desire to please the queen, to be safe, rich, and graced by her favor. In a most revealing letter, Sidney confesses to his father-in-law that his radical Protestant activism, his very self, is more important to him than her favor. Elizabeth was perhaps very wise when she refused to reward such lack of devotion.

I had before cast my court of dang[er] want and disgrace, and before God Sir it is trew [that] in my hart the love of the caws doth so far over-ballance them all that with Gods grace thei shall never make me weery

of my resolution. If her Majesty wear the fowntain I woold fear consi-
diring what I daily fynd that we shold wax dry, but she is but a means
whom God useth and I know not whether I am deceaved but I am
faithfully persuaded that if she shold with draw her self other springes
woold ryse to help this action. For me thinkes I see the great work
indeed in hand, against the abusers of the world, wherein it is not
greater fault to have confidence in mans power, then it is to hastily to
despair of God work. I think a wyse and constant man ought never to
greev whyle he doth plai as a man mai sai his own part truly though
othgers be out but if him self leav his hild becaws other marriners will
be ydle he will hardli forgive him self this own fault. For me I can not
promise of my own cource no nor of the my[   ] because I know
there is a hyer power that must uphold me or els I shall fall, but certainly I trust, I shall not by other mens wantes be drawn from my
self. . . . I understand I am called very ambitious and prowd at home,
but certainly if thei knew my hart thei woold not altogether so judge
me. (*Works* 3:166–67)

21. Sidney's works went through nine editions in the next century, while
Spenser had only three editions and Shakespeare four; of them all, only Sidney
was translated into foreign languages, including French, German, Dutch, and
Italian. See Ringler, *Poems of Sir Philip Sidney*, p. 440.

22. Ronald A. Rebholz, *The Life of Fulke Greville, First Lord Brooke* (Oxford:
Clarendon Press, 1971), pp. 211–16, discusses Greville's "self-centered" account
and argues that he depresses his worth to elevate Sidney's and with it his own in
relation to the age of James.

23. The recent publication of the two versions of the *Arcadia* in accessible
paperback format may change our sense of Sidney's achievement from poetry to
prose—a distinction, of course, he held to be moot.

24. Jonathan Goldberg, *James I and the Politics of Literature* (Baltimore: Johns
Hopkins University Press, 1983), pp. 23–24, traces James's own anti-Petrarchan
poets and contrasts James and Elizabeth's styles of self-presentation.

25. See Tennenhouse, *Power on Display*, p. 34, and Louis A. Montrose, "Of
Gentlemen and Shepherds: The Politics of Elizabethan Pastoral Forms," *ELH* 50
(1983): 441–48, for comment on the political function Petrarchism had during
the reign of Elizabeth.

26. Pierre Bourdieu, "The Economics of Linguistics Exchanges," tr. Richard
Nice, *Social Science Information* 16 (1977): 545–68.

27. I am indebted to Margreta DeGrazia for suggesting the possible ordinari-
ness of the pun to me. In "Prelexical Possibilities in Shakespeare's Language," a
paper delivered to the Shakespeare Association of America, March 1985, De-
Grazia specifically argues that none of the rhetorical figures that name wordplay
of various sorts (syllepsis, antanaclasis, paranomasia, significatio, traductio) describe what we postdictionary readers and speakers identify as a pun—that is,
two separate words that are spelled and spoken identically. Sixteenth-century
logic maunals do discuss the homonym but define it as "one word that signifieth

diverse things," a very different sense from ours; as DeGrazia puts it "what a prelexical age considers one word, a postlexical age considers two or more words." According to the *OED*, the term "pun" was first used in 1660.

28. Ringler, *Poems of Sir Philip Sidney*, p. 447.

29. Arthur F. Marotti, "'Love Is Not Love': Elizabethan Sonnet Sequences and the Social Order, *ELH* (1982): 396–428; hereafter cited in the text.

30. Ann Rosalind Jones and Peter Stallybrass, "The Politics of *Astrophil and Stella*," *SEL* 24 (1984): 53–68. See also Nancy J. Vickers, "Diana Described: Scattered Woman and Scattered Rhyme," *Critical Inquiry* 8 (Winter 1981): 265–79.

31. For a discussion of Laura's uncertain identity, see Robert M. Durling, *Petrarch's Lyric Poems: The Rime Sparse and Other Lyrics* (Cambridge: Harvard University Press, 1976), p. iv.

32. A dependent of his wife's powerful brother the earl of Essex, Rich acquiesced in his wife's later long-term liaison with Sir Charles Blount, yet he did not remain loyal to Essex's followers when the earl was executed for treason. As Ringler puts it, "he was zealous in religion and affected the air of a Puritan, but like Malvolio he was more of a 'time-pleaser' than anything else" (*Poems of Sir Philip Sidney*, p. 445).

33. Marotti, "Elizabethan Sonnet Sequences," p. 406. Poems from the sequence do not appear in contemporaries' manuscript collections until after Sidney's death, while other poems of his come into these miscellanies earlier. Ringler notes that Sir John Harington copied eight poems by Sidney into his collection. He himself first copied "Certain Sonnets 3" (on fol. 34), and then Song 10 from *Astrophil and Stella* (on fol. 36ᵛ). As Ringler notes, Harington apparently did not know that Stella was Lady Rich at the time he first copied the poem, because he headed it "Sʳ Philip Syd: to the bewty of the worlde"; subsequently, he copied *Astrophil and Stella*, Sonnet 1 (on fol. 155) and headed the poem "Sonnets of Sʳ Philip Sydneys ~~vppon~~ to yᵉ Lady Ritch." It is fascinating to see Harington hesitate in his designation of Penelope Devereux's relationship to the first poem. Is she its subject ("upon") or its addressee ("to")? Harington's confusion about how to state the relationship of the real, historical Stella to the poem (which does not, in fact, address her) nicely demonstrates the unstable position of the female with respect to the male poet of the Petrarchan tradition, an instability just as problematic for sixteenth-century as for later readers.

34. P. J. Croft, *The Poems of Robert Sidney* (Oxford: Clarendon Press, 1984).

35. Sir Walter Ralegh owed his later prominence as favorite to his cultivation of the cult of Elizabeth; his fragmentary "Cynthia" may stand as testimony to his sense (however disproved) that direct address in poetry could win back the queen's favor. Sidney addressed no poem to Elizabeth, save for *The Lady of May*.

36. Sidney's actual marriage to Sir Francis Walsingham's daughter Frances (when Sidney was age thirty and she sixteen) does not seem to have been based on love, for it obeyed all the tenets of a patriarchal match, save one: Queen Elizabeth, official patriarch of her society, was not notified. When the queen objected that she had not been asked her approval of this signal traffic in women, Walsingham explained that, the principals being of such low birth, he had not

thought it necessary to obtain her permission. The maneuver is so like the suppression of Elizabeth's remarks about the choice of a husband for the Lady of May, one cannot help but wonder if the source was the same. Once again the hierarchy can be manipulated from below.

37. Ringler, *Poems of Sir Philip Sidney*, p. 443.

38. Interspersed between the first two children Penelope Devereux bore Blount was the birth of the final child she had with Lord Rich (in all, she bore the two men ten children). She was accepted by both the courts of Elizabeth and James as Blount's official mistress until the two illicitly got married after her divorce from Rich in 1605. Only after they were married were she and Blount ostracized. William Laud, who performed the ceremony and later became archbishop, kept the wedding anniversary, according to Ringler, as a day of penance (*Poems of Sir Philip Sidney*, pp. 445–46).

39. Both Lady Rich and Frances Walsingham helped Robert Sidney during his period of political unpopularity when even Essex had dropped his support; see Croft, *Poems of Robert Sidney*, p. 83. Walsingham's father also had a hand in arranging Robert's marriage against Elizabeth's express wishes (pp. 70–71).

40. Until Penelope married Blount, she never suffered any punishments, either for her adulterous liaison or for her loyal support of her brother or of Robert Sidney. Marrying only to legitimate their children (as Blount had himself succeeded to an earldom), she was punished for this transgression only; no more than Elizabeth could she bestow herself where she might wish.

41. I am grateful to Richard Strier for this final formulation as well as for other suggestions, clarifications, and corrections.

"The Sun in Water": Donne's Somerset Epithalamium and the Poetics of Patronage

Some say the world will end in fire,
Some say in ice.
From what I've tasted of desire
I hold with those who favor fire.

Robert Frost, "Fire and Ice"

I

"After I was grown to be your Lordships, by all the titles that I could thinke upon," Donne wrote to his patron Rochester, "it hath pleased your Lordship to make another title to me, by buying me."[1] Donne, like the rest of the court, no doubt considered the marriage of Rochester (by then elevated to earl of Somerset) and Frances Howard a subject more fit for censure than celebration; nonetheless, in return for the favors mentioned in the bitterly sweet letter that I just quoted, he composed an epithalamium for the occasion. Most readers have interpreted this poem as the outward and visible sign of the subjection to which that letter refers.[2] Enslaved and enchained by the patronage system, the argument goes, a great prince in prison lies: Donne jettisons both personal integrity and poetic skill in writing the Somerset epithalamium. Or as one scholar, generalizing about the works that poet wrote for his patrons, put it, "the desire to please brought out the worst in Donne."[3] In contrast, a few other readers, alluding in passing to the Somerset epithalamium, have described it as a consummately successful response to the exigencies of patronage.[4] In fact, however, the poem resists both of these readings: it is far more complicated, poetically and politically, than its commentators have acknowledged. And the significance of those complications extends beyond this particular lyric. No poem in the canon better illuminates Donne's responses to that "desire to please" imposed by patronage. In so doing it clarifies as well more general issues about the relationship between patrons and their suitors and about the problems of studying those relationships.

The poem was composed late in 1613 or early in 1614, a period when Donne's need to please a patron was acute.[5] He had been trying without success for several years to obtain an attractive appointment. Sir Robert Drury, who had at first seemed a promising avenue to preferment, had proved a virtual liability to those associated with him; he was viewed as too hot tempered and indiscreet to fill the responsible positions he himself desired. Donne's tract *Pseudo-Martyr* inspired the king to recommend religious appointments for its author, not the secular ones he had been so sedulously and so unsuccessfully pursuing. Though actively considering the obvious alternative of entering the church, Donne remained hesitant about that decision. Under these circumstances, Rochester may well have seemed his last hope for secular preferment.

He was also in some senses Donne's best hope. After initially attracting the king's attention by injuring his leg in a tournament, Rochester had become James I's favorite. The significance of that fact emerges when we contrast the Jacobean court with the Elizabethan one. As many historians have pointed out,[6] for most of her reign Elizabeth skillfully juggled a number of favorites and permitted several factions, so there were many paths to her ear and hence to royal patronage. James I, in contrast, indulged in single-faction rule: it was through the support of his particular favorite of the moment that one could attract the king's interest and secure his largesse. At the time Donne was courting the favor of Rochester, then, that nobleman was in a singularly good position to obtain for Donne the preferment that he had been seeking. Hence the pressure to please him was particularly intense, a fact that may help to explain why the compliments in this work are more fulsome than those in many of its author's other epideictic poems, such as the epithalamium on the marriage of Princess Elizabeth and the Elector Palatine.

Yet it is more than possible that Donne also recognized the fragility of Rochester's power. The shelf life of courtly favorites, after all, was not always long, as Rochester's own fall was soon to demonstrate. Recent shifts in the center of power at court, notably those occasioned by the death of Prince Henry in 1612,[7] testified to the slipperiness of courtly ladders as eloquently as Wyatt's extraordinary lyrics on the subject a century earlier. Such perceptions did not prevent Donne from seeking to please Rochester, but, as we will see, they help to explain certain characteristics of the resulting epithalamium.

If the circumstances of Donne's own career made composing that poem virtually unavoidable, the circumstances of Rochester's wedding made doing so singularly unattractive.[8] In reviewing the background to that marriage one is tempted to sympathize with the descendent of the bride who fastidiously declared, "Nor shall I dwell upon the disgusting particulars,"[9] for an account of those particulars makes the *National Enquirer* seem restrained and elliptical. Having established a liaison with Rochester while she was married to the earl of Essex, Frances Howard attempted to dissolve her marriage on the grounds of her husband's impotence and her consequent virginity. When the bishops conducting the hearing did not seem disposed towards a favorable verdict, James, like many sovereigns after him, packed the court with more tractable men of God. Some of the evidence presented to them suggested that Frances Howard had tried to induce impotence with drugs obtained from that dubious character Simon Forman. Whatever the truth of the accusations, shortly after the marriage she was found guilty of a far more serious crime: the murder of Sir Thomas Overbury, once a confidante of Rochester, who had been thrown in the Tower after opposing the marriage. In short, though Donne knew which side his bread was buttered on, he also must have recognized that in this instance Rochester could bestow only the most rancid of spreads.

The problems of writing about so unsavory an occasion were intensified by some of the literary skills and techniques at Donne's disposal. As Barbara Kiefer Lewalski has shown, he had developed what she terms "symbolic praise" as a strategy for preserving his integrity while complimenting his patrons and patronesses.[10] But that type of praise depends on building up the subject of the poem into an ideal, a process that would evidently be rendered singularly difficult when writing about a patron who was a fitter subject for formal verse satire than epideictic poetry. Nor could Donne rely on the technique he had used in certain verse letters to sidestep flattery: composing a philosophical essay only marginally related to the recipient. The conventions of the lyric epithalamium were well established, and one of the most central was that the poem should bestow extensive praise on the couple.

Those generic conventions posed other problems as well for Donne. Hence to interpret the Somerset epithalamium it is as important to understand the form in which Donne was writing as the event about which he was writing. Based primarily on Catullus 61, the norms of what has been termed the lyric epithalamium (in contrast to the epic form the genre sometimes assumes) had been well established by 1613.[11] Lyric epithalamia typically trace the events of the wedding day in chronological order: the rising of the sun, the dressing of the bride, the celebrations and ministrations of young boys and girls and of matrons, the ceremony itself, the ensuing feast, and finally the consummation of the marriage. The speaker serves as both participant and master of ceremonies, commanding the bride to awake, the members of the community to join in the procession, and so on. The genre is also characterized by

equally significant though more subterranean motifs. One of the principal ones is its emphasis on the harmony between various conflicting
forces. In particular, epithalamia typically celebrate the reconciliation of
sexual drives and social norms; sexuality is sanctioned by marriage and
channeled into the production of heirs. This reconciliation in turn con-
tributes to a broader one: the potential conflict between outside (whether
it be represented by physical nature, by alienated members of the culture,
or by sexual drives) and inside (represented by the participating members
of society) is mediated and resolved in several ways. Thus, for example,
epithalamia number among the wedding guests both representatives of
the natural world, like nymphs, and members of the community itself;
they describe the bride passing over the threshold of the house and hence
traveling from outside to inside; and the poems themselves represent a
generic dovetailing of outside and inside in that they conjoin motifs of
pastoral and of courtly epideictic poetry.

As this summary of the genre would suggest, adapting it to celebrate
the wedding of Rochester and Frances Howard was a perilous undertak-
ing. For instance, the prayer for children, so central in other epithalamia,
was a potentially explosive motif since it drew attention to the putative
impotence of Frances Howard's first husband. (Chapman had gotten into
trouble because his own contribution to the occasion, a long poem called
Andromeda Liberata, portrays Frances Howard as chained to a "barraine
Rocke";[12] in fact, so tactless is the work in this and other ways that one
suspects a desire, conscious or not, to subvert the praise to which the
poem is ostensibly devoted, a kind of passive-aggressive response.) Nor
could Donne readily posit a reconciliation of sexual urges and social values: the events behind this particular wedding exemplified an intensifi-
cation of that conflict, not its resolution. Similarly, the convention of
portraying a community happily celebrating the wedding was inappropriate in this case: the marriage certainly occasioned lavish festivities, but
contemporary reports of scandalized gossip suggest that the court hardly
responded with uncritical enthusiasm to those events.[13]

Yet if generic conventions created problems for Donne (or for any
writer commemorating the wedding of Rochester and Frances Howard),
they also offered solutions to those very dilemmas. When we examine
the poem more closely we discover that Donne repeatedly invokes the
motifs of the epithalamium in order to comment on the peculiarities of
this particular wedding, as well as on the more general problems of complimenting a patron. To borrow a phrase that Annette Kolodny uses in a
very different context, it is in large part by adapting generic norms that
Donne performs the feat of "dancing through the minefield."[14]

II

In a letter no less revealing than the one on which this essay opened, Donne hints at his ambivalence about celebrating the marriage of Rochester and Frances Howard: "I deprehend in my self more then an alacrity, a vehemency to do service to that company; and so, I may finde reason to make rhyme."[15] One denotation of "deprehend" is to "to catch . . . in . . . some evil or secret deed,"[16] a meaning underscored by "vehemency," with its suggestions of a loss of reason and balance, and by the denigration of the artistic process implied by "make rhyme." The ambivalence suggested in this letter is writ large in the poem to which it refers. Neither the humiliating sycophancy that most readers have found in this lyric nor the tact and integrity that others claim for it adequately describes the complexity of the Somerset epithalamium. Instead Donne's responses to the problems of patronage variously range along the entire spectrum between uncritical adulation and uncompromising criticism.

It must be said, first of all, that he often flatters the couple openly and uncritically. Many of these compliments are based on the pattern of imagery that structures the poem: references to fire, light, and the sun.[17] In several other poems, Donne also describes the court in terms of heat and fire, but there the connotations are typically negative; in a verse letter to Sir Henry Wotton, for instance, he disparages "Courts hot ambitions,"[18] while in his elegy on Lord Harrington he refers to the "calentures [a tropical fever] / Of hot ambitions."[19] In the Somerset epithalamium, in contrast, the imagery in question is often the vehicle for compliments that testify that one of Donne's principal responses to the pressures of patronage was simply to yield to them.

> First her eyes kindle other Ladies eyes,
> Then from their beames, their jewels lusters rise,
> And from their jewels, torches do take fire,
> And all is warmth, and light, and good desire.
> (lines 29–32)[20]

It is striking that the flattery in this poem is much more blatant and extensive than the compliments to the Princess Elizabeth and her bridegroom, the Elector Palatine, that are infused into the epithalamium that Donne wrote less than a year before.[21] The Palatine epithalamium devotes less space to praising the couple; for example, its first stanza evokes a delightful natural scene, ignoring the wedding itself until the final two lines, while the corresponding stanza of the Somerset poem focuses on a compliment to the bride and bridegroom.

Haile Bishop Valentine, whose day this is,
    All the Aire is thy Diocis,
    And all the chirping Choristers
And other birds are thy Parishioners,
        Thou marryest every yeare
The lirique Larke, and the grave whispering Dove,
The Sparrow that neglects his life for love,
The household Bird, with the red stomacher,
        Thou mak'st the Blackbird speed as soone,
As doth the Goldfinch, or the Halcyon;
The husband Cocke lookes out, and straight is sped,
And meets his wife, which brings her feather-bed.
This day more cheerfully then ever shine,
This day, which might enflame thy self, Old Valentine.
        (Palatine epithalamium, lines 1–14)

Thou are repriv'd, old yeare, thou shalt not die,
        Though thou upon thy death bed lye,
        And should'st within five dayes expire,
    Yet thou art rescu'd by a mightier fire,
        Then thy old Soule, the Sunne,
When he doth in his largest circle runne.
The passage of the West or East would thaw,
And open wide their easie liquid jawe
To all our ships, could a Promethean art
Either unto the Northerne Pole impart
The fire of these inflaming eyes, or of this loving heart.
        (Somerset epithalamium, lines 1–11)

The differing tones of these opening stanzas point to a distinction that continues to demarcate the two lyrics: the compliments in the Palatine poem are more playful and more restrained. Donne's increasing desperation about preferment may help to explain this contrast between his wedding poems; the patronage system could evidently affect a writer very differently at different moments in his career. One suspects, too, that Donne's distaste for the Somerset wedding led him to overcompensate with particularly fulsome compliments.

Many of the flattering tributes in the Somerset epithalamium are directed to the king himself. At first this appears curious: the wedding of James I's daughter Elizabeth would have seemed a more obvious opportunity for such compliments, yet the Palatine epithalamium contains very few of them. It is only at one point in that entire poem that we are even reminded that the bride is indeed a princess.

One reason the Somerset wedding poem includes such tributes is that the king himself was indirectly implicated in the dubious events behind the wedding, having favored the bridegroom and supported his attempts to marry the notorious Frances Howard. To praise him was to acknowledge and implicitly accept his responsibility for the marriage. In addition, as we have seen, it is likely that when he wrote the Somerset epithalamium Donne was even more desperate about patronage than he had been a year earlier and hence more eager to scatter compliments as widely as possible. Perhaps, too, his nervousness about the political longevity of any of James's favorites encouraged him to cover his options by flattering the ultimate source of bounty rather than simply devoting the poem to praising its conduit.

The epithalamium also responds to the pressures of patronage in a second way: in addition to praising the happy couple (and the monarch who gave his blessing to their match), it performs the more subtle and no doubt more useful service of implicitly defending Somerset and Howard from the accusations that had been leveled against them. Donne does so, for example, through one image that cleverly implies that their wedding does indeed involve the conventional reconciliation of social and sexual forces.

> Our little Cupid hath sued Livery,
> And is no more in his minority,
> He is admitted now into that brest
> Where the Kings Counsells and his secrets rest.
> (lines 87–90)

In more senses and more ways than one, these lines civilize the god of love. By describing him as "our little Cupid," an epithet that may suggest fondness or condescension or both, the passage effectively tames him; sexuality becomes not an enemy of the court and its values but rather its pet (*"our* little Cupid"). The assertion that he "hath sued Livery" also defuses the threats he might otherwise represent. One editor interprets this image as a statement that Cupid, no longer a minor, has filed a legal application to leave the system of wardship; another glosses "livery" as the clothes of a retainer.[22] Both readings are possible, and both make Venus's son seem less menacing than readers of Renaissance texts—or readers of the cultural text at hand, the wedding of Somerset and Howard—might otherwise assume. If Cupid is petitioning the legal system, he is not an opponent of society but rather a participant in it. Furthermore, he is petitioning it because he "is no more in his minority"; this suggests that he has traded the childish fecklessness and recklessness normally associated with him for adulthood. And it is an adulthood presented in terms of legal rights and political responsibility, not the irresponsibility manifested by the adults to whom this poem refers. Alternatively, if we read the lines as an affirmation that Cupid is—by choice—clothed, then the image is a literalized version of one way Donne defends the couple throughout the poem: here and elsewhere he suggests that the raw forces of sexuality choose to wear the vestments of society, of respectability. Our impression that this Cupid will not threaten society is intensified by "is admitted," where the passive implies that Cupid did not shove or shoot his way into the hearts of the bride and bridegroom but rather entered politely, at their pleasure.

The epithalamium deploys other generic norms as well to suggest that sexuality is controlled, subdued. In many wedding poems the speaker urgently anticipates the wedding night and complains about the events that delay it. In the Palatine poem Donne himself writes, "and night is come; and yet wee see / Formalities retarding thee" (lines 71–72); the implication is not that the bride is hesitant about going to bed but rather that the events of the day are impeding her. In the Somerset epithalamium, in contrast, the speaker chastises the bride for her apparent reluctance to consummate the marriage: "What mean'st thou Bride, this companie to keep? / To sit up, till thou faine wouldst sleep? / Thou maist not, when thou'art laid, doe so" (lines 193–95). On a very subterranean level the passage acknowledges one tension associated with this wedding: it posits a clash between the demands of society, of "companie," on the one hand and the demands of sexuality on the other. But of course Donne is reversing the way that tension actually functioned in the events behind that marriage: he suggests that Frances Howard is prone to fulfill her social duties at the expense of her sexual drives, not vice versa. Thus the passage serves to obfuscate and even deny her actual behavior. These and subsequent lines attribute to Frances Howard a singularly improbable maidenly modesty—a point made more explicitly in what is undoubtedly the most outrageous lie of the poem: "Their soules, though long acquainted they had beene, / These clothes, their bodies, never yet had seene" (lines 210–11).

Similarly, the poem plays down the prayer for heirs that features so prominently in many other wedding poems: "Raise heires, and may here, to the worlds end, live / Heires from this King, to take thankes, you, to give" (lines 177–78). The syntax is knotty, but the main point seems to be that the heirs of the couple will serve those of the king; the lines devote more attention to courtly services than to the offspring as such. In so doing they allow Donne again to compliment the king, hence cutting his losses if Rochester himself proved a less helpful patron than Donne hoped. But the passage also serves other functions, permitting Donne to touch only lightly on a subject rendered delicate by Frances

Howard's accusations of her first husband and, more to our purposes here, deflecting attention from the sexual act necessary for the production of heirs.

Another way Donne develops generic conventions to lend respectability to the couple is by playing up the church ceremony. He spends very little time on that episode in his Palatine wedding poem and hence implies that the emotional and physical union of the couple is far more important than the way the priest joins them together. In contrast, in the Somerset epithalamium the church service becomes as central as it is in Spenser's "Epithalamion," though it is central for very different reasons: Donne is stressing that the church is blessing this marriage and hence lending respectability to it. In so doing he also defies the bishops who had in fact opposed the match.[23]

In addition, Donne uses religious references to defend the couple— and his own speaker. The act of writing the poem is repeatedly described as sacerdotal: "this poore song, which testifies / I did unto that day some sacrifice" (lines 103–4), "I will lay'it upon / Such Altars, as prize your devotion" (lines 234–35), and so on. Such a claim deepens the implication that this wedding is a sacred event, not a sordid one.

Besides whitewashing the behavior of the couple in that way, the lines in question attempt to perform the same service for their own writer: the imagery of priests and altars suggests that his art is not a token in the demeaning financial transactions of patronage but rather a ritual in the holy ceremony of matrimony. Yet, as is so often the case in this poem, excuses are undermined even as they are proffered: "sacrifice" hints that his devotion to Rochester is not without its price. Donne's own debates about taking holy orders lend resonance to these lines. On one level they anticipate his role as priest. On another level this metaphor draws attention to a kind of metaphoric substitution occuring in Donne's life: he is officiating at courtly altars as an alternative to doing so at spiritual ones, seeking secular offices rather than performing holy ones.

We have seen that Donne uses generic conventions and other literary devices both to praise the couple and to defend their behavior. A third point along the spectrum we are tracing is represented by the many observations that slip back and forth between compliment and criticism. Thus his refrains repeatedly refer to the couple's "inflaming eyes." On the one hand, this is yet another tribute to the charms of Frances Howard and Somerset; on the other hand, when we remember the Renaissance notion that the eye-beams of lovers become entangled when they fall in love, we sense that the lines in question contain a subterranean rebuke, a reference to the illicit passion that lies behind this wedding. But this criticism is limited, subdued by the fact that the refrains are fourteeners.

The resulting langorous movement lessens the impression of passion contained in the imagery of flames: "Since both have both th'enflaming eyes, and both the loving heart" (line 126). On the prosodic level, as on so many others, the poem attempts to contain the fires ignited by this wedding, to turn a conflagration into a hearthside glow.

Even more suggestive—in both senses of that term—are the lines that invite the bride to weep because the spectators cannot otherwise safely look on her sunlike glory.

> For our ease, give thine eyes, th'unusuall part
> Of joy, a Teare; so quencht, thou maist impart,
> To us that come, thy'inflaming eyes, to him, thy loving heart.

Her Apparrelling

> Thus thou descend'st to our infirmitie,
> Who can the Sun in water see.
> (lines 146–50)

In one sense, this is simply a tribute to the bride's radiant charms, a compliment intensified by adducing the Platonic passage that lies behind this image: she is, the lines imply, like the Idea that cave dwellers would find it difficult to look upon.[24] Yet just as Plato's imprisoned characters would be hurt by looking at the light, so, Donne's image hints, looking directly at Frances Howard could blind us. One implication is that it is in general dangerous to be too close to the powerful, too much in the sun; another, that we dare not gaze at this particular woman, whether because what we see would be frightening or because we might be burned by the fire emanating from her. This second implication most obviously connects her power with that of male sun-gods, though an allusion to Medusa may be present here as well[25]—an especially telling resonance when we recall that, as Freud among others has argued, Medusa is associated with sexual threats. But these suggestions remain subdued, ambiguous. And so the lines also at once allude to and embody one way the poem works: it handles sensitive issues indirectly and hence renders them safe for the poet to touch and safe for the audience to observe, like a sun in water. By indirection he—and we—find direction out.

Another sign of the ambiguous commingling of praise and blame that characterizes this poem is that the wedding is distanced from the speaker, the community that is evoked, and the reader. As we have observed, in most epithalamia, including Donne's own poem on the Palatine wedding, the speaker actively participates in the events, acting as both master of ceremonies and a guest at the festivities. In the Somerset wedding poem, in contrast, he generally assumes the more distant role of observer: "let me here contemplate thee" (line 129), "wee which doe behold" (line 152), and so on. Only at a few points does he issue the type of commands that recur so often in other epithalamia.

In other works in the genre, members of the community participate actively in the events. Here, however, they do not fill many of the functions customarily assigned to them. Matrons undress the bride in the Palatine epithalamium; no such figures are present here. When this lyric does allude to members of the community, it does so in terms so vague and general that they play down the presence of the personages they ostensibly evoke: "to all which come to look upon" (line 144), "For every part to dance and revel goes" (line 188).

The responses of Donne's audience mime those of the fictive audience at the festivities, for the reader, too, is distanced from the events. Donne adopts the unusual strategy of prefacing each stanza with a title: "the time of the Mariage," "Raysing of the Bridegroome," and so on. The very existence of such titles frames the action, removing the reader from it so that we, too, feel like detached observers. Moreover, because so many of those titles are gerunds, the wedding comes to seem like a series of static tableaux; this epithalamium has comparatively little of the urgency that characterizes most other wedding poems. These effects are intensified by the fourteeners that, as we have observed, conclude each stanza.

The functions of these distancing strategies are as varied as those of the words "the sun in water." The distancing involved in substituting the role of observer for that of master of ceremonies may suggest the speaker's awed respect. Another effect of this technique, however, is to enact the doubts about participating in the occasion that Donne himself no doubt experienced. By turning the wedding into tableaux Donne is encouraging us to see it as a glorious spectacle, a masque, and hence bodying forth in his lyric genre the kinds of theatricality that, as many recent critics have demonstrated, characterized the Jacobean court.[26] But the same strategy drains the event of the vitality and energy that enliven the weddings evoked in other epithalamia and thus, one suspects, reflects Donne's own distaste for the proceedings. And the absence of a community at the points in the poem where one would expect to find it hints that Donne's contemporaries, too, found participation in the events unattractive.

In addition to overt praise and complex juxtapositions of praise and rebuke, the spectrum of Donne's responses to patronage also includes a far pole that most readers have neglected: uncompromising criticism of his patron. One of the speaker's injunctions to Frances Howard is less ambiguous than the lines we have been examining.

> Pouder thy Radiant haire,
> Which if without such ashes thou would'st weare,
> Thou, which, to all which come to looke upon,
> Art meant for Phoebus, would'st be Phaëton.
>
> (lines 142–45)

On one level, these lines merely refer to a common method of adorning the hair, but it is surely no accident that ashes are traditionally associated with penitence. This passage subtly but unmistakably warns the bride that only repentance will preserve her from danger: she must control her passions (and also, perhaps, beware of her desire to be too close to the sun, in the sense of the powerful members of the court) lest she be destroyed as tragically as that arrogant young astronaut Phaëton.

Both the facts behind this wedding and the traditions behind Donne's genre intensify the force of this warning to the bride. Hair often represents sexuality, so a statement that the bride's beautiful hair is potentially dangerous acquires troubling resonances when one considers the circumstances of this marriage. Furthermore, at the wedding Frances Howard wore her hair flowing down her back, the sign of a virgin;[27] hence the lines comment as well on her deceptive semiotics, suggesting that predilection for falsehood represented by her hair needs to be controlled, chastened.

Moreover, if generic traditions lie behind the praise of the bride at other points in the poem, here they implicitly contribute to yet another rebuke. English epithalamia frequently suggest that it is the bride's chastity that controls lust.

> There Vertue raynes as Queene in royal throne,
> And giueth lawes alone.
> The which the base affections doe obay.
>
> (Spenser, "Epithalamion," lines 194–96)[28]

> That's her *Vertue* which still tameth
> Loose desires, and bad thoughts blameth.
>
> (Wither, "Epithalamion," lines 67–68)[29]

In other words, in other works in the genre the bride controls the fires of passion emanating from others, while in this instance the fires emanating from her might endanger those around her, just as Phaëton's flight through the skies kindled a conflagration. Thus the allusion to Phaëton is the dark side, the demonic parody, of the earlier compliments that suggest that Frances Howard's eyes inflame the rest of the court. Similarly, Donne further criticizes the wedding by writing,

> Plenty this day
> Injures; it causes time to stay;
> The tables groane, as though this feast
> Would, as the flood, destroy all fowle and beast.
> (lines 182–85)

These lines may be playful, but they also hint at a negative judgment on the lavishly expensive festivities associated with this wedding. And in another sense, too, this allusion to the destructiveness of gluttony has a sharp and sombre edge to it, reminding us of the destructiveness of the other deadly sin in which the couple has indulged. The excesses of the feast recall the excesses of the bride and bridegroom—and perhaps, too, those of the poet when he bestows hyperbolic praise.

But it is above all through numerology that Donne censures the wedding. Most readers have ignored this aspect of the poem, in part because they have not anticipated and hence have not found any negative commentary on the couple and also perhaps in part because the extreme claims of certain numerological studies have made many critics suspicious of the whole enterprise. Alastair Fowler, the one scholar who has paid any attention to the numerology of the poem, interprets it only positively, finding triumphal forms in the ordering of the stanzas.[30] But it is no accident, I would suggest, that eleven of those stanzas, each consisting of eleven lines, comprise the poem. For, as Saint Augustine, whose work Donne knew well, declares, "Surely then the number eleven, passing ten as it does, stands for trespassing against the law and consequently for sin."[31] Mystical philosophers of the Middle Ages develop this connection between eleven and sin.[32] Writers, too, pick it up; as one critic has pointed out, the evil monsters in *The Faerie Queene* often appear in the eleventh canto, and another scholar demonstrates that some of the measurements of Dante's hell are based on multiples of eleven.[33]

How, then, does Donne himself play on the significances of eleven? In the Palatine epithalamium, the fourteen-line stanzas remind us that the wedding takes place on Valentine's Day, February *14,* with the beneficent Bishop Valentine as its presiding deity. In contrast, when we turn to the Somerset epithalamium we find that the length of the stanzas invokes the concept of trespass; just as that number goes beyond the decalogue and hence represents sin, so the couple have gone beyond the decalogue, especially its seventh commandment, in committing their own sins. And the allusion may include an autobiographical reference as well: Donne is violating his own moral dictates in praising the couple.

III

The Somerset epithalamium comments on patronage in another way as well. Always intensely self-conscious, Donne incorporates into his poem an examination and critique of his own participation in the courtly system that inspired it. The epithalamium proper is encased in a curious framework. A character named Allophanes rebukes one called Idios for absenting himself from the wedding and retiring to the country in the worst season, "whilst Flora herselfe doth a freeze jerkin weare" (line 8). Idios rejoins that he was not in fact absent, since the country is an epitome of courts. Answering that objection, Allophanes proceeds to sing the glories of James's court and, in particular, of the wedding that has just taken place there. Idios declares that it is precisely because he agrees that he left the court.

> I knew
> All this, and onely therefore I withdrew.
> To know and feele all this, and not to have
> Words to expresse it, makes a man a grave
> Of his owne thoughts.
>
> (lines 91–95)

As this passage suggests, the pastoral world in this poem exemplifies the pathetic fallacy; its deathlike coldness and barrenness mime the mental landscape of Idios, who was referred to in the opening line of the poem as "statue of ice."[34] That character proceeds to explain that after retiring to the country he did in fact write an epithalamium, which he then apparently shows Allophanes. Idios attempts to burn the poem, but in the final line of the eclogue Allophanes declares he himself will instead present it at court.

The few readers who comment on the eclogue at all tend to read it as a straightforward apology for an absence, occasioned by illness, from court and from the wedding.[35] Such readings typically adopt Sir Herbert Grierson's interpretations of the personages in the poem: Idios (the "private man") is Donne himself, while Allophanes ("in another voice") is probably Sir Robert Ker, a friend of Donne's with the same name as the bridegroom.[36] But Donne could have apologized for missing the wedding and submitting his epithalamium late merely by incorporating a few lines to that effect within the poem. The eclogue in fact serves far more complex functions, and the identification of its characters is correspondingly more complex than we have acknowledged.

One of the roles of the eclogue is to intensify the distancing that the poem achieves in so many other ways as well. The pastoral framework offers a strategy, though a transparent one, for excusing the distasteful act of composing the poem: it was presented at court against Idios's will. That character's geographical separation from court provides a metaphor for the psychological separation he—and Donne himself—wish to achieve.

But the main function of the eclogue is to express and embody the problems of courting a patron. Some of that commentary is autobiographical. To the extent that Idios represents Donne, his problems in writing the epithalamium evidently mirror the poet's own; indeed, Donne's characteristic self-involvement is reflected in the fact that even when writing an epithalamium, one of the most public of forms, he opens and closes with allusions to his own situation. Though the references to death and icy coldness recur throughout Donne's poetry, it is very possible that here they have a more local significance as well, representing metaphorically a sense of sterility or perhaps an actual writing block.[37] Donne may well have reacted to the problems of praising this wedding by having trouble writing. Such hypotheses must be approached cautiously: after all, the "inexpressibility conceit" is a common literary convention, and one could make a case that Donne is mechanically adducing it. Fortunately, however, one is not forced to choose between formal and psychological explanations: events in writers' lives and configurations in their sensibilities may lie behind their attraction to a given formal strategy. That is, I would suggest, the case here; Donne utilizes a conventional conceit to express his own responses to the problems of praising Rochester and his blushing bride.

Yet why should we assume that only Idios represents Donne? Another interpretation of Allophanes' name is that he is an alternative side of Idios, an alter ego.[38] And in fact the conversations between these two characters do enact dialogues like those that may well have taken place within their creator. Thus Allophanes stands for the attraction to the court that motivated so many of Donne's actions, while Idios bodies forth the reluctance to participate in that world to which Donne's verse letters often testify. Allophanes' insistence on bringing the epithalamium to court represents the willingness to please a patron that led Donne to write the poem, while Idios's desire to burn it expresses the poet's doubts about that task. Allophanes is the successful courtier Donne wanted to be, while Idios is the failed courtier he sensed he really was.[39] And in another sense these conflicting voices may mirror a specific period in Donne's career: during the Mitcham years he seesawed between living at court like Allophanes and eschewing that world like Idios.[40] In any event, the author who delights in yoking together disparates on linguistic levels, here does so on a dramatic level, through the evocation of two characters who are different yet the same. Once again the reactions of an idiosyncratic writer to an idiosyncratic wedding find apt expression in well-established generic conventions. The epithalamium is a fundamentally dialogic medium: the dialogue that occurs explicitly in Catullus 62 and imitations of it is manifest as well in the paired opposites we find in other versions of the genre: nature against society, male against female, and so on. In the Somerset epithalamium Donne adapts this predilection of his genre to express the personal tensions he brings to it.

The dialogue between Idios and Allophanes also raises another question about patronage, whether it is indeed possible to escape the court and its patronage system. The poem does not offer a clear or definitive answer; the paradoxes in Idios's responses (as we have seen, he variously claims that he is away from court and that he is there, that he was unable to write an epithalamium and that he in fact did so) reflect, one suspects, the contradictions in Donne's own reactions. Despite these paradoxes and contradictions, however, the primary implication of the eclogue is that it is difficult and painful to distance oneself, literally or metaphorically, from the court. The poem recurs repeatedly, if not obsessively, to the problems and perils of doing so, even as it attempts to establish its own distance from the court through criticisms of the wedding and through the rhetorical strategies I have charted, such as appending titles to its stanzas.

Thus the apparent alternatives to the court, the poem reminds us, are unattractive; the "world elsewhere" to which Idios retreats is not the *locus amoenus* of many other pastorals but rather a wilderness. Indeed, the imagery of the poem associates that wilderness with barrenness, with death itself; rather than tending his flocks while melodious birds sing madrigals, Idios becomes a "statue of ice" (line 1). To describe leaving the court as a type of death is on one level to offer a tribute to that world but on another, of course, to remind us that leaving from the court could in fact involve the death of one's political hopes. (Being banished from court was in fact a punishment inflicted on courtiers for many types of infractions, such as breaking the law against dueling.)[41]

Moreover, throughout the poem attempts to escape the court are subverted, whether by internal forces or by external ones. Idios, a master (and a slave) of occupatio, writes a courtly poem that is in part devoted to his unwillingness to write a courtly poem. His own attitudes to that text are also revealing. At one point he declares, "As I have brought this song, that I may doe / A perfect sacrifice, I'll burne it too" (lines 226–27). On their primary level, of course, these lines are merely a witty joke,

Idios's clever way of opposing Allophanes, and yet, as we have already seen, they are not without other resonances. His language suggests at once a desire to destroy the·poem (like its creator, it will be dead once it has been burned), and hence not participate in the event, and a desire to assume that sacerdotal role that we examined earlier. In any event, whatever Idios's attitude to the poem may be, Allophanes triumphs: he wrests the text from its author and lays it on those "Altars" (line 235).

These ambiguities and tensions reflect the fact that Donne was pulled between the moral necessity to condemn the wedding and the financial necessity to praise it—and also, perhaps, between his desire to absent himself from the court and his urge to participate in courtly rituals, even morally dubious ones. In any event, it is clear that he—and, by implication, other courtiers—did not find it easy to achieve that world elsewhere. Or, as Donne puts it in one of the most revealing lines of the poem, "And yet I scap'd not here" (line 97).

IV

If Donne's lyric reveals the difficulties Renaissance poets confronted if they wished to survive within the patronage system, the poem as a whole demonstrates as well the difficulties modern literary critics confront if they wish to study it. In particular, the Somerset epithalamium implicitly warns us that we need to temper our generalizations on the subject of patronage with a number of qualifications and cautions about both literary and historical methodology. Both formalism and that sibling with which it enjoys so uneasy a relationship, New Criticism, have recently become unfashionable; jokes directed against New Criticism are virtually obligatory in many literary circles, much as architects often feel obliged to share witticisms directed against the International Style. The Somerset epithalamium, however, reminds us how much certain contemporary schools of criticism may in fact depend on their more traditional forebears. It is by deploying the generic conventions analyzed by formalists and the verbal ingenuity beloved of New Critics that Donne explores the social and political tensions that interest so many critics today. Hence it is by studying the conventions and techniques that concerned formalists and New Critics that we ourselves can explore those cultural tensions.

The Somerset epithalamium also invites us to rethink some of our approaches to the historical facts behind patronage and, indeed, behind many other cultural institutions. Despite the current interest in history, shared by many literary critics, in one important regard we tend to interpret Renaissance culture unhistorically: that is, we often focus on what is static about it at the expense of change. A number of critics who would be prone to question many assumptions of structuralism nonetheless adopt its predilection for the synchronic study of a system, in this case the system or systems of Renaissance society, over the diachronic. Not only does this approach obscure the concern for the sources and forces of change that is so central to historical studies in general; it also neglects the fact that many historians have recently been investigating certain issues that militate against broad generalizations about Renaissance culture, notably the problems of periodization and the coexistence of many conflicting value systems or intellectual models.[42]

If we adduce the results of such investigations when studying patronage, we will acquire a salutary suspicion about generalizations that attempt to encapsulate the workings of patronage in Renaissance England at the expense of observing changes and variations in that system or, more precisely, systems.[43] Thus, as many historical studies remind us, Elizabethan patronage differed significantly from its Jacobean single-faction counterpart—a concept that immediately demands the further qualification that towards the end of her reign Elizabeth's approach to patronage anticipated that of her Stuart successor. These distinctions are relevant to the Somerset epithalamium and, one suspects, to many other works in that and in other genres: I have suggested that appreciating the unique role that Rochester enjoyed because of the patronage system helps us to understand the pressures that faced Donne when he celebrated that favorite's wedding. But we need to be even more specific about historical periods and the subdivisions within them; the death of Prince Henry, for instance, significantly affected the tenor of Jacobean patronage (one critic, in fact, has traced some of the changes in Ralegh's *A History of the World* to the demise of that exemplary prince).[44] In other words, patronage might more fruitfully be studied in terms of decades, or even years within a decade, than in terms of the Renaissance as a whole. And if participating in the patronage system was very different at different moments in history, so too events in one's own history could significantly affect one's responses; by comparing the Palatine wedding poem, we have seen that the Somerset epithalamium in no small measure reflects the particular moment in Donne's life when he composed it.

The Somerset epithalamium also testifies that we need to think further about the roles of criticism in the poetry of patronage. Though that issue has not been wholly neglected, our examination of it has too often been limited by certain assumptions: poets confronted a binary system of submission to the patron or subversion, and that subversion was itself typically permitted, channeled, and contained by those in power. These assumptions, however, need to be challenged. If we approach patronage with the presupposition that those in a position to bestow it will inevitably and successfully repress rebellions against their power, we may misread the poetry of patronage by neglecting or misinterpreting its reactions against that system. In the case of the Somerset epithalamium, such predilections would lead us to read the poem—as critics influenced by a range of methodologies have in fact done—as wholly adulatory; or, alternatively, we would assume that whatever criticisms do occur pale to insignificance beside the fact that Donne yielded to the pressure of praising Rochester. Mimetically, we ourselves suppress dissent, dismissing all but the ideology currently dominant in our own field. But the truth, as we have seen, is more complex. So interwoven, so counterbalanced are the elements of flattery and criticism in that poem that it would be as dangerous to label it a mere token in the patronage system, the tune that Donne sang for his dinner, as it would be to hail it as a wholly successful rebellion against that system.

Several recent studies have suggested more complex and more promising models for studying how poets criticized their patrons. Thus Annabel Patterson has posited a system of, as it were, licensed license, in which writers and political leaders agreed to an "implicit social contract" that determined what could and could not be said; ambiguities were skillfully marshalled to facilitate censure.[45] The Somerset epithalamium suggests that, in some instances at least, poets and their patrons may have approached the process of criticism with more ambivalence and less control than this model implies; but, more to our purposes here, the concept of the contract serves the essential function of reminding us how much dissent and criticism was in fact possible within the poetry of patronage. Contemporary historical work, too, could fund our evaluations of the role of dissent in the poetry of patronage. Many scholars in that field have traced instances in which rebellious lower-class assumptions and values, far from yielding to the culture of the powerful, remained potent.[46] These interpretations are themselves problematical, and a scholar who bases uncritical generalizations on them risks substituting one type of orthodoxy for another. But such studies do warn us against unthinkingly anticipating only a submission to power, only a containment or deflection of rebellion. This is relevant to patronage in that clients, though generally not lower class, were evidently in a potentially submissive role that in some senses parallels that of Menocchio, the extraordinary Italian peasant who offers so intriguing an instance of the survival of dissent.[47]

When read in light of recent studies like these, the Somerset epithalamium invites us to investigate further a whole series of questions about the role of criticism and dissent within poetry addressed to a patron. To what extent and under what circumstances was dissent seen as an alternative to courtly praise, to what extent and under what circumstances a subdivision within it, much as anti-Petrarchism is often regarded as a branch of Petrarchism? How much did the possibility of such dissent ease a poet's concern about praising an unpraiseworthy patron or event? To which of his multiple audiences, internal and external, did that poet address his criticisms?

However we eventually answer these broader questions raised by the Somerset epithalamium, it is apparent that Donne's poem marries praise and criticism and that this is a marriage as complex in its implications and its consequences as the one the poem itself is commemorating. For on the one hand the lyric Donne wrote for the wedding of Frances Howard and Somerset is packed with sycophancy blatant and clumsy enough to dismay us. The fact that Rochester's fortunes were so high in 1613 and Donne's so low undeniably invited the most demeaning sort of flattery. Yet on the other hand, lines like the reference to Phaëton demonstrate that Donne could achieve a measure of integrity and independence despite the exigencies of patronage—and could achieve it in the very poem that also includes the lies and evasions bred by those pressures. If this epithalamium testifies that the pressures on a client could be even more intense than we sometimes remember, it simultaneously reminds us that patronage could allow more room to maneuver than we sometimes acknowledge. When he writes passages like that description of Phaëton and when he adduces strategies like his numerological code, Donne, though a "statue of ice," manages to play with fire without being melted by its power.

Notes

1. John Donne, *Letters to Severall Persons of Honour* (London, 1651), p. 290.
2. See, e.g., Arthur F. Marotti, "John Donne and the Rewards of Patronage," in *Patronage in the Renaissance,* ed. Guy Fitch Lytle and Stephen Orgel (Princeton: Princeton University Press, 1981), p. 230.
3. Patricia Thomson, "The Literature of Patronage, 1580–1630," *Essays in Criticism* 2 (1952): 280–81.
4. For instance, Joseph H. Summers asserts that the poem "contains not a single lapse, social or literary" (*The Heirs of Donne and Jonson* [London: Chatto & Windus, 1970], p. 33).
5. On this period in Donne's life and on Drury's own professional problems, see R. C. Bald, *John Donne: A Life* (Oxford: Clarendon Press, 1970), p. 238 and chap. 11.
6. For background on the distinctions between Elizabethan and Jacobean patronage see Wallace T. MacCaffrey, "Place and Patronage in Elizabethan Politics," in *Elizabethan Government and Society: Essays Presented to Sir John Neale,* ed.

S. T. Bindoff, J. Hurstfield, and C. H. Williams (London: Athlone Press, 1961), esp. pp. 97–98; J. E. Neale, *Essays in Elizabethan History* (New York: St. Martin's, 1958), esp. pp. 74–84. For a revisionist interpretation of those distinctions, see two studies by Linda Levy Peck, *Northampton: Patronage and Policy at the Court of James I* (London: George Allen & Unwin, 1982), pp. 215–16; and "Court Patronage and Government Policy: The Jacobean Dilemma," in *Patronage in the Renaissance*, Lytle and Orgel, esp. pp. 28, 41–46.

7. On the significance of this death, compare Marotti, "Rewards of Patronage," p. 230.

8. For a summary of these circumstances, see Bald, *John Donne*, pp. 273–74, 313–14; and David Harris Willson, *King James VI and I* (London: Jonathan Cape, 1956), pp. 338–43.

9. Quoted by Edward Le Comte in his account of the marriage. *The Notorious Lady Essex* (Robert Hale & Co., 1969), p. 14.

10. Barbara Kiefer Lewalski, *Donne's "Anniversaries" and the Poetry of Praise: The Creation of a Symbolic Mode* (Princeton: Princeton University Press, 1973).

11. Useful summaries of the conventions enumerated in this paragraph may be found in Thomas M. Greene, "Spenser and the Epithalamic Convention," *CL* 9 (1957): 215–28; Virginia Tufte, *The Poetry of Marriage: The Epithalamium in Europe and Its Development in England*, University of Southern California Studies in Comparative Literature 2 (Los Angeles: Tinnon-Brown, 1970). The more subterranean motifs that I subsequently discuss, however, have been neglected.

12. George Chapman, *Andromeda Liberata; or, the Nvptials of Persevs and Andromeda* (London, 1614), B4ᵛ.

13. See, e.g., Thomas Birch, ed., *The Court and Times of James the First*, 2 vols. (London: Henry Colburn, 1848), 1:269–89.

14. Annette Kolodny, "Dancing through the Minefield: Some Observations on the Theory, Practice, and Politics of a Feminist Criticism," *Feminist Studies* 6 (1980): 1–24.

15. Donne, *Letters*, pp. 180–81. Also cf. the letter on pp. 270–71.

16. *OED*, s.v. "deprehend."

17. Other critics have observed this pattern, though their explanations of it differ from mine. See esp. Margaret M. McGowan, "'As Through a Looking-glass': Donne's Epithalamia and Their Courtly Context," in *John Donne: Essays in Celebration*, ed. A. J. Smith (London: Methuen, 1972), p. 210. Also cf. John Carey's analysis of Donne's references to the sun (*John Donne: Life, Mind, and Art* [New York: Oxford University Press, 1981], p. 119).

18. John Donne, "Sir, more then kisses," line 60, in *The Satires, Epigrams, and Verse Letters*, ed. W. Milgate (Oxford: Clarendon Press, 1967), p. 72.

19. John Donne, *The Epithalamions, Anniversaries, and Epicedes*, ed. W. Milgate (Oxford: Clarendon Press, 1978), p. 70, lines 124–25. All citations from Donne's epithalamia and funeral poems are from this edition.

20. I am including quotations from the eclogue that frames the epithalamium proper since, as I argue below, they constitute a unified poem.

21. Compare my article "Tradition and the Individualistic Talent: Donne's 'An Epithalamion, Or mariage Song on the Lady Elizabeth . . . ,'" in *The Eagle and*

the Dove: Reassessing John Donne, ed. Claude J. Summers and Ted-Larry Pebworth (Columbia: University of Missouri Press, 1986). When comparing Donne's epithalamia I do not include the "Epithalamion made at Lincolnes Inne" because of the debate about whether that poem is parodic. On that controversy see David Novarr, "Donne's 'Epithalamion made at Lincoln's Inn': Context and Date," *RES* 7 (1956): 250–63; and my article "Donne's 'Epithalamion made at Lincolnes Inne': An Alternative Interpretation," *SEL* 16 (1976): 131–43.

22. See, respectively, Milgate, *Epithalamions,* p. 121; John T. Shawcross, ed., *The Complete Poetry of John Donne* (New York: New York University Press; London: University of London Press, 1968), p. 180.

23. On Donne's allusions to the bishops, cf. Carey, *John Donne,* p. 87.

24. Plato, *Republic* 7.515–16.

25. On Medusa-like women see Marjorie Garber, *Shakespeare's Ghost Writers: Literature as Uncanny Causality* (London: Methuen, 1987), chap. 5. It is suggestive that, as she reminds us, the Medusa is related to fears of castration, since disapproval of Frances Howard's sexual license may well have involved a sense that she was sexually threatening. But such hypotheses are very speculative, especially since the allusion to Medusa, if it is in fact present in the poem, is very subterranean.

26. See, e.g., Stephen Greenblatt, *Renaissance Self-Fashioning from More to Shakespeare* (Chicago: University of Chicago Press, 1980), pp. 162, 227–32; and his essay "Invisible Bullets: Renaissance Authority and Its Subversion," *Glyph* 8 (1981): 40–61.

27. See Carey, *John Donne,* p. 87.

28. *The Works of Edmund Spenser,* 11 vols., ed. Edwin Greenlaw, Charles Grosvenor Osgood, Frederick Morgan Padelford, and Ray Heffner (Baltimore: Johns Hopkins University Press, 1932–57).

29. George Wither, *Ivvenilia* (London, 1622), Gg3ᵛ–Gg4.

30. Alastair Fowler, *Triumphal Forms: Structural Patterns in Elizabethan Poetry* (Cambridge: Cambridge University Press, 1970), pp. 71–73.

31. Saint Augustine, *The City of God against the Pagans,* 7 vols., tr. George E. McCracken et al. (London: Heinemann; Cambridge: Harvard University Press, 1957–72), 4:535.

32. See Vincent Foster Hopper, *Medieval Number Symbolism: Its Sources, Meaning, and Influence on Thought and Expansion* (New York: Columbia University Press, 1938), p. 101.

33. On Spenser see Alastair Fowler, *Spenser and the Numbers of Time* (London: Routledge & Kegan Paul, 1964), p. 54, and on Dante see Hopper, *Medieval Number Symbolism,* p. 152. Fowler's argument about Spenser is complicated by the fact that a basic principle of narrative—the climax occurs shortly before the denouement—can explain why monsters appear in canto 11. But this explanation need not preclude numerological ones as well.

34. Several critics have commented on the uses of pastoral in courtly poetry. See esp. Frank Whigham, *Ambition and Privilege: The Social Tropes of Elizabethan Courtesy Theory* (Berkeley: University of California Press, 1984), p. 128.

35. See, e.g., Bald, *John Donne,* p. 274.

36. Herbert J. C. Grierson, ed., *The Poems of John Donne*, 2 vols. (Oxford: Clarendon Press, 1912), 2:94.

37. In one of his letters he does declare he could write an epithalamium for the occasion were his muse not dead (Donne, *Letters*, p. 270), but it is hard to be sure that reference serves to allude to his trouble in writing rather than merely excusing his reluctance to do so. Donne's verse letters also mention unproductive periods ("To Mr. Rowland Woodward" ["Like one who'in her third widdowhood"], pp. 69–70, lines 1–3).

38. Tufte touches on the possibility that the speakers may body forth Donne debating with himself but then limits the significance of this insight by asserting that "Idios [is] expressing [Donne's] actual viewpoint and Allophanes . . . arguing against it" (*Poetry of Marriage*, p. 227). After completing this essay, I heard the paper Annabel Patterson presented at the 1985 MLA convention, "Donne: The Self and the Other"; she too acknowledges the possibility that Allophanes may be a mask for Donne.

39. On the ways courtiers attempted to cope with failure at court, cf. Whigham, *Ambition and Privilege*, p. 22.

40. See Bald, *John Donne*, chap. 8.

41. Peck, *Northampton*, p. 163.

42. For a useful summary of these and other trends in historiography, see Michael Kammen, "Introduction," in *The Past before Us: Contemporary Historical Writing in the United States*, ed. Kammen (Ithaca: Cornell University Press, 1980).

43. I am grateful to David Harris Sacks and Wallace MacCaffrey for useful suggestions about this section of my essay.

44. Leonard Tennenhouse, "Sir Walter Ralegh and the Literature of Clientage," in *Patronage in the Renaissance*, Lytle and Orgel, pp. 253–58.

45. Annabel Patterson, *Censorship and Interpretation: The Conditions of Writing and Reading in Early Modern England* (Madison: University of Wisconsin Press, 1984).

46. See, e.g., Richard Hoggart, *The Uses of Literacy: Aspects of Working-Class Life, with Special Reference to Publications and Entertainment* (London: Chatto and Windus, 1957); and Eugen Weber, *Peasants into Frenchmen: The Modernization of Rural France, 1870–1914* (London: Chatto and Windus, 1979).

47. Menocchio is discussed by Carlo Ginzburg in *The Cheese and the Worms: The Cosmos of a Sixteenth-Century Miller*, tr. John and Anne Tedeschi (Baltimore: Johns Hopkins University Press, 1980).

Law and Ideology: The Civil Law and Theories of Absolutism in Elizabethan and Jacobean England

This essay discusses the influence that the study of civil law had on English political thought in the late sixteenth and early seventeenth centuries. By selecting such a topic, I have in a certain sense placed myself outside the mainstream of English legal and political thinking. Of all the countries of western Europe, England has been the least influenced by Roman or civil law.[1] It alone did not experience a reception of Roman law between the thirteenth and sixteenth centuries; it alone did not train its lawyers in what we have come to call the civil law tradition; it alone has resisted the adoption of those procedures that are an important part of that tradition. The repeated failure of Roman law to penetrate the English world has had a lasting effect on the legal and political culture of England and America. It explains, for example, why the idea of codification has never attracted wholehearted support in either country.[2] It also explains why neither the idea nor the reality of "the state" has found fertile ground in either country.[3] I am aware that much more can be said about the failure of Roman law in England than about its success, and that hostility to Roman law—which can be seen most clearly in the writings of men like Sir John Fortescue and Sir Edward Coke—played a much larger part in English political history than did an admiration for it. My purpose, however, is not to study Romanophobic or Romanoid attitudes in England but to explore the ways in which the study of Roman law did influence political thought during the reigns of Elizabeth and James I.

Historians have not been entirely silent on this subject. Whig historians, in particular, have often claimed that the theories of absolutism articulated by James VI and I and by a growing number of political writers in the early seventeenth century were inspired at least to some extent by the study of the civil law. C. H. McIlwain, for example, asserted that "the struggle for the prerogative" could only be understood "in combination with the royalist zeal for the absolutist principles of the Roman law."[4] To Whig historians the formulation of such ideas was of monumental significance, since these ideas generated intense political conflict that not merely foreshadowed, but actually caused, the civil war that lay some forty years in the future.

The Whig version of early seventeenth-century English history has come under severe scholarly criticism, especially in recent years.[5] Much of this criticism is valid. Revisionist historians have shown, for example, that the constitutional and religious divisions within the body politic during the early years of James I's reign were not as deep as Whig historians have traditionally claimed. Revisionists have also shown that it is difficult to establish causal connections between those ideological divisions and the events of the 1640s. Nevertheless, Whig historians have made an important point in identifying the civil law as a source of some of the new constitutional ideas that began to circulate at the end of Elizabeth's reign and at the beginning of James's. These ideas, I shall argue, were not so absolutistic or conducive to tyranny as either contemporaries or subsequent historians have asserted. Nor were they the exclusive property of the English civil lawyers. But they did represent a significant development in the history of English political thought; they did generate a certain amount of political tension; and they did contribute in an indirect way to the origins of the English civil war.

Before exploring these "civilian" ideas and discussing their significance, it is important to establish exactly what is meant by the civil law and to determine how widely it was known in England. The main component and foundation of this law was the *Corpus juris civilis,* the great code of Roman law compiled by legal scholars during the reign of the emperor Justinian in the early sixth century and published at Constantinople in 533. The study of this law was revived in the West in the eleventh and twelfth centuries and became the subject of an enormous legal literature—glosses and commentaries which acquired a certain amount of authority in and of themselves. Roman law consisted of a large amount of private law, the basic principles of which were contained in the first three sections of the *Institutes* (the law of persons, of things, and of obligations), but it also contained a great deal of public law, the law that governed princes, officials, and the political life of the community. Roman law also embodied the *jus gentium,* a term of various meanings which in its most general sense denoted the basic principles of justice shared by all peoples. Since Roman law was originally concerned with cases that arose between Romans and foreigners, it was only natural that it should have sought to establish such principles. Moreover, the high intellectual quality of the Justinianic code, which was influenced by Greek notions of natural law, made Roman law appear to be the equivalent of the natural law of reason. The rational, philosophical character of Roman law, together with its systematic arrangement, explains its great appeal to scholars, while its identification with the *jus gentium* made possible its adoption in various degrees by most European nations.

In addition to the Roman law of Justinian and the commentators, the civil law was thought to embrace, or at least to be closely associated with, three other legal traditions. The first was the canon law of the Roman Catholic church, which was modeled to a great extent upon Roman law and which followed procedures that were essentially Roman. In England, of course, this law underwent significant modifications at the time of the Reformation and acquired technical autonomy as English ecclesiastical law. The second tradition was the commercial and maritime law of medieval Europe. Roman law included a good deal of early commercial law, since it regulated contracts between foreigners and Romans, but this body of law had developed a life of its own in the Middle Ages and was referred to by some lawyers as *jus gentium*. Finally, the civil law included international law, a body of rules governing relations between states. This law originated in the *jus inter gentes* of Roman law, but like the commercial law, it acquired a certain measure of autonomy when the state system of modern Europe began to emerge at the time of the Renaissance.[6]

Knowledge of the civil law was much more limited in England than in the other countries of western Europe. England, unlike those countries, never experienced a reception of Roman law, the process by which both the substance and the procedures of Roman law were written into the national or municipal law of individual European states. The main reason for this failure was that English national law, the common law, had developed into a mature legal system at a relatively early date, before Roman law began to be received in the kingdoms and principalities of western Europe.[7] England also had developed its own law schools, the Inns of Court, which trained prospective lawyers and judges in the common law, but not Roman law. From an early date the Inns adopted a jealous attitude toward the common law and resisted attempts to introduce Roman elements into it.

Roman law was taught in England at Oxford and Cambridge. It was, therefore, known to the small group of students at each university who pursued either the baccalaureate or the doctorate in civil law. The great majority of these men studied the law to prepare for careers as proctors, advocates, or judges in the ecclesiastical and admiralty courts or as diplomats in the service of the crown. The statutes of the university attempted to make their education as professionally relevant as possible by stipulating that the regius professor of law should lecture on those parts of the *Corpus juris civilis* that had a bearing on English practice.[8] There is some evidence that Alberico Gentili, the regius professor at Oxford from 1594 to 1608, lectured extensively on those aspects of Roman law that touched on wills and international relations. It is difficult to escape the general conclusion, however, that the education of legists at Oxford and Cambridge was not very practical. Instead of being trained in English ecclesiastical law or mercantile and maritime law—which is what they needed to know as prospective lawyers—law students at Oxford and Cambridge spent most of their time studying a code whose value in England was primarily jurisprudential.[9]

Those who received law degrees from Oxford and Cambridge were not the only Englishmen who had some knowledge of the civil law in the late sixteenth and early seventeenth centuries. A substantial number of common lawyers also appear to have been fairly well read in this area, although it is often difficult to establish the extent of their knowledge and the means by which they acquired it. The only solid evidence we have comes from the upper echelons of the legal profession, men who served in judicial and administrative positions and who wrote legal or political treatises. Lord Ellesmere, Sir John Doddridge, Sir John Davies, Sir Francis Bacon, and Sir Thomas Fleming all gave ample evidence that they were widely read in the Justinianic texts and in the works of Continental civilians.[10] Whether the run-of-the-mill common lawyer shared their knowledge is much more difficult to establish. Certainly he did not *need* to know any civil law in order to function as a common lawyer. The common law was a self-contained system of national law, and its practitioners did not have to know any civil law in order to maneuver within it.[11] A few common lawyers acquired a knowledge of the civil law through their studies at the universities. This number was, however, much smaller than one might expect. Of the 107 Oxford legists who proceeded no further than the degree of B.C.L. between 1571 and 1603, only eight went on to the Inns of Court.[12] There were of course many common lawyers who received degrees in the arts, but the curriculum for that degree did not include instruction in the civil law. If a common lawyer wished to acquire a knowledge of civil law, therefore, he usually had to do it on his own, through a program of private reading conducted either at university or the Inns. We know for certain that this is how Ellesmere acquainted himself with the civil law,[13] and it is likely that Davies and Doddridge did so in similar fashion. When William Fulbecke, a scholar who was knowledgeable in both the common and the civil laws, recommended that law students read the *Digest* and the *Institutes* of Justinian, he was probably considering this mode of instruction.[14] Indeed, the only other way in which a prospective common lawyer might have acquired a knowledge of the civil law was through the public readings or lectures that formed part of the learning exercises at the Inns. Although these readings did occasionally include references to the civil law,[15] they were hardly ideal vehicles for a deep understanding of the subject.

We shall never know how many English common lawyers became familiar with the texts of Justinian, but their numbers are not what really matter. The important consideration is that, at the end of Elizabeth's reign and the beginning of James's, there was a cluster of common lawyers, notably those who were judges and those who had an interest in legal scholarship, who had a knowledge of the civil law. To what precise uses they put this knowledge we cannot be sure. Unlike the civilians themselves, they did not have a jurisdictional area, such as the ecclesiastical or admiralty courts, where the civil law prevailed. When they used the civil law, therefore, they did so in subtle, indirect, and perhaps even subconscious ways. It is possible, for example, that when common law judges made new law by means of judicial decisions, which was only when precedent was lacking, they drew upon civilian sources, which might easily be regarded as reflections of natural law.[16] It has been suggested that even Coke, who apparently knew a good deal of civil law, did this occasionally.[17] It is not my concern here to test this proposition or, for that matter, to discuss the impact that the civil law had on the substantive development of the common law. Attempts to locate civil law sources for common law doctrines have not been very successful, if only because it is often just as easy to locate a common law source for the same doctrine.[18] What I do wish to explore is how the civil law that both the civilians and the common lawyers studied helped to shape their political ideas.

My thesis is that the study of the civil law provided a number of late Elizabethan and early Stuart writers with a set of questions, a vocabulary, and in some cases a set of political principles with which they approached some very difficult constitutional questions around the turn of the seventeenth century. In so doing they created a certain amount of political tension and established a framework for political discussion. Before providing support for this thesis, I must make two preliminary qualifications. The first is that the ideas of the men whom I shall be discussing—Smith, Gentili, Cowell, Davies, Fleming, Bacon, and Doddridge—had many different sources. They were in a certain sense multilingual, and the civil law was only one of their languages. Being men of broad education, they were widely read in the classics, scholastic philosophy, Scripture, and history, not to mention the common law and the political treatises drafted by common lawyers. Because of the variety of their sources it is often difficult to identify the origins of some of their ideas, and for the same reason it is possible to discuss the works of these men without any reference to the civil law. Indeed, most treatments of Smith and Bacon pay little attention to this source of their thought. What I have to say about these men, therefore, does not so much contradict as supplement the work of others. It is important to keep in mind, however, that all these men were lawyers, judges, or legal scholars, and therefore they tended to approach constitutional and political matters at least to some extent from a legal perspective.

The second qualification is that even when these political thinkers were influenced by the civil law, that law did not necessarily turn them into royal absolutists. The civil law has long been recognized as the source of absolutist thought, mainly because it contains two statements that appear to give the prince the power to impose his will on his subjects arbitrarily. The first is the declaration in the *Institutes,* duplicated almost verbatim in the *Digest,* "quod principi placuit legis habet vigorem" (whatsoever has pleased the prince has the force of law).[19] The second is the statement in the *Digest,* "princeps legibus solutus est" (the prince is not bound by the laws).[20] Taken by themselves, these statements appear to support a form of government in which the prince rules autocratically and despotically, and these texts have been used by princes who did in fact rule or try to rule in precisely that way.[21] But when considered in the total context of the Justinianic code, and when considered in light of the interpretations that glossators and commentators have placed on them, the texts do not necessarily lead to such conclusions.[22] Indeed, the texts of Justinian have served the cause of modern constitutionalism just as effectively as they have the cause of absolutism. For example, Roman law could easily be used to show that the people translated all authority to the prince, but a long line of commentators argued with equal force that the people never completely surrendered their power but merely delegated it and could therefore recall it.[23] Similarly it could be shown that what the civilians called *merum imperium,* or full power, could either be assigned to the prince as part of his sovereign power or shared by lesser magistrates.[24] And even when these texts were seen as endorsements of absolutism, there were many other texts, most notably the *digna vox* of Justinian's *Code,*[25] which stressed the subordination of the prince to the law.[26] Taking a more general view, one can say that the most enduring legacy of Roman law is the sharp distinction it makes between the public and the private spheres (*res publica* and *res privata*). This distinction is generally viewed as being conducive to absolutism, since it allows public law and the state to develop autonomously, without reference to, or a foundation in, private right. On the other hand, the distinction between the public and private realms has also laid the basis for a theory of private interest, a recognition of the unconditional nature and hence inviolability of private property, and in the long run the rise of economic liberalism. We are so accustomed to thinking of the connection between Roman law and absolutism that we forget that one of the historic critiques of it as a legal system was that it sanctioned laissez-faire capitalism.[27]

While knowledge of the civil law did not necessarily turn its students into royal absolutists,[28] it did encourage them to think about political and constitutional questions in a certain way. Therein lies its significance for late sixteenth- and early seventeenth-century English political thought. Because it contained a large amount of public law, because it involved a significant amount of international law, and because it contained a number of texts that at least suggest that the prince is sovereign, it encouraged its readers to inquire into the nature of sovereignty, to ask where it was located in the state, and to determine exactly the relationship of the king to the law. English thought on such questions in the sixteenth century was, to say the least, vague. Everyone admitted that the king was a sovereign in the sense of being both an independent prince and the highest person in the kingdom, but the idea of his possessing an absolute and undivided sovereignty, such as that which the French political theorist Jean Bodin claimed must exist in every ordered commonwealth, was alien to the sixteenth-century English political mind.[29] The king, to be sure, had a constellation of specific feudal and political powers, termed collectively his prerogative, which gave him political preeminence and a certain amount of legal privilege. But these powers, many of which arose out of the king's private property rights, were considered to be part of the laws of the land and regulated by that law in one way or another.[30] On the other hand, the prerogative, being a mysterious and in some sense a reserved power, was not entirely defined by that law.

As far as lawmaking was concerned, which was at the very center of the new theories of sovereignty that were emerging on the Continent, the English situation was equally confusing. Everyone admitted that the king made laws with the consent of the Lords and Commons in Parliament. This meant, as Fortescue explained, that the king of England was a limited or constitutional monarch.[31] But the actual relationship between the king and the two houses of Parliament was never made clear, and references to the supremacy or even the sovereignty of the king-in-Parliament (a notion that combined the ideas of Parliament as a superior court or jurisdiction, the king as the chief lawmaker, and the Lords and

Commons as effective but nevertheless subordinate restraints on the king's power) did more to disguise than resolve the confusion. Useful as the phrase "constitutional monarchy" has proved to be for both contemporaries and later historians, it does not say much more than that sovereignty in England was shared in some unspecified way.

In the work of Sir Thomas Smith we meet the first attempt in the late sixteenth century to resolve some of these ambiguities, but unfortunately Smith does not get us very far. Smith was a civilian, the regius professor of civil law at Cambridge, and an advocate of the new humanistic school of jurisprudence that was developing in France. Surprisingly, however, Smith's most famous work, *De Republica Anglorum,* which was written in France in 1565, does not bear many signs of a civilian mentality. As one of his modern editors has indicated, Smith is remarkably "unjuristic in his method." [32] This is not to devalue a remarkable piece of work which offered an informed comparison between English government and the government of those countries that followed Roman or civil law; it is only to suggest that Smith was much more concerned with proving that the English style of government was most appropriate for the English people than he was in resolving the ambiguities of the Tudor constitution. Only in two places does Smith appear to be using his legal knowledge to resolve the problem we have been describing. The first is where he describes the English Parliament as "the most high and absolute power of the realm." [33] Whether this represents an attempt at a theory of legislative sovereignty is difficult to determine. Smith may have been trying to apply a concept drawn from the civil law to English politics, the result being a doctrine of parliamentary rather than royal sovereignty. [34] It is possible, however, that in referring to the absolute power of Parliament, Smith was thinking of nothing more than its jurisdictional preeminence over other tribunals.

The second place where Smith gives evidence of his civilian background is in his discussion of the power of the king. In order to establish the discretionary authority of the king in making war and peace and in coining money, Smith makes reference to the "absolute power" of the king. The use of the term "absolute" once again suggests that he may have been thinking in terms of sovereignty, but Smith does not use this opportunity to establish the king's freedom from, or supremacy over, the law. In light of his general emphasis on the limited nature of English government, one would not expect him to have taken such a position. His general approach to the royal prerogative was that of Sir William Stanford and other Tudor theorists. Smith considered the prerogative to be a body of special rights and privileges that were a part of the law and limited by it, noting that "the rights and preeminences of the Prince are

declared particularly in the books of the common laws of England."
Only in "war time and in the field," when proceeding by martial law, did
the king have such power that "his word is a law."[35]

The traditional, moderate, and even unjuristic character of Smith's
book becomes even more apparent when we compare it with the political
treatises written by Alberico Gentili in 1605. Like Smith, Gentili was a
regius professor of civil law, but that is where the similarities end. Gentili
was an immigrant, an Italian by birth, who had studied at the University
of Perugia. The legal tradition with which he identified was that of the
Bartolists, the school of legal commentators against which the French
legal humanists and Smith had reacted. He also was, unlike Smith, a
prolific and important *legal* writer, who is widely recognized as one of
the founders of modern international law.[36] Even in his political works,
which are our concern, Gentili's juristic approach is as prominent as it is
lacking in Smith, while the numerous citations of the *Corpus juris civilis*
and civilian commentators, also absent in Smith, confirm the importance
of civil law sources in the formation of Gentili's ideas. Another difference, one of great importance, is that Gentili was writing almost forty
years after Smith in a quite different intellectual and political environment. In the realm of political ideas, two major developments had oc-
curred. First, Bodin's *Les Six Livres de la République,* with its conception
of legislative sovereignty and theory of royal absolutism, had appeared in
1576 and, if we can judge by both statements of contemporaries and
citations in published works, had a profound impact on English thinking.[37] Second, the political writings of James VI, now James I of England,
were becoming fairly well known in the southern kingdom. I shall not
discuss James's political ideas here, both because they are already well
known and because they do not appear to have been inspired to any great
extent by the civil law. James is of course famous for his praise of the
civil law, and he is often identified with the threat that many scholars
believe the civil law represented to the common law at that time. James's
political views do not, however, betray much of a civilian mentality, and
it is better to think of him as writing in a theological and a patriarchal,
rather than a legal, tradition.[38] Nevertheless, his views, which were
clearly absolutistic and derogatory of Parliament, created quite a stir in
the first decade of the seventeenth century. They drew a number of angry
responses from members of the House of Commons, and they also encouraged men who had royalist sympathies to develop their own political
ideas, sometimes with the ulterior motive of currying favor with the
king.[39]

It was in this intellectual and political environment that Gentili wrote
his *Regales disputationes tres* in 1605. It would not be an exaggeration to

claim that it was the most absolutistic piece of writing that appeared in England in the early seventeenth century. Armed with quotations from the *Corpus juris civilis*, including the famous "quod principi placuit" and "legibus solutus est," Gentili identified the sovereign power of the state or *majestas* with the king's prerogative, an extraordinary power that was free from the law. Gentili did not free the king from natural or divine law, but no one, either in the civil law or common law tradition, had ever done that. Parliament, which figured so prominently in Smith's treatise as the most high and absolute power of the kingdom, was relegated to the subordinate status of a consultative body.[40]

If Gentili had been the only civil lawyer to express ideas like these at the beginning of the seventeenth century, we might be inclined to minimize the significance of his views. Gentili was, after all, a religious refugee, a foreigner who apparently had little knowledge of the common law or the traditions of English government. Unlike Smith, who was a privy councillor, and the great majority of English civil lawyers, who held office in the king's government, Gentili was a purely academic civilian who never joined Doctors' Commons, the professional society of civil law practitioners in London, and whose legal activity outside the university was restricted to some pleading in the Admiralty Court on behalf of the Spanish government.[41] His treatises, written in Latin, apparently attracted little or no attention in England until after the outbreak of the civil war, when an anonymous pamphleteer discovered them and claimed that they were the ideological inspiration of the royalist cause.[42] It is tempting, therefore, simply to dismiss Gentili as atypical and uninfluential. But however atypical Gentili may have been, his views were not without support in England. Most notably, they were shared by his counterpart at Cambridge, Dr. John Cowell.

Cowell, whom his great antagonist Sir Edward Coke called Dr. Cowheel, is one of the most maligned figures in seventeenth-century English history; Whig historians have consistently depicted him as the implacable foe of parliamentary liberty. It is not surprising that he, rather than Gentili, became the butt of parliamentary criticism during the early years of James's reign. Cowell, unlike Gentili, was a native Englishman who had a deep knowledge of the common law and a long record of service in local and central government.[43] A protégé of Archbishop Bancroft, he held a number of administrative positions in the English church and served on the Court of High Commission from 1605 to 1611.[44] It was not easy, therefore, to dismiss Cowell's political views, and since his most controversial work was written in English and widely circulated, it was not easy to ignore them either.

Cowell's controversial political ideas originated in his efforts to reconcile the civil law that he taught at Cambridge with the common law. Cowell was one of a small group of English scholars, a group that included Gentili's student William Fulbecke, who endeavored to illustrate the compatibility of civil law and common law as manifestations of the *jus gentium.* Their work can be broadly described as Bartolist, in that it resembled the efforts of Bartolus of Sassoferrato to fuse Roman and canon law with the customary law of the Italian states. Fulbecke, who has been nicknamed "the Bartolist Bee" for his efforts to extract the good juice out of the better flowers or laws of England,[45] was the first scholar to develop this approach in his *Parallele or Conference of the Civill Law, the Canon Law, and the Common Law of England.* In 1605 Cowell continued the work that Fulbecke had begun by publishing a Latin treatise, *Institutiones juris Anglicani,* in which he tried to place the common law within the framework of Justinian's *Institutes.* This effort at codification had the ultimate purpose of preparing for a possible union of English common law and the more civil law–oriented system of Scotland, a project of James I that was ultimately unsuccessful.[46]

In his second and more politically controversial book, *The Interpreter,* which was published in 1607, Cowell continued his efforts to reconcile civil and common law. *The Interpreter* was a law dictionary, intended for the use of common lawyers, which illustrated a number of similarities between civil and common law. Since many of the defined terms, such as "prerogative of the king", "subsidy," and "Parliament," were terms that dealt with public law, the book gave Cowell an opportunity to apply the vocabulary and the principles of the civil law to the English constitution. The result was a statement of royal absolutism no less potent than that of Gentili. As far as Cowell was concerned, the king of England had the same regalities as "the most absolute prince in the world." He had the power to make law by himself, he made laws with Parliament only out of his own benignity, he could dispense with statutes by his own will, and, most important, he was above the law by his absolute power.[47]

In all of Cowell's political statements the influence of the civil law and of Bodin's writing is clear. It is no wonder that one of Cowell's parliamentary critics inquired whether he had "confederates . . . from beyond the sea."[48] At the same time, however, Cowell argued that his position had a solid foundation in the common law. This is the claim that made his work so interesting, so important, and from the perspective of many common lawyers, so offensive. The way in which Cowell combined the civil law and the common law in his definitions is best illustrated by his most significant and controversial entry, that of "prerogative": "Prerogative of the King (*Prerogativa Regis*) is that especial power, preeminence, or privilege that the King hath in any kind, over and above other persons and above the ordinary course of the common law, in the right of his crown. And this word (*prerogativa*) is used by the civilians in the same sense . . . so our lawyers *sub prerogativa regis* do comprise also that absolute height of power that the civilians call *majestatem vel potestatem vel jus imperii.*"

There is no question that Cowell's application of civilian learning to English politics presented his common law audience with some relatively unorthodox political ideas. Instead of having a limited monarch, they were now being told, as they had been by Gentili (and in a somewhat different way by James I), that he was absolute; instead of that monarch being described as a ruler who had an obligation to obtain the consent of both Lords and Commons to legislation, he was now being described as being "above the Parliament"; and instead of being under the law, as Bracton and everyone else had always insisted, the monarch was now being proclaimed "above the law by his absolute power." Now it can certainly be argued that some of Cowell's statements had more of a foundation in the common law and in conventional English political thought than they appear to have when taken at face value. There was, for example, a certain sense in which the English king had always been above the law, since he could not be held legally accountable for his actions.[49] Also, he was in a certain sense above his Parliament, since he could always veto the bills they passed. But Cowell did nevertheless introduce some revolutionary ideas into the English political arena. Most important, he changed the definition of the prerogative from a power that was part of the law and limited by it to a much more general power that was free from the ordinary course of the common law. Possession of this power was, by itself, the mark of an absolute king.

Cowell's views were considered so extreme that some of his critics in the Parliament of 1610 allegedly wanted to hang him. In the end they had to settle for the suppression of his book by royal proclamation. The proclamation did not condemn all of Cowell's constitutional ideas. It did not, for example, accuse him of exalting the power of the king. Instead it charged that he had submitted the royal prerogative to definition and had inquired into the "mysteries" of kingship. But the edict did accuse Cowell of being "too bold with the common law" and of mistaking the "fundamental and original grounds and constitutions of the Parliament," and therefore it did go a long way toward appeasing the wrath of his critics.[50]

It was relatively easy for members of Parliament to mount a campaign against Cowell, a civil lawyer who had spoken "unreverently" of the common law. It was much more difficult to deal with very similar ideas expressed by a common law judge, Sir Thomas Fleming, the year before

The Interpreter was published. Fleming advanced his views in the speech he gave deciding *Bate's Case,* which determined that the king could levy impositions without the consent of Parliament on the grounds that the king, by virtue of his prerogative, had the right to regulate trade. The decision was based to a great extent on technicalities, but in a famous *obiter dictum* Fleming discussed the power of the king in terms similar to those of Cowell and Gentili and with specific reference to the civil law.

> The King's power is double, ordinary and absolute, and they have several laws and ends. That of the ordinary is for the profit of particular subjects, for the execution of civil justice, the determining of *meum;* and this is exercised by equity and justice in ordinary courts and by the civilians is nominated *jus privatum,* and with us common law; and these laws cannot be changed without Parliament; and although their form and course may be changed and interrupted, yet they can never be changed in substance. The absolute power of the King is not that which is converted or executed to private use, to the benefit of any particular person, but is only that which is applied to the general benefit of the people, and is *salus populi* . . . and this power is guided by the rules which direct only at the common law and is most properly named policy and government; and as the constitution of this body varieth with the time, so varieth this absolute law, according to the wisdom of the King for the common good; and these being general rules, and true as they are, all things done within these rules are lawful.[51]

Now it is possible to accommodate much of what Fleming said within the traditional framework of the English constitution. Indeed, McIlwain has traced Fleming's ideas back to Bracton and has anchored them in a solid tradition of medieval constitutionalism.[52] Further support for the relative moderation of Fleming's views comes from the recognition that he did not claim that in matters of state "the King's discretion was unfettered in all respects."[53] The reason why so many historians have thought this is that when G. W. Prothero edited Fleming's speech, he inserted the word "not" in brackets in the sentence that asserts that the king's absolute power was guided by the rules of the common law.[54] What Fleming meant was that when the king was using his prerogative he was not subject to the coercive power of the law, but that his actions were *guided* or directed by the rules of the common law. The insertion of the word "not" before "guided," however, made it appear that Fleming was giving the king the freedom to do anything he pleased whenever he was dealing with matters of state.

Nevertheless, Fleming was espousing some rather untraditional views.[55] Instead of describing the royal prerogative as a constellation of specific rights, he was conceiving of it in much more general, abstract terms and asserting that it could be exercised whenever "matters of state" needed to be resolved. He was, in other words, helping to modernize the theory of royal power in the Continental mode, just as Gentili and Cowell were, and just like Cowell and Gentili, Fleming was using ideas from the civil law in order to achieve this new definition. In his *obiter dictum* he resorts to the important civilian distinction between public and private law, a distinction that was only dimly perceived in English law at this time. His application of this analysis to English law is not very convincing, since he is forced to identify the entire common law administered in the courtroom with *jus privatum,* thereby failing to distinguish which aspects of common law may be labeled private and which public. Yet the distinction he makes does enable him to introduce into the common law itself a new definition of royal power and a concept analogous to the Continental theory of "reason of state."

Besides its reliance upon the distinction between public and private law, Fleming's theory of absolute power had other roots in the civil law tradition. As Francis Oakley has shown, the distinction between the ordinary and the absolute power of the king had a distinctly civilian pedigree. Instead of having its roots in the Bractonian tradition of medieval constitutionalism or in the distinctions between common law and equity, it had much more direct sources in the writings of the French royalist political theorists of the sixteenth century (Gentillet, Chasseneuz, and Bodin), in the legal writings of Baldus, and ultimately in the canonists rather than the civilians of the thirteenth century.[56] Where Fleming got his ideas we shall never know. It is unlikely that he was widely read in the early canonist literature, but it is quite possible that he was familiar with the work of Baldus and the sixteenth-century French writers. Perhaps he got them from Gentili, who made the same distinction and revealed Baldus and Bodin as his sources.[57]

If the common lawyer Fleming can be grouped with the civilians Cowell and Gentili in a general effort to modernize the concept of royal power by using terms and concepts borrowed from the civil law, the question arises whether any other seventeenth-century royalists shared their views.[58] As one might expect, a number of civil lawyers, most notably John Hayward and Richard Zouche, wrote treatises and gave speeches that identified them clearly with Cowell and Gentili. Concerning the politics of the English civil lawyers I have written elsewhere, and much of my analysis explains their political behavior in terms of their close professional connections with the court and their need for royal patronage.[59] But my emphasis on their preoccupation with professional survival was not in any way intended to deny that these men derived political ideas from the law that they studied and that in many cases (although hardly in all) these ideas were absolutistic. Even in the 1660s, when it appeared that the question of royal absolutism had been settled once and for all in England, candidates for the degree of doctor of civil law at Oxford, as part of their formal academic exercises, were defending the proposition that the king was free from the laws.[60]

But what of the common lawyers? If we are going to claim that the novel, at least partially civilian ideas of the early seventeenth century were not atypical, then we must identify other common lawyers who shared Fleming's views on absolute power, and we must ask whether their ideas were inspired by the study of the civil law. There is evidence that Sir John Doddridge, Sir Francis Bacon, and Sir John Davies, all of whom could be generally described as royalists in the early seventeenth century and all of whom had more than a passing acquaintance with the civil law, shared at least some of Fleming's ideas. Of the three, Doddridge is the most interesting, not because his views were so extreme, which they were not, but because he wrote first, before the death of Elizabeth. In his treatise on the royal prerogative, which identifies numerous civilians, canonists, and French lawyers as his sources, he anticipates much of what Fleming was to say a few years later, distinguishing between the absolute and the ordinary powers of the king in the characteristically civilian mode, and laying the basis for later claims that the king had a general prerogative that he could exercise for the welfare of the people.[61] The only difference between Doddridge and Fleming is that Doddridge still conceived of the prerogative as being "preserved in divers particulars," whereas Fleming had transformed the prerogative into a more general power.[62]

With Bacon we are on more uncertain ground than with Doddridge, since the sources of Bacon's political thought are more difficult to detect and, with all due respect to Doddridge, more varied. Bacon's thought is also more difficult to label than that of other royalist writers, since he tends to combine absolutist and constitutionalist ideas and he speaks of the necessity of preserving both the king's sovereignty and the liberty of the Parliament.[63] But Bacon's views on the royal prerogative, which are contained in the appendix to his *Preparation for the Union of Laws* and in his defense of the Council of the Marches in Wales, bear many markings of a civilian attitude.[64] The most important of these is his recognition that the absolute power of the king, which he also refers to as his sovereign power, was qualitatively different from his ordinary or "limited" power, which was "declared and expressed in the laws."[65] The crux of the distinction was whether or not the king's power could be contested in a court of law. Bacon explained that "though other prerogatives by which he claimeth any matter of revenue or other right pleadable in his ordinary courts of justice may be there disputed, yet his sovereign power, which no judge can censure, is not of that nature."[66] This sovereign power, which is inherent in the king's person, was not only "exempt from controlment by any court of law" but also capable of staying suits at the common law, changing the common law for the public good, and even suspending parliamentary statutes.[67] For Bacon, therefore, the king was in a very real sense above the law by virtue of his absolute power, just as Cowell had insisted.[68]

The third of the common law royalists who can be identified with Fleming's point of view is Sir John Davies, the attorney general for Ireland, who is best known to legal and political historians for his high praise of the common law. Yet Davies was learned in the civil law and in fact used the authority of civilian writers in arguing cases in Ireland.[69] His learning in the civil law appears to have led him to adopt absolutist views that were analogous to those of Fleming. He too, like Doddridge and Bacon, made the distinction between the absolute and ordinary powers of the king, using the distinctly civilian phrase, *merum imperium*, to describe the former, which, as he explained, was not bound by the positive law. Davies also placed his discussion of the king's absolute power in the context of an argument that drew further inspiration from the civil law. We have seen that one of the components of the civil law was the *jus gentium*, the law of nations, which many civilians equated with the natural law of reason.[70] According to Davies this law was the original law, and since it was the source of the king's absolute power, it gave him a position of precedence in relation to the common law, which came after the establishment of the monarchy and placed limitations upon it.[71]

Davies's views are important not simply because they echo Fleming's but also because Davies formulated them more than a decade after *Bate's Case* was decided. The theories of absolutism that appeared in 1605, 1606, and 1607, in other words, were not a temporary aberration. Quite to the contrary, the new view of the royal prerogative that Gentili, Cowell, and Fleming articulated became the very basis of the royalist theory of sovereignty in the 1620s and 1630s, which was developed by judges like Sir Robert Berkeley and Sir Francis Crawley.[72] Concerning this later development I shall not elaborate, but I do wish to mention that while transforming the ideas of Fleming and the civilians into a general theory of sovereignty, Berkeley drew directly on another civilian idea, that of the king as *lex loquens,* or *lex animata,* which Ernst Kantorowicz has shown to lie at the center of the Continental theory of the absolute state.[73]

What can we conclude from all this? First, the study of the civil law and the works of the theorists who relied upon it was a formative influence in English political thought at the end of the sixteenth and the beginning of the seventeenth century. There were, to be sure, many other strains of thought, especially theocratic ideas of divine right, that were of equal or greater importance, but the ideas, the principles, and the vocabulary of the civil law helped a large number of political writers, common lawyers as well as civilians, to clarify their ideas regarding sovereignty and absolute power in the English constitution. Indeed, it was largely because of these ideas that English political thought in the early seventeenth century assumed contours that distinguished it clearly from what went before and from what was to follow. As many authors have noted, there was a distinct difference between the theories of the Tudor period, which celebrated the supremacy of Parliament and the superiority of mixed government, and those of the early seventeenth century, which emphasized the power of the king and the limitations, large or small, that were placed upon it.[74] I would contend that the civil law had a great deal to do with this transition, for it focused attention on the king as sovereign and had difficulty accommodating a theory of mixed government.

Above and beyond this, I would argue that the new theories influenced by the civil law that emerged in the early seventeenth century played a significant part in causing the political divisions and tensions that arose before the civil war. Cowell's book in particular contributed to the growth of constitutional fear—the fear of absolutism—which can be detected in Parliament as early as 1604 and which was later aggravated by the political and religious policies of Charles I.[75] This fear is a central theme of early seventeenth-century political history, and it provides an element of continuity between the early parliaments of James's reign and those of the late 1620s and early 1640s. In addition to heightening this fear, however, the new view of the prerogative which emerged from the statements of Fleming and others initiated a constitutional debate that was conducted in Parliament and in the courts during the next four decades, a debate that centered on the nature and the extent of the royal prerogative and on the location of sovereignty in the state.[76] Because Cowell, Gentili, and Fleming had helped to start this debate, and because the vocabulary and the concepts of the civil law affected their thought, we might wish to reconsider the argument of the parliamentarian pamphleteer who accused Alberico Gentili of causing the English civil war by inspiring Charles I's supporters with absolutistic theories taken from the civil law. It is easy to criticize this pamphlet as bad history, since it takes Gentili out of context and greatly exaggerates the influence of his thought. Nevertheless, the pamphlet had something important to tell us.

What is suggests, in opposition to many historians today, is that there was serious constitutional conflict in the early seventeenth century, that this conflict did contribute to the growth of political tension in the 1610s, 1620s, and 1630s, and that, in the final analysis, there was some connection between the lectures of the regius professors of civil law at Oxford and Cambridge and the civil war which brought about the destruction of royal absolutism in England.[77]

Notes

1. For a discussion of those influences see Peter Stein, "Continental Influences on English Legal Thought, 1600–1900," *La Formazione Storica del diritto moderno in Europa; Atti del III congresso internazionale della Societa Italiano di Storia del diritto* (Florence, 1977), pp. 1105–11; and Thomas E. Scrutton, *The Influence of Roman Law on the Law of England* (Cambridge: Cambridge University Press, 1885).

2. Barbara Shapiro, "Codification of the Laws in Seventeenth-Century England," *Wisconsin Law Review* 2 (1974): 428–65.

3. Kenneth H. F. Dyson, *The State Tradition in Western Europe* (Oxford: Martin Robertson, 1980), pp. 113–15.

4. Charles H. McIlwain, ed., *The Political Works of James I* (Cambridge, Mass.: Harvard University Press, 1918), p. xli.

5. See for example Conrad Russell, "Parliamentary History in Perspective, 1604–1629," *History* 61 (1976): 1–27.

6. The term *jus gentium* could also be used to denote international law. See Arthur Nussbaum, *A Concise History of the Law of Nations* (New York: Macmillan, 1962), p. 101.

7. On the importance of chronology in this regard see R. C. van Caenegem, *The Birth of the Common Law* (Cambridge: Cambridge University Press, 1973), pp. 90–91.

8. Andrew Clark, ed., *Register of the University of Oxford*, vol. 2, pt. 1 (Oxford: Oxford Historical Society, 1988), p. 113.

9. Brian P. Levack, *The Civil Lawyers in England, 1603–1641: A Political Study* (Oxford: Clarendon Press, 1973), pp. 16–18.

10. John Aubrey claimed that John Selden and Sir Matthew Hale were "good civilians" and that Sir John Maynard was "pretty well acquainted" with the civil law (Bodleian Library, Aubrey MS. 10, fol. 68). On Hale's knowledge of the civil law see Peter Stein, *Roman Law and English Jurisprudence Yesterday and Today* (Cambridge: Cambridge University Press, 1969), pp. 7–8.

11. J. G. A. Pocock, *The Ancient Constitution and the Feudal Law* (Cambridge: Cambridge University Press, 1957), p. 90.

12. John Barton, "The Faculty of Law," in *The History of the University of Oxford*, vol. 3, *The Collegiate University*, ed. James Kelsey McConica (Oxford: Clarendon Press, 1986), p. 282.

13. Louis A. Knafla, *Law and Politics in Jacobean England: The Tracts of Lord*

Chancellor Ellesmere (Cambridge: Cambridge University Press, 1977), pp. 39–40, 49. For a seventeenth-century guide to private study in the civil law see Queen's College, Oxford, MS. 478.

14. William Fulbecke, *A Direction or Preparative to the Study of the Law* (London, 1600).

15. Louis A. Knafla, "The Matriculation Revolution and Education at the Inns of Court in Renaissance England," in *Tudor Men and Institutions,* ed. Arthur J. Slavin (Baton Rouge: Louisiana State University Press, 1972), p. 252.

16. See Brian P. Levack, "English Law, Scots Law, and the Union, 1603–1707," in *Law-Making and Law-Makers in British History,* ed. Alan Harding (London: Royal Historical Society, 1980), p. 116.

17. See Hans S. Pawlisch, "Sir John Davies, the Ancient Constitution, and Civil Law," *Historical Journal* 23 (1980): 694.

18. Charles Donahue, Jr., "The Civil Law in England," *Yale Law Journal* 84 (1974): 168, 179.

19. *Institutes* 1.1.6, *Digest* 1.4.1.

20. *Digest* 1.3.31.

21. Quentin Skinner, *The Foundations of Modern Political Thought* (Cambridge, 1978), 2:124; Myron Gilmore, *Argument from Roman Law in Political Thought, 1200–1600* (Cambridge, Mass.: Harvard University Press, 1941), p. 131.

22. See, for example, Brian Tierney, "'The Prince Is Not Bound by the Laws': Accursius and the Origins of the Modern State," *Comparative Studies in Society and History* 5 (1963): 378–400.

23. J. W. Allen, *A History of Political Thought in the Sixteenth Century* (London: Methuen, 1957), p. 281.

24. Gilmore, *Argument from Roman Law,* passim.

25. *Code* 1.14.4.

26. For an English civilian's use of this text see William Clerke, "Ancillans Synopsis," Trinity College, Dublin, MS. 635, title page.

27. H. F. Jolowicz, "Political Implications of Roman Law," *Tulane Law Review* 22 (1947): 62–63.

28. See for example, Levack, *Civil Lawyers,* pp. 86–121.

29. On the development of Bodin's political thought see Julian H. Franklin, *Jean Bodin and the Rise of Absolutist Theory* (Cambridge: Cambridge University Press, 1973).

30. G. R. Elton, "The Rule of Law in Sixteenth-Century England," in *Tudor Men and Institutions,* Slavin, p. 277. The view that the prerogative is completely subsumed within the law is a Tudor novelty, the product of the legalism of the age. See Donald W. Hanson, *From Kingdom to Commonwealth: The Development of Civic Consciousness in English Political Thought* (Cambridge, Mass.: Harvard University Press, 1970), pp. 288–89.

31. Sir John Fortescue, *The Governance of England,* ed. C. Plummer (Oxford: Clarendon Press, 1885).

32. L. Alston, introduction to Sir Thomas Smith, *De Republica Anglorum* (Cambridge: Cambridge University Press, 1906), p. xiv.

Law and Ideology

33. Smith, *De Republica Anglorum*, p. 48.

34. For William Petyt's later use of Smith to establish such a doctrine see Corinne C. Weston and Janelle R. Greenberg, *Subjects and Sovereigns: The Grand Controversy over Legal Sovereignty in Stuart England* (Cambridge: Cambridge University Press, 1981), p. 192.

35. Smith, *De Republica Anglorum*, pp. 58–62. In dealing with monarchy in general, Smith establishes the importance of restricting the absolute power of the king. See pp. 16–18.

36. See Gezina van den Molen, *Alberico Gentili and the Development of International Law* (Amsterdam: H. J. Paris, 1938).

37. George L. Mosse, "The Influence of Jean Bodin's *République* on English Political Thought," *Medievalia et Humanistica* 5 (1948): 73–83. The first English translation of this work was published in 1606.

38. For the alleged influence of Roman law on James see McIlwain, *Political Works of James I*, p. xlii.

39. The development of John Hayward's political thought can be interpreted in this way. See Levack, *Civil Lawyers*, pp. 113–15.

40. Alberico Gentili, "De potestate regis absoluta," in *Regales disputationes tres* (London, 1605).

41. Alberico Gentili, *Hispanicae advocationis libri duo* (Hanover, 1613).

42. *Englands Monarch* (London, 1644).

43. Levack, *Civil Lawyers*, p. 221.

44. Cowell dedicated *The Interpreter* to Bancroft, and consequently the archbishop was suspected of sharing Cowell's views. See Elizabeth R. Foster, ed., *Proceedings in Parliament, 1610* (New Haven: Yale University Press, 1966), 1:18, 23–24, 188.

45. Daniel R. Coquillette, "Legal Ideology and Incorporation, I: The English Civilians, 1523–1607," *Boston University Law Review* 61 (1981): 69.

46. Brian P. Levack, *The Formation of the British State: England, Scotland, and the Union, 1603–1707* (Oxford: Clarendon Press, 1987), pp. 68–101.

47. John Cowell, *The Interpreter, or booke containing the signification of words* (Cambridge, 1607).

48. *Journals of the House of Commons* 1:400.

49. Even the moderate constitutionalist William Camden argued that the king was above the law in this regard (F. S. Fussner, "William Camden's 'Discourse concerning the Prerogative of the Crown,'" *American Philosophical Society Proceedings* 101 [1957]: 213–14.)

50. James F. Larkin and Paul L. Hughes, eds., *Stuart Royal Proclamations* (Oxford: Clarendon Press, 1973), 1:243–45; Foster, *Proceedings in Parliament* 1:28–31; S. B. Chrimes, "The Constitutional Views of Dr. John Cowell," *EHR* 64 (1949): 461–75.

51. T. B. Howell, ed., *A Complete Collection of State Trials* 33 vols. (London: Longman, 1809–26), 3:389.

52. Charles H. McIlwain, *Constitutionalism Ancient and Modern* (Ithaca: Cornell University Press, 1947), pp. 67–130.

53. David S. Berkowitz, "Reason of State in England and the Petition of Right, 1603–1629," in *Staatsräson: Studien zur Geschichte eines politischen Begriffs*, ed. R. Schnur (Berlin, 1975), p. 176.

54. G. W. Prothero, ed., *Select Statutes and Other Constitutional Documents Illustrative of the Reigns of Elizabeth and James I*, 4th ed. (Oxford: Clarendon Press, 1913), p. 311. Both J. R. Tanner, ed., *Constitutional Documents of the Reign of James I* (Cambridge: Cambridge University Press, 1930); and J. P. Kenyon, ed., *The Stuart Constitution* (Cambridge: Cambridge University Press, 1966), have preserved Prothero's insertion in their collections.

55. Margaret Atwood Judson, *The Crisis of the Constitution* (New Brunswick, N.J.: Rutgers University Press, 1949), pp. 112–13, considers Fleming's statement to be "the clearest and fullest statement of the royalist position during the whole period of controversy."

56. Francis Oakley, "Jacobean Political Theology: The Absolute and Ordinary Powers of the King," *Journal of the History of Ideas* 29 (1968): 323–46.

57. Gentili, "De potestate," pp. 10–11.

58. Elton, "Rule of Law," p. 276–77, argues that Cowell and Fleming were "not typical even of early-Stuart opinion."

59. Levack, *Civil Lawyers*, passim.

60. Bodleian Library, Oxford University Archives, Congregation Register 1659–69, fol. 175.

61. Judson, *Crisis of the Constitution*, p. 115.

62. British Library, Harleian MS. 5220, fol. 9v.

63. See, for example, Gerald R. Cragg, *Freedom and Authority* (Philadelphia: Westminster Press, 1975), pp. 77–78.

64. On the influence of the civil law on Bacon see Paul H. Kocher, "Francis Bacon and the Science of Jurisprudence," *Journal of the History of Ideas* 18 (1957): 3–26; Coquillette, "Legal Ideology," p. 9n.

65. *The Works of Francis Bacon*, 15 vols., ed. James Spedding, Robert Leslie Ellis, and D. D. Heath (Boston: Brown & Taggard, 1860–64), 15:377.

66. *The Letters and Life of Francis Bacon*, 7 vols., ed. James Spedding (London: Longman, 1861–74), 3:371.

67. Ibid., p. 373.

68. Bacon also claims that the king is above the law, "for it may not correct him for any offence" (*Works*, 15:377).

69. Pawlisch, "Sir John Davies," pp. 689–702.

70. Bacon made the same equation (Kocher, "Bacon," pp. 10–11).

71. Sir John Davies, *The Question concerning Impositions* (London, 1656), pp. 29–31.

72. See Sir William Holdsworth, *A History of English Law*, 16 vols. (London: Methuen, 1936–66), 6:19–55.

73. Judson, *Crisis of the Constitution*, p. 137; Ernst Kantorowicz, "Kingship under the Impact of Scientific Jurisprudence," in *Twelfth-Century Europe* (Madison: University of Wisconsin Press, 1966), p. 104.

74. R. W. K. Hinton, "English Constitutional Theories from Sir John Fortescue to Sir John Eliot," *EHR* 75 (1960): 410–25. For general treatments of the rise

of absolutist thought in the early seventeenth century see J. P. Sommerville, *Politics and Ideology in England, 1603–1640* (London: Longman 1986), pp. 39–46; and Robert Eccleshall, *Order and Reason in Politics* (Oxford: Oxford University Press, 1978), pp. 76–96.

75. For this fear in connection with Cowell's *Interpreter,* see the speech of Richard Martin in Foster, *Proceedings in Parliament* 2:328. For a general discussion of constitutional conflict and fear during this entire period see Derek Hirst, "Revisionism Revised: The Place of Principle," *Past and Present* 92 (1981): 79–99, esp. pp. 87–90.

76. On the later influence of Cowell's views see Sommerville, *Politics and Ideology,* pp. 126–27.

77. An early version of this paper was presented to the seminar on political thought in the Elizabethan age at the Folger Institute Center for the History of British Political Thought in February 1985. I am grateful to Professor Donald R. Kelley and the members of the seminar for their criticisms and comments.

"Subject to Ev'ry Mounters Bended Knee": Herbert and Authority

In 1631, two years before his death, Herbert addressed a letter to Anne Clifford, the countess of Pembroke and Montgomery. This letter, written from the country at Bemerton where Herbert was parson to a great lady at court, measures in reverse the geographical, social, and linguistic distance covered by Herbert's career. "A Priests blessing," remarks Herbert, "though it be none of the Court-stile, yet doubtless Madam, can do you no hurt."[1] Herbert develops this opposition between the blessings of a priest and "the salutations, and complements, and formes of worldly language" in *The Country Parson,* his manual of conduct for rural clergy, asserting that "if a Minister talke with a great man in the ordinary course of complementing language, he shall be esteemed as ordinary complementers; but if he often interpose a Blessing, . . . this unusuall form begets a reverence, and makes him esteemed according to his Profession" (pp. 285–86). Herbert suggests that religious and social discourse are different, and that the parson, by replacing the compliments through which one renders respect to "a great man" with the novelty of religious blessing, accents this difference; at the same time, he signals his separation from ordinary men, and so attains the reverence of that superior from whom ordinary compliments would elicit only common esteem.

These discourses, however, and the experiences they represent, are not as discrete as Herbert or his critics would like to make them. Even religious language remains, in the words of Joseph Summers, an "incorrigibly social medium,"[2] inevitably implicating the otherworld in the terms of this one. While Herbert opposes the "unusual form" of blessing to the deferential compliments of ordinary discourse with superiors, he nevertheless reveals the motives of both—winning the good will and respect of superiors—to be astonishingly alike. Benediction, finally, is recommended because it fulfills this social and rhetorical function more effectively than ordinary compliments. A priest's blessing, it turns out, has more to do with "the Court-stile" than Herbert's letter to Anne Clifford would reveal.

As Herbert's dialogue with authority in *The Country Parson* blurs the distinction between social and religious demeanor that it attempts to draw, so throughout *The Temple* Herbert's intimate experience of political authority infiltrates and enriches his discourse with divinity. In an important but overlooked essay on Herbert, Kenneth Burke asks, "Where matters of 'reverence' are concerned, should we not consider such possibilities of fusing social eminence with divine eminence as would be indicated by the similarity between 'My Lord' and 'milord'? . . . why should we not consider also such relationships between the language of worldly hierarchy and the language of the supernatural hierarchy, each with its great stress upon the exercising of one's desire freely to praise?"[3] As Burke's questions indicate, the two discourses that Herbert wishes to separate—the courtly and the religious—share similar motives and a common rhetoric. In both, praise of and reverence for hierarchical authority are expressed in a nearly identical vocabulary of submission. Bemerton may be far removed from the court, but both Bemerton and the court require the continual subordination of the self to superior power.

In "The Priesthood," for example, the poem in which Herbert most forthrightly ponders changing a secular for a sacred vocation, the terms he uses to denote these different careers nevertheless stress their continuity. This lyric is remarkable not only for its demonstration of how fully Herbert's purported turn from the world is involved in the discourse of this world, but also for its perception of the potentially insidious consequences of aligning behavior towards earthly and heavenly authority. Herbert depicts the contemplated career change as an "exchang[e]" of his "lay-sword / For that of th' holy Word." The sword, an emblem of social and martial power, is traded in for a "sword of the spirit," but the visual and auditory rhyme between "word" and "sword" emphasizes their likeness. Besides, *sword* encloses the *Word* to which it is opposed, the *Word* that should contain it.[4] The conclusion of the poem, moreover, reinstates the courtly values ostensibly surrendered with the gentleman's "lay-sword." Both attracted and repelled by the awesome power and responsibility of the priesthood, Herbert can only prostrate himself before his heavenly superior: "I throw me at his feet." Yet in this posture of complete submission, he discovers a method for ingratiating divine authority that is strikingly similar to secular and courtly strategies of social climbing.

There will I lie, untill my Maker seek
For some mean stuffe whereon to show his skill:
Then is my time. The distance of the meek
Doth flatter power. Lest good come short of ill
In praising might, the poore do by submission
        What pride by opposition.

Deference functions as a device for celebrating sacred as well as secular power. The calculated observation of occasion ("Then is my time") and hierarchical distance, so much a part of behavior in the world of the "lay-sword" allegedly abandoned, is fused with the ideal of Christian patience.[5] The distinctions between praise and flattery, good and ill, submission and opposition, begin to dissolve in a world of political and spiritual opportunism. Just as social concerns constantly interpenetrate the sacred world to which they are contrasted, so are devotional postures of submission continually contaminated by the subtle forms of opposition or ambition they both enable and disguise. Surprisingly, the submission of the poor and the opposition of the proud have the same outcome, however different they may be in appearance and intention: the flattery of might and power, whether secular or sacred.

Such scrupulous attention to the affinity between obedience and opposition, between placating authority and challenging it, could only come from one who had practiced the manipulative powers of submission in his own career. The shape of Herbert's biography and the vitality of his poetry are, I want to argue, intimately related. His political experience begins with the confident assertion that secular office might be integrated with sacred duty; the "dignity" of University Orator, Herbert promises his stepfather Sir John Danvers, "hath no such earthiness in it, but it may very well be joined with Heaven" (p. 370). Yet in this secular occupation Herbert learned that submission is indeed an act of opposition, that deference and praise are tactics for manipulating authority, and self-deprecation a way to scale both the social and the religious hierarchy. Thus, when Herbert asserts in "The H. Scriptures (I)" that the Bible, the ultimate authority, the word of the King of Kings, is "Subject to ev'ry mounters bended knee," he acknowledges not only the striking availability of Scripture to the humble but also the coercive power that gestures of humility can exert over figures of authority. As "The distance of the meek / Doth flatter power," so is the bended knee the mark of the social and spiritual mounter, he who would attempt to acquire power over those powerful personages to whom he submits. By examining closely Herbert's verbal performances before secular authority, we can more fully comprehend the accomplishment of poems such as "The Thanksgiving" and "The Reprisall," in which Herbert exposes the political presumption and social aggression inherent in the lexicon of gratitude, submission, and dependence. The lyrics of *The Temple* do not occupy a realm of discourse completely separate from the court; rather, they concatenate, and consummate, Herbert's social and political experience.[6]

I

Herbert's reputation as an Anglican saint has hindered our understanding of his poetry by diverting attention from the amount of time and energy he invested in the world. Even Izaak Walton, whose hagiography initiated this approach, credits Herbert with desiring courtly promotion (although he does so only to increase the value of Herbert's retirement from the world of the court, and to encourage other similarly gifted young men to join the church).[7] The concept of two Herberts, like that of the two Donnes on which it is modeled, provides a convenient way for selves and for critics to organize experience. The reality, however, is more complex and more compelling.

Herbert's social status and political situation forced him to practice daily the modes of submission to authority that the divine poetry exploits. As an aristocrat, Herbert would have nourished great expectations for his political future (two of his brothers, in fact, became influential court figures—Edward was ambassador to France, and Henry was Master of the Revels—by successfully translating verbal talent into political place). Yet as a younger son, Herbert possessed few means to fulfill these expectations, save his ability to ingratiate his superiors.[8] Herbert did receive an annuity of thirty pounds, but this was apparently insufficient (considering Herbert's many pleas for money in his letters) and often tardy.[9] In a social structure composed of a chain of dependence leading up to the monarch, the only theoretically self-sufficient figure, Herbert had to rely upon his ability to please potential patrons for his very sustenance.[10]

Equipped with great verbal dexterity and a talent for witty praise that pleased both the intellect and the vanity of many Renaissance superiors, Herbert wisely attempted to win the good graces of those in authority. In what may have been his first public performance, Herbert, as Reader in Rhetoric at Cambridge, was appointed to give the "Barnaby" lectures, in which he was expected to "expound in English, for the special benefit of first-year students, such authors as Cicero or Quintilian."[11] Herbert, however, chose as the appropriate text for analysis not the classical orators but instead the words of his monarch, King James I. The oration, unfortunately, has not survived, but an account by one of Herbert's classmates—John Hacket—has. In writing about James's address to the Parliament of 1624, Hacket recalls a day six years earlier when Herbert had praised James's eloquence: "Mr. *George Herbert* being praelector in the Rhetorique School in *Cambridg anno* 1618. Pass'd by those fluent Orators, that Domineered in the Pulpits of *Athens* and *Rome,* and insisted to Read upon an Oration of King *James,* which he Analyzed, shew'd the concinnity of the Parts, the propriety of the Phrase, the height and Power of it to move Affections, the Style utterly unknown to the Ancients, who could not conceive what Kingly Eloquence was, in respect of which those noted Demagogi were but Hirelings, and Triobulary Rhetoricians."[12] We do not know whether James was in attendance, or even if word of this speech got back to him. But two years later Herbert had been elected to the position of University Orator, an office requiring just the kind of artful flattery apparently displayed by his explication of James's eloquence.

The oratorship, observes A. G. Hyde, "was instituted as a practical means of securing the good-will of influential persons in the outer world by paying them compliments (in elegant Latin) when they visited the University. The writing of letters, in the same tongue, to obtain privileges for the academic body, or to defend or maintain its existing privileges, was an especially important part of the office, together with conveying thanks for services rendered by Secretaries of State and others, and for gifts of all kinds."[13] Performance of such tasks, concludes Hyde, demanded "the courtier's gifts as well as the graces of scholarship." As such, the position provided an appropriate transition between the academic hierarchy of the university and the political hierarchy of the court. Indeed, the two previous holders of the office—Sir Francis Nethersole and Sir Robert Naunton—had ascended from the oratorship into positions as secretaries of state, and Herbert had no reason to think that he would interrupt that pattern.

In the letters to Danvers in which Herbert discusses his hopes for the position, we can glimpse the developing political acumen of an aspiring and gifted twenty-six-year-old excited at the prospect of the civic world opening up to him. "The Orator's place," Herbert tells Danvers, "is the finest place in the University, though not the gainfullest . . . but the commodiousness is beyond the Revenue; for the Orator writes all the University Letters, makes all the Orations, be it to King, Prince, or whatever comes to the University; to requite these pains, he takes place next the Doctors, is at all their Assemblies and Meetings, and sits above the Proctors, is Regent or Non-regent at his pleasure, and such like Gaynesses, which will please a young man well" (pp. 369–70). To Herbert, the primary value of the oratorship is not in its monetary reward (equal to his annuity) but in the political importance of those whom it gives him the privilege to address ("King, Prince, or whatever") and in the physical and social place it grants him ("next the Doctors . . . above the Proctors"). Even as he attempts to distance himself from the ambitious young man who would be pleased with such "gaynesses," Herbert acknowledges that the "commodiousness" of the post is not so much the revenue it bestows as the honor it confers.[14]

In the conclusion of this letter, Herbert asks Danvers to send on a letter to Sir Francis Nethersole as soon as possible, "that I may work the heads to my purpose." The phrase cunningly recognizes the kinds of political manipulation required to ascend the hierarchies of university and court. And Herbert continued to "work the heads" on behalf of the university, and himself, once he had been officially elected to the position. In the first letter that Herbert wrote as University Orator, he thanks King James for donating a copy of his *Opera Latina* to the university library. He apostrophizes James as "incomparable wisdom," apparently aware of James's desire to be considered the English Solomon, and declares in an epigram that Cambridge now has the equal of the Vatican and the Bodleian libraries, because James's volume is a library unto itself. Herbert also praises James for a creative, life-giving power that approaches divinity: "your right hand alone . . . quickens the globe with life and action." He suggests that by becoming an author, James displays a Christlike condescension towards his creatures: "laying aside thy majesty, thou dost offer thyself to be gazed upon on paper, that thou mayst be more intimately conversant amongst us. O astonishing benignity!" Herbert concludes with a prayer "that to your crown, civil and literary, He [God] may at a far-off hour add a third, celestial (crown)."[15]

This circumspect commingling of sacred and secular power is on one level simply a presentation of James as he most wanted to be imagined: a kind of god on earth.[16] Herbert's exuberant praise of James's nearly divine might sanctifies political ascension while flattering authority, thus permitting Herbert to implement his desire to join the civil office of Orator with the divinity of heaven. Another manifestation of this desire may be glimpsed in the *Musae Responsoriae,* Herbert's only work of explicit theological controversy. Commencing with flattering dedications to King James, Prince Charles, and Bishop Andrews and concluding with equally laudatory epigrams to James and to God, the volume attempts to span the range of political, ecclesiastical, and heavenly authorities upon whose favor opportunity for preferment would depend.[17] The text itself—a witty if immature defense of Conformist liturgy against the Puritan Andrew Melville's censure—bestrides the boundary dividing political from spiritual pursuits. Moreover, as Arthur F. Marotti argues in his provocative study of Donne, "the very act of composing sacred verse in the reign of a monarch [such as James] who had himself written religious poetry and especially favored pious and polemical writing was a political gesture."[18] In this context, Herbert's vindication of Conformist worship in Latin verse can be seen to reflect royal generic taste as well as Herbert's own liturgical preferences. The entry into religious disputation is also a gesture paying court to secular authority.

The performance of effusive praise and official apology, however, must also have been the source of much apprehension and resentment. In his only gossip-laden letter, written to Sir Robert Harley at Danvers's request, Herbert relates in noteworthy detail an incident that demonstrates his awareness of the difficulties and dangers of attempting to translate linguistic talent into political reward at the Stuart court. "There is a Frenchman," Herbert reports, "who writt a poem heere in England & presented it to the King, who because of his importunities gaue him a reward, but not so great as he expected & therfore he grumblingly said that if he had giuen it to the pope he should haue had a greater reward. upon this he was forbid Court & kingdome, yet was seene lately neere the king, wch some observing who heard the interdiction denounced to him, told the King & so he is committed to prison" (pp. 368–69). Herbert's surprising fascination with this anonymous foreigner betrays a preoccupation with the acute political anxieties that were an inevitable part of the Renaissance literary network.[19] Unable to escape the pull of the very court that disappoints and then banishes him, this unfortunate figure allows his disgruntlement to surface. As a result, his poetic labors are requited not with promotion but with prison. Like so many Englishmen who attempted unsuccessfully to attain appropriate recompense for the exercise of their verbal abilities, this Frenchman testifies to the centripetal attractions and pressing dangers of the court.

Despite such dangers, Herbert persevered in his bid for the favor of those in authority over him. This political climate, however, necessitated the development of a mode of discourse through which one could articulate such anxieties in a language of submission and ingratiation. Hutchinson cites a contemporary account of the circumstances in which Herbert presented an oration to King James that illuminates the inherent theatricality of the Orator's role while elucidating the ways such a discourse might be attained. After having observed the performance of a Latin play entitled *Loiola,* and expressing "no remarkable mirth thereat," the king was brought "to the door, entring into ye Court, where his Coach did wait for him: but his Majesty was pleased to stay there, while the Orator Mr. Herbert did make a short Farewell Speech unto him. Then he called for a copy of the Vice-Chancellor's Speech, & likewise for an Epigram the Orator made."[20] Following directly a dramatic performance, the oration is in fact another performance, an entertainment intended to please the king. The epigram that James apparently relished, "Dum petit Infantem," wittily compares Prince Charles's visit to Spain in search of a spouse with King James's visit to Cambridge. "The question is," asserts Herbert, "whose loue the greater showes," James's or Charles's; Herbert then answers the question by opting for James, whose "wit's more / Remote from ours, then Spaine from Britains shoare."[21] Both Charles and James are adroitly praised for a beneficence towards their creatures that the Orator intends to encourage.

Herbert's ingenious and successful encomium of James, however, leaves open the possibility that the recognition of distance between James's wit and that of the members of the university denigrates rather than celebrates the royal intelligence. The ambivalence that the brilliant young orator must have experienced, faced with the task of praising the intellect of his intellectual inferior while surrounded by some of the best minds of the kingdom, reflexively permeates the terms of his praise. Whether intentionally or not, the epigram equivocates on the question of James's wit, allowing Herbert to flatter and belittle the king in a single utterance. Concurrently eulogizing and satirizing the mental capacity of his political superior, Herbert uses "the distance of the meek" to praise and oppose power. Hostility to authority is vented in a discourse that is nevertheless acceptable and pleasing to authority.[22]

Indeed, in the next and final extant oration given by Herbert, praise of and opposition to power are so completely enmeshed that many scholars have suggested it as the major reason for Herbert's apparent loss of favor at court.[23] The occasion of this oration was the return of Prince Charles and the duke of Buckingham from Spain, angry at their failure to complete negotiations for a Spanish marriage, and intent upon war. As University Orator, Herbert was placed in a politically sensitive and rhetorically difficult situation: by advocating war, he would alienate the peace-loving King James, but by counseling peace, he would antagonize the already indignant Prince Charles. Herbert responded by praising the prince fulsomely, but for an attribute more appropriate to the king: the desire for peace. As S. R. Gardiner explains, "Herbert disliked war, and he could not refrain from the maladroit compliment of commending Charles for going to Madrid in search of peace."[24] In this oration, Herbert attempts to command authority by commending it for qualities it lacks in the hope that it will then try to live up to the terms of the praise. Such a tactic supplies one of the few means by which a dependent might sway a superior without losing his favor. Francis Bacon, for example, recommends that courtiers deal with authority through the tactic of "*laudando praecipere,*" when by telling men what they are, they represent to them what they should be."[25] Herbert's coercive praise, however, was unsuccessful. Perhaps the aging King James appreciated Herbert's extensive praise of peace, but "from Charles, rushing headlong into war, the lover of peace had no favour to expect."[26]

Yet the oration is curious not only for its impolitic praise of peace but also for its disingenuous declaration of plainness amidst such covertly manipulative tactics: "I do not speak to rustics or to barbarians, whom it were easy to circumvent by the grandeur of a statement, and to astonish their inexperienced minds by the force of (mere) words. . . . I do not play the orator, O collegians. . . . that wild folly and empty noise of words I have long ago laid aside; bubbles and rattles are for boys. . . . I truly am conscious both who I am myself (a beard, alas, so grave!) and amongst whom I am speaking—men of polished and nice ear, whose gravity and position [purple robes] I will not trifle with."[27] Although conventional, Herbert's protestation of candor and simplicity far exceeds the needs of the convention or the occasion. This overwrought refusal to "play the orator" adumbrates a deep discomfort with the project of praising superiors who may not necessarily merit it. Furthermore, even as he covertly attempts to counsel royalty by extolling Charles for seeking "peace at the risk of his own life," Herbert declares that the counsels of ordinary mortals "lie open," but "hidden are the counsels of gods and kings."[28] Such irony inexorably percolates through the prior and subsequent praise of Charles for qualities that contravene those the prince exhibits. Herbert's own complex motives are revealed even as they are veiled by his declarations that they are untainted by the orator's art.

Ultimately, such masterful subterfuge enables Herbert to claim for his own status an authority equal to that of the royal audience he essays to manipulate. In describing how Charles represented the king in Spain just as the Orator speaks on behalf of Cambridge, Herbert discovers a parallel between their respective missions: "kings have ambassadors, stationary and resident, which position our sweetest prince occupied; he himself acted the orator, that I may glory a little in this title."[29] As he endeavors to manipulate authority through strategies of indirection and praise, Herbert discovers a model for his own authority. By means of complex rhetorical gestures expressing "the distance of the meek," Herbert attempts simultaneously to applaud and to appropriate power.[30]

The "respective boldnesse" Herbert displays towards "great persons" in his oration upon Charles's return from Spain is precisely the demeanor towards authority that Herbert advises in "The Church-porch" (line 235). "That temper," Herbert counsels, "gives them theirs, and yet doth take / Nothing from thine" (lines 254–55). But as Herbert discovered, that *via media* of behavior was enormously difficult to sustain. Although his oration delicately interlaced respect and boldness, adulation and admonition, it must have only infuriated the already irate prince. Authority, Herbert learned, was subject to him only as long as he exuded praise and reverence unadulterated by resentment or assertion; as long, in other words, as his bended knee did not stiffen or ache.

Herbert's subsequent political life leaves few other records. He does represent Montgomery in Parliament in 1624, resulting in an enthusiastic endorsement of the educational value of parliamentary experience: "there is no School to a Parliament."[31] Herbert retained the position of Orator until 1628, but apparently fulfilled few if any of its duties.[32] When King James died in 1625, Herbert Thorndike, not George Herbert, delivered the official funeral sermon at Cambridge. The promising youth who had attracted the notice of the king then becomes nearly invisible to the public and to history until his ordination as priest in 1630, when presented with the living of Fugglestone-with-Bemerton.[33] There in the country, where Herbert spent the last three years of his life, emerges the legend of saintly Parson George, a figure whose shadow has nearly effaced the experiences of the first thirty-seven years, but whose poetry and prose reflect, and reflect upon, those experiences. Unlike Donne, whose appointment as dean of Saint Paul's was not so much an alternative to as a fulfillment of his secular goals, providing him with the courtly audience he had sought so fervently throughout his career, Herbert concluded his career and his life at a great social and geographical distance from the court, among country people, whom he characterized as "thick, and heavy" (*Country Parson,* p. 233). Rather than rubbing elbows with the rich and powerful of the realm, Herbert as country parson had to learn to disdain not "to enter into the poorest Cottage, though he even creep into it, and though it smell never so lothsomly" (p. 249). Yet the sacred poetry produced before and during these last three years at Bemerton exerts great verbal and spiritual labor in the effort to ingratiate a monarch who bears at times an unsettling resemblance to the inscrutable, praise-loving, godlike king whose favor Herbert had originally sought.[34] Much of the power of this poetry derives from Herbert's intimate acquaintance with the world of political power.

II

"The *Poet,*" observes Ben Jonson in the *Discoveries,* "is the neerest Borderer upon the Orator, and expresseth all his vertues."[35] This is certainly true in Herbert's case, although the very real differences in style, tone, and content between Herbert's Latin performances as Orator and his English poems have prevented readers from exploring this rich border territory. Even those critics who have noted Herbert's relationship with the world have concentrated on its renunciatory elements. M. M. Ross, for example, although correctly claiming that "too little attention has been given to any concern Herbert may have shown in his poetry for the world about him," proceeds in his reading of Herbert to explore only "the antihistorical note of withdrawal in Herbert."[36] Similarly, while Leah S. Marcus properly looks to the social ramifications of Herbert's use of the persona of a child throughout *The Temple,* she nevertheless describes this persona as a "retreat," an "escape," a "refuge" from "encroaching political and religious chaos."[37]

In *The Temple,* however, Herbert not only turns away from the social and political world but also turns the language of this world into the medium for his lyric worship of God. Herbert's intention to implicate his discourse with God in the strategies by which a social inferior petitions and gratifies his superior can be glimpsed in the very first poem that the reader of *The Temple* encounters: "The Dedication." This poem, modeled closely on the language by which secular authors address their literary performances to figures of superior power in hopes of protection and reward, aligns Herbert's devotional productions with the matrix of social and political motives of authorship in Renaissance England.[38] The following poem—"The Church-porch"—is primarily a versified courtesy book in miniature, offering shrewd advice on comportment in a variety of situations.[39] Despite its surprising emphasis on social cunning, "The Church-porch" is, as its architecturally liminal status would indicate, contiguous with rather than divorced from the sacred lyrics it introduces. In admonishing the reader to "Doe all things like a man, not sneakingly," for example, Herbert declares, "Think the king sees thee still; for his King does" (lines 121–22). Similarly, Herbert encourages prompt arrival at church because "God then deals blessings: If a king did so, / Who would not haste, nay give, to see the show?" (lines 389–90). Behavior before God is coterminous with behavior towards earthly authority. Power, whether secular or sacred, monitors and rewards human conduct.

Yet it is within "The Church," rather than in the text on conduct prefacing it, that Herbert most effectively capitalizes on the political sophistication acquired in his traffic with secular authority. "The Thanksgiving," for example, is a poem whose situation and motives correspond closely to those Herbert confronted in the social world. A figure of superior power, here a "king of grief," has performed an act of beneficence that requires in return a proffer of gratitude. In this poem Herbert attempts a conventional tender of thanks; yet he also exploits his experience of gratitude in the political world to reveal the aggressive aspects of giving thanks, of offering requital, of imitating a superior's munificence. At the same time, he dramatizes the psychological burden that acts of un-requitable beneficence place upon the recipient.

The speaker of "The Thanksgiving" asks his sovereign, "But how then shall I imitate thee, and / Copie thy fair, though bloudie hand?" He views emulation as a proper response to his superior's largesse, and portrays the giving of thanks as a literary performance (copying the bloody hand-writing and imitating what the bloody hand has written).[40] In like man-ner, Herbert begins his first letter to Danvers with the question of his own ability to express appropriately witty gratitude—"though I had the best wit in the World, yet it would easily tyre me, to find out variety of thanks for the diversity of your favours" (*Works*, p. 363)—and concludes by promising Danvers that "I will strive to imitate the compleatness of your love, with being in some proportion, and after my manner, Your most obedient Servant" (p. 364).

The predicament of answering the favors of a superior—whether di-vine or mortal—is voiced in strikingly similar terms. In the letters to Danvers, however, Herbert wants to conceal the manipulative and com-bative impulses inherent in expressions of gratitude; in "The Thanksgiv-ing," by contrast, he chooses to expose them. The immediate response of the speaker of "The Thanksgiving" to his rhetorical question allows the politically competitive potential of the desire to *give* thanks to surface: "Surely I will revenge me on thy love, / And trie who shall victorious prove." The speaker proposes to engage in a contest with his monarch, to pit his own abilities against those of his king in what "The Pearl" calls "vies of favours." He will *revenge* himself on his monarch (a verb with intentionally violent as well as imitative connotations) through the ac-complishment of a series of purportedly pious resolves.

> If thou dost give me wealth, I will restore
> All back unto thee by the poore.
> If thou dost give me honour, men shall see,
> The honour doth belong to thee.

As Richard Strier asserts, "Herbert is presenting the desire to imitate Christ as the essence of misguided good intentions."[41] Yet in these lines, the speaker also endeavors to appeal to the self-interest of his monarch by suggesting what profits future acts of beneficence would achieve. As he presumptuously pretends that his own good deeds do not depend (politically and grammatically) upon a prior act of beneficence by his superior ("*If* thou . . . *then* I will . . ."), so does he promise to return to his superior whatever gifts that superior bestows upon him.

The speaker attempts, in other words, to make his offering of thanks

coercive and to reject an acknowledgment of his own inability to reciprocate. He does this because such an acknowledgment would also require
the recognition of his own complete subordination. Lorenzo Ducci, author of the *Ars aulica*, asserts that man naturally resists a status of indebtedness: "that facultie wherein thankfulness and gratitude reside, doth not
desire by nature (which makes us ever strive to be more than other men)
onely to give equall recompense with the benefit, but much more then
what hath beene received . . . so that in love he answereth not alone in
just proportion to his dutie, but by the foresaid reason endevours to outstrip the same."[42] The competitive gratitude manifested by the speaker of
"The Thanksgiving" derives from a desire to "outstrip," to be superior
to, his monarch. What appears to be a humble offering of thanks and a
pledge of pious performance is in fact a covert bid for political superiority, as the speaker chafes against the weight of indebtedness placed upon
him by his superior's beneficence.

Even gifts, Herbert demonstrates in "The Thanksgiving," can oppress.
The dynamics of potlatch exchanges demand that when one receives a
benefit, he is both materially enriched and politically impoverished by
it.[43] Milton's Satan rebels against the beneficent king of heaven because
his favors force Satan to assume, and continually confess, "The debt im-
mense of endless gratitude, / So burdensome still paying, still to owe."[44]
In the letters of thanksgiving to Danvers, glimmers of the onerous nature
of the favors that Danvers graciously bestows upon his stepson emerge
from the language of Herbert's proffered gratitude. When the young
Herbert wittily suggests that Danvers's gift of a horse "come[s] a Horse-
back," the image of a burden can be discerned. This image is developed
in a later letter, where Herbert asserts that "this Week hath loaded me
with your Favours" (*Works*, p. 369). Moreover, as the monarch of "The
Thanksgiving" "preventest" (meaning both "to go before" and "to hin-
der") the speaker's attempts to respond in kind, so does Danvers's beneficence disable Herbert's effort to express appropriate gratitude: "I can
never answer what I have already received; for your favours are so ancient, that they *prevent* my memory" (p. 367). The inexpressibility topos,
employed often by Herbert as University Orator, functions rhetorically
to flatter authority and politically to remind authority that one is accepting, by declaring one's inability to respond properly, a status of inferiority.[45]

Yet rather than rest in a confession of his inability to utter sufficient
gratitude, as Herbert does with Danvers and with the benefactors whom
he addressed as Orator, the speaker of "The Thanksgiving" refuses to
accept the political liability and social subordination such a confession

would incur. His desire to equal and surpass his monarch interlards the ridiculous and the sublime:

> For thy predestination I'le contrive,
>   That three yeares hence, if I survive,
>   I'le build a spittle, or mend common wayes,
>   But mend mine own without delayes.
> . . . .
>   My musick shall finde thee, and ev'ry string
>   Shall have his attribute to sing.
> . . . .
>   Nay, I will reade thy book, and never move
>   Till I have found therein thy love,
> Thy art of love, which I'le turn back on thee:
>   O my deare Saviour, Victorie!

Yet this exclamation of victory over his sovereign proves to be premature: "Then for thy passion—I will do for that— / Alas, my God, I know not what." That quality of his monarch with which the poem begins—his suffering—proves inimitable and unrequitable.

In attempting to imitate the actions of his heavenly monarch, the speaker of "The Thanksgiving" not only engrosses the *imitatio christi* devotional tradition; he also employs a tactic for ingratiation recommended by many courtly commentators. As Lorenzo Ducci observes, the courtier who desires the favor of his monarch "is to adapt and fit himselfe by all the meanes he may unto his will, and make himselfe, if he bee possible, the very portract [*sic*] of his properties and fashions."[46] By imitating one's monarch, one subordinates one's desires and inclinations to those of the monarch. Such subordination wins the favor of superiors, explains Ducci, "because selfe *love* which is the roote of all other loves, chiefly extends it selfe unto his like, and more towards those who conforme themselves in manners and natural inclination thereunto."[47] Just as Herbert's orations and letters praising James manage to present back to James the very image the king most desired to project, so does the successful courtier, finally, fashion himself into a flattering mirror of his superior.

Yet there is in the imitation of authority a danger that Herbert exposes in "The Thanksgiving": the ease with which imitation becomes emulation, and reproduction precipitates rivalry. A gesture by which the self is shaped and subordinated to the whims of authority can nevertheless threaten that authority with supplantation or appropriation. If one imitates one's prince too well, one may equal or even surpass the prince, and so subvert the hierarchical subordination one's imitation was intended to express. George Puttenham, for example, asserts that while one should study to imitate the prince in matters "wherein the Prince would seeme an example of vertue, and would not mislike to be egalled by others," one should also remember that princes "must be suffred to have the victorie and be relented unto," and that "in gaming with a Prince it is decent to let him sometimes win of purpose, to keepe him pleasant."[48] Similarly, Denys de Refuges warns in his *Treatise of the Court* that "as soone as [our prince] knowes that wee surpasse and excell him" in any enterprise, "he will begin to looke on us with frowning eye."[49] If *sprezzatura* is the capacity to accomplish difficult actions with apparent ease, then what is required, finally, of the expert courtier is a kind of inverted *sprezzatura*, by which one deliberately tries and fails to imitate the monarch, thus declaring simultaneously the monarch's exemplary and inimitable nature. As de Refuges advises, "it sufficeth not to stoope and yeelde to [the prince] in words: but wee must likewise in effects and deedes make it appeare, that in all things wee are inferiour to him: yea, and in plaine earnest, doe something grossely and sleightly, so it may please him."[50] Or, as Berowne observes in *Love's Labor's Lost,* "'tis some policy / To have one show worse than the King's and his company."[51]

Such policy would have been particularly pertinent for behavior at the Jacobean court, presided over by a king who prided himself on his innate superiority to other men. "Two sorts of men King James never had kindness for," remarked one contemporary, "those whose hawks and dogs flew and run as well as his own, and those who were able to speak as much reason as himself."[52] To perform before this figure without upstaging him, to show one's wit to him without showing him up, would have required heroic self-control. For an educated, intelligent, and ambitious young man such as Herbert, the necessity of expressing artful yet submissive gratitude and praise to so vain a monarch must have exerted tremendous intellectual and psychological pressure.

This pressure is assessed and recorded in "The Thanksgiving." By attempting to offer gratitude befitting the sacrifice of his king through a mixture of ludicrous and pious proposals, Herbert demonstrates the impassable gulf separating him from his sovereign. Yet in the discovery of his inability to imitate his superior's behavior, the speaker of "The Thanksgiving" is forced into a sputtering acknowledgment of his sovereign's absolute superiority. Finally, then, "The Thanksgiving" fulfills the speaker's purported intention of praising his "king of griefs," but only in the painful discovery of his inability to imitate his monarch or to offer appropriate thanks. "The Thanksgiving" is an act of gratitude and praise despite, rather than because of, the speaker's behavior.

In "The Church-porch," Herbert advises, "Envie not greatnesse: for thou mak'st thereby / Thy self the worse, and so the distance greater" (lines 259–60). This is exactly what happens to the speaker of "The Thanksgiving." In his envy and emulation of divinity, he exposes the vast distance separating him from divinity. Unintentionally, then, he dramatizes the distance of the meek. The submission of the poor and the opposition of the proud are revealed not only to have the same outcome— flattery of superior power—but in fact to be one and the same gesture. In "The Thanksgiving," Herbert shows how genuflection is not only a gesture of reverence and submission but also a posture of social climbing. He punctuates the worldly cynicism of one of the *Outlandish Proverbs* he collected: "He that followes the Lord hopes to goe before" (no. 994, p. 354).

"The Reprisall," the poem immediately following "The Thanksgiving" and originally entitled "The Second Thanks-giving," appears to resolve many of the dilemmas plaguing its predecessor. Yet as C. A. Patrides notes, "'reprisal' is used in the (military) sense of retaliation as well as in the (musical) sense of returning to the original subject."[53] Although more successful than "The Thanksgiving" at disguising its aggression, "The Reprisall" is nevertheless a reprise, in a more compliant key, of its contentious energies, as well as a retaliation for their repudiation. It begins with an acknowledgment of the failure of "The Thanksgiving" to offer gratitude suitable to the Lord's beneficent suffering.

> I have consider'd it, and finde
> There is no dealing with thy mighty passion:
> For though I die for thee, I am behinde;
> My sinnes deserve the condemnation.

By admitting defeat, the speaker endeavors to recoil from the coercive and competitive discourse practiced in "The Thanksgiving." Yet this sincere confession of inability is at the same time a rhetorical figure entitled "Paramologia, or the figure of Admittance," described by Puttenham as "when the matter is so plaine that it cannot be denied or traversed, it is good that it be justified by confessall."[54] Even the effort to escape a coercive discourse is enclosed by that discourse. Moreover, the language of quantification ("I am behinde") and requital ("My sinnes deserve the condemnation") reiterates rather than rejects the terminology of rivalry in "The Thanksgiving." Although earnestly attempting to renounce the manipulative motives of "The Thanksgiving," "The Reprisall" replays them under the colors of submission and confession.

As if acknowledging the calculated nature of his surrender, the speaker sues to be cleansed of such motives: "O make me innocent, that I / May give a disentangled state and free." But the request replicates the situation of "The Thanksgiving." The speaker of "The Reprisall" wants to be made innocent so that he will be able to *give* to God from a "state," or status, that is "free," not "entangled" in debt. Like the speaker of "The Thanksgiving," he hopes through an act of benefaction to avoid acknowledging his own subordination. But even as he voices this wish, the speaker of "The Reprisall" realizes the impossibility of its fulfillment: "And yet thy wounds still my attempts defie, / For by thy death I die for thee." The two meanings of "attempt" active here—"endeavor" and "assault upon a person's life"—underscore the aggression lingering in his poses of submission. The speaker's realization of his own utterly subordinate status forces a bitter sigh from him.

> Ah! was it not enough that thou
> By thy eternal glorie didst outgo me?
> Couldst thou not griefs sad conquests me allow,
> But in all vic'tries overthrow me?

While conceding his lord's supremacy in "eternal glorie," the speaker wonders why his lord must also flaunt his preeminence in grief. The speaker self-centeredly suggests that Christ suffered only to "outgo" and "overthrow" him. Moreover, he displaces onto Christ his own competitive motives, implying that the reprisal of the title may include not only human retaliation against God but also God's retaliation against humanity.[55]

The final stanza of "The Reprisall" appears to elude the quandary of gratitude exposed in "The Thanksgiving".

> Yet by confession will I come
> Into thy conquest: though I can do nought
> Against thee, in thee I will overcome
> The man, who once against thee fought.

Rather than attempting to outstrip his maker, the speaker pledges to cultivate a discourse of his own inferiority. Although his competitive tendencies are not completely purged, the speaker does promise to direct them towards himself, "The man who once against thee fought," rather than towards his superior. Yet the language by which the speaker distinguishes his submissive and aggressive selves demonstrates the difficulty of keeping them apart. The proximity in sound and location of "Against thee, in thee," for example, blurs the distinction between submission and aggression that the speaker is attempting to draw. Likewise, the consonance of "conquest" and "confession" belies the contrast between the conquering and confessing selves on which our sense of the resolution of the poem depends. Moreover, the emphasis upon the "will" of the speaker sounds suspiciously like the catalog of actions the speaker of "The Thanksgiving" promises to perform. The tangled syntax and intricate acoustics suggest some of the difficulty of the project that the speaker of "The Reprisall" has set out for himself: disentangling from his gestures of submission the agonistic and manipulative motives voiced in "The Thanksgiving."[56]

As University Orator, Herbert had responded to the situation of complimenting a superior for an accomplishment or award by identifying with the superior's success. In a letter to Buckingham congratulating him on his marquisate, for example, Herbert declares, "Marquis, thy glory we account our own, and in thy honours we congratulate our own advantage."[57] The speaker of "The Reprisall" attempts in like manner to assimilate the success of his superior. He desires, in the words of the speaker of "The Thanksgiving," to "side with thy triumphant glorie." His surrender is simultaneously tactical and sincere, an act of legitimate resignation and a Pyrrhic defeat exercising the pragmatic wisdom of one of Herbert's *Outlandish Proverbs:* "Sometimes the best gaine is to lose" (no. 224, p. 328). Like so many of Herbert's poems, including the poem it purports to resolve, "The Reprisall" contains both submissive and aggressive impulses. Although voicing a genuine wish to utter submission untainted by resentment or the desire for power, the poem nevertheless implicates its gestures of compliance in the covertly manipulative discourse with authority that it ostensibly rejects. It sublimates, but does not fully subordinate, its insurgent energies.

As in "The Thanksgiving" and "The Reprisall," so in the series of reprisals that comprise the lyrics of *The Temple* does Herbert express his devotional anxieties in the vocabulary of his social and political experience. In "Affliction (I)," for example, Herbert translates the attractions and frustrations of courtly service into a bitter indictment of divine authority. Likewise, the two poems entitled "Employment" depict the desire for devotional fruitfulness in terms of a wish for gainful office (a particularly poignant wish for a younger son).[58] The speaker of "Praise (1)" promises greater glory to his divine superior if this superior will only "mend" the speaker's "estate." "Submission" pleads for, then retreats from, the desire for "Some place or power" by which the speaker might more effectively serve and praise his sovereign. "Providence," on the other hand, discovers a political and spiritual place for man as "Secretarie of thy praise"—a title certainly possessing special resonance for Herbert, who as University Orator had ascended to a place that required the continual performance of praise and that was generally viewed as preparation for promotion to the post of secretary of state. Even "Jordan (I)," with its plea for honesty and simplicity and its implicit criticism of courtly entertainment, is, as Anthony Low reminds us, "a divine masque, designed as a compliment to God the King as the court masque compliments His human shadow."[59] To read Herbert's panegyrics of divine power without hearing a reverberation of the covertly coercive praise that Herbert performed before secular power is to divest the poetry of much of its subtlety and vigor. As "Dedication," the first lyric of *The Temple,* signals the involvement of the discourse between God and man in the dialect of social supplication, so does "Love (III)," the final lyric of *The Temple,* employ the politically charged language of courtesy to represent the divine-human encounter.[60] Between these two works, almost every poem in *The Temple* registers in some manner Herbert's dexterity with the language of social hierarchy and his experience of political authority.

In his introduction to the first edition of *The Temple,* Nicholas Ferrar, Herbert's good friend, declares that he feels compelled to give some details of Herbert's life for the reader's benefit: "onely for the clearing of some passages, we have thought it not unfit to make the common Reader privie to some few particularities of the condition and disposition of the Person" (*Works,* p. 3). This paper has proceeded from a related set of assumptions: that literature is neither created nor read in a vacuum, but is inextricably bound up with political, social, and biographical circumstances; that religious and political discourse are intertwined like the aristocratic "silk twist" let down from heaven to Herbert in "The Pearl"; that Herbert lived not only in those "sacred volumes of Divinity" for which he seeks money in his letters but also in the acts of supplication represented by these letters, and in the complex, hierarchical culture that continually demanded such conduct. Ferrar also notes that Herbert, "to testifie his independencie upon all others . . . used in his ordinarie speech, when he made mention of the blessed name of our Lord and Saviour Jesus Christ, to adde, *My Master*" (p. 4). The assertion of dependence upon divine authority sanctions the expression of independence from secular authority. Yet the term representing divine authority—master—is indistinguishable from the forms of political dependence that it purportedly escapes. Even as secular and sacred subordination are segregated, they are admixed.

Herbert's age was intensely preoccupied with the rhetorical and theological aspects of conduct. The plethora of courtesy literature telling one how to behave towards one's superiors is surpassed only by the remarkable outpouring of devotional manuals advising one how to behave before divine authority.[61] The lyrics of *The Temple* are perched, emphatically if precariously, on the cusp of these two projects, addressing heavenly authority in a language at times strikingly similar to that used before political authority. The penetrating and unforgiving gaze to which Herbert subjects his own gestures of devotion throughout *The Temple* was made possible by his acquaintance with a social world that demanded daily declarations of submission and dependence. Herbert never allowed himself the illusion of having attained in his poetry what Kenneth Burke terms an act of "pure persuasion," that is, "the saying of something, not for an extraverbal advantage to be got by the saying, but because of a satisfaction intrinsic to the saying."[62] By exposing rather than repressing the impure, insurgent, advantage-seeking tendencies of the language of submission made available to him by his society, Herbert achieves in his poems a spiritual rigor and lyric intensity that continue to impress readers who may not share his religious beliefs and who inhabit a public world quite different from the social hierarchy of early seventeenth-century England. At once devious and devout, these poems translate the particular idiom of Herbert's social, political, and theological experience into the familiar vocabulary of negotiation between an intractably beneficent being and an impertinently recalcitrant self. The capacity of the poems of *The Temple* to transcend their culture is largely a function of the degree to which they are embedded in that culture. By construing them as a product of rather than an escape from their historical moment, we glimpse the mysterious consubstantiation of local and indigenous matter into legible, perhaps even universal, phenomena.

Notes

1. *The Works of George Herbert,* ed. F. E. Hutchinson (Oxford: Clarendon Press, 1941), p. 377. All citations of Herbert's English works are to this edition, and all citations of the Latin works will be cross-referenced to it.

2. Joseph Summers, *The Heirs of Donne and Jonson* (London: Oxford University Press, 1970), p. 16.

3. Kenneth Burke, "On Covery, Re- and Dis-," *Accent* 13 (1953): 222. Burke's essay is actually a review of Rosemond Tuve, *A Reading of George Herbert* (Chicago: University of Chicago Press, 1952).

4. See John Knott, *The Sword of the Spirit: Puritan Responses to the Bible* (Chicago: University of Chicago Press, 1980), for the religious associations of this phrase. On the importance of enclosure as an architectonic and metaphorical component of Herbert's poetry, see Robert Higbie, "Images of Enclosure in George Herbert's *The Temple,*" *Texas Studies in Literature and Language* 15 (1974): 627–38; and Frank L. Huntley, "George Herbert and the Image of Violent Containment," *George Herbert Journal* 8, no. 1 (1984): 17–27.

5. Ps. 37:34 (Authorized Version)—"Wait on the Lord, and keepe his way, and he shall exalt thee to inherit the land"—along with Luke 12:36–37—"And ye your selves like unto men that waite for their Lord. . . . Blessed are those servants, whom the Lord when he commeth, shall find watching"—provide the

biblical foundation for this ideal. This concept receives its consummate literary statement in the final line of Milton's Sonnet 19: "They also serve who only stand and wait" (*John Milton: Complete Poems and Major Prose*, ed. Merritt Y. Hughes [New York: Macmillan, 1957], p. 168).

6. My sense of the potential interpenetration of devotional and social experience is indebted to Stephen Greenblatt's brilliant discussion of Wyatt's translations of the penitential psalms in *Renaissance Self-Fashioning from More to Shakespeare* (Chicago: University of Chicago Press, 1980), pp. 115–56.

7. Izaak Walton, "Life of Mr. George Herbert" (1670), in *Lives,* ed. George Saintsbury (London: Oxford University Press, 1927), pp. 251–339. As David Novarr demonstrates in *The Making of Walton's "Lives"* (Ithaca: Cornell University Press, 1958), pp. 301–61, Walton emphasizes Herbert's worldliness "in order to show that even so noble and brilliant and worldly a man can see fit to renounce the worldly life for the holy one" (p. 353).

8. Joan Thirsk, "Younger Sons in the Seventeenth Century," *History* 54 (1969): 358–77, explores the precarious economic and social status of younger sons such as Herbert.

9. Amy M. Charles, *A Life of George Herbert* (Ithaca: Cornell University Press, 1977), pp. 48–49, 101, examines the circumstances of Herbert's annuity and compares it to the support received by some contemporaries. Many of Herbert's letters to Danvers ask him to advance money against the annuity (see *Works,* pp. 364–65, 367).

10. Perez Zagorin characterizes the social world of the early seventeenth century as one stratified by status, a stratification "entail[ing] the result that an acknowledged personal dependence should exist between those in authority and their inferiors . . . . Persons desiring success in a suit of advancement attached themselves to men of rank in order to obtain their recommendation" (*The Court and the Country: The Beginning of the English Revolution* [New York: Atheneum, 1971], p. 42). On the systems of Renaissance patronage, see also the essays collected in *Patronage in the Renaissance,* ed. Guy Fitch Lytle and Stephen Orgel (Princeton: Princeton University Press, 1981); Linda Levy Peck, *Northampton: Patronage and Politics at the Court of James I* (London: Allen & Unwin, 1982), and "'For a King Not to Be Bountiful Were a Fault': Perspectives on Court Patronage in Early Stuart England," *Journal of British Studies* 25 (1986): 31–61; and Derek Hirst, *Authority and Conflict: England, 1603–1658* (Cambridge: Harvard University Press, 1986), pp. 30–33.

11. *Works,* p. xxvii.

12. John Hacket, *Scrinia Reserata,* 2 vols. (London, 1693), 1:175; quoted in Charles, *A Life,* p. 98, and in *Works,* p. xxvii. Charles is surely right, contra Hutchinson, that Hacket means to praise rather than "comment severely" on Herbert's choice of a subject. Hacket prefaces this entry by observing of James's speech to Parliament—"his Majesty Feasted them with a Speech, then which nothing could be apter for the Subject, or more Eloquent for the matter. All the helps of that Faculty were extreamly perfect· in him, abounding in Wit by Nature, in Art by Education, in Wisdom by Experience"—and concludes by noting—"the Speech which was had at the opening of this Parliament; doth com-

mend Mr. *Herbet* [*sic*] for his Censure." These statements allow us to glimpse how a contemporary could accept, unashamedly and approvingly, such effusive flattery.

13. A. G. Hyde, *George Herbert and His Times* (New York: G. P. Putnam's Sons, 1907), pp. 65–66.

14. This eager and somewhat inexperienced Herbert apparently would have disputed the cynicism of one of the *Outlandish Proverbs* he was to collect: "Honour without profit is a ring on the finger" (no. 230; *Works*, p. 328).

15. *The Complete Works in Verse and Prose of George Herbert*, 3 vols., ed. A. B. Grosart (London: Fuller Worthies' Library, 1874), 3:448–51 (*Works*, pp. 458–59). All translations of Herbert's Latin works are from this edition.

16. Jonathan Goldberg, *James I and the Politics of Literature* (Baltimore: Johns Hopkins University Press, 1983), explicates the strategic relationship between literary representations of James and the ways in which James presented himself. On James's particular interpretation of divine right, see his speech to Parliament, 1610, in J. P. Kenyon, ed., *The Stuart Constitution* (Cambridge: Cambridge University Press, 1966), pp. 12–14. See also J. N. Figgis, *The Divine Right of Kings* (Cambridge: Cambridge University Press, 1914); and G. R. Elton, "The Divine Right of Kings," in *Studies in Tudor and Stuart Politics and Government*, 2 vols. (Cambridge: Cambridge University Press, 1974), 2:193–214.

17. Charles, *A Life*, p. 91, remarks that this "triple dedication . . . could be construed as an attempt to gain royal or ecclesiastical favor," but reminds us that the work "did not appear in print until many years after Herbert's death."

18. Arthur F. Marotti, *John Donne, Coterie Poet* (Madison: University of Wisconsin Press, 1986), p. 246.

19. Frank Whigham, *Ambition and Privilege: The Social Tropes of Elizabethan Courtesy Theory* (Berkeley: University of California Press, 1984), expertly analyzes the social pressure exerted by the need to perform continually at court, and the rhetorical strategies that evolved from this pressure.

20. *Works*, pp. 598, 600, citing a letter by Joseph Mede to Martin Stutevile (B.M. Harl. MS. 389, fol. 298), and a letter from Thomas Baker, Cambridge Collections (B.M. Harl. MS. 7041, fol. 38ᵛ).

21. In *Works*, p. 598, Hutchinson is noncommittal on the question of whether the translation of "Dum petit Infantem" first printed with the Latin is by Herbert.

22. In *The Politics of Mirth: Jonson, Herrick, Milton, Marvell, and the Defense of Old Holiday Pastimes* (Chicago: University of Chicago Press, 1986), pp. 8–11, Leah S. Marcus argues that James in fact tolerated a remarkable degree of freedom in his subjects' discourse about him as long as this freedom could be contained within a framework upholding his authority.

23. Those who see this oration on Charles's return as the watershed of Herbert's political and religious careers include Joseph Summers, *George Herbert: His Religion and Art* (Cambridge: Harvard University Press, 1954), pp. 40–42; Marchette Chute, *Two Gentle Men: The Lives of George Herbert and Robert Herrick* (New York: Dutton, 1959), pp. 83–84; and Charles, *A Life*, p. 100. Both Summers and Charles stress the strong personal reason that may have disposed Her-

bert to speak out against war—he had lost two brothers, Richard and William, in battle. Kenneth Alan Hovey explores Herbert's use of the terminology of war and peace in this oration in "Holy War and Civil Peace: George Herbert's Jaco-bean Politics," *Explorations in Renaissance Culture* 11 (1985): 112–19. Herbert's antiwar sentiments are also vented in *Lucus*, no. 32, "Triumphus Mortis"; see Hovey, "'Inventa Bellica' / 'Triumphus Mortis': Herbert's Parody of Human Progress and Dialogue with Divine Grace," *Studies in Philology* 78 (1981): 275–304.

24. Samuel R. Gardiner, *History of England from the Accession of James I to the Outbreak of the Civil War: 1603–1642*, 10 vols. (London: Longmans, Green, 1883–84), 7:266. On the bitter public outcry against the search for a Spanish marriage and the spontaneous rejoicing that overtook the country when Charles returned from Spain without a bride, see Roger Lockyer, *Buckingham: The Life and Political Career of George Villers, First Duke of Buckingham, 1592–1628* (London: Longman, 1981), pp. 125–97; and R. Malcolm Smuts, *Court Culture and the Origins of a Royalist Tradition in Early Stuart England* (Philadelphia: University of Pennsylvania Press, 1987), pp. 32–36.

25. "Of Praise," in *Francis Bacon: A Selection of His Works*, ed. Sidney Warhaft (New York: Odyssey, 1965), p. 179. In the *Discoveries*, Ben Jonson also recom-mends that the courtier should counsel his prince "not with insolence, or precept; but as the *Prince* were already furnished with the parts hee should have, especially in affaires of *State*" (C. H. Herford, Percy Simpson, and Evelyn Simpson, eds., *Ben Jonson*, 11 vols. [Oxford: Clarendon Press, 1925–52], 8:566).

26. Gardiner, *History of England* 7:267.

27. *Complete Works* 3:399; *Works*, p. 445.

28. *Complete Works* 3:406–7; *Works*, p. 447.

29. *Complete Works* 3:408; *Works*, p. 450.

30. The oration contains many other oddly subversive passages: an attack on intemperate princes, "effeminate Caesars," which sounds very much like Puritan criticisms of the excesses of the Jacobean court (*Complete Works 3:411; Works*, p. 452); a reminder, indecorous to the aging king and inappropriate to the young prince, that "in that last dissolution there is no distinction of people or prince. . . . The vapours from slaves exhaled into the clouds will produce equally loud thunder with the vapours from kings" (*Complete Works*, 3:411; *Works*, p. 452); and a warning that "flattery and flatterers . . . are always tickling the ears of princes" (*Complete Works*, 3:412; *Works*, pp. 452–53). Those who have suggested the oration was unwelcome at court simply because of its untimely expression of antiwar sentiment have missed the threads of resentment and criticism woven into its fabric of praise.

31. *Works*, p. 277. This Parliament, described by an "old Scottish courtier" as one that "dois evrye daye grate upone the King's prerogative soe mutche" (quoted in Zagorin, *Court and the Country*, p. 64), was also marked by the disso-lution of the Virginia Company, in which both Nicholas Ferrar and Sir John Danvers had been major figures. See Robert E. Ruigh, *The Parliament of 1624: Politics and Foreign Policy* (Cambridge: Harvard University Press, 1971).

In "Herbert's Experience of Politics and Patronage in 1624," *George Herbert Journal* 10, nos. 1 and 2 (1986/87): 33–45, Diana Benet suggests that Herbert's parliamentary experience precipitated his apparent disillusionment with state employment, and his subsequent turn to the church. But Herbert's country parson is far less a figure in retreat from the political currents of his time than such a pattern assumes. He encourages the youth of his parish not only to "endeavour by all means" to participate in Parliament but also (albeit less avidly) to encounter the court: "sometimes he may go to Court, as the eminent place both of good and ill" (p. 277).

32. Herbert may have delivered the oration at Buckingham's installation as Chancellor of Cambridge in 1626, but the oration is not extant. See Charles, *A Life*, p. 121.

33. In 1626 Herbert contributed "In obitum incomparabilis Francisci Vicecomitis Sancti Albani" to an unofficial tribute to Sir Francis Bacon from members of Cambridge, *Memoriae Francisci, Baronis de Verulamio, Vice-Comitis Sancti Albani Sacrum* (London, 1626). Bacon had died earlier that year in disgrace. In 1627 Herbert published *Memoriae Matris Sacrum*, his Latin verse elegy to his mother, alongside the text of Donne's funeral sermon for her.

34. In contrast, Richard Strier stresses Herbert's "flouting of decorum" and his analysis of "the difference between God's values and behavior and those of earthly lords" in poems such as "Redemption," "Gratefulnesse," "Prayer (II)," and "The Storm" (*Love Known: Theology and Experience in George Herbert's Poetry* [Chicago: University of Chicago Press, 1983], pp. 57–58, 179–88). The impact of this divine disregard for decorum depends upon the expectation that earthly standards of behavior do apply to heaven. In "Ritual Man: On the Outside of Herbert's Poetry," *Psychiatry* 48 (1985): 69, William Kerrigan offers a compelling if somewhat different model from my own for apprehending continuity between Herbert's secular and sacred careers: "whether at Cambridge or Bemerton, as Claudian or as Aaron, orating in Latin or sermonizing in English, Herbert presided over ritual occasions."

An eloquent statement of the orthodox idealization of Herbert's transmutation of his social experience is available in Graham Parry, *The Golden Age Restor'd: The Culture of the Stuart Court, 1603–1642* (New York: St. Martin's Press, 1981), p. 243: "In contrast to the earthly Court that had been so unresponsive to his pleas, in the poems that form the record of his spiritual life Herbert was to envisage an ideal Court, whose lord was the King of Kings. . . . In the service of the Lord there is always satisfaction and reward, and the Lord of the heavenly Court is always attentive." Such spiritual quixotism is developed at length in Marion White Singleton, *God's Courtier: Configuring a Different Grace in George Herbert's "Temple"* (Cambridge: Cambridge University Press, 1987).

35. Herford, Simpson, and Simpson, 8:640.

36. M. M. Ross, *Poetry and Dogma: The Transfiguration of Eucharistic Symbols in Seventeenth Century English Poetry* (New Brunswick, N.J.: Rutgers University Press, 1954), pp. 141, 153. Ross's emphasis upon the abjuratory aspects of Herbert's poetry has received sophisticated endorsement in Richard Strier, "George

Herbert and the World," *Journal of Medieval and Renaissance Studies* 12 (1981): 211
36. Similarly, in "Herbert's 'Decay' and the Articulation of History," *Southern Review* 18 (1983): 3–21, the only vestige of history that Jonathan Goldberg finds in *The Temple* is "the story of salvation played out in the Bible" (p. 3). A useful catalog of the images of aristocratic and courtly activity in Herbert's poetry is available in Ivan Earle Taylor, "Cavalier Sophistication in the Poetry of George Herbert," *Anglican Theological Review* 39 (1957): 229–43. Karen L. Wadman, "'Private Ejaculations': Politeness Strategies in George Herbert's Poems Directed to God," *Language and Style* 16 (1983): 87–106, offers an interesting attempt to analyze Herbert's discourse with divinity in the terminology of interactional sociology.

37. Leah S. Marcus, *Childhood and Cultural Despair: A Theme and Variations in Seventeenth-Century Literature* (Pittsburgh: University of Pittsburgh Press, 1978), pp. 95, 97, and 94–120 passim. In her "George Herbert and Anglican Plain Style," in *"Too Rich to Clothe the Sunne": Essays on George Herbert,* ed. Claude J. Summers and Ted-Larry Pebworth (Pittsburgh: University of Pittsburgh Press, 1980), pp. 179–93, Marcus profitably returns Herbert to the world of ecclesiastical controversy. For provocative studies of the complex relationship between public and private experience in Herbert, see Summers and Pebworth, "Herbert, Vaughan, and Public Concerns in Private Modes," *George Herbert Journal* 3, nos. 1 and 2 (1979): 1–21, and "The Politics of *The Temple*: 'The British Church' and 'The Familie,'" *George Herbert Journal* 8, no. 1 (1984): 1–15; and Sidney Gottlieb, "Herbert's Case of 'Conscience': Public or Private Poem," *SEL* 25 (1985): 109–26. In "The Social and Political Backgrounds of George Herbert's Poetry," in *"The Muses Common-Weale": Poetry and Politics in the Earlier Seventeenth Century,* ed. Summers and Pebworth (Columbia: University of Missouri Press, in press), Gottlieb unearths covert reference to political controversy in Herbert's poetry.

38. On the close relationship between Herbert's "Dedication" and secular dedications, see my "Submission and Assertion: The 'Double Motion' of Herbert's 'Dedication,'" *John Donne Journal* 2, no. 2 (1983), pp. 39–49.

39. In "Sanctifying the Aristocracy: 'Devout Humanism' in François de Sales, John Donne, and George Herbert," *Journal of Religion* (January 1989), Richard Strier corrects the traditional perception of "The Church-porch" as a prosaic work of pious moral counsel, suggesting that it is concerned more with negotiating a perilous social world than with avoiding sin.

40. In "Versions of Imitation in the Renaissance," *RQ* 33 (1980): 1–32, G. W. Pigman III explores the competitive and submissive aspects of literary imitation in Renaissance theory. See also Thomas Greene, *The Light in Troy: Imitation and Discovery in Renaissance Poetry* (New Haven: Yale University Press, 1982).

41. Strier, *Love Known,* p. 50. Ilona Bell, "'Setting Foot into Divinity': George Herbert and the English Reformation," *Modern Language Quarterly* 38 (1977): 219–44, views "The Thanksgiving" as an attack upon the presumption inherent in the Catholic *imitatio christi*. Both her argument and Strier's provide theological corollaries to my claims about the politics of the relationship between the speaker and his "king of grief."

42. Lorenzo Ducci, *Ars aulica; or, The Courtiers Arte,* tr. [Ed. Blount?] (London, 1607), pp. 226–27. This translation is dedicated to Herbert's two noble kinsmen, William Herbert, earl of Pembroke, and Philip Herbert, earl of Montgomery.

43. On the political superiority of giving to receiving, see also Aristotle, *Nichomachean Ethics,* tr. Martin Oswald (Indianapolis: Bobbs-Merrill, 1962), pp. 96–97; and Marcel Mauss, *The Gift: Forms and Functions of Exchange in Archaic Societies,* tr. Ian Cunnison (New York: Norton, 1967), pp. 72–73. Goldberg, *James I,* pp. 134–39, perceptively inspects the discourse of gratitude and giving in the relationship between King James and Buckingham. William Nestrick has written a stimulating study of prestation in Herbert's poetry, "George Herbert—The Giver and the Gift," *Ploughshares* 2, no. 4 (1975): 187–205. In *The Country Parson,* Herbert assimilates these political lessons to religious goals, arguing that the parson is to win the respect of others, "despite the general ignominy which is cast upon his profession," by "doing kindnesses, but receiving none . . . for this argues a height and eminency of mind, which is not easily despised" (p. 268).

44. John Milton, *Paradise Lost* 4:52–53, in *Complete Poems,* p. 278.

45. On the inexpressibility topos, see Ernst Robert Curtius, *European Literature and the Latin Middle Ages,* tr. Willard R. Trask (Princeton: Princeton University Press, 1953), pp. 159–62. On Herbert's employment of this topos, see the two letters to King James (*Complete Works* 3:450, 452; *Works,* pp. 458–59, 460), and a letter to George Abbott, archbishop of Canterbury (*Complete Works* 3:458; *Works,* pp. 466–67).

46. Ducci, *Ars aulica,* p. 111. Baldassare Castiglione similarly suggests that the good courtier "must evermore set all his diligence to be like his maister, and (if it were possible) chaung him selfe into him" (*The Book of the Courtier,* tr. Thomas Hoby [1561; reprint, London: Dent, 1928], p. 45).

47. Ducci, *Ars aulica,* pp. 111–12.

48. George Puttenham, *The Arte of English Poesie,* ed. Gladys Doidge Willcock and Alice Walker (Cambridge: Cambridge University Press, 1936), pp. 293, 295–96. As Daniel Javitch argues in *Poetry and Courtliness* (Princeton: Princeton University Press, 1978), Puttenham conflates the art of poetry with the art of courtly conduct.

49. Denys de Refuges, *A Treatise of the Court; or, Instructions for Courtiers,* tr. John Reynolds, 2 vols. (London, 1622), 2:186.

50. Ibid. 2:187.

51. *Love's Labor's Lost* (5.2.512–13), cited from *The Riverside Shakespeare,* ed. G. Blakemore Evans et al. (Boston: Houghton Mifflin, 1974), p. 207.

52. Quoted in Marjorie Cox, "The Background to English Literature: 1603–1630," in *From Donne to Marvell,* ed. Boris Ford (Harmondsworth, England: Penguin, 1982), p. 25.

53. C. A. Patrides, ed., *The English Poems of George Herbert* (London: Dent, 1974), p. 57n.

54. Puttenham, *Arte of English Poesie,* pp. 227–28.

55. "The Reprisall" could thus be seen to fulfill the ambiguous revenge threat-

ened by the suffering Christ in the final stanza of "The Sacrifice": "Onely let others say, when I am dead, / Never was grief like mine." On the terrifying ambivalence of this stanza and this poem, see the brilliant reading by William Empson, *Seven Types of Ambiguity* (New York: New Directions, 1947), pp. 226–33.

56. This difficulty is reproduced in the wide range of critical reactions engendered by the poem's close. Stanley Fish, for example, suspects the speaker of rationalizing "if you can't beat him, join him" (*Self-Consuming Artifacts: The Experience of Seventeenth-Century Literature* [Berkeley: University of California Press, 1972], p. 183). Michael McCanles is even more skeptical of the speaker's sincerity: "by 'confessing' Christ's transcendent redemption he may conquer the 'man, who once against thee fought'; but he may also become Christ's secret enemy in still hoping to make his own part something to be valued, to 'come / Into thy conquest' in a way that would 'conquer' God by the very act of flourishing his humility before Him" (*Dialectical Criticism and Renaissance Literature* [Berkeley: University of California Press, 1975], p. 82). Yet other readers have found the conclusion to offer a valid response to the devotional obstacles exposed in "The Thanksgiving." Louis Martz, for example, states that "The Reprisall" "solves the dilemma of gratitude for the Passion with which the first Thanksgiving, with a witty inconclusion, ends" (*The Poetry of Meditation* [New Haven: Yale University Press, 1962], p. 292). This view has recently been affirmed by both Barbara Leah Harman and Richard Strier; Harman asserts that "the speaker does find an authentic and acceptable labor . . . the task of overcoming the self who produces poems like this" (*Costly Monuments: Representations of the Self in George Herbert's Poetry* [Cambridge: Harvard University Press, 1982], p. 61), while Strier argues that "The Reprisall" achieves "a true rather than an 'incomplete' resolution" (*Love Known*, p. 53). Such interpretive disparity provides, I would argue, the best gauge of the indeterminacy of the speaker's aspirations.

57. *Complete Works* 3:433; *Works*, p. 456. See also the letters to Thomas Coventry (*Complete Works* 3:439; *Works*, p. 465), to Robert Naunton (*Complete Works* 3:441; *Works*, p. 465), and to James Leigh (*Complete Works* 3:462; *Works*, p. 468).

58. In *The Country Parson*, Herbert demonstrates great concern about the employment prospects of younger sons (pp. 277–78).

59. Anthony Low, "Herbert's 'Jordan (I)' and the Court Masque," *Criticism* 14 (1972): 118.

60. On "Love (III)" and the discourse of courtesy as a medium for exercising political superiority, see my "Standing on Ceremony: The Comedy of Manners in Herbert's 'Love (III),'" in *"Bright Shootes of Everlastingnesse": The Seventeenth-Century Religious Lyric*, ed. Claude J. Summers and Ted-Larry Pebworth (Columbia: University of Missouri Press, 1987), pp. 116–33.

61. Louis B. Wright, *Middle-Class Culture in Elizabethan England* (Chapel Hill: University of North Carolina Press, 1935), explores in detail both "Handbooks to Improvement" (pp. 121–69) and "Guides to Godliness" (pp. 228–96).

62. Kenneth Burke, *A Rhetoric of Motives* (New York: Prentice-Hall, 1950), p. 268. Daniel Javitch, "The Impure Motives of Elizabethan Poetry," in *The Forms of Power and the Power of Forms in the Renaissance*, ed. Stephen Greenblatt (a special

issue of *Genre* 15 [1982]: 225–38), suggestively employs the concept of impure persuasion in relation to Elizabethan secular poetry. On pure persuasion in a theological context, see also Burke, *The Rhetoric of Religion: Studies in Logology* (Berkeley: University of California Press, 1970), pp. 34–35n.

Part Four

Humanism and Its Discontents

Barbarous Tongues: The Ideology of Poetic Form in Renaissance England

I

Midway through one of his letters to Harvey, Spenser exclaims, "Why a God's name may not we, as else the Greeks, have the kingdom of our own language?"[1] For years bits of this sentence have been running through my head. Here, it has seemed to me, Spenser gave voice to the generative impulse that lay behind not only his own career but also the whole extraordinary development of English poetry in his time—and, indeed, the very emergence of England itself as an autonomous and powerfully self-conscious realm. This is, I realize, a large claim to make for so little, but the more closely I have looked at the sentence itself and the further I have gone in tracing its reverberations the more fully justified my initial feeling has seemed. Spenser had, of course, only a limited responsibility for all those momentous events. Not even the shape of his own poetic career depended entirely on him. But he was very much a part of what was happening to him and around him, and he here expressed with marvelous economy both the ambition and the situation of those of his own generation who shared his involvement.

Consider for a start those last six words, "the kingdom of our own language." They carry us from an essentially dynastic conception of communal identity ("the kingdom") to an assertion of what we recognize as one of the bases of postdynastic nationalism ("our own language"). A kingdom whose boundaries are determined by the language of its inhabitants is no longer a kingdom in the purely dynastic sense, but neither, so long as it goes on identifying itself with the person of a hereditary monarch, is it quite a nation. Nor are the representational resources of this phrase exhausted by the extremes of "kingdom" and "language," for between them comes that first-person plural "our" with its suggestion of shared participation and possession. King, people, and language—which is in charge? From this formulation it is impossible to tell. But even a small acquaintance with the history of England in the next century or so will remind us that conflict was to develop along precisely the lines suggested by these few words, between royal prerogative, subjects' rights, and the cultural system.[2]

So attached have I become to this phrase that I feel a pang each time I must reinsert it into its original context, for immediately it loses its evenhanded representational character and is captured by a purpose that upsets the delicate dynamic equilibrium that had been so finely achieved. In Spenser's impatient question, "the kingdom" does not, after all, initiate the semi-autonomous noun phrase we have been regarding, a stable syntactic and conceptual entity to which further qualification (as, for example, "the *glorious* kingdom of our own language") might be added. No, rather it belongs with the verb *have*. Spenser wants to "have the kingdom" of his own language; he wants to exercise sovereignty over English, wants to make it do what he wants it to do. Of the triangularly balanced forces that weigh against one another in "the kingdom of our own language," Spenser selects one and asserts its priority. "Our" makes a claim to omnipotence which reduces "kingdom" to the role of action and "language" to that of object. But if there is semantic loss here, there is also gain. Instead of an ideal representation, the larger sentence presents a dramatic expression of ambition, cultural envy, and frustration. The Greeks had the kingdom of their own language. Why, Spenser asks, can't we? Why must we be consigned to perpetual subjection and inferiority? This pressure, this tension, this conflict of aspiration and insecurity, brings us close to the crisis from which Elizabethan poetry emerged, close to the desperately hopeful sense that, were England to rival the greatness of Greece or of Rome, something decisive needed to be done.

And what was that something? To have the kingdom of our own language. To govern the very linguistic system, and perhaps more generally the whole cultural system, by which our own identity and our own consciousness is constituted. To remake it, and presumably ourselves as well, according to some ideal pattern. An extraordinary ambition! But, for most readers, its edge will be blunted, its momentous significance reduced to antiquarian peculiarity, as we step back further to take in more of the surrounding context. "I like your late English hexameters so exceedingly well," Spenser writes to Harvey, that I also inure my pen sometime in that kind, which I find indeed, as I have heard you often defend in word, neither so hard, nor so harsh, that it will easily and fairly yield itself to our mother tongue. For the only or chiefest hardness, which seemeth, is in the accent, which sometime gapeth and, as it were, yawneth ill-favoredly, coming short of that it should, and sometime exceeding the measure of the number, as in *carpenter,* the middle syllable being used short in speech, when it shall be read long in verse, seemeth like a lame gosling that draweth one leg after her. . . . But it is to be won with custom, and rough words must be subdued with use. For why a God's name may not we, as else the Greeks, have the kingdom of our own language and measure our accents by the sound, reserving the quantity to the verse? (10:16)

So *that* is what Spenser was talking about: the comically misguided effort to base English prosody on the rules of ancient quantitative meters. How can anything said in such a context be taken seriously?

Yet Spenser himself seems to have been quite serious about it. The greater part of both his published letters to Harvey is given over to detailed and enthusiastic discussion of this project. He assures Harvey that he is "of late more in love with my English versifying than with rhyming" (10:6), gives several brief examples of his work in this reformed mode, promises to send a more substantial "token" of "what and how well therein I am able to do" (10:17), and names as fellow partisans not only Harvey himself but also Sidney and Dyer. That Harvey and Dyer should have been mistaken in this way causes us no concern. Nor are we much bothered at finding elsewhere in these letters and in other documents the names of Drant, Preston, and Still, of Stanyhurst, Puttenham, and Webbe associated with the quantitative movement. Even Greville and Campion are figures small enough to have erred thus greatly without provoking much alarm. But Sidney and Spenser! If, as I have been assuming and as most commentators since the end of the sixteenth century itself have agreed, modern English literature got its first solid foundation in the second half of Elizabeth's reign, these two men have the best claim to being its founders. A project that concerned them deeply just at the moment when their careers were beginning and their most significant works were bring written is perhaps less negligible than we are sometimes inclined to think.

To a student of English literary history, the correspondence between Spenser and Harvey comes heavy with the promise of things shortly to be known. When the first of Spenser's letters was written toward the end of 1579, *The Shepheardes Calender* was as yet unpublished. Indeed, the question of whether to publish at all is among the issues he most worriedly discusses. In these letters, too, we find the earliest reference to *The Faerie Queene*, mentioned along with Spenser's *Slomber*, his *Dying Pellicane*, his nine comedies, and a whole collection of other words that, like these, have disappeared leaving no other trace behind. What if their fate had been shared by *The Shepheardes Calender* and *The Faerie Queene*? How different the course of our literature would have been! The future that to us is known as a secure past, so familiar that it seems inevitable, was in those years no less laden with uncertainty than with promise. Harvey, who, like Spenser, then stood on the threshold of what appeared a likely, even brilliant, career and whose ambition was, if anything, still greater than Spenser's, went on to a series of failures and public humiliations that have made him a near joke to posterity, saved from total ridicule by little more than his association with Spenser.

A similar fate has, of course, overtaken the quantitative movement. It now seems no less foolish than Harvey, no less futile than the *Dying Pellicane*. Success has a way of making failure look silly. But what if success needs failure as the guarantor of its own identity, the comic (yet still fearful) double that tells what success is not but might have been, tells of the historical abyss into which all ambition threatens to fall? The works that were finally not written, the vocational ambition that was not rewarded, the verse form that was not adopted stand to their successful counterparts as the sounds and meanings that we don't make or intend stand to those that we do. They enable by their absence and difference the production and reception of an intelligible message. For Spenser and Harvey it was, of course, not yet clear which of their many projects would succeed and which would fail—indeed, not clear that any would surely succeed or fail. But already they were ascribing meaning to various attitudes and undertakings by opposing them to others. Harvey does this when he prefers Spenser's "nine English comedies" to *The Faerie Queene*. The meaning of each is defined by its difference from the other. In a similar but more elaborate way, the two correspondents define themselves in terms of their differences, Spenser playing giddy Petrarchan love poet to Harvey's wise counselor and learned scholar, "our age's great Cato." So, to quote Harvey, "our new famous enterprise for the exchanging of barbarous and balductum rhymes with artificial verses" (10:463) derives its intelligibility as much from what it opposes as from what it supports. Rhyme can be seen as crude and trashy only in contrast to the fine artifice of quantitative verse.

In the more than four centuries since the letters between Harvey and Spenser were published, *The Faerie Queene*, Spenser's poetic identity, and English rhyming verse have entered into many new systems of difference, altering their meanings as they prospered, while the nine comedies,

Harvey's reputation for wisdom, and the dream of English verse in quantitative meters have dropped almost completely from memory, to be recalled only with amusement and wonder. But if we are to understand why in 1580 Spenser should have so ardently wished to have the kingdom of his own language and what that ambition meant for the development of his career and for the more general development of English poetry and English national self-consciousness, we need at least to entertain the possibility of valuing the terms that have failed, as both Spenser and Harvey apparently did, over those that have succeeded.

Not that the two letter writers always agreed with one another in their own valuation. On the crucial matter of having the kingdom of their own language, Harvey, though the earlier and keener partisan of the quantitative movement, thought Spenser went too far.

> In good sooth and by the faith I bear to the Muses, you shall never have my subscription or consent (though you should charge me with the authority of five hundred Master Drants) to make your *carpĕnter*, our *carpĕnter*, an inch longer or bigger than God and his English people have made him. Is there no other policy to pull down rhyming and set up versifying but you must needs correct *magnificat* and against all order of law and in despite of custom forcibly usurp and tyrannize upon a quiet company of words that so far beyond the memory of man have so peaceably enjoyed their several privileges and liberties without any disturbance or the least controlment? (10:473–74)

Where Spenser had used the language of sovereign power eager to subdue rough words and have the kingdom of them, Harvey responds in terms made familiar by centuries of resistance to royal encroachment, terms that would become still more familiar in the first half of the next century. He accuses Spenser of usurpation and tyranny, locates authority not in the king but in "God and his English people," proclaims the value of custom and the order of law, supports the peaceful enjoyment of immemorial privileges and liberties. Against Spenser's version of the absolutist cultural politics of antiquity, he sets, without quite calling it that, a Gothic, common law tradition. If quantitative verse means correcting *magnificat*, Harvey opposes it. His is, of course, a local response to a very particular provocation. He never develops its implications. Indeed, his arguments elsewhere contradict them. But the intervention is nevertheless significant. For here Harvey discovers, almost inadvertently it would seem, an oppositional politics of national literary self-representation, a politics that would later become far more open and explicit. And in doing so, he suggests one way of reversing the Renaissance hierarchy of values that had prompted him to try quantitative verse in the first place.

In the debate over quantitative meter, as perhaps nowhere else in Eliz-

abethan literary history, the great issues of national self-making came
into focus—issues that would prove central to such diverse cultural phenomena as the establishment of the Anglican church, the defense of the
common law tradition, the spread of English antiquarian study, the neochivalric cult of Elizabeth and the Jacobean reaction to it, the carto-
graphic and chorographic description of Britain, the celebration of British navigation, and the dreams of an English overseas empire. In each of
these areas the contribution of men born within just a few years of Spenser and Harvey was especially large. Richard Hooker, Sir Edward Coke,
William Camden, John Norden, John Speed, Richard Hakluyt, and Sir
Walter Ralegh, all belong to the generation that came of age in the second
half of Elizabethan's reign, and all were involved, to a degree that could
be equaled by only a very few men of any preceding generation and with
a success that could be equaled by none, in a complex and multifaceted
articulation of England, a generational project of national self-fashioning
in which the effort to found an art of English poetry had a significant,
but by no means isolated, place. When Spenser, upset at his inability to
make *carpenter* scan the way the rules of classical versification told him it
should, impatiently asks why the English can't have the kingdom of their
own language as the Greeks had the kingdom of theirs, he evokes a
model of self-making that was widely shared by his contemporaries and
that for a while governed many of their attempts to lift England to the
status of its ancient and modern competitors. And when Harvey answers
in the name of immemorial custom, he draws on what would shortly
emerge as the principal countermodel. Between these two models, these
two ways of asserting and maintaining identity, the struggle for supremacy that we saw latent in the last six words of Spenser's question, the
struggle between king, people, and cultural system, would be waged.

II

For those involved in the quantitative movement, the most influential
expression of the two opposed models came from a book of their fathers'
generation, a book that had great currency in the crucial decade of the
younger Elizabethans' coming of age, a book that in many ways shaped
their nonliterary, as well as their literary, self-presentation. That book is
Roger Ascham's *Schoolmaster* (1570). Written by the queen's tutor, dedicated to her Principal Secretary, prompted by a discussion that involved
a number of the most prominent officeholders in the realm, and based on
the ideas of leading English and Continental humanists of the first half of
the sixteenth century, *The Schoolmaster* spoke with the unmistakable
voice of cultural authority. A young man, who, like Spenser or Harvey,

aspired to occupy a position of such authority himself and who knew that his success would depend in large part on the approbation of those publically identified with Ascham's book, could hardly have ignored its recommendations. Spenser and Harvey clearly did not ignore them. On the contrary, they each refer specifically to Ascham and his views. In him they recognize the first begetter of the quantitative movement to which they both subscribe. But Ascham did not only "exhort the goodly wits of England" to "give themselves" to the task of "making perfect . . . this point of learning in our English tongue."[3] He also linked his particular exhortation to a more general choice of cultures and, indeed, to the very possibility of cultural choice itself. "Now," he wrote, "when men know the difference and have examples both of the best and of the worst, surely to follow rather the Goths in rhyming than the Greeks in true versifying were even to eat acorns with swine when we may freely eat wheat bread amongst men" (p. 145). Knowledge of historical difference is what, for Ascham, distinguished his moment from all previous moments in English history. And such knowledge brings with it the possibility of choice. Ascham thus presents that active model of self-fashioning to which Spenser, in seeking to have the kingdom of his own language, fits himself—a model based on choice and imitation. What Ascham most despises is the passive acceptance of "time and custom," eating acorns with swine. What he most admires is the "forward diligence," as he calls it, of those who choose to eat wheat bread amongst men, those who make themselves over in the likeness of a pattern of civility superior to what mere barbarous custom affords.

The deliberate fashioning of oneself and of others is what *The Schoolmaster* is all about. A schoolmaster is, after all, a professional molder of selves, and Ascham is particularly concerned with the process by which such molding is accomplished. He does, however, recognize the importance of natural differences. Many pages of the first half of his book, the section on "the bringing-up of youth," are given over to a detailed discussion of differing temperaments and their effect on learning. But Ascham's purpose is to upset expectation, to argue that hard wits make better pupils than quick ones. In going against the grain, a schoolmaster can make his most lasting impression. Translated to the cultural realm, this argument would seem to suggest that the very resistance of English speech and perhaps English institutions as well to the classical pattern might be evidence of their long-term aptness. Like hard wits, they are "hard to receive but sure to keep" (p. 24). Before Virgil and Horace corrected it, Latin, Ascham tells us, was as rude and barbarous as English. And though he does not himself make this point, many others claimed that Homer had similarly reformed Greek. This is what Spenser has in mind when he talks of the Greeks having had the kingdom of their own language. And given the way the Elizabethans pronounced the classical languages, particularly Latin, it must have seemed to them that the ancients' wielding of authority over their tongues was as much an act of arbitrary will as would be their own imposition of quantitative rules on English.[4] What, after all, distinguishes wheat bread from acorns but the planting, the harvesting, the threshing, the grinding, the sifting, and the baking? Acorns are barbarous and natural—barbarous *because* natural. They are fit food for Goths and for swine. To eat wheat bread is to give a sign of one's superiority over nature, a sign of one's power to make, ultimately to make oneself. "Follow[ing] the Greeks in true versifying" provides another sign of the same distinctly human power.

Power and its institutional embodiment are as central to the Spenser-Harvey correspondence as they were to *The Schoolmaster*. Spenser's two letters are dated from Westminster and from Leicester House, and they speak mysteriously of "his excellent Lordship" and, no less mysteriously, "of my late being with her Majesty" (10:5, 6). Ascham's project of English self-making was conceived in just such a setting, near the center of power, and Spenser lets us know that the project is being carried on there by this new generation. The quantitative movement chooses for itself the language appropriate to this setting and to its own absolutist ambition, the language of power. Its two leading advocates, Sidney and Dyer, have, Spenser tells us, "proclaimed in their Areopagus a general surceasing and silence of bold rhymers and also of the very best too, instead whereof they have, by authority of their whole senate, prescribed certain laws and rules of quantities of English syllables for English verse" (10:6). No one has known quite what to make of the Areopagus. Was it a formal society, an informal group of friends, or merely a name jokingly created by Spenser in this letter for some still less structured association? Without more evidence we will never know. But it is clear that the word is Greek and the action peremptory. In both respects it conforms to Ascham's model of self-fashioning.

Ascham's influence did not limit itself to Spenser, Harvey, Sidney, and Dyer. Nor, though the active involvement of these men was short-lived, did interest in English quantitative meter stop with them. In 1582 Richard Stanyhurst, quoting from the Spenser-Harvey correspondence and claiming to have taken it upon himself "to execute some part of Master Ascham his will," brought out his hexameter translation of the first four books of the *Aeneid*. Four years later, William Webbe, again with specific reference to both the Spenser-Harvey correspondence and Ascham, made the reformation of prosody the principal desideratum of his *Dis-*

course of English Poetry. George Puttenham in his *Art of English Poesy* (1589) was a less ardent partisan of what he called "Greek and Latin feet"—in fact, he began as an opponent—but he too ended by advocating their adoption, and he supplied six chapters of detailed discussion.[5] The publication in the next few years of much highly accomplished English rhyme, among it *Astrophel and Stella* and the first books of *The Faerie Queene,* seems to have temporarily stilled the call for a new prosody, but in 1599 the anonymous author of the *Preservation of Henry VII* attempted to reignite the issue, and Thomas Campion took it up with greater skill and greater vehemence in 1602. And through all these years poems in quantitative verse continued to be written, not only by these self-acknowledged advocates, but also by many others including the countess of Pembroke, Fulke Greville, Abraham Fraunce, Robert Greene, Thomas Lodge, and even the Marprelate combatants.

A few bits of this verse still make good reading. Others have become, as Nashe said of Stanyhurst's lumbering hexameters, "famously absurd."[6] Most have been quietly forgotten. But if we measure success in other terms, this very active movement can be considered extraordinarily successful. It succeeded, though not quite single-handedly, in putting English poetry high on the list of projects to be completed in the course of England's self-making. It furthermore succeeded in directing attention to technical questions of prosody that would have to be answered were English poetry itself to succeed. (It thus makes sense that Sidney and Spenser, the two main contributors to the development of that poetry and particularly to its metrical development, were also deeply involved in the quantitative movement.) And it succeeded in serving as a principal focal point for the discussion of national self-fashioning itself. This last is, of course, my main concern here. The rivalry between quantitative meter and rhyme was caught up in a much larger rivalry between two ways of being—between active self-making on the human-Greek-wheatbread model and passive acceptance of time and custom on the swine-Goth-acorn model. Now, of course, put in this Aschamite way, it was not hard to make a choice. And for some time English poets, like Spenser and Sidney, sided with Ascham or at least made no frontal attack on his values, even though they might in practice go against his particular precepts regarding prosody. But there were other values that could be attributed to even his terms, crushingly unequivocal though he meant them to be, and other terms that could equally alter the polarity he sought to establish.

Take, for example, the opposition between wheat bread and acorns. Nearly sixty years after the publication of *The Schoolmaster,* Ben Jonson can still use it with just Ascham's meaning. "Say that thou pourest 'hem wheat," he writes in the angry "Ode to Himself" that was prompted by the theatrical failure of his *New Inn* in 1629.

And they would acorns eat:
'Twere simple fury still thyself to waste
On such as have no taste,
To offer them a surfeit of pure bread,
Whose appetites are dead.
No, give them grains their fill,
Husks, draff to drink and swill.
If they love lees and leave the lusty wine,
Envy them not; their palate's with the swine.[7]

Not only is "pure bread" firmly identified with Jonson's classical (though not, of course, quantitative) art, but in the poem's concluding stanza that art is further associated with the absolute power of the king, with "the acts of Charles his reign." Here then the cluster of linked terms that so impressed Spenser, Harvey, and their contemporaries recurs. But difference marks this recurrence, for in 1629 both Jonson and his king were on the defensive. Just a year earlier Parliament had faced Charles with a Petition of Right that defended the privileges and liberties of Englishmen against royal usurpation in much the way that Harvey had defended the "privileges and liberties" of English words against Spenser's attempted tyranny. And, of course, Jonson had been pushed from the chair of wit. In such circumstances, neither the king nor his poet could speak with Ascham's settled authority.

The half century that separates Ascham and Jonson had granted even the lowly acorn more favorable associations. It reminds Don Quixote, as it must have reminded many Elizabethans, of the Golden Age, a distant time of innocence and perfection that found its modern expression in poetic depictions of shepherds and goatherds. Acorns may also have been linked in the minds of some Elizabethans to the *siliquae porcorum,* the swine's food envied by the prodigal in Saint Luke's Gospel.[8] Prodigal-son fiction and pastoral poetry were two of the literary kinds most favored by Spenser's generation, each of which figures a testing and often a revision of the midcentury humanist values most fully expressed by Ascham. Representing themselves as prodigals or as shepherds (and sometimes as both at once), Spenser, Sidney, and many other younger Elizabethans rebelled against paternal admonition and paternal expectation, sought a refuge from which they might examine their relation to a system of authority that at once provided only the narrowest definition of fit employment (one that excluded rhyming along with much else) and then denied them access to even such limited employment when they dutifully sought it.[9]

In begging Harvey to play Cato and to dissuade him from the folly of love, Spenser casts himself in precisely this prodigal role (a role he plays again as Colin Clout in *The Shepheardes Calender*) and seeks redemption. His efforts at quantitative verse are meant to signal this salutary turn. But if his aim was promotion in the courtly world of power, he need not have bothered. The cultural instability that could make even the barbarous acorn a sign of pristine innocence or of a fortunate fall was affecting the whole constellation of values represented by Ascham. Though Ascham located his humanist *Schoolmaster* at court, an actual humanist who tried to exhibit his schoolmasterly attainments in that region would have been in for a rude shock. At court, not the lover dedicated to pleasure and driven by passion but rather the upright Cato with his stiff hexameters and classical learning was in need of reform, for the court wanted elegant entertainment, not grave counsel or pedantic display, of its habitués. G. K. Hunter has argued this point at length in the well-known opening chapter of his book on John Lyly, and the two parts of Lyly's own *Euphues* furnish a diagrammatic example of an actual Elizabethan's discovery of its truth.[10] The first part, heavily and quite obviously influenced by Ascham, affirms the humanist lesson by taking a quick-witted young man from "Athens" to courtly "Naples" where unhappy experience teaches him to embrace the precepts he had rebelliously neglected. The second part, *Euphues and His England,* reverses that lesson. It celebrates love, exposes the inadequacy of classical learning, and advertises the skills of courtiership. It sets, moreover, England against Greece so that a representative of the latter ends by singing the praises of the former. Instead of making England over in the image of Greece, as Ascham himself, the Aschamite Spenser of the Harvey correspondence, and the equally Aschamite Lyly of the *Anatomy of Wit* all seemed intent on doing, the author of *Euphues and His England* wants us to laugh at the foolish Greek for not becoming wholly English.[11] Such laughter is precisely what greeted the unreformed Harvey when he brought his graceless learning to court.

It would, of course, also turn itself on the quantitative movement. We already sense something of this transmutation of values in Puttenham's juxtaposition of the two sorts of poetry. "Now passing from these courtly trifles," he says at the conclusion of his discussion of various sorts of artful rhyming stanzas, "let us talk of our scholastical toys, that is of the grammatical versifying of the Greeks and Latins and see whether it might be reduced into our English art or no."[12] Already quantitative verse, whose great claim to authority resided in its presumed association with imperial power, finds itself banished from court and forced to content itself with the schoolhouse. And though Puttenham thinks such verse can be naturalized in English, he does not wish that it "be generally applauded at to the discredit of our forefathers' manner of vulgar poesy or to the alteration or peradventure total destruction of the same." The possibility of English verse in quantitative meter furnishes rather another, by now almost superfluous, bit of evidence that an "art of English poesy" is not a ridiculous misnomer. In his *Defense of Poesy,* Sidney, who just a year or two earlier had been proclaiming reform and promulgating new laws, is equally cool, and he too gives more credit for eloquence to "smally learned courtiers" than to official "professors of learning."[13] In the course of very few years from the late 1570s to the early 1580s, humanist learning and courtly advancement have come to a parting of the ways. English rhyme follows the lead of the court, while quantitative verse is left to take the path that leads away from power. In these circumstances, the charge of barbarousness loses its force. If acorns are being consumed at court, they are by that very fact made courteous and civil.

III

The adoption of rhyming verse by the court and by courtiers, or at least the close association of one with the other, obscured for a while the issue that had been so clear in Ascham. In the interim a vast amount of highly accomplished rhyming verse was written and published—the most impressive and influential examples of it written by those two former partisans of the quantitative movement, Sidney and Spenser. But if their achievement went a long way toward making the earlier controversy moot, it did not erase that controversy. Under the aegis of pastoralism, Petrarchan prodigality, and chivalric romance, none of which Ascham would have approved, rhyme prospered, first at court and then in the literate community generally. But the particular terms of Ascham's argument remained unanswered—indeed, unaddressed.

The undiminished cultural prestige of classical antiquity, particularly when combined in the late 1590s with the much-diminished prestige of the royal court, made this a perilous situation. On what foundation of authority could English rhyme depend? Was the mere fact of Sidney's and Spenser's accomplishment enough to turn what even they had thought barbarous into a mark of civility? How could the taint of cultural inferiority be removed from rhyme in the face of its undoubted medieval origin? How for that matter, could that taint be removed from the identity of England itself, since its language seemed irradicably bound to a barbarous and "inartificial" mode of literary expression?

Though Sidney and Spenser had written much and written well, they had failed in their attempt to "have the kingdom of [their] own language." What significance was to be attributed to that failure? Was the original project misguided? Or had they simply given up too easily and too soon? Or, more worrisome, was English nature unalterably resistant to the nurture of civility? "You taught me art," the pupil nation might say to the master races of antiquity, "and my profit on't is I know how to rhyme."

To my knowledge, no Englishman was willing to speak of himself and his countrymen as cultural Calibans, a vile race deservedly confined to their island rock. But they did suspect that others saw them this way, and sometimes their suspicion found galling confirmation. On a trip to Italy early in the 1590s, Samuel Daniel heard the poet Guarini "oft embace the virtues of the North, / Saying our coasts were with no measures graced, / Nor barbarous tongues could any verse bring forth."[14] Just a few years later Daniel put a similar charge in the mouth of the worldly-wise Philocosmus, the antagonist of his poetry-loving spokesman, Musophilus.

> Is this the walk of all your wide renown,
>   This little point, this scarce discerned isle,
> Thrust from the world, with whom our speech unknown
>   Made never any traffic of our style?
> And is this all where all this care is shown,
>   T'enchant your fame to last so long a while?
> And for that happier tongues have won so much,
>   Think you to make your barbarous language such?
> Poor narrow limits for so mighty pains.[15]

Nor could the accomplishment of the greater Elizabethans silence doubts like these. "How many thousands never heard the name / Of Sidney or of Spenser or their books? / And yet brave fellows . . ." (p. 81). Undoubtedly the grounds for a defense of English rhyming poetry were far more solid than they had been twenty years earlier when Sidney and Spenser began their literary careers. But that defense had still to be made. As it happens, it was Daniel himself who made it—though not until he had been provoked by Thomas Campion's renewal in 1602, the last year of the old queen's reign, of the campaign for English verse based on the ancient model.

In dedicating his *Observations in the Art of English Poesy* to Lord Buckhurst, Burghley's successor as Lord Treasurer and one of the small inner circle of privy councilors who dominated affairs in Elizabeth's declining years, Campion not only attempted to associate his views with a representative of royal power. He also evoked that early Elizabethan moment, before the arrival on the literary scene of either Sidney or Spenser, when humanist values were exercising their strongest attraction. Forty years before receiving the dedication of Campion's *Observations,* Baron Buckhurst, then Thomas Sackville, had collaborated with Thomas Norton on *Gorboduc,* the most nearly regular of English tragedies. It is to the clearly articulated clash of cultures characteristic of that moment that Campion returns. Once again rhyme is stigmatized as "vulgar and inartificial" and quantitative meter praised as the "true form of versifying."[16] And once again the humanist story of European cultural development, the story of monkish decline and classical revival, is rehearsed.

In his *Defense of Rhyme,* Daniel flatly denies the assumptions that governed this story, boldly rejecting the whole set of historical premises on which the quantitative movement had depended. Though he was no less deeply bothered than Ascham or Campion by the charge that England was a barbarous nation, Daniel's response to that charge is the opposite of theirs. Where they sought to rip out barbarous custom and impose in its place the civility of Greece and Rome, he celebrates the cultural accomplishments of the barbarians themselves. "All our understandings are not," he says, "to be built by the square of Greece and Italy. . . . The Goths, Vandals, and Longobards, whose coming down like an inundation overwhelmed, as they say, all the glory of learning in Europe, have yet left us their law and customs . . . which well considered with their other courses of government may serve to clear them from this imputation of ignorance. . . . Let us go no further but look upon the wonderful architecture of this state of England and see whether they were deformed times that could give it such a form" (pp. 139–40, 145).

But Daniel does not only dismiss the historical basis of the Ascham-Campion argument. He also rejects its humanist and absolutist model of self-making. Far from wishing to "have the kingdom of our own language," Daniel accepts and delights in a form of verse that, as he puts it a few years later in a poem prefaced to his *Certain Small Works* (1607), "Confirmed by no edict of power doth rest / But only underneath the regency / Of use and fashion." (p. 5). He evokes the language of royal power only to deny its relevance, to depose the monarchic (or Areopagite) pronouncer of edicts. At the origin of English rhyme is not the act of a primal lawgiver or a sovereign maker but rather the immemorial workings of custom and nature, "custom that is before all law, nature that is above all art" (p. 131). Like Harvey, who in responding a quarter of a century earlier to Spenser's attempt to bend *carpenter* to his will had defined Spenser's act as tyrannous usurpation and had defended the privileges and liberties of English words, Daniel couches his argument in specificially legal and political terms. For both Harvey and Daniel, as for their opponents, the form of English verse was as much a political as an aesthetic matter. Indeed, they could understand the aesthetic only as a subset of the political. The distribution of syllables in a line of verse inevitably figured the distribution of power in the state. Innovation in either carried with it the threat (or the promise) of disruption in the other.

In the *Defense of Rhyme,* political innovation seems to worry Daniel still more than the changes in verse form that Campion was suggesting. And well it might. Only a few months before the book was published a reign that had lasted longer than Daniel's life had finally ended and a new monarch, a foreigner, had assumed power. It is to this event that Daniel attributes the augmentation and publication of his treatise, which he claims to have first written a short while earlier as a private letter. "The times," he says, "promise a more regard to the present condition of our writings, in the respect of our sovereign's happy inclination this way, whereby we are rather to expect an encouragement to go on with what we do than that any innovation should check us with a shew of what it would do in another kind" (p. 127). By that "happy inclination," Daniel may have been thinking not only of James's more general reputation for learning but also of his specific support for rhyme in his *Short Treatise of Scottish Poesy* (1584). If, however, James's "prentice" view of poetry was comforting, his views on government may not have been, at least not to one who had attended to them carefully. Thus Daniel's emphasis on the danger of innovation, on "the plain tract . . . beaten by custom and the time" (p. 147), on laws that have "ever been used amongst us time out of mind" (p. 150) responds directly to concerns aroused by the accession to power of a king who claimed ancestral conquest as the ultimate sanction of his authority, a king who thought his will should be law. In opposing "the unjust authority of the law-giver" Campion (p. 149), Daniel also implicitly opposes any comparably tyrannous act on the part of the new sovereign. England's verse is Gothic, and so is the English state. To alter either, even according to a plan borrowed from classical antiquity, would be to do "wrong to the honor of the dead, wrong to the fame of the living, and wrong to England" (p. 153). "Here I stand forth," he declares, "only to make good the place we have thus taken up" (p. 155).

That Daniel was quite consciously taking his stand in the face of the new king is further suggested by the company in which the *Defense of Rhyme* first appeared. It was printed (and quickly reprinted) as the last work in a small volume that began with "A Panegyric Congratulatory to the King's Most Excellent Majesty." The concerns of this poem are precisely those of the *Defense,* though it prudently assumes that the king, unlike Campion, will be in full agreement. "We shall continue," says Daniel, speaking out of this far-from-proven assumption,

> and remain all one,
> In law, in justice, and in magistrate;
> Thou wilt not alter the foundation
> Thy ancestors have laid of this estate,
> Nor grieve thy land with innovation,
> Nor take from us more than thou wilt collate;
> Knowing that course is best to be observed,
> Whereby a state hath longest been preserved.[17]

From a situation (the situation that produced Spenser's letters to Harvey) in which authority was thought to reside in innovation, in institutions as yet unfounded and which thus depend for their very existence on the exercise of sovereign will, we arrive at one in which even the sovereign's will is made subject to institutions that are said to date back to "time out of mind." Reversing the humanist call for action, Daniel denies that any action is wanted. In neither poetry nor politics does England need to make itself. It needs only to recognize, value, and use the self it already has.

Nearly a decade before they argued over rhyme, Daniel and Campion had been publicly linked. Both published their first poems as addenda to Thomas Newman's edition of *Astrophel and Stella* (1591). Campion's five poems are all experimental in form; two are in quantitative meter. Daniel's twenty-three are all Petrarchan sonnets. Both sets owe an obvious debt to Sidney: Campion's to the experimental verses of the *Arcadia;* Daniel's to *Astrophel and Stella* itself. Between them they divide the Sidneian legacy and reveal the rift within it and within the larger literary and cultural project to which it belonged. Campion follows the "Greek" line; Daniel, the "Gothic." What this collection of poems makes clear, and what Daniel so marvelously obscures in his *Defense of Rhyme,* is that neither was particularly English. Rhyme itself had been borrowed from the French little more than two centuries earlier, and the form that rhyme most often took, the form of the fourteen-line sonnet that Campion attacks and Daniel practices, was a still more recent acquisition. To identify immemorial custom with the sonnet was to invent history.

This was the final and most decisive triumph of the quantitative movement—to make an import scarcely older than itself appear native and natural. Translated into the terms of the confrontation between Goth and Greek, French and Italian poetic form came to stand for the customary and the unmade, for the purely English. Sidney and Spenser had succeeded in having the kingdom of their own language *because* of the failure of their quantitative experiments, had succeeded so thoroughly that they made it appear that their language had had the kingdom of them. To this accomplishment Daniel's *Defense* adds the finishing touch. By asserting continuity and calling this Renaissance medieval, Daniel makes their work the sign of a community whose authority can both enable other poets, like Daniel himself, and repel the encroachment of royal invaders who might try to do to English law what Campion wanted to do to English verse. Like many later nationalist movements, this early one established its legitimacy through the invention of tradition, the invention, in this case, of a Gothic past to which some of its most recent cultural innovations might be attributed.[18]

IV

Let's take a quick look over the ground we have covered. In the 1570s young Englishmen were presented with a clear choice of cultures. Dine on wheat bread with Greeks and men or on acorns with Goths and swine. A quarter of a century later the choice was once again clear, and the significance of the opposing terms was, in at least one respect, precisely what it had been. Once again Greek stood for active self-making; Goth, for passive acceptance of time and custom. But in the *Defense of Rhyme* authority shifts sides.

Not all Daniel's readers would have accepted this shift. Ben Jonson, whom we have noticed defending his own art in terms that could easily have been borrowed from Ascham, told Drummond that "he had written a discourse of poesy both against Campion and Daniel, especially this last," and late in his life he talked of reviving the quantitative experiment.[19] Nor was Jonson's classicism an isolated phenomenon. He shared it with his literary generation—a generation that defined itself in opposition to the practices of Sidney and Spenser—and, in a more general way, with his monarch. James may have defended rhyme, but he did not otherwise much favor the Gothic. In contrast to the neochivalric mode that had dominated Elizabethan court pageantry from the late 1570s on, the new king affected a Roman manner.[20] But by 1603 the Gothic had taken too firm a hold to be easily dislodged. As a result, a cultural divide that could be seen in opposed styles of architecture and in opposed legal systems, as well as in differing modes of pageantry and poetry, opened between court and country. When Jonson, who appreciated the power of the values he sometimes disdained, set Gothic Penshurst against its newer neoclassical rivals, against buildings adorned with touch and marble, polished pillars and roofs of gold, he employed precisely the system of differences we saw at work in the quantitative controversy, an opposition between deliberate making ("their lords have built") and an acceptance of what time and custom have already made ("but thy lord dwells").[21] And when in the Parliament of 1628 the great common lawyer Sir Edward Coke struggled on behalf of the "immemorial rights" of Englishmen in opposition to Stuart absolutism, an absolutism that yearned for Roman civil law as eagerly as Ascham had yearned for Roman measures, these were still the terms he used, terms that had been shared by humanists, poets, architects, lawyers, and kings for over fifty years.[22]

Spenser died long before the open break between court and country. He died even before the exchange between Campion and Daniel. But his work (particularly *The Faerie Queene*) was already moving, despite his own advocacy of the humanist model, in the direction that Daniel and Coke would take. Harvey (himself a student of Roman civil law as well as a partisan of quantitative verse) seems to have felt something of this when he objected that in preferring his *Faerie Queene* to his presumably more classical nine comedies Spenser had let "Hobgoblin run away with the garland from Apollo" (10:472), and eighteenth-century readers were still aware of it when they called *The Faerie Queen* "Gothic." *The Faerie Queene* is Gothic, and intentionally so, though it is also intentionally Greek. Unlike Daniel or Coke, Spenser does not decide in a final or definitive way between these opposing models of self-fashioning, but he does make *The Faerie Queene* a scene for their encounter. His own literary ambition, his intention of making himself a great English poet, depended both on the general success of English poetry and on the success of England itself—as their success depended in turn on his. He was aware of this mutual dependence and shaped his greatest poem in response to it.

The very richness of that response and its influence on the subsequent development of English self-understanding make the *The Faerie Queene* the first literary text we should consult if we are to appreciate the extraordinary irony that underlies this whole clash of cultures as it developed from the mid-sixteenth to the mid-seventeenth century: the fact that the Gothic image of England, which as time went on became more and more closely associated with the anticourt and finally antimonarchic faction, grew up under the sponsorship of perhaps the most effective and certainly the most celebrated royal government England has ever known, the government of Queen Elizabeth. Thanks to these remarkable developments, English rhyme—like English common law, English parliamentary practice, English Gothic architecture, and English chivalric pageantry—came to be seen as *both* Elizabethan and antimonarchic, at least as the Stuarts understood monarchy. These cultural forms entered into a specifically nationalist discourse, a discourse that lent its authority to the whole nascent enterprise of English poetry. In the end, Sidney, Spenser, and their followers had the kingdom of their own language precisely by pretending not to, by submitting to an identity that they first created.[23]

Notes

1. *The Works of Edmund Spenser: A Variorum Edition,* 11 vols., ed. Edwin Greenlaw et al. (Baltimore: Johns Hopkins Press, 1932–57), 10:16. Subsequent quotations from this edition will be identified in the text. Spelling and punctuation have been modernized throughout, with the single exception of titles of Spenser's individual works which I have allowed to retain their familiar archaic appearance. Titles in the notes follow the spelling of the edition cited.

2. Compare King James's formula, "king, people, law" (*law* here representing the cultural system, as language does in Spenser), in the preface to his *Basilikon Doron* (*The Political Works of James I,* ed. C. H. McIlwain [Cambridge: Harvard University Press, 1918], p. 7.

3. Roger Ascham, *The Schoolmaster,* ed. Lawrence V. Ryan (Ithaca: Cornell University Press, 1967), p. 151. Subsequent quotations from this edition will be identified in the text.

4. See Derek Attridge's discussion of pronunciation in his *Well-Weighed Syllables: Elizabethan Verse in Classical Metres* (Cambridge: Cambridge University Press, 1974), pp. 21–40. Attridge's book provides the best introduction available to the quantitative movement in Renaissance England.

5. In G. Gregory Smith, ed., *Elizabethan Critical Essays,* 2 vols. (Oxford: Clarendon Press, 1904), 1:137 (Stanyhurst), 1:240, 266–90 (Webbe), and 2:117–41 (Puttenham).

6. "Master Stanyhurst (though otherwise learned) trod a foul, lumbering, boisterous, wallowing measure in his translation of Virgil. He had never been praised by Gabriel [Harvey] for his labor if therein he had not been so famously absurd" (Nashe, ibid. 2:240).

7. *Ben Jonson,* 11 vols., ed. C. H. Herford, Percy Simpson, and Evelyn Simpson (Oxford: Clarendon Press, 1925–52), 6:493. I have adopted a few minor variants from the earliest edition cited by Herford and Simpson in their textual notes.

8. See, for example, *The Works of Thomas Nashe,* 5 vols., ed. Ronald B. McKerrow and F. P. Wilson (Oxford: Clarendon Press, 1958), 2:250.

9. The issues raised in this paragraph are central to my *Elizabethan Prodigals* (Berkeley: University of California Press, 1976).

10. G. K. Hunter, *John Lyly: The Humanist as Courtier* (London: Routledge, 1962), pp. 1–35. For a discussion of the more positive effect of the court on poetry, see Daniel Javitch, *Poetry and Courtliness in Renaissance England* (Princeton: Princeton University Press, 1978).

11. I discuss the relation of the two parts of *Euphues* in greater detail in *The Elizabethan Prodigals,* pp. 58–78.

12. Smith, *Elizabethan Critical Essays* 2:116.

13. Philip Sidney, *An Apology for Poetry,* ed. Geoffrey Shepherd (Edinburgh: Nelson, 1965), pp. 140, 139.

14. *The Complete Works in Verse and Prose of Samuel Daniel,* 4 vols., ed. Alexander B. Grosart (London: Spenser Society, 1885–96), 1:280.

15. Samuel Daniel, *Poems and A Defence of Ryme,* ed. Arthur Colby Sprague (1930; reprint, Chicago: University of Chicago Press, 1965), p. 81. Subsequent quotations from this edition will be identified in the text.

16. *The Works of Thomas Campion,* ed. Walter R. Davis (Garden City, N.Y.: Doubleday, 1967), p. 291.

17. Daniel, *Complete Works* 1:153.

18. See Eric Hobsbawn and Terence Ranger, eds., *The Invention of Tradition* (Cambridge: Cambridge University Press, 1983).

19. Attridge, *Well-Weighed Syllables,* pp. 127–28.

20. Jonathan Goldberg discusses the king's taste for the Roman in *James I and the Politics of Literature* (Baltimore: Johns Hopkins University Press, 1983). See especially chap. 4, "The Roman Actor."

21. Don E. Wayne discusses both the architecture of Penshurst and Jonson's poem in *Penshurst: The Semiotics of Place and the Poetics of History* (Madison, Wis.: University of Wisconsin Press, 1984).

22. On the opposition between Roman civil law and English common law, see F. W. Maitland, *English Law and the Renaissance* (Cambridge: Cambridge University Press, 1901); and J. G. A. Pocock, *The Ancient Constitution and the Feudal Law* (1957; 2d ed. Cambridge: Cambridge University Press, 1987).

23. An earlier and much briefer version of this paper was read as part of the Spenser sessions at the International Congress of Medieval Studies (Western Michigan University, May 1984) and published in *Spenser at Kalamazoo* 9 (1984): 68–79.

Sir Philip Sidney and the Uses of History

Herschel Baker in *The Race of Time,* the notable Alexander Lectures which he delivered at the University of Toronto in 1965, begins by locating "a pair of ancient commonplaces that underlie most Renaissance discussions of historiography." According to Baker,

> one is that the historian, unlike other writers, has a special obligation to ascertain and state the truth of things. The other is that such truths are exemplary: they are paradigms of moral and political behavior, which, authenticated by famous men's experience, provide patterns that can shape our own response to perennially recurring situations. Thus history, unlike more imaginative kinds of literature, was thought to be both true and useful. It had a dual sanction, and generations of humanists, politicians, and moralists—who by no means represented mutually exclusive categories—concurred in celebrating it.[1]

One of the chief celebrants was Sir Philip Sidney, but he at once complicates such simple notions as those of his contemporary historiographers. Sidney first discusses history in his citation of Xenophon's *Cyropaedia* as a new *paedeia* in the *Defence of Poetry.* This ideal portrait of Cyrus shows the ideal man as political leader and as soldier. At the same time, and more openly, more personally, Sidney directed his younger brother Robert to a somewhat different use of history. He writes to Robert from Leicester House, London, on 18 October 1580,

> Then to consider by that   as yow not your selfe, Zenophon to follow Thucidides, so doth Thucidides follow Herodotus, and Diodorus Siculus follow Zenophon. So generally doe the Roman stories follow the Greeke, and the perticuler stories of present Monarchies follow the Roman. In that kinde yow have principally to note the examples of

vertue or vice, with their good or evell successes, the establishments or ruines of greate Estates, with the cawses, the tyme and circumstances of the lawes they write of, the entrings, and endings of warrs, and therin the stratagems against the enimy, and the discipline upon the soldiour, and thus much as a very Historiographer. Besides this *the Historian makes himselfe a discourser for profite and an Orator, yea a Poet sometimes for ornament.*[2]

In both instances, turning to the great, directive texts of the past we pass through history and, so instructed, come back into historical time again. I want to argue that this double-focused, history-based poetic of past and present is worked out in greatest detail by Sidney in *The Countess of Pembroke's Arcadia,* and that if we do not read the work this way, as Mary Sidney was expected to read it—if we do not see how it points us back to certain events in the recorded past to tell us how best to live, but also identifies the significance of the most pressing Tudor issues of governance and religion and so firmly provides a blueprint for the present and immediate future of current history—we miss the meaning of Sidney's most important poem altogether.

I

Sidney's *Arcadia* draws upon those histories that Sidney mentions to his brother. Xenophon, for instance, was a set text for history at Shrewsbury School when Sidney went there; Thelma N. Greenfield notes that from the *Cyropaedia* Sidney learned "Xenophon's indefatigable ingenuity as he varies Cyrus's problems from episode to episode and through his hero's unfaltering wisdom creates unpredictable solutions."[3] But the primary model was not Xenophon but the Greek historian Thucydides, who was taught both at Shrewsbury and at Christ Church, Oxford, where Sidney later attended. Although largely unrecognized as a source, Thucydides' history provides Sidney's own with pattern and proceeding, characterization, and even particular references, as *Pyrocles,* suggesting *Pericles,* may be meant to convey. Pericles' deeply moving funeral oration, for example, a chestnut in Tudor schoolrooms for its fine sentiment and its extraordinary power, underscores the premise of much of the *Arcadia.* "Each individual," says Pericles, "is interested not only in his own affairs but in the affairs of the state as well: even those who are mostly occupied with their own business are extremely well-informed on general politics."[4] Such ideas take concrete historical form with those who died in the Athenian cause during the Peloponnesian War.

What we ought to remember first is their gallant conduct against the enemy in defence of their native land. They have blotted out evil with good, and done more service to the commonwealth than they ever did harm in their private lives. No one of these men weakened because he wanted to go on enjoying his wealth: no one put off the awful day in the hope that he might live to escape his poverty and grow rich. More to be desired than such things, they chose to check the enemy's pride. This, to them, was a risk most glorious, and they accepted it, willing to strike down the enemy and relinquish everything else. As for success or failure, they left that in the doubtful hands of Hope, and when the reality of battle was before their faces, they put their trust in their own selves. In the fighting, they thought it more honourable to stand their ground and suffer death than to give in and save their lives. So they fled from the reproaches of men, abiding with life and limb the brunt of battle; and, in a small moment of time, the climax of their lives, a culmination of glory, not of fear, were swept away from us. (Pp. 148–49)

Such are the heroic credos in Sidney's *Arcadia* too, the glamour and richness of tournaments and lists fading before the necessity of battles for what is good and just. The fact that Pyrocles and Musidorus fight to defend a land that is not native to them only reinforces the glory of their heroism and the value of their service. Rather than fear the forces of Amphialus, they trust the causes for which they battle, a trust that does not fade when they are put to trial by Philanax and judged by Euarchus.

Yet there are far more specific connections to be made: Pericles' speech also anticipates the kernel of *Arcadia* 5. "We give our obedience to those whom we put in positions of authority" Pericles remarks, like Sidney's Basilius and Philanax, "and we obey the laws themselves," as Sidney's Euarchus insists, "especially those which are for the protection of the oppressed" to which Euarchus will pay no heed, "and those unwritten laws" to be cited in Sidney by Pamela, "which it is an acknowledged shame to break" (p. 145). This last—a sense of mercy that allows reasoned exceptions to the law—is Pericles' most vital point, and it is important to note that it is altogether missing in the analogous speech, by Euarchus, in *Arcadia* 5's grand trial. For the Tudors who read Sidney's manuscript, this is a telling indicator of how we are to judge Euarchus in turn. For just this sense of mercy was very important to Thucydides. He reiterates it at a key juncture, one that became another Tudor chestnut— the Mytilenian debate in book 3. There Cleon, the son of Cleaenetus, speaks for the Athenians with ideas that are especially apposite to the final scenes of the *Arcadia*. "We should realize," he says, "that a city is better off with bad laws, so long as they remain fixed, than with good laws that are constantly being altered, that lack of learning combined with sound common sense is more helpful than the kind of cleverness that gets out of hand" (p. 213), giving historically credible and respectable precedent to Euarchus's literal and absolute judgment according to Arcadian law on the lives of his son and nephew. Cleon continues, "Let there be no hope, therefore, held out to the Mytilenians that we, either as a result of a good speech or a large bribe, are likely to forgive them on the grounds that it is only human to make mistakes." In view of this narrow application of law without equity, Sidney may have discovered one of those fundamental issues of Elizabethan life that seems to have governed much of *Arcadia 5*. Cleon remarks further that "as for compassion, it is proper to feel it in the case of people who are like ourselves and who will pity us in their turn, not in the case of those who, so far from having the same feelings towards us, must always and inevitably be our enemies" (p. 216). This is undermined, however—today we say appropriated or subverted by—the memorable, pointed Melian dialogue of book 5, by which Thucydides deliberately balances the Mytilenian debate and so introduces a serious equivocation. The Melians, too, argue the best principles of what is just and what is permissible in a stable government. "In our view," they insist, "it is at any rate useful that you should not destroy a principle that is to be the general good of all men." Nevertheless, "in the case of all who fall into danger there should be such a thing as fair play and just dealing [Peter R. Pouncey translates this "equity and justice"[5], and that such people should be allowed to use and to profit by arguments that fall short of a mathematical accuracy [in Pouncey, "the scope of vengeance"] that narrowly argues a life for a life" (p. 402).

Such elaborate arguments—of which there are many in Thucydides until book 8—at once raise particular actions in history to universal principles and make them recurring judgments. Yet the most startling and most unforgettable part of Thucydides' history is the plague that intrudes, horrible and causeless, between the fine words of Periclean oratory and the formalized debates with the Melians and Mytilenes. This inexplicable disease tests and undermines all their finest sentiments, much as the battles of the revised *Arcadia 3* test and undermine the discussions that precede and succeed them. "At the beginning," Thucydides tells us, "the doctors were quite incapable of treating the disease because of their ignorance of the right methods. In fact mortality among the doctors was the highest of all, since they came more frequently in contact with the sick. Nor was any other human art or science of any help at all. Equally useless were prayers made in the temples, consultation of oracles, and so forth; indeed, in the end people were so overcome by their sufferings that they paid no further attention to such things" (pp. 151–

52). Much of the haunting power of the revised *Arcadia 3* is our growing awareness of how ugly, corrupt, and vicious even those with the best of motives become: how selfishness corrupts and how corruption can become contagious. Irrational hatred and random death and destruction are perhaps best captured in the ideal marriage of Argalus and Parthenia, ruined by the indulgences of others; such examples show us only that no ideal is safe and that heroism exists only at the terrible price of possible death. (We do well to recall that the *Arcadia* remained the most popular English novel well into the eighteenth century and that Argalus and Parthenia likewise remained popular, Francis Quarles's epic poem about them second only to *Paradise Lost* as the most-read poem of the seventeenth century.)

What is even more striking for our purposes is that the precise concerns of malice, of random death, and of our slender hold on mortality, which take the center stage in both Thucydides and the revised *Arcadia,* would, for Sidney and those who knew him, not simply look back on the instructive ancient account of the Peloponnesian War but forward, biographically, into the current state of Sidney's own family and, autobiographically, into his own condition. Sidney's grandfather, for instance, knew something about plague when he wrote Cecil on 2 June 1552 about the sweating sickness and the sudden death of a daughter.

> First, the night before she died, she was as merry as any child could be, and sickened about three in the morning, and was in a sweat, and within a while after she had a desire to the stool; and the indiscreet woman that attended upon her let her rise, and after that, she fell to swooning, and then, with such things as they ministered to her, brought her again to remembrance, and so she seemed for a time to be meetly well revived, and so continued till it was noon, and still in a great sweating; and about twelve of the clock she began to alter again, and so in continual pangs and fits till six of the clock, at what time she left this life. And this morning she was looked upon, and between the shoulders it was very black, and also upon one side of her cheek. . . . This (is) as much as I am able to express.[6]

Sidney's mother, Lady Mary, was suddenly, inexplicably disfigured for life by an epidemic of smallpox while she was tending the queen, who also suffered but was not permanently marked in any way. Sidney too suffered from the same disease, which indelibly scarred his face; only the diplomatic paintings that have come down to us have wiped away the pockmarks that stained his once-handsome visage. These facts, witnessed by those who knew Sidney, would only reinforce the fact that the battles in the new *Arcadia 3* are deliberately parallel in placement to their model in Thucydides, while this sense of remaking the Greek historian means strongly to suggest that the manipulations of Cecropia and the foolishness of Basilius before, and the absolute judgment of Euarchus later, portray a kind of corruption of reason that leads to malice (willfully or not) and the possibility of undeserved pain or death. Contagion is not only random but chosen, not only transhuman but personal, too.

Thucydides subtly shapes his *History of the Peloponnesian War* to insist on the plague as an overarching symbol. Pouncey begins his fine reading with just the concerns we have been reviewing.

> After the Funeral Oration (2.35–46) comes the Plague (2.47–55). Death for a known and honorable cause gives way to random death by a mysterious disease, solemn rites of burial in an ancestral tradition (2.34) to indecent, makeshift expedients (2.52.4), claims to respect for authority and law (2.37.3) to actual lawlessness (2.53), and the most elaborate rhetorical construction to the most detailed clinical narrative. The two passages are brought directly into line against each other on a moralistic axis, the speech asserting the virtues of Athens, and the plague canceling them. Taken together, they display Thucydides' power and versatility as a writer, and make a challenging point of entry into his *History*. (p. 31).

But with Sidney the issue is at once more complex and more lucid. In the *Arcadia* he finds no easy answers to explain the nature of some wicked or envious men (such as Clitophon or even Philanax), nor the failings of those who (like Amphialus) are suddenly subject to passion or (like Cecropia) confuse means and ends in determined self-justification—men and women not unlike the Greeks portrayed by Thucydides. Yet Sidney's characters lead us, as the poet's images come alive with *significatio*, to the exemplary Euarchus, long awaited and much heralded, who is rendered helpless to save his own kin (and kind) in the face of foreign (but not alien) laws. The lessons Sidney takes, in an act of humanist *imitatio*, from the history of Thucydides are far more than of form alone. They involve the intricate interpenetration of the personal and autobiographical with the impersonal and fictional (even, perhaps, the fabulous); they show the harsh necessity of considering the planned actions of men and the unforeseeable circumstance. Most important of all, they show how, following Aristotle, narrative can combine story and explore idea, in an act of continual reconstruction and re-creation. History as a means of coordinating various (and sometimes opposing) levels of conceptualization gives to Sidney, following hard upon the poetics of the *Defence*, a new and vital means by which to bring past life and present poetry into close and provocative conjunction.

II

In his earlier years as a poet, Sidney had not confronted the truths of history directly. Instead he, like his forebears—his great-grandfather, Edmund Dudley, later earl of Northumberland, privy councillor to Henry VII and author of *The Tree of Commonwealth,* a treatise in favor of absolute monarchy; his grandfather, John Dudley, earl of Warwick, and Lord High Chamberlain and president of Wales under Edward VI; his father, Sir Henry Sidney, Lord Deputy of Ireland; and his uncle, Robert Dudley, privy councillor under Elizabeth I—had paid frequent tribute to the monarch. True enough, two of the Dudleys had eventually been accused of treason, and this legacy, too, pressing on him, must have urged him on to defend Elizabeth's absolutism with the sort of lavish praise that had become conventional. He is not quite so extreme as Job Throckmorton, whose prayer in his parliamentary speech of 1587 seems the "quintessence" of the Virgin Queen's mystique: "that, if it so pleased God, the last day of Queen Elizabeth's life might be the last day of this earth," and "that when she fleeteth hence . . . we may then behold . . . Jesus sitting in His throne of judgment, to our endless and everlasting comfort."[7] Nonetheless, his praise is extravagant enough. We have, for instance, the "Supplication" of *The Lady of May.*

> *Most gracious Sovereign:*
> To one whose state is raised over all,
> Whose face doth oft the bravest sort enchant,
> Whose mind is such, as wisest minds appal,
> Who in one self these diverse gifts can plant:
>   How dare I, wretch, seek there my woes to rest,
>   Where ears be burnt, eyes dazzled, hearts oppressed?
> Your state is great, your greatness is our shield,
> Your face hurts oft, but still it doth delight,
> Your mind is wise, your wisdom makes you mild;
> Such planted gifts enrich even beggars' sight:
> So dare I, wretch, my bashful fear subdue,
> And feed mine ears, mine eyes, mine heart in you.[8]

There is also the allusion to the queen in "The Four Foster Children of Desire" as "moste renowned and devine Beautie, whose beames shine like the sun."[9]

But Fulke Greville tells us that by the time of the *Arcadia*—he means the revised *Arcadia*—Sidney was determined "lively to represent the growth, state, and declination of Princes, changes of Government, and lawes: vicissitudes of sedition, faction, succession, confederacies, plantations, with all other errors, or alterations in publique affaires."[10] There, even with the entrance of Euarchus in old *Arcadia 5,* Greville sees "dark webs of effeminate Princes [who may] be dangerous forerunners of innovation, even in a quiet, and equally tempered people" (p. 13), so that Euarchus's case stands as "desolate" (p. 14). Greville has caught nicely Sidney's changing attitude. For by 1580, when he began work on the old *Arcadia,* Sidney's "Letter to Queen Elizabeth" had similar forebodings— and may contain a veiled warning. "The longer a good prince reigns," Sidney writes to the queen,

> it is most certain the more he is esteemed; for there is no man ever weary of well being; and good increased to good makes the same good both greater and stronger, for it useth the mind to know no other course, when either men are born in the time, and so never saw other, or have spent most part of their flourishing time, and so have no joy to seek other. In evil princes abuse growing upon abuse, according to the nature of evil, with increase of time ruins itself. But in so rare a government, where neighbours' fire gives us light to see our own quietness, where nothing wants that true administration of justice brings forth, certainly the length of time rather breeds a mind to think no other life but in that, than any tediousness in so fruitful sweetness. Examples of all good princes do ever confirm this, who, the longer they reigned, the deeper still they sank into their subjects' hearts. Neither will I trouble you with examples, being so many and manifest. (*Miscellaneous Prose,* pp. 53–54)

The ordering of the argument subtly moves to question the insight or blindness of a monarch whose own habits progressively distance him or her ever more from reality. A "neighbours' fire" is hardly proper enlightenment for the realistically wary and so continually reliable monarch, and the breeding of habit, given the opposing definitions of good and evil rulers, surely implies that they are as easily hardened to tradition as cautious to individual circumstances. His conclusion, then, is a stark one when withdrawn from its conventional context, and itself unconventional in the irony it harbors: "you shall be as you be" (p. 57).

In time, however, and perhaps also at the suggestion or under the tutelage of Languet, Sidney and the intellectual circle about him began to show considerable interest not merely in antique historians like Thucydides but in the contemporary, radical Protestant historians and political theorists such as George Buchanan and, perhaps to a lesser degree, Bodin. This too we know from his 1580 letter to Robert: "For the method of writing Historie, Boden hath written at large, yow may reade him and gather out of many wordes some matter" (*Prose Works* 3:130).

He also urges Robert to set down a "table of remembrance" of his reading, for a particular and pragmatic end: "So likewise in politick matters, and such a little table yow may easelie make, wherwith I would have yow ever joyne the historicall part, which is only the example of some stratageme, or good cownsaile, or such like" (3:132).

This was a lesson Philip Sidney himself would follow more and more. Using his privileged position, Sidney suggests to the queen, as he suggests more generally in the *Arcadia,* that royalty should exercise to know virtue and wisdom just as men (according to the *Defence of Poetry*) do. Although the queen ruled through reinforcing hierarchies which she alone headed—through appointing and approving nobility who vowed their obedience to her; through appointments to high office, the royal household, embassies, military commands, expeditions, and regional jurisdictions; through the granting of patents, economic sanctions, and trade restrictions; through the statute of artificers regulating the crafts and proclamations touching on the behavior, food, and dress of her people generally; and, finally, through church appointments, the Book of Common Prayer, and state-written homilies read at required church services—she nevertheless remained, always, in need of the trust and respect her subjects paid her.[11] "The power wielded by such a monarch," Steven Mullaney has written, "the power she was invested with, was to a large degree invested in her by the gaze of her subjects; the royal image and identity were not wholly at the Queen's command, but in part the projection and hence the product of those subjects. . . . She ruled not so much by 'the arduous and constant wooing of the body politic,' as Wallace MacCaffrey once suggested, as by inducing it to woo her."[12] Although we lack any firm evidence on her response to Sidney's "Letter," yet we do know from countless occasions that she would brook no opposition to her carefully regulated society. When Sidney challenged the earl of Oxford to a duel, her wrath was immediate. The sympathetic Greville records that "the Queen, who saw that by the loss, or disgrace of either, she could gain nothing, presently undertakes Sir *Philip;* and (like an excellent Monarch) lays before him the difference in degree between Earls, and Gentlemen; the respect inferiors ought to their superiors; and the necessity in Princes to maintain their own creations, as degrees descending between the peoples licentiousness, and the anoynted Soveraignty of Crowns: how the Gentlemans neglect of the Nobility taught the Peasant to insult upon both" (pp. 67–68). Sidney's aging Continental mentor Hubert Languet gives him a similar warning: "one who wishes to live free of scorn in the courts of mighty kings must govern his emotions, swallow many vexations, very carefully avoid all motives of controversy, and cultivate those men in whose hands supreme power lies."[13] Such enforced patience is a growing concern by book 3 of the old *Arcadia,* where the heroes privately withhold their identities (as in the extended scene with Mopsa) and publicly withhold political action (when Cleophilia denies Basilius) as if here, too, Sidney wishes to work out the means and consequences of undesired but discreet or expedient silence.

Sidney's temper putatively arose when Oxford cast slurs on the Puritan faction at court, the faction identified with Sidney's uncle, the earl of Leicester, with Sir Francis Walsingham, later his father-in-law, and with Sidney himself. As for the queen's wrath, it doubtless arose from her growing fears that Tudor Protestants were fast establishing a hierarchy of their own that in time would threaten and perhaps even rival hers. A decade before, in the early months of 1570, Thomas Cartwright had delivered his famous lectures at Cambridge, in which his exegesis of the Acts of the Apostles gave biblical direction to congregational polity for Tudor churches. By 1576, Elizabeth's own Archbishop Edmund Grindal was circulating a letter from Canterbury favoring preaching exercises, or prophesyings, which the queen saw as a "vehicle of subversion."[14] While such a mounting Puritan force helped the queen in keeping Mary Stuart off the throne and the Irish, the Spanish, and the Guise faction in France all at bay, they also swung her closer to open political or military alliance with the besieged Netherlands and added to the influence and power of Leicester, whose family had already tried unsuccessfully to take the throne under Edward. We must not forget that while the queen showed an ascertainable fondness for Leicester, he nevertheless, according to Lawrence Stone,

> has been described as "the keystone of the whole edifice of Elizabethan Puritanism." As the leader of the moderate Puritan group in the Privy Council, he could block moves to persecute his protégés, and could get them out of prison; he could see that their books passed the censor, and as Chancellor of the University he could find them jobs at Oxford. In 1564 he is said to have stopped the Privy Council from authorizing Parker's Advertisements. He was the patron not only of Field and Cartwright, but also of scholars and educators like Laurence Humphrey, the Puritan president of Magdalen College at Oxford, and William Fulke, the Puritan Master of Pembroke Hall at Cambridge.[15]

In addition, Leicester was the primary patron of Rowland Hall, printer of the Geneva Bible; and it was no accident that Arthur Golding dedicated to Leicester his translations of Calvin and Mornay. Wallace T. MacCaffrey adds that "from 1572 onwards Leicester became increasingly drawn away from domestic Protestantism to the larger international concerns of the reformed religion. More and more he was consumed by the ambition to play a grand role on this international stage. Most immediately he pressed Elizabeth to intervene in the Low Countries."[16] Walsingham, too, had been an exceptionally strong advocate of international Puritan activities since his days as a Marian exile in Geneva.

Family ties and political associations were thus sufficient to bring Sidney into alliance with the growing Protestant movement both at home and abroad. But if he also saw poetry flowing out of history, clarifying it and in turn shaping it, as I have been arguing for the *Arcadia,* then there are deeper philosophical reasons as well. For one thing, the repression of the new religion by the old, beginning with the massacre on Saint Bartholomew's Day in 1572, which he witnessed—James M. Osborn thinks he may even have made the rounds the following morning to see at closer range the Huguenot dead (p. 70)—must have looked very much like the tyranny of evil rulers he would record in the *Arcadia.* And tyranny had been a subject for Sidney since he took up Aristotle's *Politics* at Oxford. Jan Van Dorsten, to cite one other example, notes "a slightly erratic quotation" from Seneca's *Oedipus* concerning tyranny that appears in both the *Defence* and *Certain Sonnets* and adds that this "powerful summary of tyranny's self-destructiveness appears to have been very much in Sidney's mind—presumably in the months when he was doomed to be 'idly' looking on 'our Neighbours' fires,' discussing poetry and politics and writing the *Arcadia.*"[17]

And he had much to think about, much of it in his own country. The queen had mounted a serious campaign against Puritans following the *Admonition to Parliament* in 1570; by October 1573 she passed a royal proclamation ordering the suppression of all "contentious sects and disquietness" and then appointed "special commissions to ensure compliance."[18] Such increasing restriction by the Tudor monarchy must have reminded Sidney of the tyranny he had witnessed under the Guises during his grand tour of the Continent, when he was eighteen, and giving much added force to the memory was Leicester's increasing anxiety regarding the Spanish threat to the Protestants' cherished liberty in the Low Countries. Consciences seemed everywhere to be bent or threatened by political will. As a direct consequence, the revised *Arcadia*—begun surely by 1584—examines in detail many forms of moral and physical repression in the acts of Erona, Andromana, and Artaxia (notably, all women) as well as Plexirtus, Anaxius, and Zoilus. Sidney seems desirous here to show how characters potentially more sympathetic—such as Gynecia, who falls passionately in love, or Cecropia, who feels betrayed by her brother and is protective of her son—can fall to evil thoughts and actions in such a world. Tyranny is not only ugly; it is, like the Thucydidean plague, contagious. We can measure with some accuracy Sidney's concern and despair when, even in the original version of *Arcadia,* in the patently transparent character of Philisides, he tells the story of mankind as an allegory of tyranny. In a recent study centered on this poem, Martin N. Raitere relates it to God's warning to an apostate Israel. "This shall be the maner of the king that shall reigne over you: he will take your sonnes, and appoint them to his charets, and to be his horsemen. . . . He will also take your daughters . . . And he will take your fields, and your vineyards, and your best olive trees . . . the chief of your yong men, and your asses, and put them to his work. He will take the tenth of your sheep, and ye shall be his servants. And ye shall cry out at that day, because of your king, whome ye have chosen you, and the Lord will not heare you at that day (1 Sam. 8:11–18)."[19] Calvin made much of this text in his gloss to the Geneva Bible used throughout England by the Puritans, while Sidney—first in his discussion of Basilius's surrender of the throne in book 1 of the old *Arcadia* and later in Zelmane's address to the rebellious mob in the revised *Arcadia* (bk. 2, chap. 25)— likewise discusses surrender or mob rule as other forms of apostasy. As for tyranny, Sidney centers and ends on that, by making Euarchus's absolute application of Arcadian law the subtlest and thus the most attractive and dangerous tyranny of all.

It is, in fact, in this matter of law that Sidney's firm advocacy of liberty and Puritanism come through most strongly. We have paid too little attention to the fact that the *Arcadia* was written during the strong conflict in England between chancery and the courts of common law as they vied for judicial supremacy: chancery even overturned judgments by courts of common law on occasion, if illegally, and such reversals were becoming more and more frequent by Sidney's day. From what must have seemed time immemorial, common law upheld the monarchy, as Charles E. Phelps showed us long ago.[20] Common law rested on two key principles: strict adherence to precedent and the uniform enforcement of the letter of the law. Over centuries, unyielding reliance on precedent gave to common law a stability that guaranteed consistent enactment of institutional and monarchical policies, since judges feared that any exception or deviation would result either in contradiction or ambiguity that would undermine the very validity of the law. Regardless of circumstances, judges applied a law—imposed might be a better term— with equal definition and force. As Sir William Holdworth has it, "narrow-minded judges, quibbling and overapprehensive, gradually surrounded each action with a mass of requirements of form. Each common law action had its own precedents, and the judges refused to admit a case was good in law if it did not rigorously meet the construction of the writ and the conditions laid down by precedent."[21]

In sharp contrast, chancery supported the individual application of the law and the individual determination of justice by closely examining surrounding, even mitigating, circumstances. It involved its own term— equity—a principle that caused the strictness of traditional justice to be tempered by mercy; the Court of Chancery, in fact, was popularly called the "Court of Conscience," according to William Harrison in his *Description of England* (1587).[22] Nor was this misleading: the Court of Chancery, unlike courts of common law, had decidedly Christian roots, going back to the ecclesiastical appointments to the Lord Chancellorship first made by Henry III in the thirteenth century. The custom was interrupted in 1532 when Wolsey, as archbishop, appointed the secular statesman Thomas More to the position, but the ecclesiastical tradition was so strong that it continued to operate into Sidney's day and, beyond that, well into Francis Bacon's. Chancery's jurisdiction, in fact, was at first little more than the power to intervene in cases of royal interest in which the harshness of the law necessitated the employment of equity to favor the crown itself; but chancery came over the centuries to be thought— however accurately—to be the arm of justice affiliated with the church. By the time of the *Arcadia,* chancery had become, by natural extension, the means by which Puritans insisted on individual legal justice compatible with and congruent to the individual consciences they proclaimed for the practice of religion. (It is just this distinction between unalterable law and its literal interpretation in courts of common law and the explosively multiplying cases of equity, of individual exception and mercy in chancery, that is Shakespeare's basis for the great debate in the trial scene of *The Merchant of Venice.*)

The natural and progressively active collusion between chancery and Puritanism can be seen to be anticipated very early indeed, in Christopher St. Germain's *Doctor and Student* (1523, 1530), a humanist apology for English law printed partly in Latin and partly in English "for the profyte of the multytude" (1530 ed., p. 177). St. Germain introduced the word "conscience" into the English legal vocabulary as that divine spark "in the midst of every reasonable soul, as a light whereby he may discern and know what he ought to do, and what he ought not to do."[23] The conscience was therefore a kind of shorthand for equity itself as St. Germain popularly defined it: "Equytye is a ryghtwyse that consideryth all the pertyculer cyrcumstaunces of the dede the whiche also is temperyd with the swetnes of mercye. . . . And the wyse man sayth: be not ouer moch ryghtwyse for the extreme ryghtwysenes is extreme wronge (as who sayth of thou take all that the wordes of the law gyueth the thou shalte somtyme do agaynst the lawe)" (pp. 96–97).

St. Germain's treatise was supplanted in time by *The Commentaries, or*

Reports of Edmund Plowden (1571 et seq.) and a subsequent work by Edward Hake, *Epieikeia: A Dialogue on Equity in Three Parts*. "In the said highe Courte the decrees . . . sholde be deryued vpon conscience, euen the conscience of the judge there, directed with all good circumstances of facts, which shoulde be euermore accompanied with comiseration and pitye," Hake notes; "No more can the wordes of the lawe without *Equity* to dyrecte yt to the righte sense thereof be said to be the lawe then the bodye of a man withoute reason to directe yt in the actions of a man maye be said to be a man" ("To the Reader," p. 2, 12). In this way, equity was analogized, by saying that it fulfilled the body and practice of common law, to Calvin's notion that the New Testament fulfilled the meaning and prophecies of the Old (*Institutes* 4.8.7); in the language of *The Merchant of Venice,* Portia's Nazarene interpretation extends, modifies, and reifies the law of "a very Daniel." So popular did the legal notion of equity become as an analogy to the Christian concept of mercy—it will be almost commonplace by the time of Spenser's Mercilla as well as Shakespeare's Portia[24]—that as the case loads in chancery increased to staggering numbers (by the time of Sir Francis Bacon, 16,000 cases were pending at one time), the Court of Requests also began to take up those alleged to involve equity.

The Protestant cause led by Leicester, Walsingham, and Sidney, then, found a means through Elizabethan law and the Tudor court system to ground a rival hierarchy of enforced power of conscience that did, in fact, directly challenge Elizabeth's traditional authority through the absolute law of the monarchy. Yet what may have seemed not only threatening but revolutionary to her would have seemed to Sidney, steeped in classical learning, as with the equity espoused by Pericles in Thucydides' portrait of Athens, a tradition long honored by the ancients. Among classical treatises on rule, some of which were studied at Oxford, law combined with equity was found in the "mixed state" of government discussed by Cicero and others. This form was, however, usually associated with Sparta (what Sidney terms Lacedemonia and what, using the syncopated Roman form, becomes Laconia in the *Arcadia*). It was this experimental form of government, often cited in opposition to the democracy of Athens but actually resembling Periclean Athens and the Roman republic, that became a popular subject of Tudor disputations, going back to principal sources in Polybius, Plato, and Plutarch.

> According to Plutarch, Sparta achieved stability with Lycurgus' institution of a senate, "which he made to have a regall power and equall authoritie with the Kings in matters of weight and importance, and it was (as Plato sayeth) to be the healthfull counterpease of the whole bodye of the Common weale." Before Lycurgus's institution of this

senate, Sparta was "ever wavering, sometime inclining to tyrannie, when the Kings were to mightie: and sometime to confusion, when the people would usurpe authoritie." Lycurgus' reform thus created a *système équilibré*, holding in peaceful, temperate mixture the three sure kinds of government recognized by the classical theorists, with the senate (the Gerousia or council of elders) representing aristocracy, the *ephors* (magistrates appointed from the Spartan community specifically for the purpose of overseeing the kings) representing democracy, and the curious Spartan institution of double kingship representing monarchy. Since the "kinds" of government, apart from the executive, corresponded to the two principal social classes, Lycurgus's prescription guaranteed social harmony. Here in ancient Sparta, then, was a historical illustration of the virtues of the "mixed state." In such a state, opposed interests so balance themselves as to prevent any single one from usurping power. Since no one of the three different loci can, at least in theory, entirely escape the limitations posed by the other two, the rule of law is ensured—the rule of reason, that is to say, as opposed to the rule of some arbitrary interest, will, or class. [25]

Such laws as result closely resemble those urged by Plato in his trilogy on government (*Republic, Statesman, Laws*), while such harmony of balanced characteristics comes close to the concept of the Aristotelian mean (the *Ethics* and *Politics* were meant by Aristotle to be conceived as a single work). It may well be just such a state as this that Sidney saw the staunchly Protestant William of Orange fashioning for the Low Countries. In the *Arcadia,* at any rate, Laconia is the scene where the Helots gain their freedom, where Pyrocles and Musidorus are reunited, and where Clitophon is set free in the revised text (1.5–7). It is also where the first important transformation takes place in the later version, for it is here that Parthenia's scarred face is wondrously cured and her beauty wondrously returned by the physician to Queen Helen. So poetry can merge with politics.

III

When we place this variety of concerns alongside the two texts of the *Arcadia,* the poem to which Sidney devoted his greatest attention, we can see a progression of thought that seems accurately to register his increasing concerns with classical and contemporary history. The old *Arcadia,* which Jean Robertson thinks was "nearly completed" by the end of 1580, [26] announces the primary concern at the outset: "there is nothing so certain as our continual uncertainty" (p. 5). What follows is a debate between Basilius and his subaltern, Philanax, about right rule. Philanax proposes that "wisdom and virtue be the only destinies appointed to man to follow." These "guides" that "cannot fail" point "so direct a way of proceeding as prosperity must necessarily ensue" (p. 7). Basilius is concerned, however, with the determining powers of fortune. "And would you, then, . . . that in change of fortune I shall not change my determination, as we do our apparel according to the air, and as the ship doth her course with the wind?" (p. 9). But Philanax remains resolute and inflexible. He still advocates "a constant virtue, well settled, [is] little subject unto [change]"; "in great necessity" would he allow alteration and then only actions that are moderate and "well proportioned" (p. 9). The debate concludes in a stalemate, much as the historians of Sidney's *Defence of Poetry* were placed in stalemate with the moral philosophers until poetry chanced along: "'Yet the reeds stand with yielding,' said the duke. 'And so are they but reeds, most worthy Prince,' said Philanax, 'but the rocks stand still and are rocks'" (p. 9). A few pages later Musidorus notes an "alteration" in Pyrocles, who is accused of allowing his "mind [to] fall asleep" when he too wishes to retreat from the world of action to seek a "solitariness, the sly enemy that doth most separate a man from well doing" (pp. 13, 14). As Richard C. McCoy, whose argument I have been following generally here,[27] states, Musidorus's main point underscores that of Philanax. "A mind well trained and long exercised in virtue, my sweet and worthy cousin, doth not easily change any course it once undertakes but upon well grounded and well weighed causes. . . . Even the very countenance and behaviour of such a man doth show forth images of the same constancy by maintaining the right harmony betwixt it and the inward good" (p. 13). Thus in the opening pages the main themes of the old *Arcadia* are plainly set forth. The work will parallel the public responsibilities of a king with the private responsibilities of a prince, in terms of solitude versus action, right thinking versus right doing. It will test the need for constancy, moreover, and the virtue of flexibility, of "bending with the wind."

Such a summary will accommodate the first three-fifths of the old *Arcadia* and may also serve for the fourth book as well. But clearly, by the fifth book it will no longer do. Here Euarchus attempts to harmonize wise thought and just action through his enforcement of common law— of the precedents and strict rules of Arcadia. But such judgment misses the mark because Euarchus takes apparent truths (such as the death of Basilius and the guilt of Pyrocles and Musidorus) as facts. Thus he is neither wise nor just in actuality. Once he is confronted with mitigating circumstances—his blood relationship to the two young men—he is unable to draw on the pliability of Basilius, which would allow change of heart and mind, and the rigid stability of Philanax, which had already grown tyrannical in tone and untruthful in statement. Sidney has set up the terms of his fiction so that they coincide precisely with the debate of common law over chancery. The equity which chancery advocates, which Euarchus cannot hear of, supports Basilius. It also accommodates all the facts—not simply the apparent facts—of *Arcadia 5*. Equity admits flexibility and change, but it does not deny justice and stability. Equity was, after all, what the Low Countries seemed to be struggling for, what Sidney's uncle Leicester would advocate, what his father was arguing as the best means of establishing plantations in Ireland, and what his own youthful talent at negotiation and diplomacy (as practiced during his grand tour) seemed to qualify him for best.

It follows that, because of this conclusion, Sidney decided to rewrite the *Arcadia*. We have testimony to this change of intention as a substantial and important one. After Sidney's unexpected death at Arnhem in 1586, Greville sent forth what Victor Skretkowicz, Jr., calls an "urgent plea to Walsingham [as Sidney's executor] to prevent publication of the romantic though well polished *Old Arcadia* and to substitute for it 'a correction of that old one don 4 or 5 years since wch he left in trust wth me whereof ther is no more copies, & fitter to be printed then the first wch is so cōmon.'"[28] Sidney's sister Mary, countess of Pembroke, agreed and, so far as we can now tell, destroyed what copies she could of the original. What they published, with great but justifiable pride, was the "new" *Arcadia* which is, in many indicative and decisive ways, a very different work. It begins with the disappearance of Urania—of the ideal—so as to leave shepherds and princes alike in a fallen world (already anticipating the original Euarchus). The revisions that follow talk not about "uncertainty," which no man can respond to adequately, but "disfigurement," which he can. "Disfigured minds" follow "disfigured" bodies and perspectives; from the modified ideal of Kalendar's home (doubtless based on Penshurst, linking Henry Sidney with Kalendar and not with Euarchus as once thought) to the war with the Helots and the long "captivity episode" of book 3, the new *Arcadia* traces the minds and actions of men and women who are thwarted in their plans or desires, who thwart others in turn, and who, among the worst of them, set out with vengeance to rid the world of opposition. The "disfigurement" of heroes posing as a shepherd and an Amazon is no longer a condition of the plot but a consequence of shortsightedness. They betray their stations and themselves to achieve their desires when, by book 5, their actual stations and selves will more than bring them what they seek. But the outer "disfigurement" of a Musidorus or a Pyrocles and the temporarily misplaced passions of a Gynecia or a Mopsa show the fallibility and foolishness of unrestraint rather than the criminal intention or evil instincts of the more tyrannical. They are curable—obviously so, next to the parade of tyrants in the revised book 2 or the unscrupulous behavior of Cecropia and even Amphialus in the revised book 3.

Nancy Lindheim has estimated that "the *New Arcadia,* while apparently retaining a dramatic structure for its main plot, weaves into this action hundreds of pages of episodic material" and that "for Books I and II, the added material alone exceeds the original by almost one-third."[29] But she too sees this not simply as amplification but as a rethinking, what she calls a "re-vision," "something substantially new" (p. 133). Here the Phrygian citizens revolt against "chiefe instruments of Tyrannie" (2.9), supported by Musidorus who demonstrates what McCoy calls "sophisticated political insights and principles" (p. 140). In other episodes added to book 2, the blind king of Paphlagonia, also symbolically "disfigured," misjudges his two sons; Plangus misjudges Andromana; and Pyrocles misjudges Dido. In book 3, Cecropia misjudges Amphialus, while the Knight of the Black Tomb is recognized by no one until her death. If these are all "uncertainties," they also all involve some sort of tyranny, some deep need for equity. Alongside such uncertainties, which persist unchecked in the old *Arcadia,* Sidney's revision adds the trust of the heroes and the faith of Pamela in something more stable, and these new concerns are made to look forward too to the denouement already conceived as the old *Arcadia* 5. (Pamela's theology is now decidedly Calvinistic.) Philoclea, too, is reconceived. As Lindheim remarks, "Though Sidney's basic conception of Philoclea as an example of innocence and natural virtue remains fairly constant, he reworks her character to give increased emphasis to the idea of self-knowledge" (p. 58). Even Basilius's emotional decision to besiege the castle of Amphialus, despite Kalendar's counsel to withdraw and Philanax's argument to seem ready to serve Amphialus's self-interest by offering him pardon, suggests a kind of humanity that might instruct Euarchus if he could only know it. For such are the very feelings that Euarchus lacks, as Sidney tells us. "The beholders . . . most of them, examining the matter by their own passions, thought Euarchus (as often extraordinary excellencies, not being rightly conceived, do rather offend than please) an obstinate-hearted man, and such a one, who being pitiless, his dominion must needs be insupportable" (p. 414). But of course Sidney so judges him, too. Euarchus's decision hews closely to the rules of deliberative oratory set forth in another classical text studied at Oxford and one we are told that Sidney began translating—Aristotle's *Rhetoric.* But we also find, there in the *Rhetoric,* this:

> It is equity to pardon human failings, and to look at the lawgiver and not to the law; to the spirit and not to the letter; to the intention and

not to the action; to the whole and not to the part; to the character of the actor in the long run and not in the present moment; to remember good rather than evil, and good that one has received rather than good that one has done; to bear being injured; to wish to settle a matter by words rather than by deeds; lastly, to prefer arbitration to judgment, for the arbitrator sees what is equitable, but the judge only the law, and for this an arbitrator was first appointed, in order that equity might flourish.[30]

Such a position, which Euarchus disavows, is the one that Zelmane sets forth in advising the rebels, and Pamela uses in confronting Cecropia, in the revised text of the *Arcadia*. Thus the solution to *Arcadia* as worked out in the original book 5 is reinforced and predicted in the revisions of the earlier books. The old book 5 still fits in the revision, if a bit disjointedly; Sidney did not feel constrained to complete the revision because, in a very real sense, he already had. In fact, it provided him sufficient grounds to take up arms for the Protestant cause in the Low Countries, at the queen's request and with the strong approval of the Dutch government.[31] So history and poetry came together to direct Sidney's actions as well as his right thinking and writing; and they account not only for much of his life but also for his unfortunate (and accidental) death.

History could thus function simultaneously in an untold number of ways for Sidney. His contemporary Richard Stanyhurst, the translator of Vergil, writes in Holinshed's *Chronicle* that history is "the marrow of reason, the creame of experience, the sap of wisdome, the pith of judgement, the libraries of knowledge, the kernell of policie, the unfoldresse of treacherie, the kalendar of time, the lanterne of truth, the life of memorie, the doctresse of behaviour, the register of antiquitie, the trumpet of chivalrie."[32] In such a stunning but defensible catalog, we can now locate most of the ways Sidney's contemporaries could have—and doubtless did—read the revised *Arcadia*. It was a contemporary epic (despite its settings) that translated the antique past into the present's most pressing needs through the medium of verisimilar history implying moral philosophy.

Another historian contemporary with Sidney—and one related to him through family marriage—was William Camden, a "great man," Herschel Baker writes, "whose erudition was regarded as a national resource" (p. 87). Indeed, like Sidney, whose *Arcadia* would be regularly read for more than two centuries, Camden too had a great effect with his *Britannia* (1586 et seq.). According to Baker, "the six decades separating the publication of Camden's *Brittania* . . . and the start of Clarendon's work on *The History of the Rebellion* were productive not only of a staggering bulk of historical writing in both prose and verse but also of a gradual transformation in the historian's own conception of his function and procedures" (p. 17). Surely Sidney had much to do with that transformation: the *Arcadia* stands at the fountainhead of this revival of interest in history, remaining throughout not only its most extraordinary poetic expression but, quite possibly, also its most profound.

Notes

1. Herschel Baker, *The Race of Time* (Toronto: University of Toronto Press, 1967), p. 16.
2. Sir Philip Sidney, "Correspondence," in *Prose Works,* ed. Albert Feuillerat (1912; reprint, Cambridge: Cambridge University Press, 1962), 3:130–31; my emphasis. Further references are cited in the text.
3. Thelma N. Greenfield, *The Eye of Judgment: Reading the "New Arcadia"* (Lewisburg, Pa.: Bucknell University Press, 1982), pp. 124–25.
4. Thucydides, *History of the Peloponnesian War,* tr. Rex Warner (1954; reprint, Harmondsworth, England: Penguin Books, 1983), p. 147. Further passages are from this translation.
5. Peter R. Pouncey, *The Necessities of War: A Study of Thucydides' Pessimism* (New York: Columbia University Press, 1980), p. 89.
6. Quoted by Alan Kendall, *Robert Dudley, Earl of Leicester* (London: Cassell, Ltd. 1980), p. 15.
7. Sir Philip Sidney, quoted by J. E. Neale, *Elizabeth I and Her Parliaments* (London: Jonathan Cape 1957), 2:434.
8. Sir Philip Sidney, *The Lady of May,* ed. Katherine Duncan-Jones, in Sidney's *Miscellaneous Prose,* ed. Duncan-Jones and Jan Van Dorsten (Oxford: Clarendon Press, 1973), p. 22.
9. Sir Philip Sidney, "The Four Foster Children of Desire" (1581), ed. Jean Wilson in *Entertainments for Elizabeth I* (Woodbridge, England: D. S. Brewer, 1980), p. 76.
10. *Sir Fulke Greville's Life of Sir Philip Sidney,* with introduction by Nowell Smith (Oxford: Oxford University Press, 1907), p. 15. Further references are cited in the text.
11. For details, see Lawrence Stone, *The Crisis of the Aristocracy, 1558–1641,* abr. ed. (New York: Oxford University Press, 1967), pp. 18–29; Alan G. R. Smith, *The Government of Elizabethan England* (London: Edward Arnold, 1967), pp. 81–82; J. J. Scarisbrick, *The Reformation and the English People* (Oxford: Basil Blackwell 1984), p. 173.
12. Steven Mullaney, "Brothers and Others, or the Art of Alienation" in *Cannibals, Witches, and Divorce: Estranging the Renaissance,* ed. Marjorie Garber (Baltimore: Johns Hopkins University Press, 1987), p. 74.
13. James M. Osborn, *Young Philip Sidney, 1572–1577* (New Haven: Yale University Press, 1972), p. 296.

14. Claire Cross, *Church and People, 1450–1660: The Triumph of the Laity in the English Church* (London: Fontana Paperbacks, 1976), p. 147.

15. Stone, *Crisis of the Aristocracy*, pp. 340–41.

16. Wallace T. MacCaffrey, *Queen Elizabeth and the Making of Policy, 1572–1588* (Princeton: Princeton University Press, 1981), p. 440.

17. Jan Van Dorsten, introduction to *A Defence of Poetry* in Sidney's *Miscellaneous Prose*, p. 60.

18. D. M. Loades, *Politics and the Nation, 1450–1600: Obedience, Resistance, and Public Order* (London: Fontana Paperbacks, 1979), p. 292.

19. Martin N. Raitere, *"Faire Bitts": Sir Philip Sidney and Renaissance Political Theory* (Pittsburgh: Duquesne University Press, 1984), p. 74.

20. Charles E. Phelps, *Falstaff and Equity* (Boston: Houghton, Mifflin & Co., 1901); see esp. Appendix A.

21. Sir William Holdworth, *A History of English Law* (Boston: Little, Brown & Co., 1922), 2:326.

22. William Harrison, *The Description of England, 1587,* ed. Georges Edelen (Ithaca: Cornell University Press, 1968), p. 70.

23. Stuart E. Prall, "The Development of Equity in Tudor England," *American Journal of Legal History* 8 (1964): 4.

24. The definitive texts for these matters remain F. W. Maitland, *Equity,* ed. A. H. Chaytor and W. J. Whittaker (Cambridge: Cambridge University Press, 1936); and W. J. Jones, *The Elizabethan Court of Chancery* (Oxford: Oxford University Press, 1967). *The Faerie Queene,* book 5, is primarily concerned with "That part of Iustice, which is Equity" (5.7.34); cf. Proem, st. 10. Spenser was himself clerk of the Court of Chancery in Ireland. Useful discussions may be found in M. Pauline Parker, *The Allegory of The Faerie Queene* (Oxford: Oxford University Press, 1960), pp. 202–27; W. Nicholas Knight, "The Narrative Unity of Book 5 of *The Faerie Queene*: 'That Part of Justice Which Is Equity,'" *RES,* n.s. 21 (1970): 267–94; Angus Fletcher, *The Prophetic Moment: An Essay on Spenser* (Chicago: University of Chicago Press, 1971), esp. pp. 276–87. Equity is the proper contextualization for Portia's speech on mercy:

> The quality of mercy . . . becomes
> The throned monarch better than his crown.
> His sceptre shows the force of temporal power
>
> . . . .
> But mercy is above this sceptred sway,
> It is enthroned in the hearts of kings,
> It is an attribute to God himself.
> (*The Merchant of Venice,* 4.1.180–91).

25. Raitere, *"Faire Bitts",* p. 41.

26. Sir Philip Sidney, *The Countess of Pembroke's Arcadia (The Old Arcadia),* ed. Jean Robertson (Oxford: Oxford University Press, 1973), p. xix. All citations to the text are to this edition.

27. Richard C. McCoy, *Sir Philip Sidney: Rebellion in Arcadia* (New Brunswick, N.J.: Rutgers University Press, 1979), pp. 41–42, 53.

28. Victor Skretkowicz, Jr., "Building Sidney's Reputation: Texts and Editors of the *Arcadia*" in *Sir Philip Sidney: 1586 and the Creation of a Legend*, ed. Jan Van Dorsten, Dominic Baker-Smith, and Arthur F. Kinney (Leiden: A. J. Brill/University of Leiden, 1986), p. 116.

29. Nancy Lindheim, *The Structures of Sidney's "Arcadia"* (Toronto: University of Toronto Press, 1982), p. 132.

30. Aristotle, *Rhetoric*, 1.13; 1347b; quoted ibid., p. 159. Lindheim is the only other scholar who has related the classical notion of equity to the *Arcadia*, although her argument is different from mine. See also Aristotle in the *Nicomachean Ethics:* "The equitable is just, but not the legally just but a correction of legal justice. The reason is that all law is universal but about some things it is not possible to make a universal statement which is correct. . . . The error is not in the law nor in the legislator but in the nature of the thing, since the matter of practical affairs is of this kind from the start" (1137b5–1137b30).

31. I develop the case at length in "Intimations of Mortality: Sidney's Journey to Flushing and Zutphen," in *Sir Philip Sidney*, Van Dorsten, Baker-Smith, and Kinney, pp. 125–48.

32. Quoted by Baker, *Race of Time*, p. 16. I would like here to acknowledge my gratitude to Herschel Baker for intoducing me to a number of crucial issues in sixteenth-century English thought and literature.

Spenser, Bacon, and the Myth of Power

I

All ages and all nations have their political myths, shared beliefs about a society's origins and purpose, about the behavior that is expected or tolerated in its leaders, and about the character of its enemies.[1] A striking feature of the political world of the sixteenth century is the attempt of European rulers to control these beliefs by manipulating classical myth into a political vocabulary. One need only think of the triumphs and romances of the Emperor Maximilian, the masques of the Medici court, the royal entries of the Valois kings, or the various portrayals of Queen Elizabeth as Venus, Diana, and Astraea in Spenser's *Faerie Queene*.

The Renaissance humanist drawn to the active life inevitably found himself involved in these practices. He might hope to serve his prince as historian or moralist, deepening the prince's understanding of law and government with the examples of history and guiding his conscience with the precepts of ethics. But more often, the humanist was a mythographer, justifying and glorifying the deeds of the prince with the poetical trappings of classical fable. I want to look in this essay at some ways in which Renaissance humanists were caught up in fables—to suggest that they were both manipulators of political myth and were manipulated by it, and further, that they found power to be a myth, that is, something part verbal and part physical, alluring and elusive. For in the end, the wielders of power turned out to be the Machiavellians, and the humanist mythographers were cast into the role of court flatterers.

How did a poetic humanist like Edmund Spenser negotiate his conflicting impulses to offer advice or flattery, to chastize or eulogize the mighty? What role did the tension between moral aspiration and political necessity have in the genesis of the complex languages of Renaissance humanism? Should a man of learning proclaim justice or secure himself a place at the table—or do both at once? Beyond these questions, one must ask where the complex languages broke down, allowing advice to separate off from flattery, the political from the mythical, the practical from the poetic. One must ask how it became possible to imagine that learning really made one *unfit* for power, that poetry was at once impractical and sycophantic, and that some other language of political analysis was, as its polar opposite, the natural speech of those like Francis Bacon who saw reality as it was and kept their prosaic hands on the levers of power.[2]

By 1600, there had emerged within humanism two quite distinct languages about power. From Machiavelli and Guicciardini flowed a new form of political and historical discourse, rooted in the humanistic study of Livy and Tacitus, but hostile to or cynical about the humanist's ethical claims. To the practitioners of this new discourse, whom I will call *politiques,* the oratorical and poetical moralizing of the humanists seemed like unrealistic and old-fashioned posturing. From the poetic humanists still came those epics, eulogies, masques, and hymns in which princes are gods inspiring awe in their subjects and terror in their enemies. Theirs was a mythological discourse that increasingly seemed devoted to the "illusion of power," not to its substance.

Both political and mythological discourse have within the past dozen years been the objects of a sophisticated analysis that has uncovered the contradictions and enabling assumptions of Renaissance humanist ideology. While the earlier work of Hans Baron and Felix Gilbert testifies to the continuous interest that Renaissance political and historical discourse has held for historians of humanist thought, two books, J. G. A. Pocock's *The Machiavellian Moment* (1975) and Quentin Skinner's *Foundations of Modern Political Thought* (1978), stand in their different ways as the signposts of a renewed rhetorical approach. They shift from a focus on content to a focus on form and context, demonstrating that political discourse is not innocent of the devices of humanist learning. Simultaneously, Stephen Orgel's *The Illusion of Power: Political Theater in the English Renaissance* (1975) initiated a new wave of study of the political dimensions of Renaissance literature, even as it stands as the culmination of the earlier work of Orgel himself, Roy Strong, Frances Yates, and D. J. Gordon.

This new analysis of the illusion of power has uncovered the ways that poets use their learning to gild the power of princes and has revealed the propagandistic purposes that such sycophantic shows and illusions served in masking the origins and structures of power. In the process, it has had to skirt the dangers both of overestimating and of underestimating its subject. On the one hand, the metaphoric power of masques, rites, and festivities can seem so total as virtually to supplant the power of economic forces, standing armies, and bureaucratic intrigue. The danger here is of accepting the illusion's own description of the power structure and its claim to be the sole language of power. Metaphoric power becomes the only power, and the poetic language of masque, epic, and eulogy becomes a monologue from above. A more plausible view of poetic language is provided by Mikhail Bakhtin's notion of "heteroglossia," that within the language of an authoritarian ideology other voices may be heard, some subversive, some just different from the monologue of power.[3] Hence Stephen Orgel in a recent essay finds that the relationship of stage and crown in Renaissance England was "a complex mixture of intimacy and danger," and that whether a performance "constituted celebration or satire lay ultimately . . . in the eye and mind of the beholder."[4] Orgel now recognizes, in effect, a self-subverting element within the illusion of power that he delineated in his earlier work.

The Bakhtinian model is a partial solution, but it is still curiously formalist, leaving the heterodox and the authoritarian coupled within language. It tends toward a paradox dominated by the polar terms of authority and subversion, echoing perhaps a simplistic myth of modern politics and creating a duality that is almost as flattering to the central authority as an acknowledgment of total sway. To break out of the prison house, one must look beyond heterodox language to heterodox power, as Orgel hints in his gesture toward the beholder. One must move, that is, to a view of the power structure that gets behind the totalizing picture of the political myth to the network of local forces operating in any particular situation. This move in effect traces the shift from early Foucault to late Foucault, from the totalizing structure of the *episteme* to the demolition of such totalizing structures in *The History of Sexuality.*

This move from language to power confronts us with the second danger, of treating language *merely* as illusion, in contrast to "real" power, whether of money or of the sword. It is tempting to think that our critical analyses see through the mask of language and reveal the naked truth about authority. But there is no end to the illusion: the realm of action beyond language is understood only through more language.[5] The money changers, the politicians, and the military all have their ways of talking—indeed, it is in the Renaissance that they find their voices, which the political historians have long explored. As much as poets, they talk about power, and even their power is partly verbal.

Spenser's England was not yet a centralized and homogenized state, but rather several estates with an infinite gradation of "place" and prece-

dence. With those various estates and places come the various interests
and the various languages of power that are used by those who, like
Spenser, seek to pursue their own interests, on an individual or even a
class basis, without having to pay the cost in blood of challenging the
entire structure. An adequate approach to the subject requires a complication of the notion of "heteroglossia." Within any local network of
power, many groups may contend, each with its own language of power,
with each language containing its own nuances and diverse voices. The
struggle for power is both a struggle of groups and a struggle over the
definition of power, as each language provides an image of the nature of
power, within which only its native speakers can adequately perform.
Historical changes in the wielding of power can be described through the
apparent dominance or inadequacy of competing languages as much as
through changes in economic activity or constitutional structures (these
last two being themselves the hypostases of political languages). Hence,
while political systems may have many languages that are clearly heterodox, it is unusual for linguistic authority to be so monolithic that there is
only one orthodoxy. Rather, there may be—especially in the slippery
world of Renaissance and Reformation Europe—several languages in between, each proclaiming its own authority while preserving the power
to subvert the claims to orthodoxy of its rivals.

The breakup of humanist discourse in the sixteenth century into the
discourse of myth and the discourse of Machiavelli marks the creation of
two such competing groups[6] employing competing languages of power.
In those competing languages inhere two rival concepts of the operation
of power: power derived from an originating source, such as God or
justice or history, and power derived from the command of the technology of statecraft. Both, as I have said, have humanistic origins, although
the second increasingly (and still in modern practice) denies that origin.
They are not different *kinds* of language, since both employ the full range
of linguistic resources, from poetic metaphor to formal logic. They are
like regional dialects that become separate speeches as their peoples lose
contact with one another. As they do so, one group moves to the center
of power, and one to the margins.

The process of sorting out the languages of myth and Realpolitik, and
of repositioning them within European culture, was a long one, already
begun when More wrote his *Utopia* and not yet finished when Milton
wrote *Paradise Lost*. Most writers of the period cannot be simply relegated to one sphere or the other; they struggle with the residual entangle-
ment of the political and the mythical, and with the pressure to pull the
two apart. And they struggle at the same time with the various roles that
these languages permit and create for them. Hence it is not surprising

that a poet like Spenser should write both epic poetry in the *Faerie Queene* and political analysis in the *View of the Present State of Ireland,* or that the two modes should be infected by one another. Even Francis Bacon, who in virtually every aspect of his career seems to embody the new ruling technocracy, found himself compelled to confront the political dimensions of myth. In *De sapientia veterum* (*The Wisdom of the Ancients*) Bacon offers a defense of humanistic political mythography against the attacks of the politiques and a disclosure of the lessons that myth can offer to the astute prince and the subtle courtier.

Why should Bacon of all people compose such a book? A provocative answer was suggested by Charles Lemmi in 1933. Lemmi traces Bacon's frequent borrowings from the sixteenth-century mythological hand-books, especially Natalis Comes. The result is to erode the image of Bacon as a modern man of science and place him beside Edmund Spenser as one of the last medieval poets.

> Spenser is frequently declared to stand at the threshold of the Renaissance: looking forward, yet half-turning to listen to the voice of the mediaeval past. Bacon stands beside him, and one reason for his wealth of picturesque symbolism is that he also has his ear turned to the past. . . . Beside the picturesque confusion of [Spenser's] mediaeval romance you may see the perverse ingeniousness of [Bacon's] scholastic classification; beside mysticism, mysticism; beside deep piety, deep piety; beside a vision, a vision. . . . The poet and the essayist both breathe the spirit of a great enthusiasm; both speak a gorgeous language, rich with images and melodies that the age of disenchantment was not to know. *The Wisdom of the Ancients* is not *The Faerie Queene,* but we shall not understand it if we think of it as something very different.[7]

Lemmi's characterization of Bacon and Spenser partakes of a late Victorian political myth in which the poetic imagination is celebrated precisely because it is fantastic and visionary, and hence offers an escape from the industrial iron age of disenchantment. Lemmi projects the present radical split between imagination and technology back onto its earliest stages, escaping from the mystique of practicality into the countermystique of antimodernist impracticality.

Yet Lemmi's argument deserves attention for the ways in which it is right as well as for the ways in which it is wrong. Bacon is indeed far more caught up in the thought of his predecessors than he ever lets on, and *De sapientia veterum* is indeed like Spenser's *Faerie Queene*—not, I would argue, in its medievalness, but because both Spenser and Bacon share the original aspiration of the Renaissance humanist to bring classical wisdom and poetic imagination to bear on modern political and military problems. Within the problematics of the interpretation of myth, each found a key to the relationship of learning to politics. Each desires no less than to combine the insight of a Machiavelli or Guicciardini with the fabulous manner of a Vergil or Ovid. Their initial response to the fissures opening between politics and poetry was to attempt to speak across the gaps. As dual discourses emerged, they sought to empower each form with the potentialities of the other, creating complex and hybrid myths of power. For Spenser, as for Bacon, poetic myth might indeed be a language of counsel that reminds the prince of her strength and warns her of its limits. Neither goal can be achieved by simple flattery or panegyric, or pompous moralizing. Poetic language must be analytical as much as it is celebratory, laying bare the basis of power and the ways—good or bad, successful or flawed—that it is wielded by the prince or by the poet.

For all their similarity, however, Bacon does not fully share Spenser's assurance in the effectiveness of mythic analysis, for Bacon's treatise is an astute critique of the limits to our knowledge of the shadowy age of fable. In questioning the origins of myth and the correct mode of its interpretation, Bacon reopens the problem of applying those interpretations to a modern culture. In the process, he directly attacks the counsels of the poets, whether ancient or modern, for failing to realize these limits and for leading men into vain delusion and folly. Only when he has subjected Spenser's mythological discourse to the criticism of the politiques does Bacon make a last attempt to reformulate it in Machiavellian terms. By such radical surgery he hopes to preserve it as a form of political analysis, but only at the cost of demoting it to the lesser seat of "wisdom" in a new realm whose chief counsel is empirical knowledge.

II

Both Bacon and Spenser did, after all, spend the better parts of their adult lives in public service. Spenser, the elder of the two, moved quickly from Cambridge to a series of secretaryships, first to the bishop of Rochester, then to the earl of Leicester, and in 1580 to Lord Grey de Wilton when Grey was appointed Lord Deputy in Ireland. This last was a good opportunity; Sir Henry Sidney's secretary, Edward Waterhouse, had been knighted and now sat on the Privy Council of Ireland. Within days of arriving, however, Spenser managed to offend Grey's predecessor, Lord Justice Pelham.[8] After Grey's recall, Spenser stayed on and moved up in the bureaucracy: from the clerkship of the Chancery Court to the deputy clerkship of the Council of Munster to the office of Sheriff of Cork.

Around 1596 he set out a detailed analysis and policy recommendation in his *View of the Present State of Ireland,* but neither Elizabeth nor any of her chief courtiers seemed inclined to back him. Bacon simultaneously was experiencing the queen's indifference, as Essex repeatedly failed to get him an office. Under King James, of course, Bacon's rise was swift, from King's Counsel to Lord Chancellor in fourteen years. Spenser, had he lived, could have had no such hopes from a monarch who had already made a diplomatic protest over the portrayal of his mother Mary in Book 5 of the *Faerie Queene.*[9]

Generally recognized as the most political—and perhaps the most intensely mythological—part of the work is Book 5, the Legend of Artegall, or Justice. There Spenser turns to the golden age to find an adequate image of the "discipline / Of vertue and of civill uses lore,"[10] since the empirical images of modern human conduct available to him in this present age are too corrupt, too mutable, to be useful models. Spenser interprets the ancient fables euhemeristically, describing how "those great Heroes got . . . / Their greatest glory, for their rightfull deedes, / And place deserved with the Gods on hy" (5.2.1). Despite this origin in a historical process, the fables work in the poem not as history but as a kind of law, a fixed pattern for human conduct, and law, Spenser says in the *View,* "ought to be like stony tables, plain, steadfast, and unmoveable."[11]

Invoking the law, Spenser breaks it, by not binding himself to the received text of the fable. He takes an Orphic liberty to recreate the myths through a subtle and nearly invisible process of selection and adaptation. Even in recounting the fall from the golden age that justifies his use of fable, he silently reworks his source in Ovid.

> For from the golden age, that first was named,
>   It's now at earst become a stonie one;
>   And men themselves, the which at first were framed
>   Of earthly mould, and form'd of flesh and bone,
>   Are now transformed into hardest stone:
>   Such as behind their backs (so backward bred)
>   Were throwne by *Pyrrha* and *Deucalione:*
>   And if then those may any worse be red,
> They into that ere long will be degendered.
>
> (5. Proem. 2)

Ovid described how the stones thrown by Deucalion and Pyrrha turned into men, while Spenser, justifying his recourse to ancient fable, says that the men of today have turned into stones. Ovid's version, one of his few moments of direct moral commentary, suggests why our lives are hard, but holds out the possibility of regeneration, if men are kept pious by labor. Spenser holds out the opposite possibility, that if there is some lower form of depravity, men "into that ere long will be degendered." Yet the possibility of renewal is essential to Spenser's poem. How else can the image of a just ruler be fashioned? Why else bother with antique images of glory? Spenser's interpretation of the myth reveals the contradiction built into his system of application, whereby "antique praises [are] unto present persons fit." For the poem does not in fact describe a golden age: Faerieland is filled with brutes and politicians, and even its heroes behave in strange and imperfect ways. And in the historical present, where corruption reigns and justice is "for most meed outhyred," he turns for poetic inspiration to his own monarch, who somehow embodies the goddess Astraea, signifying a return of the goodness, peace, and justice of Saturn himself.

The motive for this last contradiction may seem obvious, but there is more at work than flattery—a flattery that would just confirm Spenser's thesis of moral decay. The representational process by which Spenser applies ancient fable to present reality is as circular as his time scheme. Faerieland is already the conjunction of antiquity and the present, a world as corrupt as ours, through which his virtuous heroes march. This applied myth is itself applicable to our world as a law or measurement for human conduct, and our world in turn forms the perceptual basis from which we interpret and understand fable. For all his Platonic rhetoric, Spenser's mythological imagery has an empirical basis in the public affairs of Renaissance England. In Spenser's hands, the fable's lack of textual integrity or interpretive stability is no drawback: the myth of the golden age is a conspicuous fiction or reconstruction, not an attested fact. Myth confers upon us no absolute knowledge either of the present or the past. It confers knowledge only through the momentary correspondence of empirical information with an absolute standard of truth, an insight that is epistemologically unstable. Hence a golden age filled with evil, and a universal decay in which Justice returns and reigns: Spenser delights in the vertigo his contradictions thrust upon us. If we stay balanced within the terms of his myth, his poem is an epic celebration of how transcendent truth manifests itself. If the myth opens beneath us and pitches us down, the crash is a satiric music made from the dissonance of our own fallen minds.

The two kinds of music in Spenser's poem correspond to two strains within mytho-political discourse, one celebratory and one analytical. The celebratory strain is essentially a form of propaganda, in which the political self-justification of a ruling class is wrapped in fable in order to maintain itself against scrutiny. This language works in the same way myth does to establish religion. As Natalis Comes describes it, the eagle and the thunderbolt of Jove, the cyclops, and other immortal terrors were invented to overawe the minds of women and the rabble.[12] Spenser similarly is blinded by the glory of Elizabeth whenever his poetic vision discloses to him the ways in which she mirrors divine virtue. Whatever the usefulness of such myths, they always carry the threat of deluding their inventors as well.

The propaganda value of myth lies in its capacity to create an image that prevents insight. If Spenser's myths are thereby a kind of blindness-in-seeing, he simultaneously creates an analytical discourse of political myth through metaphors of seeing in darkness. The ways of truth are obscure, the byways of Faerieland crooked, but somehow the poet will find his way and return with a truth for his audience to learn. The peril here is threefold: that the clear light of analysis will merely demolish one's own myths; that the poet will find no clear pattern at all; or that what he does find will not apply to the complexity of the present. Hence Spenser laments that evil seems to triumph as often as good in this world and that the good must be imposed upon reality with the sword.

> For vaine it is to deeme of things aright,
> And make wrong doers iustice to deride,
> Vnless it be perform'd with dreadlesse might.
> For powre is the right hand of Iustice truely hight.
>
> (5.4.1)

By interweaving the celebratory and analytical strains, Spenser thrusts his poem into the matrix of sixteenth-century dynastic mythography. Take, for instance, the flattering image of Elizabeth as Astraea. The virgin goddess of justice, Ovid tells us, has fled the earth with the coming of the iron age, and will return, Vergil prophesies, to establish a new *imperium* of universal order: "iam redit et Virgo, redeunt Saturnia regna."[13] It is specifically the imperial aspect of Elizabeth that Spenser invokes as his Muse in Book 5, the "Dread Souerayne Goddesse" who "Doest to thy people righteous doome aread, / That furthest Nations filles with awfull dread" (5.Proem.11). This Elizabeth is queen not just of England, but of Ireland, France, and Virginia, and the leader—if only the Leicester-Sidney party could have had their way—of a federation of the Protestant princes of Europe.

Frances Yates has demonstrated that this is a bit of Hapsburg mythography that Spenser and Elizabeth have appropriated.[14] Elizabeth had a habit of such filching, all the more piquant since her deadliest enemy was Philip II of Spain. Indeed, her claim to the throne, her very existence, derived from her father's repudiation of his Hapsburg queen. Yet in the so-called Sieve portrait, now in Siena, Elizabeth even adopts the personal device of Philip's father, the emperor Charles V.[15] As a point of strategy, one might wonder if it were better to acknowledge or to conceal such appropriation. Yates herself couldn't decide if it was conscious or unconscious on Elizabeth's part. To acknowledge the source might seem to be to demolish the myth, since the claim of Charles or even Philip to empire is so obviously superior to Elizabeth's. But in Spenser's hands, the juxtaposition becomes a way of investigating the origins and bases of such dynastic myths and, by implication, the political claims erected upon them.

The Hapsburg Charles V traced his family claims back to the Roman Caesar, founding his imperial pretension on bloodlines as well as on his and Caesar's analogous careers of conquest. Spenser probes into Elizabeth's claims only indirectly, through the surrogate of her knight of Justice, Sir Artegall. Artegall's rights are established purely by deeds, and the legendary predecessors Spenser provides for him—Hercules and Bacchus—are offered as analogies, not as progenitors. Hercules suggests ignorant brutality, but modern scholarship on the choice of Hercules has charted his transformation into an improbable champion of temperance and justice.[16] Bacchus is even more ambiguous: our immediate associations are of drunkenness, revelry, and the rout of women who murdered Orpheus. Indeed Spenser's Bacchus acts with "furious might" in "defacing" the "fruitful rankness" of the plant of evil. If this Bacchus is not drunk with savagery, then his actions occur in a kind of divine frenzy. In Ovid and Apollonius of Tyana, Bacchus the conqueror seems much like his son Hercules, as he is driven to swift vengeance against those who refuse to acknowledge him as the son of Jove and as their new sovereign. Inserted into the historical scheme of Spenser's poem, such unstable images form a critique of the claims of inheritance and virtue on which dynasties rest. Which is truly the child of Jove and right ruler: Philip or Elizabeth, Hapsburg or Tudor? Which is the savage aggressor, and which is moved by righteous fury?[17]

Spenser similarly exploits the ambiguous application of myth in his account of the sword Chrysaor, which is given to Artegall by Astraea.

> Which steely brand, to make him dreaded more,
>   She gaue vnto him, gotten by her slight
>   And earnest search, where it was kept in store
>   In *Ioues* eternall house, vnwist of wight,
>   Since he himselfe it vs'd in that great fight
>   Against the *Titans,* that whylome rebelled

> Gainst highest heaven; *Chrysaor* it was hight;
> *Chrysaor* that all other swords excelled,
> Well prov'd in that same day, when Ioue those Gyants quelled
> (5.1.9)

Chrysaor appears in the *Iliad* (5.509) as the sword of Apollo.[18] Spenser transfers it to Jove, invents a history for it, and passes it through the hands of Astraea, all so that his knight may have the proper arms. In the process, he clarifies the relationship of Artegall to Astraea and, by application, of Lord Grey to Elizabeth. Astraea wields a sword of her own that she could easily give to Artegall. Instead she gives him Jove's, suggesting first that she still retains her own power, and second that she, as the administrator of earthly justice, fulfills divine behest. Still, there is that odd note—she has obtained it by her "slight" and her "earnest search" out of the storeroom where it lay hidden, which reminds us that divine power is indeed an obscure force, and much diligence and cunning are required in its application.

In his focus on the sword, Spenser reminds us of the very real form such power takes. A Lord Deputy, such as Lord Grey de Wilton, was a vice-roy, who in the monarch's absence acted in the monarch's place with the monarch's power. He was invested with a ceremonial sword of state to mark his assumption of such power, a fact Spenser would not likely forget, since it was in making the arrangements for the transference of the sword to Grey that he snubbed Lord Justice Pelham. That the ceremony was regarded as a very real transfer of power, and not just an empty form, is demonstrated by the account of the Essex rebellion put together for the government by Bacon. Essex insisted that he be invested with the royal powers of justice and mercy in the specific forms of a large army and the right to pardon traitors. The pardons he would use to bind the Irish rebels to himself, and the army to invade England. Hence, wrote Bacon, a rumor arose among the Irish rebels "that the Earl of Essex was theirs, and they his: and that he would never give up the one sword, meaning that of Ireland, until he had gotten the other one in England."[19] The Lord Deputy's sword, like Chrysaor, is a metaphor for a transcendent power that is transferred to its possessor by mysterious, even magical means. Yet the power is simultaneously very real, especially when the Lord Deputy was backed by an army and the monarch was over two weeks' journey away. There really was a sword and it, or another much like it, would be put to its most unceremonious use. It was intended for the prosecution of rebels, and therefore the poet may feign that it is the very sword with which Jove smote down the Giants.

The rebels whom Grey is to smite down were of course the Irish, and smite them he did, so that within two years he was recalled by Elizabeth for his excesses of zeal and of cruelty. The most infamous incident came at the siege of Smerwick where, with Spenser at his side, Grey put to the sword four hundred Spanish mercenaries sent to aid the archtraitor Desmond. Again Spenser's image of Chrysaor is historically ironic, for again it invokes a Hapsburg device turned to Spenser's own purposes. The story of the giants' rebellion had been used to demonstrate the futility of revolt against Charles V, as in the title page of Lodovico Dolce's translation of Ovid, which shows a Hapsburg Jove hovering over Italy.[20] This dynastic reading of the myth is a secular extension of the reading prevalent before 1500, in which the story was most commonly taken as an allegory for those who rebel against God's will. And these readings depend upon a certain confusion, in which the Giants and the Titans are mixed up. For Jove as emperor is an ambiguous figure, both right ruler defending his realm and the usurper who supplanted the just Titan Saturn. Spenser repeats the confusion, using the words "Titan" and "Giant" interchangeably within four lines, but he does so in a way that brings the confusion to the surface, and analyzes the basis of sovereignty and the right of conquest.

Jove is a usurper—there is no doubt about that. He holds heaven by right of conquest, and justifies his power on the grounds of his virtue. The virtue of Jove was something of a joke in antiquity, a joke not lost on Christopher Marlowe, who in *Hero and Leander* describes "Jove slyly stealing from his sister's bed / To dally with Idalian Ganymede." But might can make right, and, as Spenser suggests in his image of Chrysaor, right can make might. Elizabeth's claim in Ireland was, like her claim to England, based on the right of conquest, derived from William the Conqueror and Henry II. Spenser outlines this claim in detail in his *View of the Present State of Ireland,* adding there and in the *Faerie Queene* a second claim based on justice.

For William the Conqueror brought with him the Norman law, which, under the name of the Common Law, says Spenser, suited the peaceful nature of the English people: "But with Ireland it is far otherwise. For it is a nation ever acquainted with wars though but amongst themselves, and in their own kind of military discipline trained up even from their youths, which they have never yet been taught to lay aside, nor made to learn obedience unto the law, scarcely to know the name of law, but instead thereof have always preserved and kept their own law which is the Brehon law."[21] Spenser has here grasped the principle of the historical and cultural specificity of laws and institutions,[22] and seen the inapplicability of English common law to Ireland. Yet he cannot go one step further and grant that the Irish should be ruled by their own customs and—to go the last step—by their own kinds. He is, at this point and at this point alone, too blinded by his own myth of the empress Elizabeth and by his own myth of Justice. For his words contrast Brehon law with absolute law, and he goes on to demonstrate how Brehon law is in fact a form of anarchy. In following their old law, the Irish violate the new and true law; old custom makes new criminal; a sovereign Titan becomes a rebellious giant.

The *View* is a policy paper, reflecting the position of the permanent colonial administration in Ireland,[23] in which Spenser held a significant place. It demonstrates Spenser's command of the historical, legal, and military discourse of the politiques. It would seem thereby to stand apart from Spenser's poetry, and indeed for many years was considered an embarrassment by literary critics. But it is apparent to more and more scholars that the mode of logic in the *View* replicates that of the *Faerie Queene*, both in its observation of cultural relativity and in its invocation of absolute standards to limit and control that relativity. As the political language of the *View* can extract from history the general principles of human behavior and reapply them to the situation in Ireland, so in the *Faerie Queene* the complex mythological image, compounded of worldly observation and heavenly principle, can be reapplied to an analysis of the world. A real sword and a divine one delineate the powers of Artegall and of the Lord Deputy. The facts of Irish customs and the ideal of law lead to the myth of the giants and to the conclusion that the Irish are rebels against Elizabeth.

Noting Spenser's recourse to the absolute in moments of difficulty, Jonathan Goldberg observes that, "to find the truth when both parties can make equally potent claims—when, in the text, they share attributes and seem to mirror each other—one must submit to the power of authority."[24] This relationship to authority within Spenser's text, he argues, conditions the relationship of Spenser's works to the authority of Elizabeth and her government. In a subtle analysis of Spenser's Machiavellianism, Goldberg finds that "in the *View*, as in Book V of the *Faerie Queene*, the premises upon which sovereign power operates are laid bare . . . the terms of the poem are those of the *Prince:* force and fraud (equity turns out to be a version of guile), fortune and the like. Further, the poem is Machiavellian in another sense: it exposes the reality of power that lurks beneath the justification of it in such myths as chivalric rescue, the dispensation of mercy, the enactment of equity."[25]

Goldberg has, like Sir Guyon, trampled down the Bower of Bliss inhabited by those who, like Lemmi so many years ago, would rather equate poetry with escapism and mystical pleasure. But having accepted the similarity of Spenser's two texts, we must still ask about the difference between them. Goldberg accepts the "usual" assumption that the *View* is "a statement of the official attitude toward Ireland" and guesses that it was suppressed because it revealed what the government could not endure to have revealed, that "decapitation, destruction, and constant surveillance are the facts upon which the [official] language rests."[26] *The Faerie Queene,* by contrast, "cannot be read as a version of the official language of state," because "the very act of reproduction of that language produces ironies and duplicities" that are subversive of the state.

Sound as it is generally, Goldberg's formulation needs to be modified on two grounds: first, that it is overdichotomized between the authoritarian and the subversive and between nonpoetic and poetic language; and second, that it contradicts Goldberg's own earlier demonstration that similar ironies and duplicities lie at the heart of the *View.* Spenser had warned in the *View* that there can be "no remorse or drawing back" in a "course of reformation," nor can there be here in the chain of argument that leads us to consider the linguisticality of power. The *View* and the *Faerie Queene* must be read as parallel statements, in two competing languages, about the origins of power and its justification. Each seeks to advise the queen and can gain the right to do so only if it meets two criteria: that it can lay bare the sources of power with sufficient clarity to lead to effective action, and that the action it leads to will indeed serve to keep the queen in power. They are what Foucault described as "different and even contradictory discourses [existing] within the same strategy."[27] *Neither* is the language of state, or of the queen herself, but each aspires to be.

Both are, in effect, subjunctive modes, spoken as if they were the official language, by those who put their recommendations in the mouth of the sovereign so that she may speak them; such advisors achieve power by denying that they have any, claiming that what they say is not theirs but the queen's.[28] But the power of the political or poetic counselor is not thereby only a projection of the queen's power. It is predicated precisely on *her* belief, and that of the Elizabethan elite generally, in the power of learning; this credulity converts the humanist's ability into authority and acknowledges in him the power to do something that the prince cannot do simply by virtue of being a prince. Elizabeth, in her wisdom, seems to have been quite happy to practice political bilingualism, espousing both myth and Machiavelli. But of the two, Machiavellian counsel, based as it is on the study of princes, does not differentiate itself from the prince's power as subtly as poetic mythography does. With its tincture of absolutism, myth was like the biblical discourse of a Knox or Calvin: it threatened the prince with moral exposure but promised that her good behavior would cause its subversive ironies to be directed against her enemies.

If both discourses in their different ways expose the realities of power, then one must ask whether this revelation is an inherently subversive act, something akin to the disclosure of official secrets, and if it opens up a dangerous and ambiguous distance between the writer and the prince he serves. But the reality of power in Tudor England does not seem to have been shocking news, for it did not lurk very far beneath the surface of things. Forced conscription, special levies of taxation, headings, hangings, and burnings would be enough to awaken even those who could close their eyes to the historical chronicles of conquest and usurpation that brought each dynasty to the throne. However much Elizabeth might protest the mildness of her private person, she never abjured the use of terror by her public self. She was constantly depicted with a sword, and no one would mistake it for a mere decoration. The danger of too public a Machiavellianism lay not in the revelation of what princes did, but in the ascription of motive, the admission that the prince might act purely to maintain his or her own power and not, as Sir Thomas Elyot so optimistically suggested, "only for the weale of his people." [29] Indeed, the peculiar value of political mythology was not that it concealed the reality of power, but that it could magnify power into an immortal terror. The thunderbolt of Jove or the wrath of Hercules are not things that the average citizen would choose to defy.

This mystification of princely might is evidenced in the two weapons that Sir Artegall has at his disposal, his sword Chrysaor and his sidekick Talus. Both are iron and irresistible, and Artegall's opponents are no sooner known than they are punished. Judgment and justice coincide exactly. If only Lord Grey de Wilton had found things so easy in Ireland. Instead of a dichotomy of the powerful and the powerless, he found in the "mere Irish" an implacable foe made all the more cohesive and infathomable by their cultural differences from the English. In his Anglo-Irish allies Grey found divided loyalties and a propensity to subvert his authority through their own connections at court. The uneven encounters of Book 5 are mythic exaggerations of the ability of the Elizabethans to extend their reach beyond the Pale, and denials of the formidable power of the Irish in resistance.

Spenser's tendency to transform military struggle into a struggle between civility and barbarism results from what Stephen Greenblatt calls his "field theory of culture." [30] In the *View*, Spenser sees the root of the conflict in the collision of two cultures and the solution in the use of military force to totally eradicate Irish ways. It is tempting for us to see here the reality of colonialism laid bare, but what Spenser's Machiavellian language has done is to create the very idea of modern colonialism by treating the Irish conflict as a foreign war waged against a barbaric and alien people. Hence he sees the Anglo-Irish as the major obstacles to victory: offspring of both cultures, they threaten to mediate his polarity, to reconcile England and Ireland.

Herein probably lies the reason for the suppression of the *View*, for Elizabeth counted on the Anglo-Irish to reconcile the two cultures. She persisted in seeing Ireland as a domestic and feudal matter. The large-scale military campaigns involved in Spenser's proposals would only mean vast expenditures and the likelihood of foreign intervention, such as precipitated the Smerwick massacre. The Anglo-Irish aristocracy had pledged loyalty to the Tudors (some of them were even related to Elizabeth), and Elizabeth preferred to rely on them to maintain order. She manipulated and dandled them just as she did the English aristocracy. She was generally willing to listen sympathetically to their complaints about the various plantation ventures, military expeditions, Lords Deputy and Lords Lieutenant sent over from London, and she was specifically worried that the "oppression and insolencies of the soldiers" might alienate her subjects.[31] The humanist-colonial analysis of the *View* challenged and disturbed Elizabeth's position in a way that the humanist-mythological analysis of the *Faerie Queene* did not.

If the special psychology of Elizabeth dictated the immediate fortunes of the *View* and the *Faerie Queene,* the mytho-political discourse of Spenser's epic was nonetheless losing out to the vocabulary of the *politiques* even as Spenser wrote. For there is, of course, a difference between them, although I do not think that one is inherently more authoritarian or more subversive or more illusory or more real than the other. Both expose the gap between what is said and what is done, but they treat that gap in fundamentally different ways. Machiavellian political discourse wishes to deny that the gap lies within itself as a language, and projects the gap outward, onto the nature of men; the prince does what she is compelled to do by circumstances and necessity. This discourse celebrates the successful prince as the virtuoso performer of the techniques of political manipulation. How much more appealing and ultimately more flattering this is to the prince than a language that delves into origins and reaches after abstractions to measure her, that tells her that power itself may not be enough.

In the *Faerie Queene,* the gap between reality and divine pattern is the basis on which Spenser's imagery is founded, and his position as an advisor rests on his ability to acknowledge and examine it. His absolute patterns threaten the prince as well as praise her. In saying so, I must acknowledge the powerful argument of Stephen Greenblatt that it is precisely this gap within Spenser's language that prevents a questioning of the ideology of the ruler. Greenblatt concludes,

> Spenserean allegory . . . opens up an internal distance within art itself by continually referring the reader out to a fixed authority beyond the poem. Spenser's art does not lead us to perceive ideology critically, but rather affirms the existence and inescapable moral power of ideology as that principle of truth toward which art forever yearns. It is art whose status is questioned in Spenser, not ideology; indeed, art is questioned precisely to spare ideology that internal distantiation it undergoes in the work of Shakespeare or Marlowe. In *The Faerie Queene* reality as given by ideology always lies safely outside the bounds of art, in a different realm, distant, infinitely powerful, perfectly good.[32]

No one could quarrel with Greenblatt's initial account of the internal distance within Spenser's art, but as his description goes on, it takes on a disturbing resemblance to Lemmi's characterization of Spenser as a medieval absolutist, though the result here of course is to hang both Spenser and medieval absolutism on the same gallows. There is, to be sure, nothing of the carnivalesque in Spenser's poetry as there is in Marlowe's or Shakespeare's, and little that is properly called subversive. Spenser's art forever yearns toward truth and towards power in the hope of uniting them in the creation of ideology. It refers the reader out to a fixed authority, but to one that it claims a role in establishing, and so it always asserts the provisional status of that fixity. His art questions the relation of power to morality, and therefore—and to that extent—is able to perceive both that ideology and that power critically.

Spenser's "field theory of culture," so aptly described by Greenblatt, and Spenser's Calvinist suspicion of secular power, alike lead him to perceive the absolute good and the earthly good in continuous dialectic. This exposure of power to the light does not make power go away, nor does the truth necessarily set one free. As Gadamer insists in his reply to Habermas, it is an illusory, anarchistic utopianism to imagine that reflection by itself demolishes power, or that authority is always wrong.[33] Spenser confronts his own illusion of power, offering the prince the chance to combine goodness with force. We may now puzzle over the word "justice" and painlessly reject any number of the things that Spenser thought good. But it is less easy to escape the challenge of his fundamental insight that, if power without justice is not enough, then neither is justice without power.

III

The issues raised by the political allegory of the *Faerie Queene*—issues about the relationship of learning to power, about the various applications of ancient myth to contemporary circumstances, and about the nature of political and poetic discourse—would inevitably occupy a man like Francis Bacon. By the time of the first publication of his *Essayes* in 1597, he had come to see the rhetorical, civic humanism taught to him at Cambridge as something that (as F. J. Levy puts it) "served best as a mask, to be put on when it could be advantageous to him."[34] In 1605, in *The Proficiencie and Advancement of Learning*, Bacon came down resoundingly on the side of the *politiques*, accepting the division between politics and humanism and summing up the charges of political uselessness brought against the poets, namely,

> that learning . . . doth mar and pervert men's dispositions for matter of government and policy in making them too curious and irresolute by variety of reading, or too peremptory or positive by strictness of rules and axioms, or too immoderate and overweening by reason of the greatness of examples, or too incompatible and differing from the times by reason of the dissimilitude of examples; or at least that it doth divert men's travails from action and business, and bringeth them to a love of leisure and privateness. . . . Out of the same conceit or humour did Virgil, turning his pen to the advantage of his country and the disadvantage of his own profession, make a kind of separation between policy and government and between arts and sciences in the verses so much renowned, attributing and challenging the one to the Romans, and leaving and yielding the other to the Grecians: *Tu regere imperio populos, Romane, memento, Hae tibi erunt artes,* etc.[35]

Bacon creates a parodic image of the scholar, twisted and perverted by his obscurantism and self-absorption, obsessed with trivia, capable only of opinionated arrogance or paralytic indecision. He seizes on Vergil's line to project all of these faults onto poetry, which yields to the needs of the nation and is subjugated to political discourse, just as Greece, for all its cultural splendor, was subjugated to Rome. Full of Ciceronian phrases and antique comparisons, Bacon's poetic humanists are suited only for *otium,* not for the active realm of *negotium.* If they are to enter the public arena, it must be merely as flatterers.

Bacon spoke as one of the masters of the new political and technological discourse. Author of the government's indictment of Essex and solicitor-general since 1607, he was an expert on the legal dimensions of political action. His *History of Henry VII* (1622) would show a command of politic history, and the *Proficiencie and Advancement of Learning* and *New*

Instauration did not so much challenge the humanist learning of Greece and Rome as declare it to be irrelevant. Yet despite the stark polarities of Bacon's language in the *Proficiencie and Advancement of Learning,* he recognized that finding the right language for the "matter of government and policy" was no simple matter.[36] The same imperviousness of public affairs to rules, axioms, and examples that thwarted the poetic humanist would frustrate Bacon's own new methods. Lisa Jardine observes that "Bacon like Aristotle accepts the fact that human behavior tends to be much more complex than the behavior of other natural phenomena. More disturbing factors interfere with the basic patterns, and the variables are less easily determined. . . . There is also a theological difficulty, since knowledge of the principles which determine human voluntary behavior is forbidden to man."[37]

Spenser's poetic language in the *Faerie Queene* inhabits this realm of human interest, mirroring both its variableness and the obscurity of its principles. And it is precisely that variableness that Bacon saw as the drawback to mythological discourse. In his preface to *De sapientia veterum,* he expressed the fear that its malleability and obscurity made it both unreliable and useless as a medium for the discovery of general truths.

> I suppose some are of opinion, that my purpose is to write toyes and trifles, and to usurpe the same liberty in applying, that the Poets assumed in faining, which I might doe (I confesse) if I listed, and with more serious contemplations intermixe these things, to delight either my selfe in meditation, or others in reading. Neither am I ignorant how fickle and inconstant a thing fiction is, as being subject to be drawen and wrested any way, and how great the commoditie of wit and discourse is, that is able to apply things well, yet so as never meant by the first Authors.[38]

To Bacon, poetic mythology was licentious, as is audible in the diction of his attack: "toyes," "trifles," "usurpe," "liberty," "Poets," "faining," "delight," "fickle," "inconstant," "fiction," "drawen," "wrested," "wit."

The root of the problem lies in those gaps in poetic language that threaten to reveal the nature of language itself, reveal that it is not stable, not *about* anything, without referentiality or certainty of application. Four years earlier, in the *Proficiencie and Advancement of Learning,* Bacon had similarly defined poetry as that branch of learning which is "extremely licensed": "[It] doth truly refer to the Imagination, which, being not tied to the laws of matter, may at pleasure join that which nature hath severed, and sever that which nature hath joined, and so make unlawful matches and divorces of things. . . . It is . . . nothing else but Feigned

History."[39] Poetic fable seems indeed to be doubly fantastic, first in its creation and again in its application, and Bacon fears that, acting merely as an interpreter of fable, he will be like the poetic creator of fable, a pleasure seeker sporting among arbitrary disconnections between words and things. That emptiness makes language useless babble, unable to do what Spenser claimed for it, either to reveal the nature of the world or to advise a prince. It is just this mental libertinism that has brought men of learning under attack from the politiques, as purveyors of curious fancies, "too incompatible and differing from the times."

If there is a bit of hysteria in Bacon's attack, it is significant that the entire preface to *De sapientia veterum* is a response to anonymous accusations[40] that Bacon himself uses his poetic imagination in applying the fables: "I suppose *some are of opinion, that my purpose is to write toyes and trifles.*" Under self-interrogation, Bacon proves self-contradictory, alternately denying and half confessing the charges, saying he *might* do it if he wished, and wondering if he is indeed "captus," "rauished," by love of antiquity.[41]

The way out is to show that poetry and the imagination are not in fact wholly licentious, and then one's complicity might be safely admitted. In the *Proficiencie and Advancement of Learning,* Bacon tries to show that the feigned history of the poets offers to the soul a heroic and virtuous image which is more satisfying than the imperfections of nature. Therefore poetry "was ever thought to have some participation of divineness, because it doth raise and erect the mind, by submitting the shews of things to the desires of the mind; whereas reason doth buckle and bow the mind unto the nature of things."[42]

Bacon's defense of poetry starts out, like Spenser's description of the golden age, with a poetic image more perfect and stable than sense perception. But Bacon is no longer certain that the imagination reflects transcendent law, and he ultimately sets its working within the limits of the mind. If Spenser's poetic mirror reflects the divine, Bacon's distorts it. By his last sentence, Bacon's defense has crumbled, and the imagination's images of virtue and vice are reduced to a condition of the mind itself, which Bacon calls an idol of the tribe, the innate desire of thought to warp perception and impose its forms upon reality.

So Bacon shifts his ground and denies that the better sort of fables are the creation of the poets at all. What if the "allusive or parabolic" fables were in fact created by men of reason? Bacon finds in the myths themselves three significant qualities: a "singular proportion between the signifier and the thing signified," an "apt and clear coherence in the very structure of them," and etymologically significant names, such as "Typhon," meaning "insurrection," or "Metis," meaning "counsel." From these qualities he infers that the allegorical sense of the fables was intended by their inventors as part of an ancient philosophy.

By tracing the origin of myth to an age of reason rather than an age of fancy, Bacon creates a feigned history for Feigned History. In the process, he transforms the problem of interpreting myth into a question of historical understanding.

> The Antiquities of the first age (except those we find in sacred Writ) were buried in obliuion and silence: silence was succeeded by Poeticall fables; and Fables againe were followed by the Records we now enjoy. So that the mysteries and secrets of Antiquity were distinguished and separated from the Records and Euidences of succeeding times, by the vaile of fiction which interposed it selfe and came betweene those things which perished, and those which are extant.[43]

Bacon's first sentence sets up a threefold division of human time: an antique age of oblivion, an age of fable, and a modern age of records. These in turn correspond to three stages of knowledge: at one extreme, an age of wisdom for which no certain evidence survives; at the other, the empirical knowledge based on written evidence; and in between, an understanding of "fables," which may contain traces of the ancient wisdom but which do not attain the status of evidence. In the next sentence, rather than define fable more closely, he collapses the middle stage, making it a mere "vaile" between things known and things lost, a veil that has not been placed there deliberately, but has "interposed it selfe." In this way, the deliberate act of meaning by the poetic transmitter of myth is effaced, and the veil is defined as a condition intrinsic both to philosophical parable itself and to our historical distance from it.

Bacon is aware that the poetic fables that come down to us in Homer and Ovid are not themselves the original myths but late literary forms; hence his skepticism toward them as "Records and Euidences" of the antique mind. He is aware that myths exist in variant forms and have been subject to even more variant interpretations. Indeed, he astutely sees their variety as evidence of their antiquity, since in a process of oral transmission "they became various by reason of the diuers ornaments bestowed on them by particular relations."[44]

Given his insight into the oral transmission of myth, one might expect that Bacon would try to control the variants and, by a careful collation, remove those acidentals and discern the earliest form of each myth as a necessary safeguard against anachronistic interpretation. Oddly, he does exactly the opposite, offering fables assembled from a variety of late sources, from Fulgentius to Natalis Comes, and concentrating on myths that are clearly allegorical and literary. Having placed fable beyond the reach of "Records and Euidences," Bacon has implicitly found all analysis of origins to be futile and all interpretations to be illusory, the momentary opinions of men, or Idols of the Marketplace. Even his interpretive canons of internal coherence and correspondence of signifier to signified are abandoned when he suggests that the absurdity of some myths argues that they must contain an allegorical justification. In this makeshift sequence of defenses, fable is rescued from the lying poets only to be left trapped behind the veil of fiction, for no record or evidence can distinguish which interpretations were originally intended and which were invented later, or when coherence is to be preferred, and when absurdity.

Having cut the fables loose from their anchor in antiquity, Bacon simultaneously uproots them from the present, giving them none of the specific application to the public affairs of England that Spenser does. His fables are, to be sure, applicable to England at every turn in a general way, but Bacon does not enmesh historical specifics in his images the way Spenser does. By maintaining the fables as a veil between past ignorance and present evidence, he creates a form rather like that of his legal maxims, which, as Paul Kocher describes them, are "middle axioms . . . arrived at by induction from . . . individual cases and then . . . applied back to determine new particulars."[45] The fables of *De sapientia veterum* summarize the knowledge of the past in a form useful to the present, without being tied at either end to specific cases. By depriving them of original authority, Bacon has reconstituted the myths as a form of the *phronesis,* or practical wisdom, that Aristotle saw as particularly appropriate to politics.[46]

De sapientia veterum is formed as a book of counsel designed to avoid the obscurity of the scholar and to provoke that "tossing and turning" of the mind that is necessary for careful deliberation. Bacon begins by examining the nature of counsel itself through the subtle juxtaposition of his fables. Beginning with a discussion of Cassandra, the true counselor who seems rebellious to the unheedful prince, he then turns to Typhon, the true rebel. Next is "the Cyclopes, or the Ministers of Terror," examples of the false counselor, followed by Narcissus, the one who neglects to take his place of duty in civil affairs. Having anatomized the types of false servants, Bacon returns to an analysis of true counsel in Machiavellian terms, in his sections on "Styx, or Leagues," and "Perseus, or Warre." From this point on, nonpolitical myths are increasingly intermingled, as the focus of the volume moves from human nature to natural philosophy.

Bacon is careful to deny his own creativity throughout the book and to disguise his ingenuity in its shaping. Each section begins with some phrase like "the poets feign," by which Bacon denies responsibility for the inventions that follow. Nevertheless, the organization of the volume is wholly Bacon's, and he selects and arranges the material within each section. In his discussion of Typhon, for instance, Bacon draws and wrests the fable to suit his desires, while appearing only to follow his source.

> The people . . . study how to create and set vp a cheefe of their own choise. This proiect by the secret instigation of the Peeres and Nobles, doth for the most part take his beginning; by whose conniuence the Commons [*populi*] being set on edge, there followes a kind of murmuring or discontent in the State, shadowed by the infancie of *Typhon*, which being nurst by the naturall prauitie and clownish malignity of the vulgar sort [*plebis*] . . . at last breaks out into open Rebellion. . . . And sometimes these rebellions grow so potent that Princes are inforc't (transported as it were by the Rebels, and forsaking the chief Seates and Cities of the Kingdome) to contract their power, and (being depriued of the Sinewes of money & maiestie) betake themselues to some remote & obscure corner within their dominions: but in processe of time (if they beare their misfortunes with moderation) they may recouer their strength by the vertue and industry of *Mercury,* that is, they may (by becomming affable & by reconcyling the minds and willes of their Subiects with graue edicts and gratious speech) excite an alacritie to graunt ayds and subsidies whereby to strengthen their authority anew.[47]

While the central conceit of Bacon's fable, the loss and renewal of "sinews," has come from Comes, he has expanded and particularized the allegory, making far more details of the myth significant and specifying their political meaning in a more exact way. Bacon has opened the myth in the direction of English politics, and his English translator, Sir Arthur Gorges, is careful to make the correct applications, as in his choice of words like "Peeres" and "Commons." Comes's "rebellion" becomes in Bacon's hands the setting on of the rabble by conspiratorial nobles. The sinews of Jove, equated vaguely with the minds of his followers, become the financial resources, the "ayds and subsidies," that maintain the king's majesty and allow him to prosecute a war.

Bacon's Machiavellian mythography avoids what seemed to him the crippling fallacies of either of its parts. Freed from the taint of pleasure, the anchor of euhemerism, and the anachronisms of application, fable is acquitted from the list of charges brought against learning by the politiques. Bacon's aphoristic phrasing and neglect of source study remove the necessity for the "tedious inquiry into many books" that is impossible for the busy man of affairs. On the other hand, the collective wisdom of generations which is summarized in the myths proves superior to the shallow cleverness of the politiques themselves, who lack the range and subtlety of insight that comes only to those who can see beyond the horizon of the instant.

In perfecting the political discourse of fable, however, Bacon has fundamentally changed the way fable operates in the political world. The interpenetration of analysis and mystification that characterizes Spenser's language is unhinged, leaving only a clear and skeptical language that is excellent as counsel and useless as propaganda. In Natalis Comes especially, Bacon confronted a claim that myth was both a plain and easy form of teaching and a dark language of secrets that defined an elite of initiates and held in awe the uninitiated. Bacon ultimately insists that fables were used "to teach and lay open, not to hide and conceale knowledge."[48]

This dispersing of the aura of myth may derive from some emotional limitation within Bacon himself, that fear of being "captus" that underlies his insistent denials of the imagination. It may also suggest why Elizabeth was reluctant to employ him, for such a man would not be held in thrall by her divinity. Published in 1609, *De sapientia veterum* stands as a judgment on the political methods of Elizabeth and as a warning to the Stuart monarchs who were struggling to appropriate the Spenserian mythography of the Virgin Queen. At the very moment that the court masques were becoming central to the cultural program of the English monarchy, Spenser's poetry was also, as David Norbrook has shown, serving as the language for opposition to the court.[49] Bacon simultaneously disowns the attempt to mystify the origins of power and warns of the dangers of an ambiguous mythography that can be exploited by multiple and competing cliques. Instead, he seeks to purify myth of the taint of its origins and to mystify the operation and exercise of power, suggesting that command of the state lies with those who command statecraft through their grasp of significant examples and their capacity to apply them to a present situation. One can only wonder whether, in his constant probing into the mind's capacity for self-delusion, he foresaw that in the decades to come the poetical myth of power would blind only the courtly elite that created it, and not the people they sought to rule.

IV

While Bacon's reformation of fable demands that it be a language of analytical clarity and not of mystification, it may at the same time suggest why this discourse was not ultimately able to sustain itself in the face of the language of the politiques. Having become intensely self-reflective, revealing its own interior logic, fable had demythologized itself, denying to itself the one form of power that it could offer and the politiques could not. But for a few decades at least, Bacon's reformulation of mytho-political discourse seems to have worked to preserve it as a viable language in its dual nature, a potential competitor with both the illusions of the masque and the pragmatism of the political treatise.

Nowhere is this more clearly demonstrated than by a curious pamphlet entitled *The Faerie Leveller,* published during the English civil war.[50] The body of the pamphlet is an excerpt from book 5, canto 2, of the *Faerie Queene,* the passage in which Sir Artegall confronts the Giant Leveller. Artegall and his squire Talus have just dismembered Pollente and Munera, who specialize in stratagems and bribery, and are displaying the severed parts in the customary English way with traitors. They then come upon the giant, who stands on the shore preaching democracy, threatening to "stirre up civill faction" (5.2.51) among those very groups—women and the lower classes—whom myth is designed to restrain. The giant argues for the existence of injustice from direct observation, concludes that the present authorities are in fact usurpers, and offers to restore equity by a simple weighing of all things in his scales of justice.

> Tyrants that make men subiect to their law,
>   I will suppresse, that they no more may raine;
>   And Lordings curbe, that commons ouer-aw;
> And all the wealth of rich men to the poore will draw.
>   (*Faerie Queene* 5.2.38)

The giant is so persuasive and dangerous because his arguments arise from the same observations and the same desires as Artegall's. He sees that nature and society have alike decayed from their original order and offers to redress the effects of tyranny and of excess concentrations of wealth, just as Artegall has done with Pollente and Munera. Unable to dispute his logic, Artegall must instead challenge the giant's ability to make empirical observations at all, and hence his right to construct from them historical schemata and abstract principles. For God, he retorts, weighed all things in the beginning and assigned them their places, and his order has lasted till the present. The inadequacy of empiricism is redressed by an appeal to first principles, and only then can the empirical data be understood.

For all of Artegall's resistance, the giant's arguments are those that within fifty years would threaten the life of the English monarchy. Hence the royalist author of *The Faerie Leveller* finds that Spenser's verses, "then propheticall are now become historicall in our dayes."[51] By Artegall, he tells us, is meant King Charles, while Talus represents the king's military forces, or even "Gregory," the common hangman of London. The Giant Leveller is of course Cromwell, and the giant's accomplices, Pollente and Munera, are respectively the Long Parliament and its tax collectors. The author dwells on the significance of that Latin word *munera,* for it is the "Countrey Committees, Sequestrators and Excise-men" who "must first be apprehended and brought to justice, ere the Army be quelled." [52] At a stroke this nameless author has joined Spenser and Bacon together, wrapping King Charles once again in the garments of Tudor iconography while showing a Baconian insight into the economic bases of power, those sinews of war that the giant rebel has stolen from Jove.

Dated 27 July 1648 by the London bookseller George Thomason,[53] *The Faerie Leveller* is a clever attempt in the midst of the Second Civil War to misrepresent the enemy. Presbyterians, Grandees, and Levellers are lumped together as forces of anarchy, leaving moderates no rational alternative to supporting the king. At the same time that it paints the antiroyalist forces all with one brush, the pamphlet seeks to divide them. Of the various ad hoc administrative arrangements made by the Long Parliament during the First Civil War, none was more controversial than the County Committees, the groups of local gentry responsible for the raising and maintenance of militia.[54] In August of 1946 and again in July of 1647 the House of Lords had introduced bills for their abolition (both tabled in Commons). Equally inflammatory was the proposal in the summer of 1647 for the confiscation and sale of the property of delinquents in order to pay the army. At the other extreme, the reluctance of Parliament to use the excise to pay the soldiers' arrears in wages had been a principal grievance of the New Model Army in its first confrontation with Parliament in 1647. Aware of his enemy's internal divisions, the pamphleteer has aimed his fable at the exact points most likely to provoke dissension and conflict. And in the summer of 1648, with Fairfax bogged down before Colchester, Cromwell's troops checked at Pembroke, and a Scottish army bearing down from the north, the hold of the king's enemies over the country seemed fragile indeed.[55]

In his few sentences, the pamphleteer has shown a humanist's skill in the drawing and wresting of his fable, and a politique's capacity for analysis. His advice is good, if a little late, for precisely at this moment both he and his king ceased to have any power to implement it. Even as the pamphleteer wrote, Cromwell was turning north to intercept the Scots. Within three weeks of the appearance of the pamphlet, the royalist armies were smashed to bits, like the Giant Leveller himself. Such is the nature of political mythography, ever duplicitous in its application. For the stern and just Artegall seems more like Cromwell than like the indecisive Charles, and the iron Talus could pass for a Roundhead trooper.

If by reason or the accidents of history we are inclined to side with the Giant Leveller's offer of equality and freedom, this merely demonstrates the delicate balance of Spenser's mode of analysis, which in scrutinizing itself is liable to reveal its own circularity, and hence the circularity of any political claims based upon it. The few pages of interpretation of the *Faerie Leveller* stand then as the epitaph of the peculiar breed of political mythography represented by the *Faerie Queene*. But it did not die before its time or before its rivals. The masque was already swept away, with the court of Charles itself. Twined also in the pamphleteer's words is the next challenge to Machiavelli, as the pamphleteer foresees institutional and economic modes of analysis for political and military power that the great Florentine never mastered. With those new languages would come new concepts of power based on vast material forces that are not readily wielded by the poet or philosopher. Instead, the power that claims to derive from God, justice, or intellectual *virtú* finds itself cut off from positive activity and forced back upon its negative capacity for examination and self-examination. We should not be surprised then if by our time humanism should espouse antihumanism and become less a mode for the exercise of power than a mode for opposition to all power, including its own.

Notes

1. I am grateful to the Herzog August Bibliothek in Wolfenbüttel, West Germany, whose invitations in 1980 and 1982 first caused me to consider this subject. For the kernel of the present argument see my paper "Spenser und Bacon: Die Wahrheit der Dichter und die Weisheit der Antike," in *Mythographie der frühen Neuzeit: Ihre Anwendung in den Künsten,* Wolfenbütteler Forschungen, vol. 27, ed. Walter Killy (Wiesbaden: Harrassowitz, 1984), pp. 115–26 (proceedings volume of the 1982 conference).

2. An issue adjacent to the creation of a poetic sphere separate from the political is the reaffirmation in the sixteenth century of a sphere of female activity separate from formal politics (or, perhaps, the creation of a formal politics separate from women). While women were barred from offices and institutions (except where the chance of family lineage might make them queens or duchesses), they might participate in the "feminized" politics of court intrigue and influence peddling. On the separation of spheres, see Sir Thomas Smith, *De Republica Anglorum: A Discourse on the Commonwealth of England* (1583), ed. L. Alston (Cambridge: Cambridge University Press, 1960), bk. 1, chap. 11 (pp. 22–23); Joan Kelly, "Did Women Have a Renaissance?" in *Becoming Visible: Women in European*

History, ed. Renate Bridenthal and Claudia Koonz (Boston: Houghton Mifflin, 1977), pp. 137–64; and Merry E. Wiesner, "Women's Defense of Their Public Role," in *Women in the Middle Ages and the Renaissance: Literary and Historical Perspectives*, ed. Mary Beth Rose (Syracuse: Syracuse University Press, 1986), pp. 1–27. On the roles of women in formal and informal politics, see Constance Jordan, "Feminists and the Humanists: The Case of Sir Thomas Elyot's *Defence of Good Women*," and my "Stella's Wit: Penelope Devereux as Reader of Sidney's Sonnets," both in *Rewriting the Renaissance: The Discourses of Sexual Difference in Early Modern Europe*, ed. Margaret Ferguson, Maureen Quilligan, and Nancy J. Vickers (Chicago: University of Chicago Press, 1986). The "feminization" of poetry is an implicit issue in Richard Helgerson, *Elizabethan Prodigals* (Berkeley: University of California Press, 1976) and the same author's "The New Poet Presents Himself: Spenser and the Idea of a Literary Career," *PMLA* 93 (1978): 893–911. I am grateful to Mary Ellen Lamb for sharing her work in progress on the circle of the countess of Pembroke, which will treat the issue at length.

3. Mikhail M. Bakhtin, *The Dialogic Imagination*, tr. Caryl Emerson and Michael Holquist (Austin: University of Texas Press, 1981), especially pp. 262–63, 301–31.

4. Stephen Orgel, "Making Greatness Familiar," in *The Forms of Power and the Power of Forms in the Renaissance*, ed. Stephen Greenblatt, special issue of *Genre* 15 (1982): 41–47.

5. I follow here Hans-Georg Gadamer's argument that "there is no societal reality, with all its concrete forces, that does not bring itself to representation in a consciousness that is linguistically articulated. Reality does not happen 'behind the back' of language" ("On the Scope and Function of Hermeneutical Reflection," tr. G. B. Hess and R. E. Palmer, in *Philosophical Hermeneutics*, ed. David E. Linge [Berkeley: University of California Press, 1976], p. 35).

6. The rival groups of the poetic humanists and the politiques cannot be differentiated on economic or social grounds. Both recruited members from among university-trained sons of the commercial and professional classes and gentry who were trained at the universities and the Inns of Court. Both depended for advancement on aristocratic patronage and such offices as clerkships and secretaryships. Their defining characteristic is that they see each other as separate groups and talk about each other in fiercely hostile terms. The two groups are in effect subcategories of the same class, divided and pitted against each other by the crown. Symptomatic is the fabled animosity between Spenser and William Cecil (by then Lord Burghley). The reality of their relationship is less important than the expectation of those around them that they should dislike one another. As Burghley, Sir Thomas Smith, and eventually Robert Cecil were the leading Elizabethan politiques, so Raleigh, Leicester, and eventually Essex emerged as the patrons of the poetical humanists.

7. Charles Lemmi, *The Classic Deities in Bacon: A Study in Mythological Symbolism* (Baltimore: Johns Hopkins University Press, 1933), pp. 212–13. Lemmi's position was expanded by Barbara Carman Garner in her article on "Francis Bacon, Natalis Comes, and the Mythological Tradition," *Journal of the Warburg and Courtauld Institutes* 33 (1970): 264–91. Garner seeks to demonstrate Bacon's

deep respect for the ancients, arguing that he conceived of a pre-Socratic age of philosophical parable that rivals or exceeds the learning of the present, including his own. Hence *De sapientia veterum,* which sets forth that learning of the past, is a necessary addition to his survey of erudition in *The Advancement of Learning,* and, like his *Essays,* constitutes a kind of dramatic counsel that persuades even as it enlightens.

8. Pelham to Grey, 5 September 1580, in *Calendar of the Carew Manuscripts at Lambreth,* ed. J. S. Brewer and William Bullen, 2 vols. (London: Longman, 1868), 2:312. Pelham complained that Grey's secretary had omitted Pelham's title of Lord Deputy before that position had actually passed to Grey. Pauline Henley, *Spenser in Ireland* (reprint, 1928; New York: Russell and Russell, 1969), p. 23, claims that Pelham's phrasing suggests that the offending party was a more experienced person than Spenser, but his words need not bear that construction.

9. James's response to the publication of Book 5 is insightfully analyzed by Jonathan Goldberg in the opening pages of *James I and the Politics of Literature* (Baltimore: Johns Hopkins University Press, 1983), pp. 1–11.

10. Edmund Spenser, *The Faerie Queene,* bk. 5; Proem, st. 3. All citations of the *Faerie Queene* are to the edition of Thomas P. Roche, Jr. (New Haven: Yale University Press, 1981), and will be cited by book, canto, and stanza.

11. Edmund Spenser, *A View of the Present State of Ireland,* ed. W. L. Renwick (Oxford: Clarendon Press, 1970), p. 33.

12. Natalis Comes, *Mythologiae* (Venice, 1568), sig. P5^r.

13. Vergil *Eclogues* 4.6. Cf. Ovid *Metamorphoses* 1.149–50: "et virgo caede madentis / ultima caelestum terras Astraea reliquit."

14. Frances A. Yates, *Astraea: The Imperial Theme in the Sixteenth Century* (London: Routledge, 1975), pp. 29–87.

15. Yates, *Astraea,* pp. 116–17. Yates associates the painting with the 1590 Accession Day Tilts. In *Gloriana: The Portraits of Queen Elizabeth I* (London: Thames & Hudson, 1987), pp. 101–7, Roy Strong attributes the painting to Cornelius Ketel, suggesting that it was executed between 1579 and 1581, while in his review of Strong, Malcolm Rogers proposes a date of 1578 ("Likeness and Likelihood," *Times Literary Supplement,* 14 August 1987, p. 867).

16. The classic treatment is Erwin Panofsky, *Hercules am Scheidewege,* Studien der Bibliothek Warburg, 18 (Leipzig, 1930); see also Jane Aptekar, *Icons of Justice* (New York: Columbia University Press, 1969), chap. 11, and Stephen Orgel, "The Example of Hercules," in *Mythographie der frühen Neuzeit,* Killy, pp. 25–48.

17. In "Reflections on the Above," delivered at the 1986 MLA in New York, David L. Miller doubted whether Spenser could have asked himself such questions, or asked them in this way. Indeed, the relatively narrow band of expression allowed in print in Elizabethan England and the national internal monologue of Elizabethan state propaganda both would seem to preclude such skeptical consciousness. But Spenser was writing in an international form, the epic, from the international battleground of Ireland. In the cacophony of Hapsburg, papal, Calvinist, Lutheran, Valois, Bourbon, and Tudor propagandas that deluged Europe, such questions were unavoidable. What are foregone are Spenser's final answers to the questions.

18. Aptekar, *Icons,* p. 30, finds no tradition of a sword of Jove in antiquity,

18. Aptekar, *Icons*, p. 30, finds no tradition of a sword in Jove in antiquity, while Thomas P. Roche, Jr., ed., *The Faerie Queene*, (Baltimore: Penguin, 1978), p. 1190, traces Chrysaor to the *Iliad*, "where it is used as the name of the sword by which Jove defeated the rebellious Titans."

19. [Francis Bacon], *A Declaration of the Practices & Treasons attempted and committed by Robert late Earle of Essex and his Complices* (London, 1601), sig. C3ʳ.

20. Lodovico Dolce, *Le trasformationi* (Venice, 1555).

21. Spenser, *View*, p. 4.

22. See, for comparison, the similar principle of cultural relativism in Jean Bodin, *Six Books of the Commonwealth*, tr. M. J. Tooley (New York: Macmillan, 1955), bk. 5, chap. 1 (pp. 145–57); and Sir Thomas Smith, *De Republica Anglorum*, bk. 1, chap. 15 (pp. 28–29).

23. The position of the *View* within the Elizabethan political context is established by W. L. Renwick in his edition, pp. 180–85 and 189–90.

24. Goldberg, *James I*, p. 7.

25. Ibid., p. 244 n. 9.

26. Ibid., p. 9.

27. Michel Foucault, *History of Sexuality*, vol. 1, *An Introduction*, tr. Robert Hurley (New York: Vintage, 1980), p. 100.

28. Compare Goldberg, *James I*, pp. 6–7: "The poem claims an unequivocal univocality giving voice to the language of sovereignty, taking on a sovereign voice of power. But to take it on entirely, or fully to voice the sovereign's voice, is, in either case, to present a masterful Machiavellian duplicity. To adopt the voice of power is, in Foucault's definition, to speak beyond oneself, ascribing one's powers elsewhere, saying one thing and meaning another. . . . Power—the ruler's, the poet's—styles itself in denial; the poet points to the ruler, the ruler to abstract principles."

29. Thomas Elyot, *The Boke named the Governour* (London, 1531), sig. A7ᵛ.

30. Stephen Greenblatt, *Renaissance Self-Fashioning: From More to Shakespeare* (Chicago: University of Chicago Press, 1980), p. 187.

31. Elizabeth to Grey, 15 July 1580, in *Carew Manuscripts at Lambeth* 2:312.

32. Greenblatt, *Renaissance Self-Fashioning*, p. 192.

33. Gadamer, "Hermeneutical Reflection," pp. 32–33, 42. Compare, interestingly, Jacques Derrida: "a deconstructive practice which would not bear upon 'institutional apparatuses and historical processes' . . . which would remain content to operate upon philosophemes or conceptual signifieds, or discourses, etc. would not be deconstructive; whatever its originality, it would but reproduce the gesture of self criticism in philosophy in its internal tradition" ("Ja, ou, le faux-bond," *Diagraphe* 11 [April, 1977], tr. Wlad Godzich, "The Domestication of Derrida," in *The Yale Critics: Deconstruction in America*, ed. Jonathan Arac, Wlad Godzich, and Wallace Martin [Minneapolis: University of Minnesota Press, 1983], p. 39).

34. F. J. Levy, "Francis Bacon and the Style of Politics," *ELR* 16 (1986): 122.

35. Francis Bacon, *The Proficiencie and Advancement of Learning, Divine and Humane*, in *Works*, ed. James Spedding and Robert Leslie Ellis (London: Longman, 1859), 3:268.

36. Levy sees the *Essayes* of 1597 as "the culmination of that study of political language which Bacon had begun in the aftermath of his rejection by the Queen four years earlier" ("Francis Bacon," p. 121). However, it is clear that Bacon could not consider the issue closed as long as he himself remained a political outsider, and his concern with the nature of political language continued for over another decade, if not for his whole life.

37. Lisa Jardine, *Francis Bacon: Discovery and the Art of Discourse* (Cambridge: Cambridge University Press, 1974), p. 150.

38. Francis Bacon, *The Wisedome of the Ancients,* tr. Sir Arthur Gorges (London, 1619), sig. a5ᵛ–a6ʳ. Gorges's translation is piquant and generally accurate, often unfolding and amplifying the implications of Bacon's Latin: "equidem existimo plaerósque in ea opinione fore, me delicias ac ludos facere; atque similem ferè licentiam in transferendis fabulis vsurpare, ac ipsi Poëtae sibi sumpserint in fingendis; quod pro meo iure sanè facere possem, vt contemplationibus magis arduis, haec ad voluptatem, siue meditationis propriae, siue lectionis alienae aspergerem. Neque me latet quàm versatilis materia sit Fabula, vt huc illuc trahi, imò & duci possit; quantúmque ingenij commoditas et discursus valeat, vt quae nunquam cogitata sint, bellè tamen attribuantur" (*De sapientia veterum* [London, 1609], sig. A8ʳ⁻ᵛ).

39. Bacon, *Proficiencie* 3:343.

40. In 1632, Henry Reynolds leveled exactly this accusation against Bacon, asking in his *Mythomystes,* "What shall we make of such willing contradictions, when a man to vent a few fancies of his own, shall tell us first they are the wisedome of the Auncients; and next, that those Auncient fables were but meere fables, and without wisdom or meaning, till their expositours gave them a meaning?" (cited by Charles Whitney, *Francis Bacon and Modernity* (New Haven: Yale University Press, 1986), pp. 152–53.) Reynolds, fervently believing that the full allegorical meaning of the myths is intended by their original authors, is merely twisting Bacon's own words to discredit his exposé of their obscurity.

41. Bacon, *Wisedome,* sig. a7ʳ; *De sapientia veterum,* sig. A9ʳ.

42. Bacon, *Proficiencie* 3:343–44.

43. Bacon, *Wisedome,* sig. a5ᵛ. "Antiquitatem primaeuam (exceptis quae in Sacris literis habemus) Obliuio & Silentium inuoluit; Silentia Antiquitatis, Fabulae poëtarum exceperunt: Fabulis tandem successêre Scripta quae habemus, Adeo vt Antiquitatis Penetralia, & recessus à sequentium Saeculorum Memoria, & euidentia tanquam Velo Fabularum discreta & separata sint; quod se interposuit & obiecit medium, inter ea quae perierunt, & ea quae extant" (*De sapientia veterum,* sig. A8ʳ).

44. Bacon, *Wisedome,* sig. a9ᵛ. "Facilè cernas . . . quod varium [est], ex singulorum ornatu additum" (*De sapientia veterum,* sig. A11ʳ).

45. Paul H. Kocher, "Francis Bacon on the Science of Jurisprudence," *Journal of the History of Ideas* 18 (1957): 7.

46. Cf. Aristotle, *Nichomachean Ethics,* 1139.24 ff and 1141.23 ff.

47. Bacon, *Wisedome,* pp. 6–8. "Id populi aegrè ferentes, & ipsi moliuntur Caput aliquod rerum ex sese creare, & extollere. Es res ex occultâ sollicitatione nobilium, & procerum ferè initia sumit, quibus conniuentibus, tum populi sus-

citatio tentatur; ex qua Tumor quidam rerum (per Typhonis infantiam significa-
tus) sequitur. Atque iste rerum status ab insitâ Plebis prauitate & naturâ malignâ
. . . nutricatur. . . . . Atque interdum Rebelliones istae tam praeualidae sunt, ut
Reges cogantur, tanquam à Rebellibus transportati, relictis Regni sedibus & ur-
bibus primarijs, vires contrahere, & in remotam aliquam & obscuram Prouin-
ciam ditionis suae se recipere, Neruis & Pecuniarum & Maiestatis accisis: sed
tamen non ita multò post Fortunam prudenter tolerantes, uirtute et industriâ
Mercurij neruos recipiunt, hoc est, affabiles facti, & per edicta prudentia & sermones benignos, reconciliatis subditorum animis & voluntatibus, subinde alacri-
tatem ad impensas conferendas, & nouum Auchthoritatis vigorem excitant" (*De
sapientia veterum,* sig. B2ᵛ–B3ᵛ). Cf. Comes, *Mythologiae,* sig. 198ʳ.

48. Bacon, *Wisedome,* sig. a11ʳ. "Atque per haec docendi ratio, non occultandi
artificium quaesitum est" (*De sapientia veterum,* sig. A12ʳ).

49. David Norbrook, *Poetry and Politics in the English Renaissance* (London:
Routledge, 1984), chap. 8 (pp. 195–214).

50. First noted by Frederick Ives Carpenter, *A Reference Guide to Edmund Spenser* (Chicago: University of Chicago Press, 1923), pp. 123, 237, 289; and discussed in Paul Gehl and Clark Hulse, *An Uncommon Collector: Frederick Ives Carpenter (1861–1925),* catalog of an exhibition at the Newberry Library (Chicago:
Newberry Library, 1985), item 22. A full bibliographic account is provided by
John N. King, "*The Faerie Leveller:* A 1648 Royalist Reading of the *Faerie Queene,*
5:2.29–54," *HLQ* 48 (1985): 297–303. King proposes one Samuel Sheppard (ca.
1624–ca. 1655) as the author/editor.

51. *The Faerie Leveller* (London, 1648), p. 3.

52. Ibid., p. 4.

53. G. K. Fortescue, *Catalogue of the Pamphlets, Books, Newspapers, and Manuscripts Relating to the Civil War, the Commonwealth, and Restoration, Collected by
George Thomason, 1640–1661,* 2 vols. (London: British Museum, 1908), 1:655.

54. Throughout this section I rely on Mark Kishlansky, *The Rise of the New
Model Army* (Cambridge: Cambridge University Press, 1979), esp. chaps. 5–7.

55. Peter Young and Richard Holmes, *The English Civil War: A Military History of the Three Civil Wars, 1642–1651* (London: Eyre Methuen, 1974), p. 276.

From Matron to Monster: Tudor-Stuart London and the Languages of Urban Description

The history of printed maps and views of London begins in the Tudor-Stuart period, with the great works of Agas, Braun and Hogenberg, Norden, Visscher, Hondius, and Hollar.[1] This is not simply an accident connected to the history of printing; not until very late in the Stuart period did printers begin to issue bucolic landscapes that could match these city views, which were, par excellence, the English image of man's habitation in the earth. London was the largest and most striking human creation in Britain; its hold upon the imagination is reflected not only in these views but also in an unprecedented volume and variety of literary works that took the city's life as a central concern. The city was a fact of life so essential and so complex as to require countless interpretations; according to the Jacobean preacher Thomas Adams, it was like "certain pictures, that represent to divers beholders, at divers stations, divers forms."[2]

One important but neglected standpoint from which writers took the measure of London is represented by the topographical description, a widely practiced genre that flourished in the hands of such major Elizabethan and Jacobean topographers as William Camden, John Norden, John Speed, and John Stow. The aims of such writers were both intellectual and patriotic. While putting the English landscape and its history at the fingertips of English readers, they also framed them in an ideology that justified the English way of life. Thus Camden, for example, explained in the preface to his *Britannia* (1586) that his motives were both "a firme settled study of the truth, and sincere antique faithfulnesse to the glory of my God and my countrie."[3] Camden evidently saw no difficulty, later in his survey of the nation, with settling the same title of "my deere natiue country" upon London, perhaps because it was for him "the Epitome and Breviary of all Britain" (pp. 437, 421). Stow was the only major topographer to publish a work devoted exclusively to "the chiefe and principall citie of the land,"[4] but London's overwhelming domination of England's economic, political, and intellectual life made it an especially pregnant crux in almost every reading of the landscape. Norden, for example, thought it "not vnfit to begin" his *Speculum Britanniae* (1593) with a volume on "MYDDLESEX, which aboue all other Shyres is graced, with that chiefe and head Citie LONDON: which as an adamant draweth vnto it all the other parts of the land."[5] London was not, however, merely a microcosm of the national body but also one among its many subject members, and thus to the extent that London's achievements might underwrite the sovereign power they might also, potentially, usurp it. Speed's *Theatre of the Empire of Great Britaine* (1611), which had originally been dedicated to James I, was rededicated by its 1676 editor to the City of London; after all, Edward Phillips asked, to whom was it more proper to dedicate "the Description of our own Countrey, than to the Powers of that Supreme City, whose prosperous Trade distributes Wealth and Honour to the whole Nation?"[6] Precisely because they were symbolizing the nation's life, topographers drew the lineaments of London with special care.

Many of the leading descriptive works of the Tudor-Stuart age were based on innovative historical and topographical research, on techniques borrowed both from major Continental writers like Ortelius and from such pioneering English antiquaries as John Leland, Matthew Parker, Alexander Neville, and William Lambarde.[7] But the often massive learning of the topographers was matched by an equally innovative concern with expository method, by an effort to shape the facts of topography—especially of urban life—into a coherent vision. For this reason, topography was neither a figure of speech (as in rhetoric) nor a science, but a mode of invention, with its own generic rules and assumptions.[8] In fact, a fundamental feature of descriptions of Tudor-Stuart London is their use of inventive models or paradigms to guide the selection and arrangement of material. Through such models, the city's life was not simply organized, but justified.

Although the models for description came from different sources— from Aristotelian ideas adapted to the needs of statecraft, from Ramist dialectic, and from ancient rhetoric—they reinforced each other in their tendency to harmonize the facts of urban culture with the laws of nature. The procedure to which they all contributed was the personification of the city as heroic matron, symbolically submissive intermediary between nature and the higher claims of political culture.

This gender-based procedure, which dominated many of the major descriptions of Tudor-Stuart London, effectively suppressed the more dynamic aspects of urban life—especially the power of the metropolitan economy both to enfranchise and to enslave individual subjects without regard to the sovereign's intent. On the one hand, the freedom of London, though subject to its own rules and restrictions, posed a challenge to the hierarchical principles of feudal domination: "such was the Custome of London, that a villen having remained there the space of one whole yeare and a day, could not be fetched or removed from thence. For so great is the prerogatives of that place, that it giveth protection to the villen or bondman against his lord while the said bondman shall be resiant there."[9] The socioeconomic corollary of this political freedom was the spectacular opportunity for mobility. But on the other hand, these liberties and the rapid growth they spawned also made London an engine potentially dangerous to the national regime. "With time," James I declared in 1616, "England will onely be London, and the whole countrey be left waste."[10] One important reason for the monarchs' repeated attempts to halt London's growth by fiat was the city's economic domination of "the other good Townes and Borrowes of this Kingdome," which "by reason of so great receit for people in and about the said City, are much unpeopled, and in their trading, and otherwise decayed."[11] But another concern, according to an Elizabethan proclamation, was that "such multitudes could hardly be governed by ordinary justice to serve God and obey her Majesty."[12] Especially troubling were the ruptures, stretches, folds, and loosened threads of the social fabric, the potentially divergent powers and interests that were geographically epitomized by the subdivision of the city into a discontinuous terrain of holdings and jurisdictions, hidden tenements, alleys, byways, straight rooms, and cellars.

The attribution of a feminine persona to the city diminished these concerns ideologically, providing not only a gender-based model of obedient submission but also a transhistorical identity which absorbed and suppressed the spatial divisions and discontinuities that manifested the city's true historic dynamism. Foucault has observed that in the analysis of intellectual history, "metaphorising the transformations of discourse in a vocabulary of time necessarily leads to the utilisation of the model of individual consciousness with its intrinsic temporality. Endeavouring on the other hand to decipher discourse through the use of spatial, strategic metaphors enables one to grasp precisely the points at which the discourses are transformed in, through and on the basis of relations of power."[13] In the reading of Tudor-Stuart London's landscape, personification counteracted in much the same way the inherently spatial bias of topography, together with its potentially disturbing emphasis on sharply divided or discontinuous political domains. By subordinating to a trans-historical, transindividual identity the viewpoint of observers historically situated in space and time, and by stretching this identity over millennia, the personification of London unified in one body the city's discontinuous spaces and naturalized the erratic development of its culture.

The dynamic contradictions in London's cultural development did not go unnoticed in other literary genres, but their incorporation into topographical writing required the dismantling of the whole framework that supported this genre, the substitution, for the city's figurative humanity, of the humanity of the individual observer situated in historic time and space. This substitution took place during the seventeenth century, as the cultural facts of urban life began to be conceptually opposed to nature, and as the human status once claimed by the city began to be appropriated to individual observers situated in an unnaturally changeful, even monstrous, landscape. I would like to trace these changing perceptions, which transformed London from a natural to a cultural fact, by examining some abstract models for describing cities and by explaining their use, meaning, and eventual demise in some major descriptions of London.

I

For Renaissance writers, the pleasures of geography were frequently the pleasures of intellectual power. Sir Thomas Elyot, for example, explained that in geography a reader was able "in one houre, to beholde those realmes, cities, sees, ryuers, and mountaynes, that uneth in an olde mans life can nat be iournaide and pursued. . . . I can nat tell what more pleasure shulde happen to a gentil witte than to beholde in his owne house euery thynge that with in all the worlde is contained." [14] This pleasurable sense of power—of appropriating a vast public space to the private recess of the study and the mind—was greatly enhanced by the typographical revolution and its treatment of the printed book as a container of knowledge readily mastered and possessed. Through the psychogeometric apparatus of print, the world was plotted and contained in the great cosmographies and atlases of Munster, Franck, Ortelius, and Mercator. [15] It was not lost on topographers like Jodocus Hondius that the powers being claimed for the genre of the printed Atlas had once been those of a Titan.

The cities of Europe, regarded as wonders of the world even in the much older chronicle tradition, [16] quickly became a special concern of the new topography. The world atlases of Ortelius and Mercator were splendidly matched by the urban atlases of Georg Braun and Franz Hogenberg (1572–1618), of Matthias Merian (1633), and of Joan Blaeu (1663). The earliest of these, Braun and Hogenberg's *Theatrum civitates orbis terrarum*, grew to six folio volumes over several decades and inspired a host of surveys of the world's cities, including those by Adriano Romano (1585), Giovanni Botero (1588), and Hippolytus Collibus (1600). Together with the routiers and roadbooks that began to appear at the same time, these works reflect a widespread tendency to organize the world as a transnational grid of urban communities. This urban network formed, as the title of one English work has it, a *Merchants Mappe of Commerce*. The settled world, James Howell explained in 1657, might be compared "to a giant piece of embroidery, enchas'd up and down, whereof the most bossie, and richest compactest parts are Towns and Cities." [17] The formal apparatus of works devoted to this network is one of their most striking features; their tendency to epitomize, list, enumerate, tabulate, forms an urbane language of description by which large things are contained and written small. [18]

What such a language must perforce assume are the conceptual means for simplifying the complex, for reducing the abundant, disparate, and changing facts of urban life to telling and economical schemes. Indeed, just as important as actual descriptions of cities were the metalanguages, the models or paradigms, that helped to structure the art of description. Behind the image of London in the works of the major Tudor and Stuart topographers of London lie a number of interrelated paradigms, which were available to these writers both directly and through the earlier descriptions from which they borrowed. Three of the most influential come from the fields of Renaissance statecraft, Ramist dialectic, and classical rhetoric. These paradigms demonstrate the exercise of powers that were not merely intellectual but ideological. Implicit in the intellectual shapes inscribed upon the cultural facts of urban life were a series of assumptions by which these facts were naturalized and subjected to the interests of economic and political power. To describe a city through such paradigms was not only to know it but, implicitly, to control it.

The first of these paradigms emerged not from the intellectual needs of the printed book but from the practical needs of Renaissance diplomacy. We owe not only a great many descriptions of Tudor London but also a basic scheme for describing cities to the Venetian senate, which around 1500 began to require detailed reports, or *relazioni*, on foreign states from the ambassadors it sent abroad. So essential was this intelligence that the Venetian authorities issued a four-part rubric for generating a relation.

I. These things are required for making a relation. First to describe the situation of the province . . . and in how many lesser regions and provinces it is divided, not omitting to name the principal cities.

II. It is necessary to treat of the quality of that province, that is to say the temperature and value of the air, likewise of the value of the waters, of the fertility or sterility of the crops.

III. It is customary to discuss the inhabitants, showing their customs, and ways, colour, stature, and character. . . .

IV. It is necessary to come to particulars of the prince . . . his person, life, and customs, . . . his revenues and expenses.[19]

In most of the surviving ambassadorial reports from England, information about the prince and politics at court dominates the other categories, yet it is rare to find a report that does not cover all four categories, usually in the specified order. London figured heavily, almost exclusively, in the part of the reports where cities should be mentioned, and quite remarkably most of the ambassadors appear simply to have applied the same fourfold scheme to the city itself, discussing first the natural features and resources of the site, second the artificial fabric, third the population, and fourth the city government.[20] Robert Dallington's tabular arrangement of a similar scheme in *A Method for Travell* (1605) suggests that these four main categories may have been produced by crossing Aristotle's distinction between *res* and *homines* (the two essential considerations in Aristotle's sketch of an ideal *polis*) with the distinction between matter and form.[21] This is confirmed by the encyclopedia of J. H. Alsted, who noted in tabular form that things in cities are to be analyzed according to *locus* and *structurae,* and that men in cities are to be analyzed according to a scale of offices that run from *agricolae* and *artifices* to *senatores* and *judices.*[22] By implication, cities convert natural resources into cultural forms, just as rulers shape inchoate political circumstance into order.[23]

This four-part rubric, which justified the city as the cultural perfection of nature and its rulers as the perfectors of its people, found its way into both manuscript and printed descriptions of London by such Latin humanists as Domenico Mancini (ca. 1487), John Major (1521), Polydore Vergil (1523), and Paolo Giovio (1548).[24] In turn, these descriptions made their way—often verbatim—into compilers like Bale, Munster, Ortelius, and Braun, who influenced Camden and his contemporaries.[25]

In addition to such embodiments in prose descriptions, however, the four-part Aristotelian model also found a reincarnation in another metalanguage—a metalanguage worked out primarily in the travel manuals and Ramist treatises of Germany. The *artes peregrinandi,* manuals designed for the aid of travelers, contained much practical and moralizing advice, but they also offered specific suggestions for what things should be observed in traveling. These guidelines were essential not only for writing the requisite journal, but also for reducing the bewildering variety of urban details to a manageable shape. The emphasis fell on method, with which, Albrecht Meier promised, "the thicke mistes of ignorance, and hard conception will soone be scattered, and the same converted into a quicke sight, and illumination of the senses."[26]

The concept of "method" in these manuals owes a great deal to the influence of Ramus. German Ramism, however, was most fruitful in the hybrid practitioners known by their contemporaries as "Mixts," who were "followers in part of Ramus and in part of Aristotle."[27] Not surprisingly, then, the four-part Aristotelian model dominates a scheme proposed by the Ramist Hilary Pyrckmair. "When the names of the city and their derivation have been examined," Pyrckmair explains, the first of the external things to be examined are the site, and then the walls, fortifications, gates, and such things; next come the streets, markets, fountains, and gardens; then the buildings, "which are either public or private. The public can best be seen divided into two parts," the sacred and the profane. Finally come the internal considerations, the people and the civic and ecclesiastical government.[28]

The power of such schemes to codify the landscape is most apparent, however, when they take their most rigidly Ramist form as dichotomous diagrams. In these diagrams, the mastery of culture over nature, and of rulers over citizens, is enshrined as the visual mastery of space over time, eternal laws over history. Identical versions of one such diagram were published by Nathan Chytraeus in 1594 and Paul Hentzner in 1627.[29] Both Chytraeus and Hentzner had in fact written descriptions of London based on their visits, and their paradigm is perhaps closest in shape to the descriptions of London by the major English topographers and antiquaries. Their scheme divides the standard topics into four basic categories: (1) the city's name, founder, and augmenters, (2) site, (3) buildings, and (4) government, education, and social life. The last three of these cover the topics in the four-part Venetian rubric as it was applied to cities (site, fabric, governed, governors), while the first repeats a feature—the city's name and founders—found throughout the German travel guides and Ramist schemes.[30] There is thus a striking persistence of both a basic set of topics and a basic order or arrangement. There seems to have been not only a core of features regarded as essential to a city, but also an overall conception of their relationship.

One such conception certainly remains the old Venetian-Aristotelian paradigm.[31] But the preoccupation with names, founders, and augmenters comes from a third framework for description—the framework of ancient rhetoric. There are in fact relatively few examples of urban description in classical literature and relatively few instructions to be found in the rhetorical treatises of Aristotle and Cicero. Quintilian, however, contains the very useful hint that "cities are praised after the same fashion as men. The founder takes the place of the parent, and antiquity carries great authority. . . . The virtues and vices revealed by their deeds are the same as in private individuals. . . . Their citizens enhance their fame just as children bring honour to their parents" (3.7.26). The *Rhetor* of Menander similarly explains that the praise of cities draws on both the rules for praising countries and "those which relate to individuals. Thus we should select 'position' [i.e., site] from topics relating to countries, and origins, actions, accomplishments from those relating to individuals."[32]

The bearing of this on the rubric of urban encomia is perhaps clarified by the schemes devised for the praise of persons by Menander's predecessors and contemporaries. For example, Aphthonius, a major influence on Renaissance rhetoric, advises that the main topics in praising a person are ancestors and parents, upbringing and the attributes that are its result, the beauties and exploits of body and mind, and finally a comparison that proves the case.[33] Interestingly enough, when Aphthonius's scheme was translated by Richard Rainolde in *The Foundacion of Rhetorike*, it was offered as a model for "the praise of all the Britaines: or of all the citezeins of London."[34] Rainolde's hint for converting praise into prosopopoeia was no idle suggestion, for in the descriptive rubrics of figures like Pyrckmair, Chytraeus, and Hentzner, the topics are disposed in just the way a person is to be praised, beginning with the city's name, founders, and augmenters. The advantages of birth and circumstance are embodied in discussion of the city's site, and the beauties and accomplishments of the person find their counterparts in the city's fabric, its government, and its worthy offspring. The personified London of Dekker's *The Dead Tearme* (1608) thus glosses the structure of her self-portrait by explaining that "because al Citties were bound in common ciuility, in pollicies, and in honour to maintaine their Names, their Callings, their Priuilidges, and those Ancient houses that Spring out of them, I wil . . . Annatomize my selfe; euen from head to foot, thou shalt know euery limbe of me, and with how many parts my bodie is deuided. My birth, my bringing vp, and my rising shall bee . . . manifest."[35]

The personification of the city is a very old tradition that originates in the myths of the Cretan and Asian goddess Cybele. In the *Aeneid*, Vergil claims that in Crete, the cradle of Trojan civilization, the ancient mother-goddess first took the form of Cybele (3.104–13); Anchises later likens Rome's surrounding wall to "Berecynthia mater . . . turrita," the great

goddess Berecynthia tower-crowned (6.784–85). Both in Vergil's narrative and in general, Cybele is "characterized by her steady movement
westward and her extraordinary assimilation into other, invariably more
austere, versions of the Great Mother."[36] Typically represented with a
towering turretlike crown and cloaked with the fruits and gems of the
earth, Cybele rides a chariot drawn by yoked lions, frequently interpreted as a symbol of wildness submitting to parental discipline. Stephen
Batman explained that "her stately sitting [in her chariot] betokeneth the
firme ground wheron is builded Cityes and townes: by her croune so
signified."[37]

What is essential to the strategy of personification is not simply that it
bestows upon the city the familiar lineaments of human nature, extended
into a lifespan that lasts for centuries, but that it subjects the city to the
ideology of gender. Cities are personified as feminine because culture
"recognizes that women are active participants in its special processes,
but at the same time sees them as rooted in, as having more direct affinity
with, nature."[38] Given this situation of female identity midway between
nature and culture, it is not surprising to find so much overlap between
the Aristotelian frameworks, which naturalize the facts of culture, and
the rhetorical schemes for personifying cities; nor is it surprising to find
this overlap inscribed authoritatively in the tables of Ramists. On the one
hand, the biological role of women in the process of reproduction provided an analogy by which to rationalize the generation of wealth. At the
same time, the domestic role of women in child rearing and family life,
understood to rest upon an affection "indifferent to sex, age, or other
possible affiliations,"[39] provided a psychic model for social communion
and thus for the conversion of nature into culture. On the other hand,
the subjection of feminine to masculine in family life could justify the
subordination of domestic loyalties to the higher claims of public life. In
the case of England, the feminine gender of London placed implicit limits on the power of the city in relation to other groups and communities
in the kingdom. By analogy to the rule of exogamous marriage, the
subordination of London to higher political powers prevented it from
being seen as a self-sufficient, closed community and stressed its bonds
of alliance—and thus loyalties—to the whole kingdom.

Insofar as it is a history of gender typing, the history of personification
is also a history of sexual ambivalence, as the book of Revelation's contrast between Jerusalem, the bride of Christ, and Rome, the whore of
Babylon, attests.[40] Thomas Dekker demonstrates this ambivalence when
he observes that London "hast all things in thee to make thee fairest, and
all things in thee to make thee foulest: for thou art attir'de like a Bride,
. . . but there is much harlot in thine eyes."[41] The literature of Tudor-

Stuart London abounds in such negative personifications as Thomas Nashe's bawdlike "Great Grandmother of Corporations, Madame Troynovant."[42] Yet such transformations of the "inlaw" into the "outlaw" feminine[43] tend to occur in satiric genres, where a different sense of temporality—a stress on contemporary life and individual experience—deprived cultural facts of their "natural" aura and put them in an irrational light. Thus the character-writer Donald Lupton, focusing on the rapid growth of London in recent memory, portrayed the city as a pregnant glutton whose "greatness doth diminish her beauty."[44] In the basically encomiastic genre of description, by contrast, a temporal framework extending the city's life over centuries suppressed the sense of contemporary experience in favor of a transpersonal identity that was orderly and submissive. The better to examine the separate incarnations and eventual demise of this identity in the works of Tudor-Stuart London's major topographers, it will be useful first to demonstrate, with reference to these writers and their contemporaries, how the Aristotelian harmonies of nature with culture and the rhetorical uses of gender coalesce as ideologies with each of the topics outlined in the idealized space of the Ramist diagram. I base my discussion on the influential table printed in Chytraeus and Hentzner (fig. 1).

II

The first of the categories in the table—name, founder, and augmenters—establish the venerable age of the city's persona. Just as the name of Rome could be traced to Romulus, or backward through the etymology of the Greek ῥώμη from Rome to army to bodily strength, so countless topographers traced the name of Trinobantia (by false etymology) to Trojan Brute, London's mythical founder. By the logic of personification, the changes in the city's name reflected her loyal submission to a series of royal masters. Dekker's London, for example, explains that she changed her name from Trinobantia to London when "Lud challenging me as his owne, tooke away none of my dignities, but as women married to great persons, loose their old names, so did I mine being wedded to that king."[45] The macaronic history of London's many different names, William Lambarde argued, was "no light Argument that [London] hath bene of great price these many Yeares,"[46] but Dekker's London was quick to add that she had "bin loued of our kings, because euer since haue [I] to our kinges bin loyall" (4:75).

The table ties the name together with the founder, and there is more involved here than the sanction of antiquity, for the notion of a founder implied that a city was not the product of organic growth but the result

I. The name of the city, and the reason for the name, if extant
   Item: the founder, augmenter (enlarger), or renewer of the place

II.
   1. Rivers, each of them, their course, length, source
   2. The seaside or harbor
   3. Mountains
   4. Woods, groves, or other things of note

III. Buildings, which are either

   public

   sacred
   - cathedrals
   - monastaries
   - churches

   secular
   - palaces
   - gates
   - squares
   - arsenals
   - fortresses
   - towers
   - means of defense

   private, or things in the private dwellings which are of note, for example, gardens, pictures, fountains, statues

IV. Method of government, and things pertaining to it
   1. The assembly, its members, and honest servants of the city
   2. Schools, method of educating and training youth
      Item. learned men and libraries
   3. Vulgar customs, food and drink
      Item: workshops

Figure 1. "Things to be noted in traveling." Translated from Nathan Chytraeus, *Variorum in Europa itinerum deliciae* (Herborn, 1594)

of a single decisive act performed on one day.[47] Through the foundation ritual, in theory, a sacred geometry was laid out at the moment of the city's foundation and fixed its identity for all time.

   The augmenters and renewers who are linked in the table with the founder further emphasize the idea of a fixed and unalterable beginning. John Guillory has recently explained that augmentation is tied to a fundamental authority, to a unique, unrepeatable event.[48] Augmentation can extend but not begin and must always be submitted to the authority of the foundation. Linguistically, augmentation permanently excludes the idea of any new beginning; it asserts the sacredness of the foundation and declares it true for all generations. Thus in countless descriptions the mythical King Lud renews London's walls and gates and gives it his name but does not alter the fundamental act of his ancestor.[49]

Through their sacralizing of space, naming, founding, and augmenting are associated with the recurrent topics of walls, shape, and gates. These appear later in a separate category, but in most of the paradigms they represent the first of the city's physical aspects to be discussed. It is here that the potentially disturbing topographical emphasis on spatial divisions and partitions was subjected to ideologies of unified order. The earliest known image of a city is an Egyptian hieroglyph which, by inscribing a cross within a circle, symbolizes the interplay between exchange and enclosure, between the intersection of common interests and the total identity this focus creates.[50] In the description of Tudor-Stuart London there are many poignant attempts to extract an ideal, symbolic figure from a misshapen reality. Nathan Chytraeus, for example, likens the city's shape to a half moon,[51] while Richard Zouche compares it to a rainbow.[52] John Stow, waxing uncharacteristically idealistic but retaining his typical eye for mundane detail, likens the city to the "forme of a bow, except that denting in betwixt Criplegate, and Aldersgate."[53] James Howell's *Londonopolis,* based on Stow, proposes nobly that London is shaped like a laurel leaf, but then goes on to add, in view of the sprawling suburbs which by 1657 had grown larger than the walled city itself, that "the Suburbs of London are larger then the Body of the City, which make some compare her to a Jesuites Hat, whose brims are far larger than the Block."[54] As for the internal geometry of London, writers remarked that London Bridge made London the crossroads of England, though they differed in where they placed the crossroads.[55]

Suppressed by an idealizing geometry, the cultural processes of growth and change were harmonized with nature in the second of the major topics, the discussion of the city's site and natural resources. In the case of London, such discussion commonly stressed the interplay between economic and aesthetic considerations, as in Camden's claim that London is "sweetly situate in a rich and fertile soil . . . on the gentle ascent and rising of a hill, hard by the *Thamis* side, the most milde Merchant, as one would say, of all things that the world doth yield: . . . A man would say that seeth the shipping there, that it is, as it were, a very wood of trees disbranched to make glades and let in light: So shaded it is with masts and sailes."[56] If the city's names and handsome shape were graces it inherited from its ancestral founders, its resources were the rightful fortune at its disposal. Nearly all the London panoramas of the period make this point by foregrounding the Thames and its shipping, thus emphasizing a fundamental reciprocity between the powers of nature and culture. River and city, fluid and fabric brought together a natural timelessness with human history.

To the realm of culture and artifice belong the buildings of the table's third major category, including the walls and gates already mentioned. In Chytraeus's table, as in most such schemes, the distinctions between public and private, sacred and profane space articulate a kind of social order.[57] Not apparent from the table, however, is the extent to which, for antiquarians like Camden and Stow, London's buildings were also a means by which time was rendered visible, by which past generations left their mark on the civic heritage.[58] This is true not only for the description of individual buildings but, as we shall see, for the temporal sequence or historical priority assigned to sacred, civic, and private construction.

The division of the city into public and private, sacred and profane space comes ultimately from Aristotle's *Politics* (7.8–9), where Aristotle notes that there are six necessary *functions* in an ideal state—agriculture, crafts, defense, government, worship, and the generation of wealth and property—but only four *parts,* since farmers and craftsmen cannot be full citizens. The remaining four parts, moreover, do not form four separate classes, but four functions of a single citizen class, divided according to age. Young citizens are soldiers, mature ones leaders, and venerable ones priests, while all three hold property. In chapters 11 and 12, when Aristotle sketches the physical outlines of a city, he assigns a proper space to each: young citizens man the public defenses on walls; priests occupy the temple on a sacred height or central spot; while leaders command the public square, from which base noncitizens are excluded, and the market square, to which they are admitted. All citizens are to own property both outside and inside the city.

In terms of the actual economy and social life of Renaissance cities, the three-part model is thus narrow and exclusive, focused solely on the civic elite and the essential spaces that are defined as theirs. Among formal descriptions of Elizabethan London we look in vain for the small retailers, craftsmen, and casual laborers, the aliens, transients, vagabonds, and paupers who likely made up more than half of greater London's population.[59] The social model implied by the division of space is not, of course, without a certain dynamism. As in Aristotle, where the divisions into sacred, public, and private merely stand for the different aspects of a citizen's life, so in the description of London they stand for the many types of association that form a citizen, from the diocese, the parish, and its vestry, to the wards, precincts, guilds, schools, and militia, to the family, the household, and the business. This dynamism is limited, however, to the citizen elite; it does not account for dislocations and asymmetries, and it moves in a general direction away from the female, domestic sphere of social communion toward a heriarchical, patriarchal political culture.

The meaning of this movement comes out most fully in the final topic of the table, the discussion of people and government. Insofar as human resources come last in a scheme dominated by the idea of personification, citizens and leaders are not so much the makers of the city as its legacy, the "famous Patriots, and Worthies, which she hath produc'd and bred."[60] In many descriptions the treatment of the city's offspring extends the role of gender to include the nurturing of an elite whose loyalties ultimately reach out beyond the city. As one verse encomium put it, "This Queene of citties, Lady of this Ile, . . . / Upon her lap did nourse those sonnes of Fame, / Whose deeds do now nobilitate her name."[61] A special stress falls upon the transition into fame and power in a 1588 manuscript description by William Smith. Smith begins with eleven pages on the site and monuments of London, but the next ninety pages are given over to a discourse "Of the State and Pollicie of London," which centers on a lengthy account of the protocols of the Lord Mayor's procession.[62] As Robert Darnton has explained, to use a procession for the purposes of description is to construct a model of society that is not so much divided into classes as segmented in graduated degrees.[63] These degrees form a syntagmatic chain that is understood metonymically as leading upward toward the elite patriarchal leadership which holds the city to obedience. Norden emphasized these circumscribing limits when he depicted a triumphal procession of the city's aldermen across the bottom of his *Civitas Londini* view and when he bordered the *Speculum Britanniae* map with the arms of London's Twelve Great Livery Companies.

The boundary of political culture placed around the city was permeable in both directions. First of all the city effected a transition that took its leading sons, if not its daughters, outside the domestic urban field and into the fields of opportunity—the court and landed aristocracy—where great prestige and power lay. It was a great tribute to London, Edmund Bolton wrote, that "all the partes of England are full of families, either originally raised to the dignity of gentlemen out of this one most famous place, or so restored and enriched as to seem to amount to an original raising."[64] Not only did attention to London's overachieving sons conceal from sight the more spectacular failures, it also implied that London was the garden where nature was nurtured. Thus William Harrison traced the rise of a new rural gentry to London, "from which (as it were from a seedplot) courtiers, lawyers, and merchants be continuously transplanted."[65]

Yet as Harrison's garden image suggests, the very metaphorical means by which London contributed to the court and monarchy provided for its cultivation by those higher powers. Placed midway between nature and culture, London's status was reinforced by a gender ideology that

made it the "nymph of Britain, graced with the seat of Kings."[66] Thomas
Churchyard wrote that London was

the Maiden toune, that keepes her selfe so cleane,
That none can touche, nor staine in trothe, by any cause or meane.
. . . .
Here is the soil and seat of Kyngs, and place of precious price.
Here worthies makes their mansions still, & buildeth stately towres,
Here sitts the Nobles of the realme, in golden halles and bowers.[67]

The visual counterpart here is not the bird's-eye views of Norden,
framed by the city's leaders or their coats of arms, but the long view of
Francis Delaram (ca. 1610), where the city appears between the legs of a
rearing horse bearing James I.[68]

III

If in some respects the topical scheme of urban description resembles a
mold into which any city might be poured,[69] the overriding trope of
personification is managed by Camden, Norden, Speed, and Stow to
elicit different personae or identities. Camden, for example, begins with
a list of epithets and names and with a discussion of the site, but then he
takes the innovative step of combining the city's topography with a narrative history. After discussing the fabulous foundation myths on which
London "fathereth her originalls," he turns to the firmer ground of recorded history and surviving monuments. He lays heaviest stress, however, on the glorious Norman period, when London "through the speciall favour and indulgence of Princes obtained verie large and great
Immunities, beganne to be called *The Kings Chamber,* and so flourished
anew with fresh trade and traffique of merchants."[70]

Topographically, this period of growth and prosperity takes Camden
outside the City proper to the new suburbs, which "stretched forth from
the gates a great length on every side but westward especially which are
the greatest, and best peopled" (p. 427). By moving topographically
westward, and by stressing the establishment of Westminster as the seat
of Norman kings, Camden implicitly traces the greatness of modern
London not to the city government, not to merchant life or trade, but to
the royal power that makes it the capital of Britannia. In other words,
London's civic and mercantile achievements are merely the by-product
of its role as capital; its powers and privileges are held at the pleasure of
England's monarchs. Only when this is established does Camden turn
finally to the fabric within the walls, to the civic and commercial buildings of the city and to the "forward service and loyalty" of London's
citizens to their prince.

Unlike Camden before him, and Speed after him, Norden does not explicitly invoke an ideology of gender, and this perhaps reflects his relatively greater emphasis on London's independent civic life. After an account of London's names and mythical history, Norden turns, like Camden, to a three-part narrative that recounts the city's early history from Roman to Saxon times and then to the Norman Conquest. Norman history culminates, however, not with the royal settlement of Westminster but with the evolution of London's government. After a series of struggles with the City, King John "granted vnto the Citie by his letters pattents, that they should yeerely choose vnto themselues, a Mayor," and "in the time of H.3. also the Aldermen of the Citie were ordeined."[71] There follows a list of the City's twenty-five aldermanic wards, to which the parishes in each are subordinated. Only after this sketch of London's civic evolution does Norden turn to the city's fabric and charitable institutions. The shape of Norden's London is no doubt a function of his segregation of Westminster for separate treatment elsewhere, yet this exclusion is itself a function of the independent status he attributes to the city.

In the hands of John Speed, the topics are aligned to produce neither a royal nor an independent London, but a providentially ordained princess of the world. In his opening discussion of the names and myths of London, Speed singles out the geographical advantage that makes her "the mart of the world: for thither are brought the silk of Asia, the spices from Africa, the balmes from Grecia, & the riches of both the Indies East & West."[72] Speed's subsequent discussion of London's fabric centers on the Constantinian and Saxon cathedrals, Saint Peter's and Saint Paul's, which, poised atop the city's two main hills, Ludgate and Cornhill, form a diptych and highlight a providential connection between the city's topography and its pious origins and soul.

Reversing the order of Norden, Speed traces from these centers *first* the 121 parish churches and *then* the city's wards and government. As if expanding outward from a religious seed to its civic fruits, Speed then makes Westminster a consequence, not a cause, of London's providential increase: "this London (as it were) disdaining bondage, hath set her selfe on each side, far without the wals, & hath left her West-Gate in the midst, from whence with continuall buildings (still affecting greatnesse) she hath continued her streets vnto a kings Palace and ioined a second Citie to her self." Following this auspicious union, the final movement in Speed's portrait carries the providential expansion outward from two sacred hills astride a river to an economic power that rules the globe: "The wealth of this Citie (as Isai once spoke of Nilus) grows from the Reuenewes and Haruest of her south-bounding Thames; whose traffique for merchandizing, is like that of Tyrus, whereof Ezekiel speaks. . . . Upon this Thamesis the Ships of Tharsis seeme to ride, and the Nauy, that rightly is termed the Lady of the Sea, spreds her saile. Whence twice with lucky successe hath bin accomplished, the compassing of the vniuersal Globe." (p. 29)

Even John Stow's monumental *Survey of London,* which ran to more than five hundred pages in the first edition of 1598, came under the influence of such idealizing schemes. In his earlier chronicles, Stow had been essentially an old-fashioned annalist, and his original research in the City's archives might have produced a misshapen catalog were it not for the well-established rubric found in Camden and elsewhere. For all its bulk, Stow's *Survey* is in structure an orderly account of London's antiquity, site, fabric, government, and worthies. There is even an attempt to sketch an ideal geometry of the city (1:113).

Stow departs radically, however, from the standard schemes in the second half of his work, a street-by-street perambulation of the wards, a technique he claims to have borrowed from William Lambarde's 1572 *Perambulation of Kent* (1:xcvii). We now perhaps associate Stow's appeal with his crusty, unadorned style and his interjection of personal memory and comment, but these stylistic aspects of Stow's persona are merely functions of a more profoundly innovative point of view. By perambulating the city street by street, he transformed what was, in the personifying rubrics, essentially a blazon or at best a triumphal procession of the city's attributes into an extended *voie* or exploration of the landscape. This not only allowed for more intimate detail but also introduced a historically situated observer into the landscape. In Camden, Norden, or Speed the city might have a history of growth like any life-form, but by stretching over several millennia the span between London's ancestors and her recent achievements and progeny, the personifying rubric paradoxically suppressed the temporal dimension of urban life. As portrayed by Camden, Norden, or Speed, the city's life is organic without being dynamic. The first half of Stow's *Survey* has the same effect, but his perambulation introduced an entirely different measure of urban temporality—the life span of the observer.

Stow was more than sixty years old when he began his work on the city in which he had been born and raised.[73] In childhood Stow had inhabited a pre-Reformation city where the old guilds still held sway and the new maritime consortia had yet to be formed. He could recall London's religious houses and their destruction, but he had also lived to see the city's new wealth and the suburban squalor brought on by a fourfold increase in population. He remembered, for example, that near the nunnery of Saint Clare, now converted to "diverse fair and large store-

houses," there had been a farm from which "I my selfe in my youth haue
fetched many a halfe pennie worth of Milke . . . alwayes hote from the
Kine" (1:126). He remembered too that part of his father's garden had
been built upon, without payment, by Thomas Cromwell and noted
"that the suddaine rising of some men, causeth them to forget themselues." (1:179) In the dedication of the *Survey* to the City of London,
Stow explained that "what London hath beene of auncient time men may
here see, as what it is now euery man doth beholde" (1:xcviii). The novelty of Stow's work was to have traversed the ground between these two
points in time. Unlike the travelogues of tourists, who observed the
sights of London for the first time, Stow's *Survey* turned on the idea of
revisiting sites to find them changed, of remarking how once "sweete
and fresh waters" were "since decaied" (1:11), how once common fields
were built up with "fayre summer houses, some of them like Midsom-
mer Pageantes, . . . bewraying the vanity of mens mindes" (2:78), and
how the now squalid suburbs were "pestered with small tenements and
homely cottages, having inhabitants, English and strangers, more in
number than some cities in England" (2:70).

By focusing on London's recent history, and especially on the changes
in his own lifetime, Stow appropriated to himself the privileged human
status that had once belonged to the personified city, and the result was
to defamiliarize, depersonalize the latter. To take the measure of the city
from the individual human perspective was implicitly to violate the rubric of personification, where the metaphoric scale of time was the mil-
lennial life span of the city. No longer strictly augmenting according to a
long established outline for description, Stow was in effect supplanting
the paradigm, sketching out a new foundation, showing that by the measure of human experience London itself had broken from its foundations
and was losing its familiar human character. In Stow's perambulation,
London acquired all the characteristics of a monstrous romance realm,
with "sudden alterations of temperature, mysterious heightenings, local
intensities, sudden drops in quality, and alarming effluvia."[74] As they
came to seem less natural, the cultural facts affecting London's growth
stood out more clearly for "*every man* [to] beholde."

While topographers like Camden and Speed were quoted and epitomized throughout the seventeenth century, it was Stow who was repeatedly updated and expanded to reflect changes in London's life. It was
Stow, too, who was the stimulus to later innovations that changed the
image of London.[75] Much that was innovative was concerned with
method,[76] a persistent concern since the Venetian rubrics, but made more
urgent by the increasingly perceived fact of rapid change in London. One
factor adding to this sense was a breakdown of the political consensus

that had defined the nature and limits of the city's power. James Howell, remarking in his *Londonopolis* that "populous Cities are alwaies subject to bring forth turbulent spirits," attempted in vain to establish a line of political continuity in Westminster when he explained that "in regard of the Royal Court once was, so the residence of the Sovereign Magistrate is still there" (pp. 40, 346). Furthermore, the changing political climate entailed a stronger emphasis on the economic roots of urban life. Even as devoted a royalist as Peter Heylyn was compelled to revise a seven-part scheme on urban wealth he had earlier borrowed from Giovanni Botero; second only to the very old category of maritime resources he placed a cause of growth whose influence was becoming recognized in Heylyn's lifetime, the development of "some Staple-Manufactures or Commodities."[77] The description prefaced to Bishop Fuller's account of London's worthies (1662) consists simply of a two-part rubric—"Manufactures" and "The Buildings." Fuller's discourse on "the Needle and the Engine," the smallest and the largest of London's manufactures, suffices as a mere synecdoche for a "labyrinth" too large to enter, but it is a striking measure of a major transformation in the tropological climate.[78] The transformation is reflected, too, in the first great statistical account of London by the virtuoso Gregory King in 1696, or in William Petty's use of statistics to transform the old mode of personified comparison in his *Observations upon the Cities of London and Rome* (1687).

Whether they stress industry or statistics, the new descriptions follow the path laid down by Stow in their focus on recent development. In 1681, for example, Thomas DeLaune published a discourse called *The Present State of London,* in which, he claimed, the matters that "lay scattered in divers Volumes [were] reduced (in a method wholly new) under their proper heads." The first two parts of DeLaune's five-part rubric, one on "the Antiquity, Original, and Name of London" and one on "the Situation" of the city, are wholly traditional, but they occupy only three pages. The next two hundred are taken up by a section on London's "Increase, Magnitude, Publick Structures and number of Inhabitants," which, as its title suggests, lays heavy stress on London's new, postfire beginnings and on changes of even more recent memory.[79] After a brief section on government, DeLaune concludes, not with an account of the city's worthy offspring, but with discourse "of the Trade of London, its Merchants, the Original of Money"; the discourse ends with prolific lists of London's exports.

Perhaps the strongest measure of Stow's influence, however, is a work written in protest against it, Daniel Defoe's description of London in the fifth letter of the *Tour through the Whole Island of Great Britain.* Approaching the "great centre of England" as he nears the center of his work,

Defoe is torn between a traditional ideal geometry and the asymmetries of London's recent growth. Viewed traditionally through the outline of its walls and liberties, the city might be described "in narrow compass," yet "in the modern acception" London is a "vast mass of buildings" extending "from Blackwall in the East to Tot-Hill fields in the West."[80] London's extent approaches the fifty-mile compass of ancient Rome, yet even "Rome, though a monster for its greatness . . . was, in a manner, round, with very few irregularities in its shape" (p. 287). As for London, sprawling irregularly in all directions, "Whither will this monstrous city then extend, and where must a circumvallation or communication line of it be placed?" (p. 288). London's outline cannot be made a pleasing figure, but only measured, and so for several pages Defoe calculates the distances from one outlying point to the next, ending with the tidy circumference of thirty-six miles, two furlongs, and thirty-nine rods.

Although he claims to be innovating, and pointedly eschews the antiquarian method of Stow's continuators, Defoe clearly adopts one of Stow's techniques by writing "in the person of an itinerant and giv[ing] a cursory view of [London's] present state" (p. 295). This street-level perspective tends to stress the dehumanizing scale of the environment, the jolting ruptures, discontinuities, and variegations that no urban perambulator can anticipate from the connected symmetries of a street map. It is the perspective adopted in Ned Ward's *London Spy* (1698), where the narrator enters London laterally, "thro' Aldgate, like a Ball thro' the Port of a Billiard Table."[81] Defoe's focus on recent changes, moreover, is justified by what he explains is "a particular and remarkable crisis, singular to those who write in this age, and very much to our advantage in writing, that the great and more eminent increase of buildings . . . has been generally made in our time, not only within our memory, but even within a few years, and the description of these oddities, cannot be improper to a description of the whole" (p. 295). The description that follows is devoted to "the new Buildings created . . . since the Year 1666" (p. 296). Yet even this proves too long a view, for Defoe's letter on London actually concludes with "an account of new edifices and public buildings erected or erecting in and about London, since the writing the foregoing account."

Defoe links the expanding physical asymmetries of London, moreover, to the dynamic asymmetries of London's changing society and economy. The dynamism that deforms London into a monstrous shape also accounts for the growing disparity between the new postfire fabric of the booming City and the decrepitude of Westminster, whose fabric, like the Westminster Hall, is "but the corpse of the old English grandeur laid in state" (p. 323). Thus are the former circumscribing powers laid to rest. Overshadowed by the great financial institutions of the City, the royal apartments have become "but little offices for clerks, rooms for coffee-houses, auctions of pictures, pamphlet and toy-shops" (p. 324).

Finally, while searching for those asymmetries that propel the city's growth, Defoe takes note of the extreme polarities of wealth and poverty, privilege and privation this growth entails. The lower orders, once unmentionable, are brought not only into Defoe's description but into close proximity to the wealth they help to generate. On London's bustling docks, for example, there are "porters, and poor working men, who, though themselves not worth, perhaps, twenty pounds in the world, are trusted with great quantities of valuable goods, sometimes to the value of several thousand pounds" (p. 313). Even more striking is Defoe's perception that "there are in London, notwithstanding we are a nation of liberty, more public and private prisons, and houses of confinement, than any city in Europe, perhaps as many as in all the capital cities of Europe put together." To have thus taken one measure of London's greatness through its toll on human lives was implicitly to have put the urban process in a different light. As Defoe wrote elsewhere, "trade is almost universally founded upon Crime." [82] It was through the personal experience of an outlaw woman, however, that Defoe reflected most acidly on the means by which the cultural (or subcultural) norm becomes the "natural." Returned in later life to the prison in which she was born, Moll Flanders decribes Newgate in terms that cast it as a microcosm of London: "how Hell should become by degrees so natural, and not only tollerable, but even agreeable, is a thing Unintelligible, but by those who have Experienc'd it, as I have." [83]

The experience of London's monstrosity had long been a powerful current in such Tudor-Stuart genres as satire and city comedy. But the exclusion of this perspective for so long from prose description is testimony both to the power of generic distinctions and to the ideological force of conceptual models through which—perhaps well past its proper prime—London retained a compelling and familiar humanized identity. The city lost this identity only as its portraitists discovered theirs.

Notes

1. See I. Darlington and J. Howgego, *Printed Maps of London, ca. 1553–1850* (Folkestone, England: Dawson, 1978); Philippa Glanvill, *London in Maps* (London: Connoisseur, 1972); Ralph Hyde, *Gilded Scenes and Shining Prospects: Panoramic Views of British Towns, 1575–1900* (New Haven: Yale Center for British Art, 1985); and E. Scouloudi, *Panoramic Views of London, 1600–1660* (London: Guildhall Library, 1953).

2. Thomas Adams, "The City of Peace," in *Works,* ed. J. Angus (Edinburgh: J. Nichol, 1861–62), 3:331.

3. William Camden, *Britain,* tr. Philemon Holland (London, 1610), unpaginated preface.

4. John Stow, *The Survey of London,* ed. C. L. Kingsford (London: Oxford University Press, 1908), 1:xcviii.

5. John Norden, *Speculum Britanniae: The firste parte* (London, 1593), p. 9.

6. John Speed, *The Theatre of the Empire of Great Britaine* (London, 1676), sig. A4.

7. See, for example, F. J. Levy, "The Making of Camden's Britannia," *Bibliotheque d'humanisme et renaissance* 26 (1964): 70–79; Levy, *Tudor Historical Thought* (San Marino, Calif.: Huntington Library, 1967), pp. 132–36; Stuart Piggott, "William Camden and the *Britannia,*" in *Ruins in a Landscape* (Edinburgh: Edinburgh University Press, 1976), pp. 33–54; and T. S. Dorsch, "Two English Antiquaries: John Leland and John Stow," *Essays and Studies,* n.s., 12 (1959): 18–35.

8. One sign that topography was considered a mode of invention is Peter Heylyn's claim that "topography is the description of some particular place or City" but that equally valid examples are "Stowes Book of *The Survey of London* . . . the description of the Vale of Tempe in the greater Ortelius: and those of the Elysian fields, the gardens of Alcinous, and the Hesperides in the ancient poets" (*Cosmographie* [London, 1652], p. 27).

9. *A Breefe Discourse, declaring and approuing the necessarie and inuiolable maintenance of certain laudable custemes of London* (London, 1584), pp. 16–17.

10. James I, speech in Star Chamber, 20 June 1616, in *The Political Works of James I,* ed. C. H. McIlwain (Cambridge: Harvard University Press, 1918), p. 343.

11. Proclamation of 12 October 1607, in *Stuart Royal Proclamations,* ed. Paul L. Hughes and James F. Larkin (New Haven: Yale University Press, 1973), 1:171.

12. Proclamation of 27 June 1602, in *Tudor Royal Proclamations: The Later Tudors, 1588–1603,* ed. Paul L. Hughes and James F. Larkin (New Haven: Yale University Press, 1969), 3:245; cf. 2:466.

13. Michel Foucault, "Questions on Geography," in *Power/Knowledge,* ed. Colin Gordon (New York: Pantheon Books, 1980), pp. 69–70.

14. Sir Thomas Elyot, *The Boke named the Gouernour,* ed. H. H. S. Croft (1883; reprint, New York: Burt Franklin, 1967), 1:76, 77–78; cf. Thomas Nashe, *Works,* ed. R. B. McKerrow (London: A. H. Bullen, 1904), 2:299; and Robert Burton, *The Anatomy of Melancholy,* ed. Holbrook Jackson (1932; reprint, London: J. M. Dent, 1977), 2:89.

15. Thus Svetlana Alpers stresses "the aura of knowledge possessed by maps as such regardless of the nature or degree of their accuracy" ("The Mapping Impulse in Dutch Art," in *The Art of Describing: Dutch Art in the Seventeenth Century* [Chicago: University of Chicago Press, 1983], p. 133). Walter Ong, from whom I borrow the term "psychogeometric," connects the spatial reorientation of knowledge by printing with "the interest in plotting the surface of the

globe which makes this same Gutenberg era the great age of cartography and exploration" ("System, Space, and Intellect in Renaissance Symbolism," in *The Barbarian Within* [New York: Macmillan, 1962], pp. 77–78). Cf. also Ong's essay, "From Allegory to Diagram in the Renaissance Mind," *JAAC* 17 (1959): 423–40.

16. The recurrence of an important early description of London in the city's legal registers, the *Liber custumarum* (1324–28) and *Liber albus* (1419), would seem in part to substantiate J. K. Hyde's view that city descriptions emerged from "the growth of cities and the rising culture and self-confidence of the citizens" ("Medieval Descriptions of Cities," *BJRL* 48 [1966]: p. 310). This description had been taken, however, from William Fitzstephen's twelfth-century life of Thomas à Becket (1173–75), and it clearly belongs to a genre of pilgrimage literature—meant to stimulate wonder and veneration—deriving from the famous *Mirabilia urbis Romae* (1143); see Antonia Gransden, "Realistic Observation in Twelfth-Century England," *Speculum* 47 (1972): 29–51. In the chronicle tradition, similarly, descriptions of wondrous cities supplement the wondrous acts of saints and kings. Caxton's version of the *Polychronicon*, for example, included "the descripcion of the vniuersal world . . . with the diuisions of countrees royaumes & empyres / noble cytees / hye mountayns famous ryuers meruayles & wondres" (*Prologues and Epilogues*, ed. W. J. B. Crotch [London: Early English Text Society, 1928], p. 67). In contrast to this chronicle tradition, the Renaissance perspective I examine here makes its appeal through the wonder of intellectual system and apparent rigor.

17. James Howell, *Londonopolis* (London, 1657), p. 382.

18. The knowledge of the urban world that is reduced from the six sumptuous folios of Braun and Hogenberg to the neat octavo of Adriano Romano's *Parvum theatrum* is taken a step further in J. C. Scaliger's *Urbes*, which is a survey of the world's cities in the form of epigrams. The logical culmination of this impulse is perhaps the international argot of the *blason populaire*, the single epigram or proverb that compares several cities; see my "Proverbs, Epigrams, and Urbanity in Renaissance London," *ELR* 15 (1985): 247–76.

19. Pietro Donazzolo, *I viaggiatori Veneti Minori* (1927), pp. 6–7, quoted in *Thomas Platter's Travels in England, 1599*, tr. Clare Williams (London: Jonathan Cape, 1937), p. 73. Cf. Marco Foscarini, *Della letteratura Veneziana* (Venice, 1854), pp. 488–91; and E. Aberi, ed., *Relazioni degli ambasciatori Veneti al Senato*, ser. 1a, 1:xx.

20. For examples, see Francesco Capello, *Relatione . . . dell' Isola d' Inghilterra*, ed. Charlotte A. Sneyd (London: Camden Society, 1847), pp. 42–46; Andreas Franciscus, *Itinerarium Britanniae*, in *Two Italian Accounts of Tudor England*, tr. C. V. Malfatti (Barcelona, 1953), pp. 32–38; and the reports in the *Calendar of State Papers, Venetian Series* by Mario Savorgnano (1533), vol. 4, no. 682; Giacomo Sorano (1554), vol. 5, no. 934; and Giovanni Michiel (1557), vol. 6, pt. 2, no. 884.

21. Aristotle's distinction between *res* and *homines* is found at *Politics* 1326a, where both are presented as material to be formed by rulers, for "the statesman

and the lawmaker must have their proper materials." The distinction between rulers and ruled, buttressed by the distinctions between form and matter and art and nature, first appears at 1254a.

22. J. H. Alsted, *Cursus philosophici encyclopedia* (Herborn, 1620), p. 1657; Alsted elsewhere invokes the four-part model of *res naturales, res artificiales, populus,* and *magistratus* (p. 23).

23. See J. G. A Pocock, "Custom and Grace, Form and Matter: An Approach to Machiavelli's Concept of Innovation," in *Machiavelli and the Nature of Political Thought,* ed. Martin Fleischer (New York: Atheneum, 1972), p. 161.

24. Domenico Mancini, *De occupatione Regni Angliae Riccardum tercium,* tr. C. A. J. Armstrong (London: Oxford University Press, 1936), pp. 125–27; John Major, *Historia maioris Britanniae* (1521), fols. 7–7v, tr. Archibald Constable, Publications of the Scottish Historical Society, 10 (Edinburgh, 1892); Polydore Vergil, *Anglicae historiae libri xxiv* (Basel, 1534), pp. 4, 24; and Paolo Giovio, *Descriptio Britanniae* (Venice, 1548), sigs. 12–12ᵛ.

25. John Bale, for example, reprinted Giovio verbatim in the 1557 Basel edition of his *Scriptorum illustrium maiores Britanniae.* Thomas Munster's *Cosmographia* (1544) took its remarks on London straight from John Major, while Ortelius took his from Vergil. Braun and Hogenberg stitched together the accounts of Vergil and Giovio, together with some chronicle material on London's mythical past.

26. Albrecht Meier, *Certaine briefe, and speciall Instructions for Gentlemen, merchants, students, souldiers, mariners, &c. Employed in seruices abrode,* tr. Philip Jones (London, 1589), sig. A3.

27. See Walter J. Ong, *Ramus, Method, and the Decay of Dialogue* (Cambridge: Harvard University Press, 1958), p. 299.

28. Hilary Pyrckmair, *De arte apodemica* (Nuremberg, 1591), pp. 21–33. A scheme virtually identical to Pyrckmair's in its categories, but slightly different in the way it arranges them, is found in *The Traueiler of Ierome Turler* (London, 1575), pp. 51–58.

29. Nathan Chytraeus, *Variorum in Europa itinerum deliciae* (Herborn, 1594); and Paul Hentzner, *Itinerarium . . . Angliae* (Breslau, 1627), unpaginated front matter.

30. As, for example, in the most massive of all tabular analyses of cities in Theodor Zwinger's *Methodus Apodemica* (Basel, 1577), pp. 187–88.

31. An intermediate source or reinforcement of the Aristotelian model may have been the architectural treatises of figures like Filarete and Alberti, who relied heavily on Aristotle; see *Filarete's Treatise on Architecture,* tr. John R. Spenser (New Haven: Yale University Press, 1965), 1:25–26; and Alberti, *Ten Books on Architecture,* ed. Joseph Rykvert (London: Alec Tiranti, 1956), pp. 65–95.

32. Menander, *Rhetor,* ed. D. A. Russell and N. G. Wilson (Oxford: Clarendon Press, 1981), pp. 32–33.

33. Introduction, ibid., pp. xxiv–xxix. The comparison of cities is not only a topic in the procedure of personification but a procedure of description in its own right. The history of this procedure extends from John Coke's *Debate Be-*

twene the Heraldes of England and Fraunce (1550), to James Howell's *Parallel by Way of Corollary Betwixt London and Other Great Cities of the World* (1657) to Sir William Petty's statistical *Observations upon the Cities of London and Rome* (1687).

34. Richard Rainolde, *The Foundacion of Rhetorike* (London, 1563), sig. K4.

35. Thomas Dekker, *Non-Dramatic Works*, ed. A. B. Grosart (London: Huth Library, 1884), 4:71.

36. Peter S. Hawkins, "From Mythography to Myth-making: Spenser and the *Magna Mater* Cybele," *Sixteenth Century Journal* 12 (1981): 52.

37. Stephen Batman, *The Golden Booke of the Leaden Gods* (London, 1577), sig. c4. This tradition is embodied in the feminine personages who mark the towns on the maps in Michael Drayton's *Polyolbion*, or in Spenser's *Faerie Queene*, where the figure of Thames wearing London on his head triumphs "Like as the mother of the Gods, they say, / . . . Old *Cybele,* arayd with pompous pride" (4.11.28). London was almost invariably personified as a woman in the city's annual mayoral pageants, though a revealing counterexample is found in Jonson's text for the coronation pageant of James I, in which the *Londinium* arch placed a female personification of "the Britain Monarchy" above "the Genius of the City, a man" (*The Magnificent Entertainment . . . upon the day of his Maiesties Triumphant Passage . . . through London* [London, 1604], sigs. B4–C2). Jonson's collaborator Dekker objected to this learned exception and urged his readers to "suppose (by the way) contrary to the opinion of all the Doctors that our Genius (in regarde the place is Feminine, and the person it selfe, drawne *Figura humana, sed Ambiguo sexu*), should at this time be thrust into womans apparell. It is no Schisme: be it so: our Genius is then a Female" (*Dramatic Works*, ed. F. Bowers [Cambridge: Cambridge University Press, 1955], 2:254–55).

38. Sherry B. Ortner, "Is Female to Male as Nature Is to Culture?" in *Women, Culture, and Society,* ed. Michelle Zimbalist Rosaldo and Louise Lamphere (Stanford: Stanford University Press, 1974), p. 73; I owe my acquaintance with this essay to my colleague Christina Malcomson. See also the several discussions of Ortner in *Nature, Culture, and Gender,* ed. Carol P. MacCormack and Marilyn Strathern (Cambridge: Cambridge University Press, 1980); cf. Edwin Ardener, "Belief and the Problem of Women," and "The Problem Revisited," in *Perceiving Women,* ed. Shirley Ardener (New York: John Wiley and Sons, 1975), pp. 1–27; and N. C. Mathieu, "Homme-Culture, Femme-Nature?" *L'Homme* 13 (1973): 101–13.

39. Ortner, "Female to Male," p. 83.

40. See William S. Heckscher, "Goethe and Weimar," in *Art and Literature: Studies in Relationship,* ed. Egon Verheyen (Durham, N.C.: Duke University Press, 1985), pp. 208–9; see also Gail Kern Paster, *The Idea of the City in the Age of Shakespeare* (Athens: University of Georgia Press, 1985), pp. 5–6, 20–21.

41. Thomas Dekker, *The Seuen deadly Sinnes of London* (1606), in *Non-Dramatic Works,* 4:10–11.

42. Thomas Nashe, *Pierce Penniless His Supplication to the Devil, The Unfortunate Traveller, and Other Works,* ed. J. B. Steane (Harmondsworth, England: Penguin, 1972), p. 78. Cf. Thomas Middleton's "lusty dame and mistress of the

land," who "lays all her foundations upon good stonework, and somebody pays well for't where'er it lands" (*The Black Booke* [1604], in *Works*, ed. A. H. Bullen [New York: AMS Press, 1964], 8:22.

43. Marilyn French, *Shakespeare's Division of Experience* (1981; reprint, New York: Ballantine Books, 1983), pp. 15–18.

44. Donald Lupton, *London and the Country Carbonadoed* (1632), in Aungerville Society Reprints (Edinburgh, 1881–82), p. 59.

45. Dekker, *Non-Dramatic Works* 4:74–75.

46. William Lambarde, *Dictionarium Anglicae topographicum & historicum* (London, ca. 1570), p. 168.

47. Varro, *De lingua Latina*, tr. Roland G. Kerr (Cambridge: Harvard Universtiy Press, 1938), 5.144; Plutarch, *Parallel Lives*, "Romulus," 9–12. See Fustel de Coulanges, *The Ancient City* (Garden City, N.Y.: Doubleday, 1966), pp. 134–43.

48. John Guillory, *Poetic Authority: Spenser, Milton, and Literary History* (New York: Columbia University Press, 1983), pp. 26–27; Guillory bases his remarks on Hannah Arendt, *Between Past and Future* (New York: Viking Press, 1961), pp. 121–22.

49. Significantly, the series of royal proclamations opposing the chaos of "continuall new Buildings, and addition and increase of Buildings" repeatedly stressed that any new building was to be "upon the foundation of a former dwelling" (*Stuart Royal Proclamations* 1:193, 267–68).

50. Robert S. Lopez, "The Crossroads within the Wall," in *The Historian and the City*, ed. Oscar Handlin and John Burchard (Cambridge: MIT Press, 1963), p. 27; cf. James Dougherty, *The Fivesquare City: The City in the Religious Imagination* (Notre Dame: University of Notre Dame Press, 1980), pp. 1–6.

51. Nathan Chytraeus, *Variorum itinerum liber*, in *Poemata* (Rostock, 1579), p. 170.

52. Richard Zouche, *The Doue; or, Passages of Cosmography* (1613), ed. Richard Walker (Oxford: H. Slatter, 1839), p. 47.

53. John Stow, *Survey* 1:9.

54. Howell, *Londonopolis*, p. 404.

55. Thomas Gainsford, for example, explained in 1618 that "from St Georges in Southwark to Shoreditch South and North; and from Westminster to St Katherines or Ratcliffe, West and east, is a crosse of streets, meeting at Leaden-Hall," the city's largest market (*The Glory of England*, [London, 1618], p. 256).

56. Camden, *Britain*, p. 422.

57. Most of the great descriptions of London embody some version of this three-part model, beginning with one of the earlier antiquarians, Lambarde, who passes from "the Bodye of the Citie," the walls and gates, to "the Residue of the publicque Buildinges," and from these "publicque Ornamentes" to "Ecclesiastical Workes" and finally to "Private Buildinges" (*Dictionarium*, pp. 171, 174, 178).

58. Thus Lewis Mumford remarks that "in the city, time becomes visible. . . . layer upon layer, past times preserve themselves in the city" (*The Culture of Cities* [1938; reprint, New York: Harcourt, Brace, and Jovanovich, 1970], p. 4).

59. Upwardly revising the estimates of earlier historians, Valerie Pearl has conjectured that in mid-seventeenth-century London, "roughly three-quarters of

the adult male householders *in the City* [italics mine] were freemen" ("Change and Stability in Seventeenth-Century London," *London Journal* 5 [1970]: 13). Recent work by Steve Rappaport confirms a similar ratio for the mid-sixteenth century ("Social Structure and Mobility in Sixteenth-Century London: Part I," *London Journal* 9 [1983]: 112). The proportion of freemen in the suburbs, however, would have been much lower (Pearl, p. 13), and recent work by Roger Finlay and Beatrice Shearer shows that "whereas in 1560 the city within and without contained three quarters of the population of the metropolis and the suburbs a quarter, by 1680 the situation was reversed, with only a quarter of Londoners inhabiting the City and three quarters in the suburbs" ("Population Growth and Suburban Expansion," in *London 1500–1700: The Making of the Metropolis,* ed. A. L. Beier and Roger Finlay [London: Longman, 1986], p. 44). Most freemen, moreover, were not "rich or even substantial men" (Pearl, p. 14); see the tabulation of occupation and status in three prosperous London wards in A. L. Beier, "Social Problems in Elizabethan London," *Journal of Interdisciplinary History* 9 (1978): 211–13.

60. Howell, *Londonopolis,* p. 1. It was common for writers who identified themselves with London to portray themselves as the city's offspring. Thomas Usk, whose *Testament of Love* was regarded as a work of Chaucer in the sixteenth century, paid tribute to "the citie of London, that is to me so dere and swete, in which I forth was growen" (*The Complete Works of Geoffrey Chaucer,* ed. W. W. Skeat [Oxford: Clarendon Press, 1897], pp. 27–28). Caxton praised London as "my moder / of whom I haue receyued my noureture and lyuynge" (*Prologues and Epilogues,* p. 77). Spenser's London is "my most kyndly Nurse" (*Prothalamion,* line 128), while Dekker's is the "Mother of my Life, Nurse of my Being" (*Non-Dramatic Works* 4:285).

61. Richard Niccols, *Londons Artillerie* (London, 1616), p. 60.

62. William Smith, *A Brieff Description of the Famous Cittie of London,* BM Harley MS. 6363.

63. Robert Darnton, "A Bourgeois Puts His World in Order: The City as a Text," in *The Great Cat Massacre and Other Episodes in French Cultural History* (1984; reprint, New York: Vintage Books, 1985), pp. 122–23.

64. Edmund Bolton, *The Cities advocate* (London, 1629), sig. K^v.

65. Quoted in Raymond Williams, *The Country and the City* (New York: Oxford University Press, 1973), p. 49.

66. Jan Sictor, *Panegyricon inaugurale* (London, 1637), sig. B2v.

67. Thomas Churchyard, *A light Bondell of liuly discourses calld Churchyardes Charge* (London, 1580), sig. D4^v.

68. See R. A. Foakes, *Illustrations of the English Stage, 1580–1642* (London: Scolar Press, 1985), pp. 16–17.

69. Nashe, for example, poured Great Yarmouth into it in the mock praise of *Nashe's Lenten Stuffe.*

70. Camden, *Britain,* p. 427.

71. Norden, *Speculum Britanniae,* p. 28.

72. Speed, *Empire of Great Britaine,* p. 29.

73. On the role of personal memory in Stow's method, see Kingsford's intro-

duction to the *Survey,* pp. xxix–xxx; and Arthur B. Ferguson, *Clio Unbound: Perception of the Social and Cultural Past in Renaissance England* (Durham, N.C.: Duke University Press, 1979), pp. 99–104.

74. Fredric Jameson, *The Political Unconscious: Narrative as a Socially Symbolic Act* (Ithaca: Cornell University Press, 1981), p. 112.

75. Camden's Latin *Britannia* made it the best-known source for London on the Continent. Johannes de Laet reprinted Camden on London verbatim at Leiden in 1630 (in *Thomae Smithi Angli De Republica Anglorum*), and in 1636 Venceslaus Clemens based on Camden a two-hundred page Latin verse praise of London, the *Trinobantias Augustae libri VI.* German travelers who borrowed heavily from Camden include the Baron Waldstein (*Diary,* ed. G. W. Groos [London: Thames and Hudson, 1981], p. 32ff.); and Paul Hentzner (see W. D. Robson-Scott, *German Travellers in England, 1400–1800* [Oxford: B. Blackwell, 1953], Appendix I). Stow's *Survey* was expanded by Anthony Munday in 1618 and 1633, while the great expansion by John Strype (1720) provoked hostile criticism from Defoe.

76. Peter Heylyn, for example, boasted that while he took the matter for his *Microcosmus* (1621) from others, "the wordes for the most part are mine owne, the method totallie" (preface). James Howell acknowledged his debt to Stow in *Londonopolis,* but claimed "the trace, and form of the Structure be mine own" (sig. b^v).

77. Heylyn, *Cosmographie,* p. 5; this same topic had been omitted from Heylyn's earlier digest of Botero in the *Microcosmus* (1621), pp. 7–8.

78. Bishop Fuller, *The History of the Worthies of England,* ed. P. A. Nuttall (London: T. Tegg, 1840), 1:333–35.

79. "In our Memory, we have seen London multiply exceedingly in beautiful Structures and numbers of Inhabitants. So that it is at present of a vast extent" (Thomas Delaune, *The Present State of London* [London, 1681], p. 5).

80. Daniel Defoe, *A Tour through the Whole Island of Great Britain,* ed.. Pat Rogers (Harmondsworth, England: Penguin, 1971), p. 286.

81. Ned Ward, *The London Spy* (November 1698), p. 4.

82. Daniel Defoe, *The Complete English Tradesman* (London, 1727), vol. 2, pt. 2, p. 108; quoted in Max Byrd, *London Transformed: Images of the City in the Eighteenth Century* (New Haven: Yale University Press, 1978), p. 19.

83. Daniel Defoe, *The Fortunes and Misfortunes of the Famous Moll Flanders, &c.,* ed. G. A. Starr (London: Oxford University Press, 1971), p. 276.

Notes on Contributors

Janel Mueller is professor of English and the humanities at the University of Chicago. She has published an edition of Donne's Prebend Sermons and *The Native Tongue and the Word: Developments in English Prose Style, 1380–1580*. She is currently at work on a study of how patriarchy configures the relations of nature, culture, and gender in Milton's major poems.

Donald R. Kelley is Wilson Professor of History at the University of Rochester and executive editor of the *Journal of the History of Ideas*. His books include *Foundations of Modern Historical Scholarship* and *The Beginning of Ideology*. He is working on a study of the European legal tradition and the human sciences.

Marjorie Garber is professor of English and director of the Center for Literary and Cultural Studies at Harvard University. She is the author of *Dream in Shakespeare: From Metaphor to Metamorphosis; Coming of Age in Shakespeare;* and *Shakespeare's Ghost Writers: Literature as Uncanny Causality*. She is at work on a book on cross-dressing from Shakespeare to Laurie Anderson.

Richard Strier, co-editor of *The Historical Renaissance,* is professor of English and the humanities at the University of Chicago. His publications include *Love Known: Theology and Experience in George Herbert's Poetry,* and essays and reviews on Renaissance poetry and on critical theory. He is currently at work on Shakespeare's critique of decorum.

Leah S. Marcus is professor of English at the University of Texas-

Austin. Her publications include *Childhood and Cultural Despair* and *The Politics of Mirth: Jonson, Herrick, Milton, Marvell, and the Defense of Old Holiday Pastimes. Puzzling Shakespeare: Local Reading and its Discontents* is forthcoming from the University of California Press.

Maureen Quilligan is professor of English at the University of Pennsylvania. She is the author of *The Language of Allegory: Defining the Genre* and *Milton's Spenser: The Politics of Reading,* and a co-editor of *Rewriting the Renaissance: The Discourses of Sexual Difference in Early Modern Europe.* She is currently at work on female literary authority and sovereignty in the sixteenth century.

Heather Dubrow, co-editor of *The Historical Renaissance,* is professor of English at Carleton College. Her publications include *Genre* and *Captive Victors: Shakespeare's Narrative Poems and Sonnets.* She is currently completing a book on the Stuart epithalamium.

Brian P. Levack is professor of history at the University of Texas at Austin. His publications include *The Civil Lawyers in England, 1603–1641: A Political Study; The Witch-Hunt in Early Modern Europe;* and *The Formation of the British State: England, Scotland and the Union, 1603–1707.* He is currently working on a study of witch-hunting in England and Scotland during the 1640s and 1650s.

Michael C. Schoenfeldt is assistant professor of English at the University of Michigan, Ann Arbor. He has published articles on George Herbert and on Ben Jonson and is currently completing a book entitled "'The Distance of the Meek': George Herbert and His God."

Richard Helgerson is professor of English at the University of California, Santa Barbara. He is the author of *The Elizabethan Prodigals* and *Self-Crowned Laureates: Spenser, Jonson, Milton, and the Literary System.* He is now completing a study of Elizabethan representations of England.

Arthur F. Kinney, the Thomas W. Copeland Professor of Literary History at the University of Massachusetts at Amherst, is the founding editor of *English Literary Renaissance* and editor of the Renaissance titles in the Twayne English Authors series. His books include *John Skelton: Priest as Poet* and *Humanist Poetics. Continental Humanist Poetics* is forthcoming in 1989.

Clark Hulse is associate professor of English at the University of Illinois at Chicago. He is the author of *Metamorphic Verse: The Elizabethan Minor Epic* and, more recently, of articles on Sidney's and on Shakespeare's sonnets. He is at work on a book about the relationship between poetry and painting in sixteenth-century England.

Lawrence Manley, associate professor of English at Yale University, is the author of *Convention, 1500–1700* and the editor of *London in the Age of Shakespeare: An Anthology.* He is completing a study of London in the literature of the Tudor and Stuart periods.